ISBN 978-1-5285-0298-6
PIBN 10919519

# 1 MONTH OF
# FREE
# READING

at

## www.ForgottenBooks.com

By purchasing this book you are eligible for one month membership to ForgottenBooks.com, giving you unlimited access to our entire collection of over 700,000 titles via our web site and mobile apps.

To claim your free month visit:

www.forgottenbooks.com/free919519

English
Français
Deutsche
Italiano
Español
Português

# www.forgottenbooks.com

**Mythology** Photography **Fiction**
Fishing Christianity **Art** Cooking
Essays Buddhism Freemasonry
Medicine **Biology** Music **Ancient**
**Egypt** Evolution Carpentry Physics
Dance Geology **Mathematics** Fitness
Shakespeare **Folklore** Yoga Marketing
**Confidence** Immortality Biographies
Poetry **Psychology** Witchcraft
Electronics Chemistry History **Law**
Accounting **Philosophy** Anthropology
Alchemy Drama Quantum Mechanics
Atheism Sexual Health **Ancient History**
**Entrepreneurship** Languages Sport
Paleontology Needlework Islam
**Metaphysics** Investment Archaeology
Parenting Statistics Criminology
**Motivational**

# Royal Irish Academy.

## TODD LECTURE SERIES.

### VOL. V.

# THE LATIN LIVES OF THE SAINTS

AS

## Aids towards the Translation of Irish Texts

AND THE

## PRODUCTION OF AN IRISH DICTIONARY.

BY

## EDMUND HOGAN, S.J.,

#### F.R.U.I., M.R.I.A.;

*Royal Irish Academy's Todd Professor of the Celtic Languages.*

49485·
1901

## DUBLIN:

PUBLISHED AT THE ACADEMY HOUSE, 19, DAWSON-STREET.

SOLD ALSO BY

HODGES, FIGGIS. & CO. (LTD.), GRAFTON-ST.;

AND BY WILLIAMS & NORGATE.

| LONDON: | EDINBURGH: |
| 14, Henrie'' street, Covent Garden. | 20, South Frederick-street. |

### 1894.

DUBLIN :

PRINTED AT THE UNIVERSITY PRESS,

BY PONSONBY AND WELDRICK.

# CONTENTS.

# PREFACE.

THE Latin Lives of the Irish Saints, and the Latin works of O'Sullevan Beare and O'Flaherty, contain a great many Irish glosses.[1] Moreover, they and the Latin *Chartæ*, *Descriptiones Hiberniæ*, and *Annales*, present us with a vast number of Irish names of persons and places. This mine has never been explored. I began to work it to get materials for some Todd Lectures ; but I found that I could not present the subject in its full light without more time than is at my disposal, and without consulting the original manuscripts, the Irish of which has been corrupted by the editors or printers. I therefore resolved to exhibit the Latin Lives under an aspect hitherto overlooked, or not sufficiently considered, that is—as translations from the Irish, or as translated into Irish; and consequently as useful aids in the interpretation of texts and in the production of a dictionary.

The equivalent Latin and Irish passages or sentences, lying side by side, or separated, in our manuscripts, would cover several hundred pages of the Todd Lecture series. If they were brought together and printed they would interpret each other, and, to use a familiar expression, would set each other off. This confrontation I have carried out within limits which the Publication Committee will readily appreciate. I have not consciously made an attempt anywhere to manufacture a version out of the elements of the Latin Lives; but where the

---

[1] Thus, in the short *Vita S. Cainnici* of the " Codex Kilkenniensis " :—" *geal-bregach* .ɪ. albus-mendax ; *achad-bo* .ɪ. agro boum ; *gall-cerd* .ɪ. mors crudelis, projecto puero super hastas stantes sursum positas ; *mochean, mochean a Chainnig* .ɪ. bene venias, bene venias, sancte Cainnice! *Caindeach mac Luigdech . . . dona fir-Ultachaib do*, etc."

equivalence was close, or where the free handling of the Irish writer was evidenced only by the use of doublets or synonyms, I have put such passages side by side, omitting those that merely reflected each other in general meaning.

By this juxtaposition I hope to flash fresh light for the dark corners of Irish texts, to illustrate the meaning and uses of Irish words or groups of words, and the sequence of sen- tences; to help students to shape the wording of their versions in accordance with the real meaning of the Irish, in place of emptying phrases of their sense by too literal a rendering, as those have done who translate *breith aithrige* by " judgment of repentance." Further, this humble work, which has proved more laborious than would be the editing and translation of texts, teaches this practical lesson—that the English versions of the Middle-Irish Lives of the Saints are, on the whole, trustworthy, even when made without opportunities of refer- ring to the old Latin lives. This is a useful lesson, since the criticisms discharged from so many quarters[1] at the versions made from the Irish have unfortunately (and unreasonably, as I think) shaken all confidence in the translators, and driven students away from their books.

It is well to bear in mind that these penetrating criticisms do not mar the goodly fellowship of Celtic scholars, nor arrest the work of interpretation, which seems to exercise on some of the keenest and best trained minds of our day a fascination from which all the spells of Saint Gall could not deliver them ; finally, that such criticisms generally touch on minor details, and are often without solid foundation. Of this last point I

---

[1] See, for instance, O'Donovan's "Four Masters," I. p. xxxi., "The Aca- demy," the " Rev. Celtique," the " Irish Eccl. Record," the " Gaelic Journal," the " Kilkenny Journal of Archæology," " Transactions of the Philological So- ciety," the German Philological Journals, Windisch's " Texte," I. 5, 197, *et passim*, and Lists of Corrigenda added to various works by the translators them- selves. See also Dr. Stokes' " Three Mid. Ir. Homilies," Preface, his " Irish Ordeals," p. 184, " Rev. Celt.," VI. p. 361, " Todd Lectures," IV. pp. 11, 32, xxii, xxiii.

will give an instance or two from the last review of the last Irish book.

In this review[1] one hundred and thirty-three "mistranslations" are quoted as "samples of what may be expected in those parts of the translation where I have not been able to consult the original."

Running my eye over the first twelve samples, I see at once, and, without any desire to meddle in a controversy between two Celtic scholars, I may be permitted to say, that in two cases the native translator is right in rendering *breith aithrige* by "penance," and *mór n-aistir* by "much toil"; and that his learned critic is mistaken in translating them respectively by "judgment of penance," and "much going astray."

*Breith aithrige* and *breitheamnas aithrige* (of the Irish Catechisms) = "pœnitentia," "penance," which is rendered "Busse" and "pénitence" in the German and French Catechisms. Thus *breitheamnus aithrige iocsláinteach*, a "wholesome penance" (Donlevy, pp. 306, 307) = eine heilsame Busse, une pénitence salutaire. So in Stapleton's "Doctrina Christiana Latino-Hibernica" (pp. 121, 122, ed. 1639), *an bhreith aithridhe chuirtheas an t-athair faoisideneach air* = "pœnam illam quam confessarius imposuerit"; *breitheamhnus aithrighe chuireas an sagart ar neach* = "pœnitentia a sacerdote imposita." See also Molloy's "Lucerna Fidelium" (pp. 211, 216), and any Irish-English Catechism. Hence "bretheamnas aithrige do chengal orum, le jugement du repentir à nous lier," of "Rev. Celt.," xv. p. 8, should be "de m' imposer une pénitence"; hence also "breath aithrige, it *seems to mean* the penance which a penitent is ordered to perform," of Dr. Stokes' glossary of "The Voyage of the *Hui Corra*," should be "it means."

As to *mór n-aistir* :—*aistear* = "labour," "travail," in Lamentations of Jeremy, iii. 5, and Exodus, xviii. 8 ; and

---

[1] "Rev. Celt," Jan. 1894.

*bean a n-aisdear cloinne* = "a woman in ·labour," O'Begley's
"Dictionary," *vide* "travel." Of course *asdior* = "journey," in
O'Brien's "Dictionary," but he adds, "it *now vulgarly* means
missing one's way."

Elucidations, such as we have got from the "Doctrina
Latino-Hibernica," and the Irish and Latin and English Bible,
will, I trust, appear in the text and word-index of these Lectures. For example :—

Issed atbert, issed roraid = dicens ; issed = et, autem,
vero.

An-nochetfanad, an-nocnited, an-dochluined, an-doadchu-
ired, an-noesed = sentiens, suspirans, audiens, revertens, gemens.

Gabais a laim ass = "manum illius apprehendens illum de
loco ejecit," confirms Dr. Stokes' version.

Dorat seirc dó, *and* tuc grad dou = "dilexit eum," show
the overliteralness of "I have levelled (ich richtete) my love
at him," "I have bestowed love upon him," &c.

Mog do magadaib (p. 81) *and* aen do mogaib (p. 80) =
"unus servorum," show that "a servant of the servants" is
too literal : cf. "aon aithne dona haitheantaib, one of the
Commandments," "aon b'all dod' b'allaib, one of thy members,"
Matth. v. 19, 29.

Leis : 1° nusbeir leis, adducit ; rosruc leis, eum duxit ; tuc
latt, porta, show that "secum," or "with him," are superfluous
in translation.

Leis : 2° ba maith leis a menma, lætatus est ; robad maith
lemsa, volo ; is maith latt, vis. Also, mór in maith, credi non
potest ; fir maith, patrisfamilias, English "goodman."

Leis : 3° co nderna-sum ernaigthi leis, et exoravit pro eo, III ;
dena ernaigthi leamsa, ora *pro* me ; guid in Coimdid lem, ora
(pro me), guidfed-su Dia letso, ego pro te rogabo ; gabuis B.
pater leis, oravit B. pro eo (p. 82). Here leis = "on his behalf," ar a son, not "with him," as it is twice rendered in
the "Lismore Lives" (p. 194), though it is translated "for"
twice in that page.

Messi fein, ego sum; mogaid-ni, nos servi sumus (pp. 60, 57).

Roslecht = "genua flexit," and also "se prostravit."

Rosocht takes a plural nominative (p. 48); and the 2nd pl. is used in speaking to one person: ni tabraid-siu, non defers (p. 48).

Tiagar, eat quis. Ní hada dúinn, non debemus, confirms Dr. Stokes' "it is not lawful for us."

Ag sud, ecce offero (p. 70).

Do fis scél (p. 69) means, I think, "to visit" = do thóruma *and* visitare, *ibi.*; cf. táinig dom' fios, "he came to see me," *and* dul d'fios, "to visit."

I select a few samples of single words on which a new light is thrown :—

Abrachtach, ánbrachtaiġe (aide), anfabrachta, anbfabrachta are rendered "consumptive" by Dr. Stokes and others; our Latin texts and the Irish context show them to mean "paralyticus."

Airilliud is rendered "property (?)" in the "Lismore Lives" (p. 384); it is = "substantia" at p. 3 of our texts; it means "meritum" (p. 71), and meritum in the sense of what one earns, acquires, and so owns.

Aislingi is feminine: "na ha."; gender not given in Windisch or Atkinson's Dictionaries.

Airge, locus in quo vaccas mulgere solemus. Windisch gives only the sense "armentum"; "a place for summer grazing," O'Brien.

Anfaitech, rusticus, and so, awkward, confirms Dr. Stokes' "incautious."

Aniar: tuc . . aníar, protulit.

Aroerachair, aroirachair "venit in," "tenuit," arroerachair, "et tenuit"; "it seems to mean *erexit*," Stokes.

Asrárachtatar (wrongly printed in Index), revixerunt.

Bachlach, "rusticus," as in O'Reilly; but "bondman" in Windisch, as if from bachall, "to clip the hair."

Béscna, mos, regula; but "jurisprudence," Stokes.

Maicc bethad = electi, mac báis, impius, are better than "sons of life," "son of death," as the words have been rendered.

Borrfad, tumor; "swelling(?)," Stokes; "indignation," Windisch.

Bunnsachaib, radiis; "darts" in *Bible Focloir*; but "Zweig" in Windisch.

Cannadus, pannus, *bis*. Dr. Stokes had translated it differently; but in Index to the "Lismore Lives," he says, "from pannus(?) seems some sort of covering for the head." It is perhaps = pannus, a "bit of cloth," a "head-band."

Co = at: co maigin itá = dú hita, 35.

Comaithgiu, "aliam gentem"; if so, Ascoli's Gl., p. 1, is incorrect: "qui una vel contigue agros conducit."

Co n = and, et: co n-(airnicc, tarut, tarfas, accai, etc.); also con-epair, con-erbairt = dicens.

Cretra = "aqua benedicta quæ ad morborum sanitatem servabatur"; blessed things would render the word better than "consecrated elements."

Decleithi (p. 40) is marked with a query by Dr. Stokes. The context of his "Trip. Life" (p. 156) points to de(g)-cleithi, "a good roof" (cf. de-gním); it might also mean "a good chief," or "two chiefs."

Dicheltair, "cloak of darkness" (Stokes), is countenanced by "quod demit ab oculis" (p. 8).

Díguind (see Index); but *di* might be intensive; cf. gand ("Irische Texte," i. 159), applied to a spear, and to the cross in *LB*. 221 b, 222 a.

Diud lai, ante prandium, shows that the Irish dined at or after nightfall.

Dofuisim seems to mean effudit. A ndorus, ante januam, ad portam; i ndorus, in porta.

Drolmach, vas ligneum apertum.

Duidlid seems to mean vagabond or robber, connected with

madudéll, or diall, or todidel gl. deerraverat of the Laurentian glosses (p. 11).·

Folamadair, " ordinavit " ; " desires " (?), Stokes.

Forbann, " order, prescription, commandment," Stokes ; but see my Index.

Greim rígda, sceptrum regale, 2, 63 ; cf. gremmae .ı. sceptri, regni, *Ml.* 110 d. Dr. Stokes renders " royal power (?)" in indexes to " Tripartite Life " and " Lismore Lives."

Imaltoir, " calix ", ciborium ; or " altar-stone " : i. cloiche forsa ndenad oiffrend cech læi, Stokes' " Trip. Life " (p. 448).

Inchoisc, indica ; " signify (?) ", Stokes.

Lista (queried by Dr. Stokes) = molesta, *vide* Index.

Miltenaib = alveariis campestribus, or "bee-hives"; "combs " (Stokes).

Molach, " molesta."

Ncm-annac, indignus, *vide* p. 90.

Tírtha : fer t., rusticus ; now *tiorthach,* " born in the country." " A drying man," of Dr. Stokes, would be *jer tirtha arbair.*

Tredenus, triduanum jejunium, cf. tregenus, " abstinence," O'Begley's " Dictionary."

Uasal-(decon, epscop, sacart) = diaconus, episcopus, sanctus presbyter ; not " archdeacon," etc.

Having so far stated the purpose and usefulness of these Lectures, and my method of dealing with my materials, I will now mention the sources from which I have drawn the equivalent Latin and Irish passages.

For the " Life of St. Patrick " I have taken: 1°. the Latin of the " Book of Armagh " (*LA.*), and the Irish of O'Curry's copy of the Egerton " Tripartite Life " (*O'C.*), which I have collated with the original *Eg.* 97, referring to O'Curry's pages as *Eg.* 97 is not paged. This text seems purer than that of Rawlinson, edited by Dr. Stokes. 2°. I take the Latin of Colgan's " Vita Secunda," " Vita Tertia," and " Vita Quarta " (*V.* 2, *V.* 3, *V.* 4), and the Irish from O'Curry's copy of the

"Tripartite Life" and from the "Leabar Breac," and somewhat from the "Book of Lismore" (*LB.*, *Lism. Life*).[1]

For the "Life of St. Martin" I give the Latin of the
"Book of Armagh" and the Irish of *LB.*

For the "Life of St. Brigit" I give the Latin of Colgan's
"Vita Tertia" with references to "Vita Quarta," and the Irish
of *LB.* and the "Book of Lismore."[1]

For the "Life of St. Brenainn"[2] I give the Latin of the
"Codex Kilkenniensis" and the "Codex Salmanticensis," and
the Irish of the "Book of Lismore."[1]

The Latin extracts on St. Columba are from Adamnan, and
the Irish from *LB.* In Adamnan I find little to my purpose.
I have added the Tripartite texts corresponding to the Index in
the "Book of Armagh." This Index, which was first noticed
and put in print and interpreted by me some years ago, shows
that some copy of the "Tripartite Life" was known to the
Armagh Scribe in 807.

A partial Index of Words is appended, with Latin equiva-
lents; it may be useful as a supplement to the dictionaries of
Middle-Irish, and a help towards the production of the Irish
dictionary.

These contractions occur through the book:—*Im.* for imorro,
which is never in full in the texts; P. = Patricius, Patraicc;
M. = Martinus, Mártain; B. = Brigita, Brigit, Brendanus,
Brenainn; *TL.* means Dr. Stokes' edition of the "Tripartite
Life." The other abbreviations will be easily understood.

In conclusion I think it proper to state that all these
Irish passages, except those from Egerton 97, have been accu-
rately edited by Dr. W. Stokes; that I have fully availed
myself of his publications, though sparingly of his "Three
Middle-Irish Homilies," which are not in the Royal Irish
Academy; and that consequently I give this book as a con-
tribution to linguistic rather than to literature.

EDMUND HOGAN.

*April* 10, 1894.

---

[1] I refer to the pages of Dr. Stokes' "Lismore Lives," which I have collated
with O'Longan's transcript in the R.I.A.

[2] This is the real form of his name; correct, p. 101, l. 4, 103, l. 10, 104, l. 10.

# IRISH AND LATIN LIVES OF THE SAINTS

## *COMPARED.*

———◆◆◆———

### LIFE OF ST. PATRICK.

1. [*O'C.* 17, 19, 18, 19.] Con-erbairt *fris*, is mithig do the*cht* conostuicce *tre* lín int ṡoscelai dochu*m* puirt bethad ... Dodecha*id* senóir tairise leis o Germa*n* fri*a* imchomet 7 fri*a* thest*us*, Segetius a ainm, 7 sac*art* o grá*d*.

Rofuid sido *i*ndi Paladius huasaldecon do praicept do Goidel*aib*. Is é *im.* airchíndech róbæ hi Roi*m* isind aims*ir* sin, Célestinus indara fer .xl. ó Petur. (Ni dó rocinn Dia a comṡo∂)[1]; ic íntud dó iar*om* *f*orculu dafarraid gal*ar* hi tírib Cr*u*ithnech *co* n*d*-erbalt de. Otchual*a* Pátraic anní si*n* 7 rofitir rombo dó roír Dia apstulacht inna hÉirend, dochúaid ... Isin láu cétna rooirdned Auxilius 7 Eisirninus 7 alaili do muintir Pátraic.

———————

1. [*LA.* 2 a.] Dicens ei adesse tempus, ut veniret et ævangelico rete eos piscaret ... Missit Germanus seniorem cum illo, hoc est, Segitium prespiterum, ut testem ac comitem haberet.

Palladius archidiaconus missus fuerat ab illo ad hanc insolam convertendam. Cælestinus urbis Romæ Episcopus, qui tunc tenebat sedem apostolicam quadragensimus quintus a Petro. Sed prohibuit illum Deus eos convertere; revertente vero eo hinc in Pictorum finibus vita functus est. Audita itaque morte Palladii Patricius, sciens quæ ventura erant declinavit iter. . . . . Etiam Auxilius, Iserninusque et cæteri inferioris gradus eodem die ordinati sunt.

———————

[1] The words in parenthesis are from "Lismore Lives," p. 7.

2. [*O' C.* 20, 21.]　Isinn aimsir sin ro bói alaile rí fe˖
gentlidi ind hEir*inn* .ı. Loigaire mac Néll, 7 is an*n* robói a ɩ
a 7 greim rígda i Temraig[1].

In rí croda-sa di*diu* rotecht drui*d*e 7 tinchitlidi doairchainti
n-a ndr*u*idec*h*t 7 tre n-a ngentle*ch*t an nobith archind dóib; Lo
7 Lucat Mæl, ithé robtar airec*h*a díib, 7 roptar auctair in dan˖
inna sæbfáth*sine*. Dofairchechnatar (s)ídi donicfed faith *for*ban
a tír, 7 forcetal n-anetarcnaid lista molach t*r*emdéa tar muir aɩ
uathad dodmb*er*ad 7 sochaidi aridféimfed 7 fogebad ermitin la
hErend 7 nólafedh na rígu 7 na fl*ath*a as a rígu, 7 nochoscerad
huili arrach*ta* nan ídal, 7 nofeidligfed a mbéscna tre bithu betha.
blia*dain* nó teora blia*dn*a ré tichtu Patraic is*ed* doairchantaiɛ
ˊˊTicfa Tailcend, a chrand cromchend, a bratt tollcend, a mía
airthiur a tigi, f*ri*s(c)érat a mu*ínt*er huili, Am*en*, Am*en*.　In

---

2. [*LA.* 2b.]　In illis diebus fuit rex quidam ferox gentili˖
in prædictis regionibus regnans in Temoria quæ erat caput r˖
Scotorum, Loiguire nomine, filius Neill.

Hic autem scivos et magos et incantatores habuerat qui pote
omnia scire[3] et prævidere præsagio ex more gentilitatis et idola
antequam essent; e quibus hi præ cæteris præferebantur[4], .i. Lo˖
et Lucet Calvus, et hi duo erant inventores doni illius.　Proɟ
tabant morem exterum futurum in modum regni cum ignota doctɼ
molesta longuinquo trans maria advectum; a paucis dictatum
multis susceptum, ab omnibusque honoratum, reges[6] subversuɼ
omnes eorum deos destructurum, et, jectis illorum artis operiˉ
in sæcula regnaturum.　In antecedentibus adventum Patricii .ii.
.iii. annis profetaverunt his verbis, ˊˊAdveniet Asciciput cum
ligno curvicapite ex sua domu[7] capite-perforata, sua mensa ex
teriore[8] parte domus suæ, respondebit ei sua familia tota, Fiat, Ƒ
Quando ergo hæc omnia fient, regnum nostrum quod est geɼ

---

[1] ˊˊin Scotia nomine Laegarius cujus
sedes erat et sceptrum regale in Temoria,ˊˊ of *Vita 2 da*, is closer than the
*B. of Armagh.*

[2] nocho scerad, *O'C.* and *Eg.*

[3] præsagire, *V.* 2.

[4] cæteris.prælati sunt, *V.* 3.

[5] *i.e.* datum, *as appears from the L*

[6] *so Brux.*, regna *in LA.*

[7] domus = casula = bratt; the L
translator thought, as *casula* m
'house' and 'mantle,' that *domus* m
them.

[8] *i.e.* eastern.

*tra* ticfat inna airde-se *con*scerthar[1] ar n-adrad-ni 7 ar ngentlecht."
Amal dorairngred di*diu*, is amlaid *for*coimnecuir 7 rócomallad. · O
fororbái · da*no* P. a im*m*ram 7 rogab port a long oc I*n*biur Dea i
cr*i*ch Laigen[2], tuc a lunga dochum thíri.   Is and sin tánic i(n)
comairle occai techt do p*r*aiceupt do Miliuc, cubaid leis, uair rofognai
do ar thús dia churp, co ro*f*ognad dia an*m*uin.   Dorat di*du* cr*an*d *f*ri
tír 7 doluid do Inis Pátraic.   Do Luid iarsin sech Conaille 7 sech or
n-Ulad co rogaib i*n* Inbiur Brénnea.   Luid iarsin co Inb*er* Sla(i)n co
rofoilgeset a lungai isin bailiu sin, 7 lotar hi tír do chor a scisi 7 do
chu*m*sanad.   Conid andsein fosfuair muccaid Díchon baile i ta saball
Pátraic i ndiu.   Dóiġ leis roptar lát*roinn* no meirrlig, co ndechaid
7 co n-ecid dia t(h)igernai.   O rodecai Díchu in*ní* Pátraic rongab
cong(an) chrídi.   Roc*r*eit *con*id hé toisech rogab c*r*eidim.

3. [*O'C.* 24, 25.]  O rocuala *im.* Mili*uc* P. do tuideċt[3], noċorb ail
do creitem dó, 7 in *for*ban*n* gentlidi in a rabi d'facbail, issí *com*airle

---

non stabit[4] eversis idulorum culturis."   Quod sic postea evenerat[5].
Consummato igitur navigio perfectoque, navis sancti in portum in
regiones Coolenorum qui vocatur Hostium Dee dilata est.   Ubi
vissum est ei nihil perfectius esse quam ut, portans servitutis ·præ-
tium terrenum et cœleste, de captivitate liberaret[6] Milcoin cui ante
captivus servierat.   Ad anteriorem insolam quæ ejus nomine nominatur prurim navis convertit.   Tum deinde Conalneos fines necnon
et fines Ulathorum in leva dimittens in Fretu*m* Brene se immisit.
Et descenderunt in terram ad Hostium Sláin, et absconderunt navi-
culam et venierunt aliquantulum in regionem ut requiescerent ibi.
Et invenit eos porcinarius viri cui nomen erat Dichu ubi nuʟc est
Orreum Patricii.   Putans eos fures ac latrones exivit et indicavit
domino suo.   Sed videns faciem Patricii, convertit Dominus ad
bonum cogitationes ejus.   Credidit præ omnibus.

3. [*LA.* 3 a.]  Audiens autem Miliucc iturum iterum, ut morem
quem nolebat faceret, instinctu diabuli[7] sponte se igni tradidit et in

---

¹ *read* coscérthar.
² in regione Lagenorum, *V.* 2.
³ venisse, *V.*, 2,c. 30.
⁴ traigfid cech flaithius, *LB.* 26 b.

⁵ completum est, *V.* 2.
⁶ *i.e.* "prædicando" liberaret Milcoin
a captivitate dæmonis ?
⁷ roaslag demun fair, *Lism. Life*, 9.

romúin Demon dosom ; luid *in* a rigthech 7 a ór 7 a argat lais
tárat fein tene fair[1].

Is an*n*sein tarr(a)sair P. dín leith a ndes do Sléib Mis, atá c*r*
isi*n* inad sin, *co* n-accai side, i*n* tenid dichéin.   Rosocht *fri* ré da *v*
an nocnited 7 an noesed isse*d* rorade :—" Tene thaige Milc*on* iar :
losc*u*d do féin, ar na roc*r*eite*d* do Día i *forc*iun*n* a áissi, ní bia rí ua
7 is a fogna*m* bías a *s*íl *tré* bithu " ; ocus ótrub*air*t na br*i*athr*a*
i*m*soi deisell 7 dothoet i*n* a *fr*ithlurg af*ri*th*i*si i tír n-Ula*d*, co tara
Mag Inis co Díchoin mac Trichim, 7 roan an*n* fri ré ciana hic si
c*r*eitme,

4. [*O' C.* 25, 26.]   O rocomaicsegestar[2] da*no* soll*omain* na Cá
rom*í*dir P. nad bái baili bád cuidbiu do árdsoll*omain* na blia*dna*,
in Cásc, do ceilebra(d) q*uam* hi Maig Breg, baili i mbai cend idlac*l*
7 druidechta na h-Eire*nn*.

Rocheilebra*i*set iarsin do Díchui*n* 7 doratsat a lui*ng* *for* mui*r*
dodechatar cor-rogabsat in Inbi*ur* Cholpthai.   *For*acabsat a lun*g*

domu in qua prius habitaverat rex congregato ad se omni instrume
substantiæ suæ[3].

Patricius (stetit) a latere dextro Montis Miss, ubi nunc cr
habetur in signum, rogum regis incensum intuitus (est).   Duas
tres horas nullum verbum proferens, suspirans et gemens, la
mansque hæc verba promens ait, " Hic rex qui seipsum igni tradi
ne crederet in fine vitæ suæ et ne serviret Deo, nemo de filiis sed*
rex, et semen[4] ejus serviet in sempiternum " ; et his dictis conve
cito iter suum ad regionem Ulothorum per eadem vestigia qui
venerat, et pervenit ad Campum Inis ad Dichoin, ibique ma
multis diebus et cœpit fides crescere ibi.

4. [*LA.* 3 b.]   Adpropinquavit autem Pascha in diebus illis ;
inierunt consilium (Patricius et socii) ubi hoc Pascha celebrare
vissum est Patricio hanc magnam sollempnitatem in Campo B
celeberari, (ubi erat) caput totius idolatriæ.

Elevata igitur navi ad mare, et dimisso in pace bono viro Dic
migrantes in portum Hostii Colpdi delati sunt.   Relicta ibi n

---

[1] succendit eam super se, *V.* 3, c. 34.       [3] con a uli arilliud, *LB.* 26.
[2] roconnaicsegestar, *Eg.* and *O'C.*       [4] a *s*íl 7 a *s*em*ed*, *O'C.* 24.

isin inbiur 7 dodechotar iar tír cor-roachtatar Fertea Fer Fécc, 7
rosaided pupoll Pátraic isin inad sein 7 roben in tenid Chascæ.
Dorala dano conid si sein aimser i celebarthai ardsollamuin na ngente
.ı. feis Temra ; tictis na ríga 7 na flatha 7 na airig co Loigairi do
Themraig, fri ceilebrad ind líthlaithi hisin ; tictis dano in druid 7
na maithmairc co mbitis oc tairchetul doib. Robáided didu tene cach
tellaig ind hErind an aidche sin ; 7 roescarad laisin ríg, na róaddaidi
tene ind hEirind ré tenid inna Temrach 7 na gebtha ór na argat óntí
noataifed, acht a techt bás ind. Amal batar ann lucht na Temrach
conaccatar an tene cháscda chosecartha uadib roaddaig P.˙ 7 rosoilsig
Mag Breg uile. "Adchím," ol na druid, "in tenid, 7 manidid-
baither, in aidchi i ndernad, ní baithfidther co bráth ; in fer dano
adannai foruaisligfe ríga 7 flatha na hEirend mani tairmiscther imbi."

5. [ O'C. 26-28.] Ótchuala in rí inni sein foruasnad co mór. Is
ann asrubairt in rí, "Ní ba ed bias de, acht regmaid-ne co romarbum
in fer noadaig in tene." Roindleta didu a charpuit don ríg, 7
dodechator .ı. in fine noctis co Fertai fer Fec. "Is foimnidi duitsiu,

---

pedestri itinere venierunt in prædictum Campum donec pervenierunt
ad Ferti Virorum Feec, fixoque ibi tentorio debita Pascae vota Deo
reddidit, et incendit divinum ignem. Contigit vero in illo anno,
quod exercerent festivitatem gentilem in Temoria ; regibus, satrapis
et optimatibus populi vocatis ad Loigaireum in Temoria (ut) excer-
cerent festitatem ; (vocatis) insuper et magis auruspicibusque. Erat
quoque quidam mos apud illas per edictum omnibus intimatus ut
quicumque in illa nocte accendisset ignem, antequam in palatio
Temoriæ succenderetur, periret anima ejus. P. pasca celebrans,
incendit ignem benedictum, qui reffulgens per plani(tiem) Campi
habitantibus visus est et a Temoria conspexerunt omnes. Magi
responderunt, "Ignis quem videmus, nisi extinctus fuerit in nocte
in qua accensus est, nunquam extinquetur in æternum. Et ille qui
incendit superabit te et omnes homines regni tui nissi extinctus
fuerit."

5. [LA. 4 aa.] His auditis, turbatus est rex valde. Et respondens
rex dixit, "Non sic erit, sed nunc nos ibimus et occidemus facientes
tantum nefas." Junctis curribus, in fine noctis perrexit Loiguire cum
magis ad Ferti virorum Feec. Dixerunt magi regi, "Nec tu ibis

tra," ol na *dr*uid, " na dechais don lucc in *n*dernad i*n* tene, ar
roadræ in fer asidanne ;[1] acht an i*m*maig, 7 cogarar duit imach,
*judicet*[2] *regem te esse illum autem subditum,*[2] 7 tacermait i*n* far fiadnais
" Is degcóma*r*le," ol sé, "dogéntar ama*l* asberid." Tancatar iar
co roscoirset an echu 7 a cairpthiu ar belaib na Fertai. Coggarar
dóib immach ; 7 rosmachtad léu ar na eirsed[3] nech ar a chi*nn*, ar
roch*r*eided dó. Atraracht *tra* P. 7 dodech*ai*d imach co n-accai
cairpthiu 7 na hecho *for* scur ; is ann rocach*ai*n in fers faithe*chd*a[4]
*in curribus et hii in equis*[5] *nos autem in nomine Domini Dei nostri*
Robatar di*diu* ar a chind, 7 ní herracht nech diib ar a chind *acht*
fer nama hi robái figuir o Día .ı. Ercc mac Dega ; is héiside í
Slani Maige Breg i *n*díu. Dorat P. be*n*nacht fair, 7 roc*r*eid do I
Dodechaid Lochru co rosir 7 co engach co cosna*m* 7 cestaib *fri*
is annsoin doréll for écnuch na hirsi cath*lacd*æ. Rofég P. iarsin

---

ad locum in quo incensus est ignis ne forte adoraveris illum
incendit ; sed eris foris juxta, et vocabitur ad te ille, ut te adorave
et ut tu ipsius dominatus fueris, et sermocinabimur invicem nos et i
in conspectu tuo." Ait rex, " bonum consilium invenistis, sic faciæ
ut locuti estis." Pervenierunt, et descendentibus illis de currib
suis et equis non intraverunt in circuitum loci sed sederunt juxi
Vocatus est P. ad regem extra locum ; et dixerunt, " Nec surgem
nos in adventu istius, nam quicunque surrexerit credet ei." Surge
denique P. et videns multos currus et equos eorum venit ad illo
huncque psalmistæ versiculum decantans, *Hii in curribus et hii*
*equis, nos autem in nomine Domini Dei nostri ambulabimus.* Illi ve
non surrexerunt in adventu ejus sed unus tantum a Domino adjuti
hoc est Ercc filius Dego, cujus nunc reliquiæ adorantur in civitæ
quæ vocatur Slane. Benedixit eum P., et credidit Deo. Loch
procax erat in conspectu sancti audens detrachere fidei catholit
tumulentis verbis. Hunc autem intuens turvo oculo, et mag

---

[1] asidan neachtan, *in Ms., read* adi-
danne (?).

[2-2] indicet *in Ms.*, the Latin passages
show that the Irish *Tripartite* was taken
from a Latin version not identical with
that of the *B. of Armagh.*

[3] ut nemo consurgeret, *V.* 2; ut nei
exurgat, *V.* 3.

[4] A curved line across the *h* in *fai*
= psalmistæ = prophetæ.

[5] in eirus, *in Ms.*

andiarid fair, 7 doriucart ó guth mór re Dia *ocus* is ed roráde, *Domine qui omnia potes* . . . . . Roimeclaigsitar na genti do ṡein.

6. [*O'C.* 28, 30.] Rofergaigestar in rí did*iu* fri P. co mor, 7 dochuaid do raith leis a marbad; ised roráde, "Marb*aid* in cl*é*rech." Otchondairc P. na genti do chomeirgi fris, doriugart ó guth mor *et dixit, Exsurgat Deus* . . . . Fo*ch*et*ó*ir dodech*aid* dorcha dar gr*é*in, 7 forcomnacair talumcumscuġud 7 arm*é*rith mor ann; *co n*-erracht cach di alailiu co rabi cach díib in *n*-ár a cheili, co torchair coica fer díib hisin coimeirgiu hisin la mallach*tain* Patraic,[1] co ndechatar na graigi hi fuascur, 7 co roimluaig[2] in goeth *inn*a cairpthiu tr*es*na maigib. Rotheichestar ass in genti *for* cach leth co nach tarrasair *acht* triar[3] namma .ı. Loeg*airi* 7 a riga*n*, 7 dias dia muintir; *et timuerunt valde. Veniensque regina ad Patricium, dixit ei, " Homo juste et potens, ne perdas regem;*[4] dorega i*n* rí cucut 7 dob*é*ra do réir, 7 slechtfaid 7 creitfid do Dia." Dodech*aid* da*n*o Loeg*air*i 7 roslecht do P., 7 dorat brecṡíth dó. Nír bú cían iarsi*n* rochoggair in rí leis

---

clamore confidenter ad Dominum dixit, *Domine qui omnia potes* . . . Et timuerunt gentiles.

6. [*LA.* 4b.] Iratusque rex Patricio super hoc voluit eum occidere, et dixit, "Injecite manus in istum perdentem nos. Tunc videns Patricius gentiles inruituros in eum surrexit claraque voce dixit, "Exurgat Deus" . . . . Et statim inruerunt tenebræ, et commotio quædam horribilis et terræ motus factus est; et expugnaverunt semetipsos alter adversus alterum insurgens, et prostrati sunt ab hac plaga, ad maledictum Patricii, septem septies viri; et præcipitaverunt se equi et currus per planitiem campi. Evasserunt, donec ipse (rex) remanserat ıv tantum hominibus, ipse et uxor ejus et alii ex sociis duo *et timuerunt valde. Veniensque regina ad Patricium, dixit ei,* "*Homo juste et potens ne perdas regem,* viniens enim rex genua flectet et adorabit Deum tuum." Et venit rex et flexit genua coram sancto et finxit se adorare quem nolebat. Et paululum gradiens vocavit rex Patricium simulato verbo volens interficere eum quomodo. Bene-

---

[1] tre mallachtain Patraic, *LB.* 27 a.
[2] agebat eos, *V.* 2.
[3] acht oen chethrur .ı. he fén 7 a ṡetig
7 dias dia muintir, *LB.* 27 a.

[4] Dodechaid in rigan co P. 7 atbert fris, "A duine fíreoin 7 a duine cumachtaig, ní ros - marba in ríg."—
*LB.* 27 a.

Patra*ic* for leith, 7 is *ed* roimraid a marb*ad*.   Dodechuid P. och
maccléire*ch* 7 Benén do gillu léu, 7 rosbendach P. ré dúide
Dodech*uid* dicheltair tairsiu *co nár* árdraig fer dib ; atohoncatar
na gentligi ocht n-aige alltaige do t(h)echt sechu fón sliab, 7 iarn
*inn* a ndegaid.   Dochuaid iarsin Loeg*aire* on dedoil dochum Temr
co mbrón 7 co mbebuil cosna huaitib noernatis leis.

Isind laithiu iarnabarach .ı. Domn*ach* Casca, dodechatar fir hÉir
dochu*m* Temr*ach* do fledól, intan ro*m*bátar oc ind fledól 7 imrac
*in* conflichta rofersatar al la riam, conaccatar P. co tarrasair for lár
Temrach *januis clausis*[1] *ut Christus in cenaculum.*

Nochon erracht nech ar a c(h)inn istaig *acht* Dubthach ma
Lugair na*m*ma rígfil*e*, 7 maothoclach dia muintir, Fíacc a ai*nm* ;
heiside atta hi Sleibti i ndiu.   In Dubthach sin da*no* is ó c*ét*na
rocr*eit* do Dia hi Te*m*r*aig* isind laithiu sin ; dorat P. b*enn*achtain f

7. [ *O' C.* 29.]   Gairmtir di*diu* P. dochum leptha ind ríg co tor
lath biad, 7 dia (f)romad hi faitsine .ı. *in venturis rebus ;* nírobai[2] d

---

dictis sociis suis octo viris cum puero venit ad regem.   Statimq
nusquam comparuerunt, dempti ab oculis regis ; sed viderunt genti
octo tantum cervos cum hynulo euntes quasi ad dissertum.
Loiguire mestus et ignominiossus cum paucis evadentibus ad Tem
reversus est diluculo.

Sequenti vero die hoc est in Die Pascæ, recumbentibus regibus
principibus et magis totius Hiberniæ, manducantibus illis et bibe
tibus, sermocinantibus aliis, et aliis cogitantibus de his quæ fa
fuerant, Patricius, in Temoria hostiis claussis venit, secundum
quod de Christo legitur.

Nemo ad adventum ejus in palatio surrexit præter unum tantu
id est Dubthoch maccu Lugir, poetam optimum, apud quem e
quidam adoliscens (poeta), nomine Feec, cujus reliquiæ adorantur
Sleibti.   Hic autem Dubthach credidit primus in illa die Deo,
benedixit ei P.

7. [*LA.* 5a.]   Vocatus est itaque P. a gentibus ad vescendi
ut probarent eum in venturis rebus ; ille autem sciens quæ venti

---

[1] doirrsib foriattaib, *LB.* 27a.          [2] *for* ni ro obai, *or* ní rohob.

anní sin dég roꞟitir inni arbíad de. Dodechaid an drúid Lucat Moel
do comól friss, fo bith robo adlaicc dó a aithi do Pátraic aní dorigne
fri a fer comtha isin lau riam; dorat dino laim di neim isinn airdig[1]
robói for láim Pátraic, conaccad cid dogenath P. friss. Roratbaid
didiu P. anní sin 7 robennach side in airdig 7 rochoteg ind línd.
Ocus roimpai[2] in lestar iarsin 7 dorochair ass in neim dorat in
drúi ind. Robendach P. daridisi ind airdig 7 rosóad in lind in a
aicned chóir[3]. "Denam," ol Lucat Moel[4], "ferta isin maig mór-sa."
Atrubairt P., "Cadet?" (A)dubairt in drui, "Tucum snechta forsan
maig."[5] Adubairt P. frissom, "Ní hail dam tichtain inaigid thole
Dé." Adubairt in drúi, "Dober-sa in snechta forsan mag ar belaib in
t-slúaig." Thindarscan iarsin inna filidechta drúidechta cor-roferustair
in snechta co toracht fernu fer. Et viderunt omnes, 7 romachtaigsetair
co mór. Adubairt P., "Atchiam inso; cuir ass, ma connice."[6] Atrubairt in drui, "Ni chuimgim-si inní sin cusin tráth-sa imbárach."

---

essent non reffellit[7] vesci. Coenantibus omnibus ille magus Lucet
Mail, qui in illa die solicitus est, extincto consocio suo, confligere
adversus Patricium, ut initium causæ haberet, immisit aliquid ex
vasse suo in poculum Patricii ut probaret quid faceret. Videnesque
Patricius hoc benedixit poculum et versus est liquor in modum gelu.
Et converso vasse cecidit gutta illa quam immisserat magus. Et
iterum benedixit poculum (et) conversus est liquor in naturam suam.
Ait magus, "faciamus signa in hoc campo maximo."[8] Ait P.,
"Quæ?" Et dixit magus, "Inducamus nivem super terram." Et
ait Patricius, "Nolo contraria voluntati Dei inducere." Et dixit
magus, "Ego inducam videntibus cunctis." Tunc incantationes
magicas exorsus induxit nivem pertinguentem usque ad zonas
virorum.[9] Et viderunt omnes et mirati sunt. Et ait P., "Ecce
videmus hoc; depone nunc." Dixit magus, "Ante istam horam cras
non possum deponere." Et ait Sanctus, "Potes malum et non bonum

---

[1] banni do neim in érdig Patraic,
LB. 27 a; for laim di neim, read loim
di neim.

[2] rosimpoi, LB.

[3] 7 attib P. in lind (LB.) = et bibit
potum, V. 3, c. 40.

[4] Lucat Calvus, Brux.

[5] Read mag, as infra and supra.

[6] si potes, V. 2, c. 39.

[7] repulit, Brux.

[8] magno, in Brux.

[9] sic Brux., pertinguentem ferenn, LA.

"Dar mo debro," ol P., "is in*n* ulc attá do chumachtai[1] 7 ní am maith.'
Rotb*end*ach P. *in* mag uad fó chetheor arda, is déniu rád rothinai[2] ir
snechtai cen flech*ad* cen gr*éi*n cen gaith.   Dodechatar iars*in* dor-
choitar[3] *for* gnuis *in* talm*an* la díchitel in druad.[4]   Rogairset na sluai£
do šen.   Adubairt P., "*Expelle tenebras.*"[5]   Adub*air*t in drui, "Noch£
cum£gaim i *n*díu."   Rogaid P. in Coim£did 7 robendach[6] am mag, ʼ
roindarpanta na dorchai, 7 doraitne in gr*ia*n, 7 dogníset atlaigthe
buidi *in*na huili.   Robatar *tra* co cíana ocon *c*honflicht so ar belait
ind ríg, *ait rex ad illos* "*Libros vestros in aquam mittite . . . aquan
enim deum habet.*"   Deg[7] rochuala s*om* is tre uisce nobaitsed.   (Tun£
dixit rex, "Cuirid bar libra in usce, 7 cibe uaib is a libair élait
dogenum-ne adrad dó."   Atbert in drai, "Dia us*ci* adras in fer-sa
7 ni rag-sa[8] im oen fuigell fris.")[9]

8. [*O'C.* 31, 32.]   *Et respondit rex, "Mittite in ignem . . . veneratur.*"   (Atbert in rí, "Curid bar libra i tenid."   "Isam erlum-sa d£

---

facere."   Tunc benedicens per totum circuitum campum, dicto citiu£
absque ulla pluvia aut nebulis aut vento evanuit nix.   Paulo pos£
invocatis demonibus induxit magus tenebras super terram.   Et clamaverunt turbæ (et mirati sunt).   Et ait Sanctus, "Expell£
tenebras."   At ille non poterat.   P. vero orans benedixit, et ex-
pulsæ sunt tenebræ, et refulsit sol ; et gratias egerunt omnes.   Hi£
autem omnibus gestis in conspectu regis, ait rex ad illos "Libro£
vestros in aquam mittite . . . . aquam enim deum habet."   Cert£
audivit baptisma per aquam a Patricio datum.   [*LA.* 5 ab, ba.]   Ai£
rex, "Libros vestros in aquam mittite et illum cujus libri inless£
evaserint adorabimus."   Respondit P., "Prumptus sum."   Magu£
dixit, "Hic homo aquam deum veneratur ; nolo ego ad judiciun
aquæ venire cum isto."

8. [*LA.* 5 ba.]   Et respondens rex ait "Mittite in ignem . . .
veneratur."   Et Rex ait, "Permittite libros in ignem."   Ait sin,'

---

[1] in malo potestatem habes, *V.* 2, c. 39.

[2] rothmai, *O'C.*

[3] Dorogart in draí demnu co tuc
dorchai for, *LB.*

[4] druag *in Ms.*

[5] Beir ass in dorchatu, *LB.*

[6] senais, *LB.*

[7] *certe* seems to mean 'forsooth, because,' = *deg.*

[8] non inibo, *V.* 4, c. 46.

[9] The words in parenthesis are fron
*LB.* 27 b.

ol P. "Ni díngen amlaid," ol in drai, "uair dia tened adras in fer-sa cech da bl*iadain*.")[1] "Nipa ed dogentar an*n*," ol P., "rega-su hi tech f*o*rdunta f*o*r leith, 7 maccléir*ech* dim muintir-se it 'arrad,[2] 7 mu chasal-sa i*m*mutsa, 7 do thonach druaḋ-su[3] i*m* mo maccléirech-sa, 7 dobérthar teine isa tech, cor-ruca Dia breth f*o*raib an*n*." Desid léo in chomairli sin; doronat[4] iarsin in tech, indala leth de cr*i*n 7 araile úr. Rofuided da*no* in drúi isa leith n-úr, 7 casal Pat*raic* i*m*bi; rofuided im. Benen isin l*e*th cr*i*n 7 tunach in dr*ú*ad i*m* suide. Roḣíadad i*n* tech iar*om*, 7 doratad crann ar chleith aire i*m*mach ar bél*ai*ḃ int-sluaig, 7 adadar tene ind. Forcaomnacair firt mór and t*r*e irnaigthe Pát*raic*, roloisced al leth n-úr den taig 7 in drúi i*m* medon na caslea, 7 ní romill a becc din chasail. Ni roloisced im. al leith cr*i*n ir-rabi Be*n*en, 7 roanacht Dia Bine*n* i*m* medón tonaigi in drúad, 7 roloisced im. in tunach co ndernai luaith di.

Rofergaigestar[5] in rí f*ri* Pát*raic* com*m*ór di marb*ud* a d*r*uad;

---

P., "Prumptus sum." Magus nolens dixit, "Hic homo versa vice in alternos annos nunc aquam nunc ignem deum veneratur." Et ait Patricius, "Non sic, sed tu ipse ibis, et unus ex meis pueris ibi tecum in separatam et conclausam domum et meum erga te et tuum erga me erit vestimentum. Sic simul incendimini in conspectu Altissimi." Et hoc consilium incedit[6], et edificata est domus, cujus dimidium ex materia viridi, et alterum dimidium ex arida facta est. Et missus est magus in illam partem ejus viridem, et Bineus cum veste magica in partem domus aridæ.[7] Conclussa itaque extrinsecus domus coram omni turba incensa est. Et factum est in illa hora, orante Patricio, ut consumeret flamma ignis magùm cum demedia domu viridi, permanente cassula tantum intacta quod ignis non tetigit. Benineus autem cum demedia domu arida non tetigit eum ignis, cassula tantum magi quæ erga eum fuerat, non sine nutu Dei, exusta est.

Et iratus est valde rex adversus Patricium de morte magi sui, et

---

[1] The words in parenthesis are from *LB.* 27 b.

[2] it tarrad *in Ms.*; *read* it farrad.

[3] tḣuiḋnech druaḋ-sa, *in Ms.*

[4] *sic* in *Eg.*, *read* doronath, *or* doronad.

[5] fergaidestar, *O'C.*

[6] *for* insedit = deisid; sedit, *V.* 2, c. 40.

[7] *aridæ* added in Brux.; read *aridam*.

atráracht 7 dochoid do raith leis a orcain, *acht* ní rochomarleicest
Dia dó.   Tre edarguidi Patraic dodech*aid* iarsi*n* ferg Dé f*o*rsin pop
n-eccraib(d)ech co n-erbalt sochaidi mór díb.

Adub*ai*rt P. *fri* Loeg*ai*ri, "Mani cr*ei*ti-siu i*n*dossa adbéla co luat
ar dorega f*er*g Dé it 'mullach." Otchuala in rí inna br*i*athra si
rongab omu*n* mór. Téit iarsin in rí hi tech n-imacallma *fri*
muintir, "Is ferr da*m*sa," ol sé, "cr*ei*tem do Dia oldáas mo marbad.
Iarsin rochreitt do Dia 7 roc*h*reitset il-mile isin láu sin. Is a*n*dsi
roráid P. re Laog*ai*ri, "Doberthar fot saoguil duit ít 'rígu; il-log i
t' anahumolloti[1] ní bía ríg uait co br*á*th."

9. [*O'C.* 131, 132.] Bói alaili duni andgaid hi tírib Ulud inta
sin .i. macc Cuill, écraibdech 7 macc báiss, nobíd ic slaitairecht
nomarbu(d) na cuitechtai. Issed roradi fri a munt*ir*, "Is hé so i
tailcend 7 in ꜱáibthaid fil ic bréccud cháich. Tiagam co tarta
a*m*mus fair dús in furtachtfaigi a Dea." Is*ed* rodolpset didu, f
dia muntir do thobairt for fuatt amal bid marb do bréccud Pátrai
7 doratsat bratt dara chorp 7 dar a gnúis. "Hícc dún," ol sí

---

inruit poene in eum volens occidere; sed prohibuit illum Deus. A
precem enim Patricii, descendit ira Dei (in populum inpium ɛ
perierunt multi ex eis.)[2]

Et ait P. regi, "Nisi nunc credideris, cito morieris quia descendɛ
ira Dei in verticem tuum." Et timuit rex vehementer. Congregatɪ
igitur senioribus et senatu suo, dixit eis rex "Melius est mihi credeɪ
me quam mori." Et credidit et crediderunt multi alii in illa diɛ
Et ait Patricius ad regem, "Prolonguentur dies regni tui; quia tamɛ
resististi meæ doctrinæ, nullus erit ex semine tuo rex in æternum."

9. [*LA.* 6 a.] Erat quidam homo in regionibus Ulothorum Patric
tempore Macuil maccu Greccæ; et erat hic homo valde impius sævu
tyrannus; tyrannidem exercebat (diberca) et transeuntes hospites iɪ
terficiens. Dicens satellitibus suis, "Ecce seductor ille ɛt perversoɪ
cui mos est ut decipiat homines. Eamus ergo ut temptemus eum ɩ
sciamus si habeat aliquam potestatem ille Deus in quo se gloriatur.
Temptaverunt itaque in hoc mudo; posuerunt unum ex semetipꜱ
sanum in medio eorum sub sago jacentem, mortem simulantem ʋ
probarent Sanctum in fallaci re. Et dixerunt ei, "Ecce unus ɛ

---

[1] *sic* in *Eg.*      [2] The words in parenthesis are in *Brux.*

*frı* Patraic, " ar fer comtha 7 dena gaidi do Choim̃ded co rutbo-
diusci a báss." "Mo debroth," ar P., "ní hingnad limm̃ cid marb."
Roláiset a munte*r* in bratt dia agid conidfuarutar secc. Roṡochtsat-
so*m* iar*um et dixerunt*, "Is duine Dé iar fír in duine-si." Rochreit
fo chétóir Macc Cuill, dorodius(c)ad da*no* Garbán a báss tria airnaigthi Pat*raic*. Dochóid *tra* Macc Cuill in laa sin for muir hi
curuch oenṡeichi, la forcongra Patraic, 7 a lám dess *frı* Mag Inis co
riacht Manaind; 7 fofuáir díis n-adamraigthi isin indsi for a chind 7
it ẹisidi rofrı́tchaiset[1] bréithir nDé hi Manai*n*d, 7 is *tre* n-a f*o*rcetul
robaitside doine i*n*na indsi sein,[2] 7 rochreitsit side[3]—Conindri 7 Romail
a n-anman*n*. Otchondarcatar di*d*u ind fir-si Macc Cuill in a churach
dofucsat din muir, ar roetatar hé co fæltæ, 7 rofoglai*n*d in mbéscnai
ndíada occu, 7 dorochaid huile aimsir a bethad occu co rogaib
epscopṓti inna (n)degaid. Is hé inso Macc Cuill dimana[4] *episcopus
et antistes Ardde Uimnen* [5*a*] *cujus nos sufragia adjuvent*[6] *sancta.*[a]

---

nobis infirmatus est, canta incantationes sectæ tuæ si forte sanari
possit." Intrepide dixit, "Nec mirum si infirmus fuisset." Et
revelantes socii ejus faciem ejus, viderunt eum jam mortuum. At
illi obstupescentes dixerunt, "Vere hic homo Dei est." In illa
hora credidit Maccuil Deo æterno. Et suscitavit mortuum Patricius
et revixit sanus. Et migravit tam cito et ascendit mare mac Cuil
in navi unius pellis secundum quod præceptum est ei, ad mare dex-
terum Campi Inis, et jecit eum ventus in Insolam Evoniam; inve-
nitque ibi duos viros valde mirabiles, qui docuerunt verbum Dei, et
baptismum in Evonia, et conversi sunt homines insolae huius in
doctrina eorum ad fidem catholicam—quorum nomina sunt Conindri et
Rumili. Hii autem videntes hominem hujus habitus, erexerunt eum
de mari suscipientes cum gaudio, ille igitur ad regulam eorum corpus
et animam exercuit, et totum vitæ tempus exegit apud istos usque
dum successeorum in episcopatu effectus est. Hic est Maccuil dimane
episcopus et antestes Arddæ Huimnon.

---

[1] *sic* in *Eg.*, *for* rophrı́tchaiset.
[2] dein *in Eg.*
[3] inside *in Eg.*
[4] de mare, *Brux.*; *cf.* din muir, *supra*.

[5] *a–a cujus* to *sancta* in *Eg.* and *Brux.*;
but not in *LA*.
[6] adimenent, *Eg.*

Ra[1] chuiḃriġsiod ag cor glais iaroinn edir a cheann 7 a chosa 7 d
cuireadh eochair an ġlais isin fairrge.    Eulais Triallach for an eachtr
i gcurach gan chodail .ı. gan chroicionn ar an fairrge timchioll Erean
siar, 7 an glas eidir a cheanu 7 a chosa gur ġaḃ port tre furtach
nDé i nDísiort Ui Triallaiġ.

10. [*O'C.* 133–138.]    Fecht rochotail il-laithiu domnaig os i
muir occ Druim Bó, co cuala fogur mór inna ngenti oc claide rathɛ
isin domn*uch*, 7 dorogart íat 7 atrub*air*t friu bith i*n* a toss.    *Ocus* noc
ndernasat aire, acht is ic fochuitbiud robátar.    *Et ait P.,* "Modebroth
*labor vestrum non proficiat.*"    *Quod probatum est.    Sequenti . . . verbu*ɪ
*Patrici.*

Bui alaili fer soi*m*m airmitnech ic Machai, Dáre a ainm.    Conait
igir P. inned a reclesa fair.    Atrub*air*t Dare, " Cia dú adcobrai?'
" Hisin tailaich mór-se thís," ol P., dú hita Ardd Macha i ndíu.    " N
t(h)ibér," ol Dare, " doḃ*er* duit chena i*n*ned do reclesa isin ráith choḃ

---

[*LA.* 6 ab.]    Conliga pedes tuos compede ferreo, et projicɪ
clavim ejus in mari et mitte te in navim unius pellis alsque guberna
culo et absque remo, et terram, in quam defferat te Divina Providentiɪ
inhabita.    Et Maccuil collegavit se jeciens clavim in mare, et ascendɪ
mare in navicula.

10. [*LA.* 6 b, 7 a.]    Alia vice requiescens juxta Collum Bovis
audivit sonum intemperatum gentilium in die dominica facientiu*n*
*rathi;* vocatisque illis prohibuit eos.    At illi non consentiebant verbiɪ
sancti, quin immo inridentes deludebant[3] eum.    Et ait P., " Mudebroth !
quamvis laboraveritis, nec tamen proficiat."    Quod completum est
In sequenti . . . verbum sancti.

Fuit homo quidam dives et honorabilis in regionibus Orientalium,·
cui nomen erat Daire.    Hunc rogavit P. ut aliquem locum ad exer-
cendam religionem daret ei.    Dixit dives, " Quem locum petis?'
" Peto," inquit Sanctus, " illam altitudinem terræ, quæ nominatuɪ

---

· [1] *From* Ra *to* end of paragraph is
inserted from the *B. of Lecan* as given
at p. 38 of Hyfiachrach ; the Latin is
from *LA.*

[2] facientes fossam .castelli, *Brux.*
[3] deridebant, *Brux.*
[4] Origentalium, *Brux.,* in Oirtheraiḃ,
*LB.* 28.

said-si thís," dú ita ind Ferta[1] i *n*díu; ro fothaig *trá* P. ré cían hi suidiu. Laa and tuctha dá ech Dare cucai i*nn* a recles *for* fér, ar rob-férach i*n*d relec. Ro fercaigestar P. fríu. Marba ind eich fó chétóir; atfét a gilla do Dáre aní sein, *dicens,* "In cristaidi so," ol sé, "romarb th'echu-sa." Forcongart Dáre for a mogaidu orgai*n* in chléirich. Dofanic tregatt obu*n*d fo cetóir co mbu comochroib báss dó. Arogart in seitig orguin Patraic, *et dixit* do Dáre co mbu hé fochun a báis tac-crad do Pátraic.

11. Robe*n*dach P. ind uisci 7 doratt donaib timthirib 7 forchongairt a thabairt tarsna heochu[2] 7 tar Dáre. *Et sic fecerunt,* 7 asrárachtatar huili a bass. Ruccad coiri umaidi do Pátraic in edbairt ó Dáre. "*Deo gratias,*" ol P. Rofiarfacht Dare dia mogadaib cid adrubairt P.[3] *Responderunt,* "*Grazacum dixit.*" "Is becc in log degcoiri insin," ol Dare. Forchongart dorithisi a choiri do thab*airt* uad.[4] "Deo gratias,"

---

Dorsum Salicis[5] et construam ibi locum." Ille noluit dare; sed dedit illi locum alium in inferiori terra ubi nunc est Fertæ[6]; et habitavit ibi cum suis. Post aliquod tempus venit eques Dairi ducens equum suum in oraculum[7] ut pasceretur in herbosso loco. Offendit Patricium[8] talis dilatio equi. Invenit eques equum jam mortuum; reversus ait ad dominum suum, "Ecce christianus ille occidit tuum equum." Dixit Daire, "Interficite eum." Dictu citius inruit repentina mors super Daire[9] et ait uxor ejus, "Caussa christiani est hæc mors; prohibe(a)ntur qui exierunt occidere eum."

11. [7 a.] Benedixit aquam et dedit ei(s) dicens, "Aspergite equum ex ista aqua." Et fecerunt sic et revixit equus, sanatusque est Dáire in asparsione aquæ sanctæ. Venit Daire portans æneum, dixitque, "Ecce hic æneus sit tecum." Et ait P., " Grazacham." Interrogavit Daire servos suos, quid dixit christianus. Responderunt, "Grazacham dixit." Et Daire dixit, "Stultus homo est qui nihil boni

---

[1] indeferta, *Eg.*

[2] darsin ech 7 darsin fer, *LB.* 28.

[3] cid atbert in clerech (?), *LB.* 28.

[4] do *in Eg., read* huad, *as infra bis.*

[5] i nDruim Sailech dú ita Ard Macha, *Lism. Life,* p. 17; Drumsailech hoc est Ard Macha, *Brux.*

[6] dorat-sum inad do P. bale ita in

Ferta indiú, *LB.* 28.

[7] Rucc gilla Dáre a ech maith isin recles dochum ind feoir díguind, *LB.* 28; I suggest, as an emendation, ducens equum suum in oraculum (= recles), for "equum suum miraculum," of *LA.*

[8] Rathoccraid sin cu mór do P., *LB.* 28.

[9] Atbail Dáre fochetóir, *LB.* 28.

ol P.  Ocus rofiarfacht Dare, cid asbert P. hic tabairt in choiri hua
*Dixerunt servi,* " Issed in cétna asbert oc a thabairt uad, .i. Graticum
"Is degbríathar leisseom," ol Dare, " .ı. Graticum ico edbairt dó
graticum o breith uad." Luid Dare iarsuidiu 7 a seitig cona ogréir
Patraic, 7 adropartadar in coiri do P., 7 in telcha[1] *con*atigair ria sur

Luid P. 7 Dare isin telchai.  Forancatar ailit *con* a loeg mag
ita in Sabull i ndíu.  Ocus dochuatar a muin*ter* dia orcain, *Et pr*
*hibuit* P. ocus rosfaid as in telchai fothuaid co maigin hitá Telach
Licci i ndíu ; *ibi magna mirabilia fecit.*

12. [*O' C.* 71.]  Ba bes dó, dobered crois Cri*st* tairis co fachét ce
lái 7 cech aidchi, 7 notheged dia chonair cid míli cheimmend nobe
in chross, acht conacced, cid hi carput nó for euch nobeth, noching
dochum cecha croissi.  Fecht and olaili laithiu rosechmall tada
croissi robói for sét dou, 7 ní fitir ara mbeth and.  Roradi a ara fri
i ndiud lái, " Foracbaiss croiss i ndíu fort'chonair cen tadall

---

dixit præter *Grazacham* pro æneo mirabili.  Addit Dare, dicens " R
portate nobis æneum." P. dixit " Grazacham." Interrogavitque Dai
dicens, " Quid dixit christianus quando reportasti æneum?" Illi respo
derunt, " Grazacham dixit et ille." Daire dixit, " Gratzacham
dato, Gratzacham in ablato—ejus dictum tam bonum est." Et ve
Daire ipsemet[2] illa vice, et portavit æneum ad Patricium et part
illam agri quam ollim petiit dedit ei.

[7 ab.] Et exierunt ambo P. et Daire et ascenderunt illam al
tudinem terræ.  Invenierunt cervam cum vitulo suo parvo in loco
quo nunc est altare sinistralis æclesiæ in Ardd Mache.  Et volueru
comites Patricii vitulum occidere.  Sed non permissit sanctus, usq
dum dimisserat vitulum in altero saltu situm ad aquilonalem plag
Airdd Mache : ubi usque hodie signa quædam virtutis ejus manen
periti dicunt.

12. [*LA.* 7b.]  Tropeo crucis in omni hora diei noctisque centi
se signans, et ad omnes cruces quascumque vidisset orationis gratia
curru discendens declinabat.  Inde etiam in die quadam ingredie
crucem quæ erat juxta viam sita non videns prætergressus est.  I
dixit auriga ante prandium, " Vidi crucem juxta viam per quam ve

---

[1] in tealach connateach fair, *Lism. Life,* p. 17.    [2] teit Dáre fén, *LB.* 28.

Farácaib P. a tech n-oiged, 7 luid for cúlu dochum na croisi; intan roboi ic airnaigthe ocun chroiss, "Adnocul so," ol P., "cia roadnacht sund?" Frisrogart as ind adnacol, "Gentlidi truag meissi 7 romadnacht sund. Alaili banscal robái hi tír chíana, 7 a macc roadnacht sund isin tír-si in a hécmais, co tanic a tírib ciana co rosuidig in chroiss for m'adnacul-sa; indar lea is for adnacul a maic dorat, ní ermadair lasin toirrsi aichni adnacuil a maic." "Is airi sein rosechmallus-(s)a in croiss," ol P. .i. a bith for adnacul in gentlidi. O esspartain aidche ndomnaig co anteirt[1] día luain ní theiged P. assin maigin im mbith. Olailiu domnuch do Patraic immaig in huair (f)escuir co rosnig flechud mór isin talmain sin, 7 nirsníg[2] isin lucc i rabi P. *sicut in concha et vellere Gedeoni accederat.*

13. [*O'C.* 72.] Fecht ann do aru(id) Patraic, téstatar a eich airi, ní chóimnacuir a fogbail la doirchi na haidchi. Tuarcaib P. a láim suas, roin(s)orchaigset a chúicc mer in mag n-uile amal bitis chóic sutralla 7 fófritha na heich foc(h)etoir.

---

mus possitam." At Patricius, dimisso hospitio per viam quam venerat ad crucem pergens oravit, et sepulcrum ibi viderat; interrogavit qua morte abierat. Respondit mortuus, "Gentilis vixi, et hic sepultus sum." Quædam etiam mulier in alia provincia degens mortuum filium, qui se longue separatus erat, habuit, et illa absente sepultus est. Post aliquot dies lugens mater omissum filium planxit et inde-creto errore sepulchrum gentilis bustum filii esse putans, crucem juxta gentilem possuit. Et ob hanc caussam, ut Patricius dixit, crucem non viderat, quia sepulturæ gentilis locus fuit. Consuetudo illi erat ut a vespera dominicæ noctis usque ad mane secundæ feriæ non ambularet. Inde in quadam dominica die, honore sacri temporis in campo pernoctans gravis pluvia accederat in tota patria, sed in loco ubi sanctus erat siccitas erat sicut in conca et in vellere Gedeon.

13. [*LA.* 8 a.] Accederat auriga, memorat equos amissos, quia illos quærere, tenebris arcentibus vissum, non poterat. Manum P. elevavit, et quinque digiti sicut luminaria ita proxima quæque inluxerant, et equos auriga invenit.

---

[1] an teirt, *O'C.*          [2] nirinig *corrected to* nirsníg *in Eg.*

[ *O' C.* 150.] Iarsna mor*m*irbailib-se *tra* rochom*f*oicsechastar láithi eidsechta Patraic ; tanic ai*n*gel adochu*m*, iss*ed* roradi fri*s*, "Eirgg fort' chulu don baili, as a ṭanac .ı. don t-S̈abull.   Dorath duitsiu d'ordan 7 t'airechas in Ard Machai ; ¹ᵃnach oen gebas do immun il-lou a etsechta . . . ; dorat duit nem d*o* Dichoin con a chlainn, 7 dorat duit cu mba tú féin bus breithem bratha ar feraib Eirenn alla sin."ᵃ  [ *O'. C.* 150, 151.] Is*ed* dorinscan techt do Ard Mach*æ* (²atchí in ṁunni for lasad ar a chind 7 ní loisced teni in muine.ᵇ   Samaiges crích fri aidchiᶜ).   Ocus frí ré da oidch̩i deucc .ı. an airet robatar sr*u*ithi hEir*end* iccó ari con i*m*naib 7 salm*aib* 7 cantaicib nocho rabi adhaig and.   Ocus atberat araili robái soillsi co cend mbliad*na* iar n-etsecht Pátraic, *quod nulli ad tanti viri meritum declarandum accidisse dubium est.*   Rochoṁocsegestar uair eitsechta indí Noeb Patraic arroét Corp Crist³ on Epscop o Thassach doréir chomarle Victoir angel.

14. [ *O'C.* 152.]  Isin cetna aidchi ai*n*gil in Choi*m*ded na ndulai robatar ic fr*i*thairi chuirp Patraic co cetlaib spirtaldaib bolomairib, 7

---

Post vero miracula tanta, adpropinquante die mortis ejus venit ad eum angelus et dixit illi : " Revertere ad locum unde venis, hoc est Sabul, et datæ sunt .ııı. petitiones tibi: ut in Ardd Machæ fiat ordinatio tua ; quicunque ymnum qui de te compossitus est in die exitus de corpore cantaverit . . . ; ut nepotes Dichon non pereant ; ut Hibernenses omnes in die judicii a te judicentur."   Inde iter carpere cœpit ad Machi ; sed juxta viam rubus quidam arserat et non combure(ba)tur. Contra noctem terminum pones.   Quia in illa die mortis ejus nox non erat, et per duodecim⁴ dies in illa provincia in qua mortis ejus exequiæ peractæ sunt nox non inruit.   Et plebs Ulod dixerunt quod usque ad finem anni totius in quo abierat nunquam tenebræ erant.   Quod ad tanti viri meritum declarandum esse dubium est.   Adpropinquante hora obitus sui sacrificium ab Episcopo Tassach, sicut illi victor anguelus dixit, ad viaticum beatæ vitæ acceperat.

14. [*LA.* 8 ab.]  In prima nocte exequiarum ejus angeli vigilias psalmi⁵ corporis fecerunt in vigiliarum et psalmorum moribus, omnibus

---

¹ *a-a from* nach oen *to* alla sin *is from* *O'C.* 67, *LB.* 28, *Lism. Life*, p. 18.

² The words in parenthesis ending (*b*) are from *LB.* 28, and (*c*), f*r*om *Fiac's Hymn*, stanza 28

³ arroet didu Commainn 7 sacarbaic,' *O'C* 99, and *Lism. Life*, 19 ; rogab comaind 7 sacarbaic, *LB.* 29.

⁴ duodecimas, *LA.*

⁵ *read* sancti (?).

ceol nan aingel dorat suan 7 failti do sruithib fer n-Erend batar ic airi
in chuirp isna haidchib iaru*m*. ¹ᵃRochometsat in corp.ᵃ Co rochomailled
f*ri*s be*n*nachtu Iacoib, "*Ecce odor*" . . . Foraccaib in t-aingel comairle oc
Pát*raic* amal noadnasta, *dicens*, "Tucaitir," ol se, " da óc*c*da*m* disciri
dó cethrai *Co*naill a F*in*dabair .ı. ó Chlochur, 7 suidigther do chorp h'i
carreni forru, 7 secip leth tiasat ind ócdaim 7 a mbaili hi tairesfet bad
a*n*dsein notadnastar 7 notabar fercubat isind adnucol arna tucait*er* do
reilci 7 do thaissi ass." Dorigned samlaid.

Bói *im.* tríall cu*im*ling móir² 7 catha etir Ulta 7 Uu Neill, 7 Airgiallu ic cosnu*m* chuirp Patraic—Airgiallu 7 Ui Neill ic triall a tab*ar*ta
do Ard Machai, Ulaid occa ostud, co ndechatur hui Néill co alaili uisci
and co tuargab ind ob f*ri*u t*ri*a n*er*t Dé. O duchóid i*n* lia as ind obai*n*d
dochuatar na slúaig fo chombáig .ı. hUi Neill 7 Ulaid do breith chuirp
Patraic. Iss*ed* tarfas do chach diib breith in chuirp leis dochum a thíri.

15. Ticced aingel dia acallaim. ³ᵇCet slechtain cech láithi 7 cét cech
n-oidche dognid*ᵇ*. ⁴ᶜForruib a choiss forsind leic ocus maraid slicht a

---

quicumque ad vigilias in illa prima nocte veniebant dormientibus.
Corpus custodierunt. Ut impleretur quod in benedictionibus Jacob
dictum est, "Ecce odor filii mei tanquam ager . . . ." Angelus
consilium sepulturæ dedit illi: "Elegantur duo instabiles juvenci de
pecoribus Conail, a loco qui Clocher vocatur ab oriente Findubrec
et stabili plaustrum gestamine humeris impossitum cum corpore
vechant, et ubicumque requiescent æclessia in honorem corpusculi tui
ædificetur; ne reliquiæ a terra reducantur corporis tui, et cubitus de
terra super corpus fiat." Quod factum est.

Dira contentio ad bellum usque perveniens inter Nepotes Neill
et Orientales de reliquiis sancti Patricii. Irarum intrat certamen
secundum fretum quoddam. Misericordia Dei surrexit freti feritas.
Freti tumore sepulto Ulaid et Nepotes Neill acriter ad certamen
ruunt et ad locum beati corporis prorumpunt. Se corpus rapere
æstimabant.

15. [*LA*. 8b.] Anguelus venire consuerat et sicut homo cum ho-
mine loquitur. Centies in die et centies in nocte orabat. Pedem super

---

¹ ᵃ⁻ᵃ in *LB*. 29.
² roas cosnam mór etir Airgiallu 7
Ultu, *LB*. 29.

³ ᵇ⁻ᵇ in *LB*. 24.
⁴ ᶜ⁻ᶜ *from* Forruib *to* cloich *in* Fiac's
Hymn and Glosses:

choss beos forsin cloich.<sup>c</sup> [*O' C.* 84.] Dochuaid P. tar Sinain*n* .L. clocc 7 .L. cailech n-altóre forácaib hi tír Condacht.    [*O' C.* 143.] Im reilcib Póil 7 Petair 7 Laurint 7 Stephain.

16. [*O' C.* 9.]   Rotècht da*no* ceithir anmand fair, Magonius·a Germano, Sucait a ainm ó thustidib, Patricius .ı. pater civium a Papa Celestino, Cothraigi iarsindi foruigenai do cetharthreib.   Rocendaig Miliuc ón triur aili 7 foruigénair-som secht mbliadna; 7 issed roherbad dó ingairi mucc, 7 rocess mór n-imned i ndithrub slébe.  <sup>1</sup><sup>d</sup>Ir-richt eoin ticed Victor aingel co Patraic, i Sciric sainriud ticed cucai.<sup>d</sup>  <sup>2</sup><sup>e</sup>Is maith dogní ernaigthe, is maith dogní aine."<sup>e</sup>  <sup>3</sup><sup>f</sup>Is fuiride didiu in long co ndiġi-sa.<sup>f</sup>

17. [*Lismore Life*, p. 8.]   Luid i tír. Dogní aoiġidecht a tiġ fir maith andsin.  Baister hé iarum.  Bái mac bec aigi, rotoltnaiġ side do Patraic 7 dobreth P. ainm fair Benignus .ı. Benén.  Gabuis in mac cos Pátraic 'n-a ucht, 7 nír æm codlud le a máthair na athair, acht nochaifeᵭ muna leicthi i fochair Pátraic hé.  Ar madain immorro cuiris P. a chois

petram ponens in Scirit; et vestigia pedis angueli iu petra hucusque manentia cernuntur.   Portavit P. per Sininn secum L. clocos, L. calices altaris et reliquit illos in locis novis.   Portavit partem de re-liquis Petri et Pauli, Laurentii et Stephani,

16. [*LA.* 9 ab.]   Inveni quatuor nomina scripta Patricio—sanctus Magonus, qui est clarus, Succetus qui est (deus belli vel fortis belli). Patricius (*i. e.* pater civium) Cothirthiacus quia servivit quatuor domibus magorum.   Et empsit illum unus ex eis cui nomen erat Milinc et servivit illi septem annis; et porcarium possuit eum multiplici labore in montanis convallibus.   Apparuit ei angelus sub specie avis in loco qui Scirech nominatur: "Bene oras et bene jejunas cito iturus eris ad patriam tuam."   Ecce navis parata est surge et ambula.

17. [*LA.* 9 ba.]   Ascendit de mari.  Vespere venit ad quemdam bonum virum, et baptizavit illum.  Invenit cum illo filium placitum sibi, et dedit illi nomen Benignum, quia collegebat pedes Patricii inter manus suas et pectus, et noluit dormire apud patrem et matrem, sed flevit nisi cum Patricio dormiret.  Mane autem facto, P. currum con-

---

<sup>1</sup> *d-d* from gloss. to l. 8 of Fiac's Hymn.    <sup>3</sup> *f-f* from *Lism. Life*, p. 6.
<sup>2</sup> *e-e* from *LB.* 24.

isin carbat,¹ iaḋaiḋ in mac bec a ḋí láiṁ im chois Pátraic,² ⁊ ised
roraid, "Romleicid aroen fria Pátraic, ár is é P. m' athair dileaṡ."
Doraid P. "Baistter in mac ⁊ doberur isin carbut, bid comarba damsa
in mac sin."

[O'C. 32.] Roanacht Dia Binen im-medón tunaigi in druad,
roloisced im. in tunach co ndernai luaith di.

[O'C. 60.] Robaitsi déchain Iúis in a sentaid Ciarán macc in tṡáir a
libur Patraic.

18. [O'C. 39.] *Venit ad Taltenam*,³ baile hi raba in t-óinach rígda
co Coirpri macc Néill, is eissidi ro-occobair orccain Pátraic ⁊ ro(ṡ)roi-
glestar muintir Patraic i sruth Séile. *Et dixit ei,* "Fognífi do sil do
silaib do bráthar, ⁊ noco bía rí dot' síl co bráth, ⁊ noco bíat brattana
isind abainn sin." Dodeochaid P. iarsin co Conall macc Neill, isann
robói a sossad, dú ita Domnach Patraic i ndiu ;⁴ ⁊ aroet hé co failti
móir ; ⁊ rombaisti P. ⁊ rosonairtnig a rígsuidi *in æternum. Ocus*
aduḃairt P. fris, "Fognífe síl do brathar dot' ṡil tre bithu ; ⁊ tech-

---

scendit, puer pedem Patricii tenuit duobus manibus strictis, et clamavit,
"Sinite me apud Patricium proprium mihi." Et dixit P. "Baḃtitzate
eum et elevate eum in currum, quia heres regni mei erit."

[10 aa.] Filius sanus effectus est fide Dei ; cassula autem magi
inflammata est circa Benignum et in cinerem finita est.

[*LA.* 9b, 12b.] Babtitzavit diaconus Iuoustus Ceranum filium
artificis in sua senectute ex libro Patricii.

18. [*LA.* 10 ab.] Venit ad Taltenam ubi fit agon regale ad Coir-
priticum filium Neill, qui voluit eum occidere et flagillavit servos ejus
in flumine Sele. Et dixit ei, "Semen tuum serviet seminibus fratrum
tuorum, et non erit de semine tuo rex in æternum, et non erunt pisces
magni in flumine Sele." Deinde venit ad Conallum filium Neill, ad
domum illius quam fundavit in loco in quo est hodie Ecclesia Patricii
Magna ; et suscepit eum cum gaudio magno, et babtitzavit illum, et
firmavit solium ejus in æternum. Et dixit illi, "Semen fratrum
tuorum tuo semini serviet in æternum ; et tu misericordiam facere

---

¹ "cum pedem in currum elevasset,"
v. 2 ?  I have lost reference.
² gebis a chois, *LB.* 26.
³ teit co haenach Taillten, *LB.* 27 b.

⁴ qui habebat sedem in loco in quo
est hodie ecclesia S. Patricii, quæ
Scotice Domnach Patraic vocatur, *V.* 4,
c. 52.

naige co *n*derna trocairi dom*m'* orbaib im degaid, 7 do meic 7 m*eic* do
mac corob dligthidi¹ suthai*n* do*m'* macaibse *c*reitmechaib." Is andsin
ro tomais C*on*all eclais do Día 7 do P. *pedibus* ejus LX *pedum, et dixit*
P., "Sicip hé dígbas in*n* eclaissi dot' síl, nocho ba fota a flaithius 7 ni ba
sonairt." [*O' C.* 40.] Ocus f*or*othaig eclais i ndú sin, 7 foracaib na t*ri*
bráithriu inti, *con* a siair, .ı. Chathaceus 7 Cathurus 7 Catneus² 7
Catnea int siur, isiedi nobliged na elte.

[*LU.* 118 b.] Ocus rohadnacht con armgasciud isin chlud imech-
trach rigratha hi Temraig hé, 7 aiged fades for Laigniu oc cathugud
friu, ar ropo náma-som na bíu do Laignib.

[*O'C.* 27.] Ocus ni herracht nech dib ar a chind a*ch*t aonfer
namá .ı. Ercc mac Dega.³

ªDochoid P. iarsin do Temraig co Loeg*uiri*, uair rogniset cairdes
etarru conná rooircthi P. in a flaithius. *Sed non potuit credere dicens,*
"Niall," ol sé, "m' athair-si ro athne dam na rochreitind, acht co
romadnaichthi i mullach Temrach amail firu cathacha," uair bá bes

---

debes hæredibus meis post me, et filii tui et filiorum tuorum filiis meis
credulis legitimum sempiternum." Pensabatque ecclesiam Deo et
Patricio pedibus ejus LX pedum ; et dixit P., "Si diminuatur
ecclesia ista, non erit longum regnum tibi et non erit firmum." Et
ibi ecclesiam fundavit in qua reliquit tres fratres cum una sorore, .ı.
Cathaceus, Cathurus, Catneus, et soror illorum Catnea, quæ emulgebat
lac de dammulis feris.

[10 ab.] Ut sepeliar in cacuminibus Temro quasi viris consistentibus in bello in sepulcris armati prumptis armis facie ad faciem pro
duritate odiui.

[*LA.* 10 ba.] Et non surrexerunt ante se nisi unus tantum, hoc
est, Hercus sacrilegus.

[*LA.* 10 ab.] Perrexitque ad civitatem Temro ad Loigairium
filium Néill iterum, quia apud illum fœdus pepigit ut non occideretur
in regno illius. Sed non potuit credere, dicens, "Nam Neel pater
meus non sinivit mihi credere, sed ut sepeliar in cacuminibus Temro
quasi viris consistentibus in bello"; quia utuntur gentiles in sepulcris

---

¹ dlidthide, *Eg.*
² Catneun, *Eg.*

³ atracht remi mac Dega .ı. Ercc fil
Slani, *LB.* 27 a.

lasna geinti an adnacal fo n-armaib *facie ad faciem usque ad diem judicii*[a].[1]

19. [*O'C*. 52.] Luith iarom P. *for* Snam-dá-én tar Sinaind, 7 is and atbath Búadmael ara Pátraiç, 7 roadnacht indú-sin, Cell Búadmáil a ainm, 7 is dílis do Patraic hí.   Luith P. iarum i crích Connacht[2] for Snam-dá-én tar Sinainn.   Otchuolatar im. *dr*uid Laegaire me*icc* Néill inna huili dogni*d* P. .ı. Mæl 7 Caplait[3] da brathair, it hé roaltatar dí ingin Loigaire .ı. Eithni Finn 7 Feidilm Dergg, 7 doratsat dorchai dluthi dar Mag n-Ái ḣuile fri ré trí lá 7 tri n-aitchi.   Doronai P. airnaigthi fri Dia, 7 rofill a glui*n*e 7 roindarbanta[4] inna huile dorchai do Mag ái, 7 dorogní atlaigthe buidi do Dia.

[*O'C*. 53.] *Ocus* dodechatar tar Sinaind co Duma Graid, is i suidiu roordne Ailbi uasalacart, 7 roinchoisc P. dó altóir chlochtha i sl(é)ib Ua n-Ailella, *inter nepotes enim Ailella fuit et baptizavit Maneum sanctum quem ordinavit episcopus Bronus filius Icni qui est ic Cassiul hIrroe, servus Dei socius Patricii.*   Luid P. do Maig Glass,

---

armati prumptis armis facie  ad  faciem usque ad diem *erdathe* .ı. judicii apud magos.

19. [*LA*. 11a.] Venitque P. ad alveum Sinone ad locum in quo mortuus est auriga illius et sepultus est ibi in quo dicitur Cail Boidmail et immolatum erat Patricio.   Venit ergo P. per alveum fluminis Sinnæ per vadum-duorum-avium in campum Ai.   Audientes hautem magi Loiguiri filii Neill omnia quæ facta fuerant, Calvus et Capitolavium, duo fratres, qui nutrierant duas filias Loiguiri, Ethne Alba (et) Fedelm Rufa, tenebras densas super totum Campum Ái fecerunt; nox longa trium dierum tot et noctium erat.   Oraculis flectenisque assiduis Deum sanctus rogabat, et discessit omnis gravitudo tenebrarum a Campo Ai; et dixit " Deo gratias."

[*LA*. 11 ba.]   Et venierunt per alveum fluminis Sinnæ (qui dicitur Bandea) ad Tumulum Gradi, in quo loco ordinavit Ailbeum sanctum prespiterum, cui indicavit altare lapideum in monte Nepotum Ailello quia inter nepotes Ailello'erat; et babtizavit Maneum sanctum, quem ordinavit episcopus Bronus, filius Icni, servus Dei, socius Patricii.

---

[1] From *a* to *a* is from Stokes' *Trip. Life*, p. 74.

[2] ad terram Connachtorum, *V*.3, c.47.

[3] Caplid, *V*. 3, c. 47.

[4] fugatæ sunt, *V*. 3.

is ann forothaig Cill Móir 7 faráccaib díis dia muintir and .ı. Conḷeng
7 Erclong. Roedbart Ono a tegdais do P., *et dixit illi* P., "Bid
bendachtha do síl 7 bíaid búaid laech 7 chleirech húait co bráth, 7
bid léu orba in luicc-se." *Et posuit ibi* . . .

20. [*O' C.* 54.] Ocus dogníth[1] altóri 7 leborchometa chethrachori
7 miassa cethrachori in honóir Patraic; 7 robui míass chethrachoiri dib
in Ard Mach*a*, 7 alaili ind Ailfind 7 alaili i nDomnach Mór Maigi
Seolæ *for* altoir Felarti *episcopi sancti*. Dochóid im. Assicus for
teithed is*in* tuaiscirt do ṡléib Liacc. Robói ⅶ *m*bliadna in insi and,
7 *c*onaigtis a manaig hé 7 fobuaratar isnaib glennaib ṡléibidib iar
soethur, 7 dofucsat léu ass, 7 atbath occu isin dithrub[2] 7 ronadnaigset
hi-Raith Chunga hi Seirthib. Ocus dorat rí in tiri dósom 7 dia
manch*aib* iar n-a écc iṅgeilt *céit* bó *cum vitulis suis* 7 xx dam i*n*
edbairt suthai*n*, ar adubairt so*m* ná ticfad doridisi im Mag n-Ai, ar in
ngói roráided uad and. Attát a thasi i Ráith Chungai, 7 la Patraic in
chell *for*dosrala muintir Col*uim* Chille 7 Aird ṡratha.

---

Venierunt ad Campum Glais et in illo possuit Celolam Magnam, et
in illa reliquit duos barbaros Conleng et Ercleng monachos sibi.
Immolavit alter sibi domum suam. Et dixit illi P., " Semen tuum
erit benedictum et de tuo semine erunt sacerdotes Domini et principes
digni in mea elimossina et tua hæreditate." Et possuit ibi . . .

20. [*LA.* 11 b.] Et faciebat altaria et bibliothecas quadratas et
patinos pro honore Patricii; et de illis tres patinos quadratos vidi, *i.e.*
patinum in Arddmache, et alterum in ecclesia Alo-find et tertium in
Ecclesia Magna Saeoli super altare Felarti sancti episcopi. Assicus iste
fecit profugam in aquilonem regionis ad Montem Lapidum. Fuit
septem annis in insola et quærebant illum monachi sui, et invenierunt
eum in convallibus montanis juxta laborem artificiorum; et abstraxerunt eum, et mortuus est apud illos in desertis montibus et sepilierunt
eum ir-Raith Chungai hi Sertib. Et dedit rex illi et monachis suis
post mortem fœnum C. vaccarum cum vitulis suis, et boum xx immolatio æterna; quia dixit quod non revertetur in Campum Ai quia
mendacium ab illo dixerunt. Sunt ossa ejus in Campo Sered hir-
Raith-Chungi. Monachus Patricii sed contenderunt eum familiæ
Colombæ Cille et Airdd Sratha.

---

[1] dognit, *in Eg.*         [2] dithrib, *in Eg.*

[*O'C.* 55.] Luith P. ó Ail-find co Dumacha óa n-Ailella 7 foro-thaig eclais and .ı. Senchell Dumaige 7 farácaib inti Maichet 7 Cetchen 7 Rodán uasal(s)acart 7 Mathona síur Benén *quæ tenuit* calle ó Patraic 7 ó Rodán 7 robo mainches dóib.

21. [*O'C.* 56.] Luid *tre* chrích úa n-Ailella 7 fothaigis *in* eolais sair hi Tamnach 7 cumdachta hí o Día 7 o dúinib. *Et ipsa fecit amicitiam* . . . *Biteus.* Doluid P. iarsin don topur .ı. Clibech i slesaib Cruachan, *fri* turcubail ngréine[1] 7 ri turcbail ngréne[2] 7 destitar *in* chlerig icon tiprait. Dolotar di ingin Loigairi m*eicc* Neill *commoch* don tiprait do nigi al-lám am*al* ba bés doib, .ı. Eithne Find 7 Feidelm Dergg; con-airnechtatar senod *in*na cleirech icon tiprait con hetaigib gelaib 7 a al-libuir ara belaib. Doruimenatar bádis fir síthe no fantaissi. Incom-aircet[3] scela do P., "Cia can duib 7 can dodechobair?"[4] *Et dixit P. eis,* "Robad ferr duib c*reittem* do Día andás imcomarc di ar ceníul-ni." Adrubairt ind ingen robu siniu[5], "Cia far nDia-si, 7 cia air*m* hítá?

---

[*LA.* 11 b.] Patricius venit de fonte Alo-find ad Dumecham Nepotum Ailello et fundavit in illo loco ecclesiam quæ sic vocatur, Senella Cella Dumiche, in quo reliquit Macet, Cetgen et Rodanum prespiterum . . . et Mathona soror Benigni quæ tenuit pallium apud Patricium et Rodanum et monacha fuit illis.

21. [*LA.* 12a.] Exiit per montem filiorum Ailello et plantavit ecclesiam liberam hi Tamnuch, et honorata fuerat a Deo et hominibus. Et ipsa fecit amicitiam . . . Biteus. Deinde autem venit P. ad fontem qui dicitur Clebach in lateribus Crochan, contra ortum solis (et) ante ortum solis, et sederunt juxta fontem. Ecce duæ filiæ regis Loiguiri, Ethne Alba et Fedelm Rufa ad fontem more mulierum ad lavandum mane venerunt; et senodum episcoporum juxta fontem invenierunt. Illos viros *side* aut deorum terrenorum aut fantassiam estimaverunt. Et dixerunt filiæ illis, "Ubi vos sitis et unde venistis?" Et dixit P. ad illas, "Melior[6] erat vos Deo confiteri quam de genere nostro interro-gare." Dixit filia prima, "Quis est Deus[7], et ubi est? Si[8] habet filios et filias, aurum et argentum Deus vester? Si vivus semper, si

---

[1] Orto jam sole, *V.* 3.

[2] ante solis ortum, *V.* 4, c. 55.

[3] interrogaverunt, *V.* 4, c. 55.

[4] qui estis vos et unde venistis, *V.* 4.

[5] major natu, *V.* 4.

[6] melius erat, *V.* 4.

[7] deus vester, *V.* 4.

[8] utrum, *V.* 4.

In failet maic ⁊ ingena lais, in fail ór *nó* airccet?   In beo é dognath
no in saothamail é, in é a macc oilfaigther na huile?   In i nim no i
tal*main*?   In fu tal*main* no for tal*main*, no hi muirib nó hi srothaib.
In hi sliabaib *no* i nglennaib? ' Abair dun co foll*us* cin*dus* docife'r é ⁊
cin*dus* gradaigt*her.* ⁊ cin*dus* dogebt*har* é, no in óge no in arsaid.''
Dofreccair *autem* Patricius, '' Ar nDia-ne Dia nan uili, Dia ni*me* ⁊ Dia
tal*man*, Dia na mara ⁊ na srothan, Dia na gr*é*ne ⁊ *in* esca ⁊ cach uili
airdren*n*, Dia na sleibti ro árd ⁊ na nglenta ísil, Dia os neim ⁊ in
neim ⁊ fó neim ⁊ ata aige tegdais[1], .ı. nem ⁊ talam ⁊ muir ⁊ cach ní
ata intu-sin. *Inspirat . . . Spiritus Sanctus.* Atcobraim-si im. far
n-accomal-si do Macc ind Ríg Nemdai ár itib ingena ríg talmo*n*. *Et*
*dixerunt filiæ* amal bid (ó) oen gein ⁊ ó óin chridi.   '' Cindus connic-
fam creitem don ríg sin *doce nos diligentissime*, con-accamar in Coi*m*did
gnuis f*ri* gnuis; inchoisc dún in mod, ⁊ dogenum-ne amal atb*er*a-su
frind.''   *Dixit P.,* '' In creiti-si[2] *tre* baithis pecad var mathar ⁊ var
n-athar do chor úaib?''   *Responderunt,* '' *Creidimus.*''   '' In creiti-si[2]
aithrigi iar pecad?''   '' *Credimus,*'' *et baptizatæ sunt* ⁊ rosen P. caille

---

pulcher, si filium ejus nutrierunt multi?   Si in cœlo an in terra?
Si in æquore, si in fluminibus, si in montanis vel in convallibus?   Dic
nobis notitiam ejus, quomodo videbitur, quomodo diligitur, quomodo
invenitur, si in juventute, si in senectute invenitur.   Respondens
autem dixit, '' Deus noster, Deus omnium, Deus cœli et terræ;
maris et fluminum, Deus solis et lunæ (et) omnium siderum, Deus
montium sublimium valliumque humilium, Deus super cælo et
in cœlo et sub cœlo habet habitaculum erga cœlum et terram et
mare et omnia quæ sunt in eis.   Inspirat . . . Spiritus sanctus.
Ego vero volo vos Regi Cœlesti conjungere, dum[3] filiæ regis terreni
sitis.''   Et dixerunt filiæ quasi ex uno ore unoque corde, '' Quomodo
credere possimus Cœlesti Regi doce nos dilegentissime ut videamus
illum facie ad faciem, indica nobis, et quomodo dixeris nobis
faciamus.''   Et dixit, '' Si creditis per babtismum patris et matris
jecere peccatum?'' Responderunt, '' Credimus.''   '' Si[4] pœnitentiam
creditis post peccatum?'' '' Credimus.''   Et babtizatæ sunt et candida

---

[1] tegais, *in Eg.*          [3] cum, *V.* 4.
[2] *sic; read* creitid-si.      [4] utrum, *V.* 4.

find for a cend.[1]  *Ocus* dorothlaichset imchaisin Críst gnuis *fri* gnuis.
*Dixit P. eis,* "Noco chumgaidsit imchaisin Críst *acht* ma blaistí bás
ar thús, 7 acht má airfemaid corp Críst 7 a fuil." *Et responderunt,*
"Tabair dún in saccarbaicc co coi*m*sam in tairgerthairig d'egad."[2]
*Ocus* arroétatár iarsin sacairbaic 7 rochotailset im mbás.  *Ocus* dosrat
fo óinbrott in óin lepaid, 7 dorigensat a carait a cóine co mór.

22. [*O'C.* 59.]  Tainic in drúi Caplait, ar is é roalt in daran-ing in,
co rabi ic cói.  Rof*r*itchai P. dou, 7 rochreit, 7 dorat P. deimess imm a
folt.  Tainic iarsin a bráthair .ı. Maol, 7 roradi, "Rocreit," ol se, "mu
brá*t*hair duitsiu ; ni geba greimm na torbu," ol sé, "dóu, dambér-
sa dorithisi hi ngentl*echt*."  *Ocus* robói hic aithisiugud Pátraic.
Rof*r*itach P. dóu, 7 rocreit do Dia in drúi, 7 romberr P., conid desin
is árasc, "Cosmail Mæl do Chaplait."[3]  *Ocus* fo*r*orbaide laithi i*n*na
cainti 7 roadnaicthe i*n*na ingena i ndú sin, 7 roedbrad Sendomnach
Maige Ai do Pátraic *in æternum,* 7, atberat alaili, tuctha taise innan
ingen do Ard Mach*e*.  Luid P. iarsin i tír Caireda, 7 forothaig eclais

---

veste[1] in capitibus earum.  Et postulaverunt videre faciem Christi
et dixit eis sanctus, "Nisi mortem gustaveritis non potestis videre
faciem Christi, et nisi sacrificium accipietis.  Et responderunt,
"Da nobis sacrificium[4] ut possimus nostrum sponsum videre."  Et
acceperunt Eucharistiam et dormierunt in morte.  Et posuerunt illas
in lectulo uno vestimento coopertas, et fecerunt ululatum et ploratum
magnum amici earum.

[*LA.* 12 b.]  Venit magus Caplit, qui nutrivit alteram et flevit.
Illi P. prædicavit, et credidit et capilli capitis ejus ablati sunt.  Et
frater illius venit Mael et ipse dixit, "Frater meus credidit Patricio, et
non erit ita."  Et ad Patricium verba dura dixit, et Patricius illi
prædicavit et convertit illum in pœnitentiam Dei, et ablati sunt capilli
capitis illius ; de hoc verbum quod clarius est omnibus verbis Scoticis,
"Similis est calvus contra Caplit" ; et crediderunt in Deo.  Et
consumpti sunt dies ululationis filiarum et sepelierunt eas ; et immolata
est (fertæ) Patricio, cum sanctarum ossibus, et heredibus ejus post se in
sæcula.  Deinde hautem venit P. ad campum Cairetho id est im Mag

---

[1] *sic* ; induit eas veste candida, *V.* 5,
c. 14.

[2] *for* d'fegad.

[3] le Chaplait, *Trias. Th.* p. 136

[4] sacrificium corporis et sanguinis
Christi, *V.* 5, c. 15.

in Ard Licce .ı. Sendomnach, 7 faracaib inti Coemán dechon. Ocus
aroerachair P. Ard Senlis, *ubi posuit Lallócc sanctam, et tenuit loccum
in campo Nento.*  Ocus dochotar la Cetheucho ep*scop* di a thír; do
ceniul Ailello a athair,[1] do ceniul Sái do Chiannacht ó Domnach
Sairigi ic Dom-liacc Cianá(i)n a máthair. Ocus ba he bes ep*scuip*
Chetheocho, isin Domnach Sái nocheilebrad in Cháisc Moir 7 ind Ath
da-Loracc i Cenandus nocheilebrad in Mincaisc *cum Comgilla*; ar
atberat muinter Chethich conid manchess do Cheithich[2] Comgilla.
Foracaib uasal-dechon dia muintir and .ı. dechain Íuis, arroerachair
Fidarta. 7 foracaib P. a lebar n-uird 7 babti*smi* occai, 7 robaitsi Húu
Mane, 7 robaitsi dechain Íuis inn a sentaid Ciarán macc in tšáir a
libur Patraic, *quia CXL annorum fuit* qua*ndo Ciaranum babtizavit ut
aiunt peritissimi.*  Frainc im. Patraic dochuatar buad .ı. cóicc bráthir
deuac 7 oen siuir .ı. Bernicius, Hibernicius 7 in tsiúr Nitria. Ocus
dorata il luic daib, óin diib-si Imgoe Baislice. Roinchoisc P. dóib

---

Cairetho et fundaverunt æcclesiam in Ardd Licce, quæ sic vocatur
Sendomnach, et posuit in illa Coimanum diaconum. Et venit Patricius
in Ardd Senlis et posuit in illo sanctam Lalocam et tenuit locum in
campo Nento. Et exierunt cum Cethiaco episcopo ad suam propriam
regionem; quia de genere Ailello ejus pater fuit et mater ejus erat de
genere Sái de regionibus Cinachtæ a Domnach Sairigi juxta Domum
Cennani, id est, Lapidum. Moris erat Cethico episcopo celebrare
circum loca Curcu Sái in Pascha Majore, et in pasca secundo fiebat in
loco Comgillæ super Vadum Duarum Furcarum, *i.e.* Dá Loargg juxta
Cenondas, quia dicunt familia Cethiaci quod Comgella est monacha
Cethiaco. Reliquit ibi Ius diaconum, et tenuit Fidard. Et dedit illi
libros baptismatis, et baptizavit Nepotes Maini, et in senectute
sua babtizavit Ciaranum filium artificis ex libro Patricii, quia. . . .[3]
Franci vero Patricii exierunt a Patricio, viri fratres duodecim cum
sorore una .ı. Bernicius et Hernicius et sororis nomen Nitria. Et
multi loci illis dati sunt, et ignoro nisi unum, id est, Bassilica sanctorum.

---

[1] a mathair, *in Eg.*          [2] *read* Ceithech ?          [3] indistinct in *LA.*

cosmailius in luicc con a méur ó chill Garat, *quia . . . . invenerunt.*
Rofothaig P. da*no* cill Garad. ·

[*O'C.* 61.] Dochóid P. íarsin co Mag Selcæ .ı. co Dumu ṡelca 7
is and robatar sé mic Brain, 7 roscr*ı*b P. *tri* anmanna i ndú sin hi
*tri* clochaib; 7 ata sude Patraic i nDumu Selcæ iter na clochai *in*
*quibus scripsit literas. Et cum illo fuerunt Bronus episcopus* Casil
Irræ, *Sachelus* Basilice Móre hi Cíarraigiu, *Bronachus prespiter*, Rodán,
Cassán, Brocaid Imlich Ech bráthair Loma(i)n Átha Truim, Benén
comarba Patraic 7 Binén brathair Cethig, Felartus episcopus, 7
caillech síur i*n*di-sin, 7 alaili síur *quæ sit* (*in*) *insola in mari*
Conmacne .ı. Croch Cuili Conmaicni, ocus rofothaigestar eclais for
Loch Selcæ .ı. Domnach Mór Maige Selce *in quo babtizavit* húu
Briúin.

23. Luid P. ig-G*r*egraidi Locho Tegett, forothaig eclais and i
nDrummæ 7 rochlaid topur occi, 7 noco techtai sruth intí ná eissi
acht lán tre bithu. Forothaig iarsin cill Attrachta, 7 ingen Taláin
inti *quæ accepit* calle de láim Patraic, ocus fa*r*ácaib teisc 7 cailech

---

Indicavit illis P. similitudinem loci digito de cacumime Garad quia
. . . invenierunt.    Fundavit sanctus ecclesiam Brer-garad.

[*LA.* 12 bb.] Venit vero P. ad Selcam, in quo sex filii Briuin,
inter lapides in quibus scripsit manu sua literas quas hodie conspexi-
mus; et posuerunt sedem in cacuminibus Selcæ inter lapides in quibus
scripsit literas.    Et cum illo fuerunt Bronus episcopus, Sachelus,
Bronach præspiter, Rodanus, Cassanus, Brocidius, Lommanus frater
ejus, Benignus heres Patricii et Benignus frater Cetheci de genere
Ailello, Felartus episcopus, et (virgo) soror ejus, et alia soror quæ sit
in insola in mari Comnacne, hoc est Croch Cuile, et plantavit ecclesiam
super Stagnum Selcæ et babtitzavit filios Broin.

23. [*LA.* 13 a.] Et perrexit ad tractum Gregrigi et fundavit ecclesiam in Drumæ, et fontem fodivit in ea et non habet flumen in se nec
ex se, sed plenus semper.    Et ecclesiam posuit in cella Atrochtæ filiæ
Taláin, et ipsa accepit pallium de manu Patricïi, (Patina et calix sunt
in Cella Atrochtæ[1]).    Et perrexit ad filios Heric.    Furati sunt equos

---

[1] The words in parenthesis are in     I either omitted them, or failed to read
Mr. Stokes' edition of the *B. of Armagh.*    ṭhem.

léa.  Dochoid da*no* co macou Eirc.  Tellsat eochu Patraic, 7 rósmall-
ach(t) P. *dicens* "Fognífi far síl do síl var mbráth*ar*."

[*O'C.* 62.]  Luid P. in Mag Airtig, *et benedixit locum.* .ı. Ailech
Airtig i Tailig na Cloch.  O*cus* dochóid i nDrum*m*ut Ciarrigi Airtig,
arránic diis m*b*rathar and ic imchlaidbed im (*f*)erann ind athar iar
n-a hécc .ı. Bibar 7 Lochru, dá m*a*cc Tamanchind di Ch*i*arr*aig*i, co
roecsat al-láma i*m*ma claidbiu conad coemnactar a síniud nach a
tairniud.  *Dixit P. eis*, " Saidid," 7 rosbendach 7 doronai sith
etturra,[1] 7 doratsat in tír do Patraic ar anmai*n* a n-athar, 7 forothaig
eclais an*n* i fail Conu soer b*rá*thair eps*cuip* Sacha(i)ll[2] .ı. Baslici.

[*O'C.* 63.]  Dochóid P. íarsin i Ciarraigi n-Airne, co tarla[2] dó
Ernaisc 7 a macc Loarnach fo bile and, 7 scríbuis P. aibgitir dó 7
anais sechtmai*n* occa di feraib déuac.  Ocus fothaigis P. eclais i ndú
sin *et tenuit illum abbatem et fuit quidam spiritu sancto plenus. . . .*
Ocus dochóid P. do Thopur Mucno, 7 róinsuidig Senchill.  *Et fuit . . .*
*diem.*  Ocus roescomlui iar sin i tír Conmaicne hi Cúil Talaith, 7
rosuidig ecailsi cethrochairi isind inut sin.  Óin díb-side Ardd Uiscon.

---

illius, et maledixit illis dicens, " Semen vestrum serviet semini fratrum
vestrorum."

[13aa.]  Et revertebatur in Campum Airthicc et benedixit locum i
Taulich Lapidum.  Et exiit ad Drummut Cerrigi, et invenit duos
viros conflinguentes (gladiis), filios unius viri, ad invicem post mortem patris eorum, qui faber æreus erat de genere Cerrigi, voluerunt
dividere hereditatem.  Et fuerunt erectæ eorum manus et non potuerunt (eas) porrigere aut colligere.  Dixit P. eis, " Sedete," et benedixit eos, et præcepit illis et ait, "Facite amicitiam."  Et immolaverunt agrum pro anima patris eorum Patricio ; et fundavit ecclesiam
ibi, et in illo loco est Coonu artifex frater Sacelli episcopi Bassilicæ.

[*LA.* 13ab.]  Perrexit per diserta Cerrigi Airni, et invenit Iarnas-
cum sub arbore cum filio Locharnach et scripsit illi elementa, et fuit
apud illum ebdomas una viris duodecim.  Et plantavit ibi ecclesiam,
et tenuit illum abbatem, et fuit quidam Spiritu Sancto plenus. . . .  Et
perrexit P. ad fontem qui dicitur Mucno, et fecit Cellam Senem.  Et
fuit . . . diem.  Et perrexit ad regionem Commaicne hi Cuil Tolat et
possuit ecclesias quadratas in illo loco.  Una earum est Ardd Uiscon.

---

[1] et fecit pacem inter eos, *V.* 3, c. 62.    [2] Sacnull ; tierla, *in Eg.*

24. [ *O' C.* 63. ] Doluid im Mag Cerai (7) tarraisetar hi Cuil Corræ,
7 forothaig eclais is ind lucc sin, *et babtizavit multos.* Íarsin dochoid
P. im Mag Foimsen conairnicc dá bráthair and .ı. Luchtæ 7 Derclam.
Fuidis Derclam a mogaid do orgain Patraic; rothairmesc im. Luctheus
imme. *Cui dixit* P., " Beitit eps*cuip* 7 sacairt dot' cheniul, bid
mallachtha im. síl do bráthar, 7 bid uathad." *Et reliquit in illo loco*
Cru*i*mthir C*o*nán, 7 dochóid iarum do thopur Stringle isin díthrub, 7
boi d*o*mnach forsin topur si*n.*

[ *O'.C.* 64. ] Luid P. co firu hUmaill do Achud Fhobair, is and sin
ro oirdned eps*cop* Senach ; is hé ainm dobert P. fair " Agnus Dei ";
7 is hé conatig trí itgi co Patraic, .ı. co na tairmthíasad fo g*rad*, 7
co(na) ruainmnigthi int ineth úad 7 anduesta dia ais-som co ndigsed
for æs a maicc Oengusa; is dó sidi roscrib P. abbgitir isind láu
rooirdned eps*cop* Senach. Folamadair P. congabad cathair ic Achud
Fobair, conerbart . . .

[ *O' C.* 65. ] Luid P. hi Cruachan Aigle, 7 boi i Cruachan cen dig
cen biud ó die sathairnd init co dia sathairnd Cascc fo chosm*aili*us

---

24. [ *LA.* 13b. ] Exiit in Campum Caeri et castrametati sunt i Cuil
Core, et plantavit ecclesiam in illo loco et babtitzavit multos. Et
exinde exiit ad Campum Foimsen, et invenit in illo loco duos fratres
.ı. Luchta 7 Derclad. Derclad mittebat servum suum ut occideret
Patricium ; Lucteus autem liberavit eum. Cui dixit P., " Erunt
episcopi et prespiteri de genere tuo, genus autem fratris tui erit maledictum, et deficient in brevi." Et reliquit in illo loco Conanum
prespiterum ; et exiit ad fontem Stringille in disertis et fuit super
ipso duobus dominicis.

[13ba.] Et exiit ad finem hUmail do Achud Fobuir, in quo ordinavit Senachum, et dedit nomen novum illi, id est, " Agnus Dei " et
episcopum fecit illum. Et ipse postulavit tres postulationes a Patricio ;
ut non peccaret sub gradu, ut non vocaretur nomen ejus super locum,
et (quod) deesset de illius ætate super ætatem filii sui veniret, Oingus
nomine; cui scripsit P. abgitorium in die in qua ordinatus est Senachus.
P. ordinavit ecclesiam in illo loco . . . in cathedra hac, ipsa est Ached
Fobuir, et dixit . . . .

[13 ba, bb.] Et perrexit P. ad montem Egli ut jejunaret in
illo XL diebus et XL noctibus Moysaicam tenens disciplinam. Et

Moysi. Ara Patraic dano atbath 7 roadnacht etir Cruachan 7 muir. I *for*ciund tra in XL laithi siu 7. in XL aidchi rolinad fair in slíab di énlaithib dubuib cona haca cungeui*n* ne*m* ná tal*main*.' [*O'C*. 69.] Dodechaid P. i· tír Chorcu-The*m*ne ocus robaitsi ilmili do dui*n*ib ann, 7 forathaig iii æclasæ .ı. teora Tuaga. Luid do thop*ur* Findmaigi .ı. Slán, adrubrad *fri* P. co n-onóraigtis in genti in topur amal dea. Cethrochoir im. in topar 7 cloch cethrochoir for a béulo 7 roch*r*eitset[1] int aos boeth co ndernai alaili fáith marb *libliothicam sibi . . . erit semen tuum benedictum in sæcula*. Cell Tog i tír Corcu The*m*na isinedi[2] rofothaig Caindech eps*cop* manach Patraic.

25. [*O'C*. 70.] Fecht do Patraic oc im*t*echt i*m* maigib m*aic* Ercæ .ı. i n-Dichuil 7 Erchuil; atchonnairc adnacol mór i*n*dib .ı. fichi traiged ar chét inn a futt.[3] Dorodiusaig P. in marb boi isind adnacol; 7 roiarfacht scela dó. *Respondit sibi dicens,* " *Ego sum Cass* macc Glaiss *qui*

———

defunctus est auriga illius hi Muiriscc Aigli hoc est campum[4] inter mare et Aigleum.[5] Et mansit ibi XL diebus et XL noctibus, et graves aves fuerunt erga illum et non poterat videre faciem cœli et terræ. [*LA*. 13 b.] Et venit in regiones Corcu-Temne ad fontem Sini in quo babtizavit milia hominum multa (et) fundavit ecclesias tres (.ı. tres) Toga et venit ad fontem Findmaige qui dicitur Slan, quia indicatum (erat) illi quod honorabant magi fontem . . . in donum[6] Dei. Fons vero quadratus fuit, et pctra quadrata erat in ore fontis; et dixerunt increduli[7] quod quidam propheta mortuus fecit bibliothicam sibi . . . . erit semen tuum benedictum in sæcula. Cellola Tog in regionibus Corcu-Teimne Patricii fuit; Cainnechus episcopus, monachus Patricii fundavit eam.

25. [*LA*. 14 a.] Et venit P. per campos in regionibus Maico hErcæ in Dichuil et Aurchuil ad sepulcrum magnum quod invenit familia ejus et mirabantur pedes traxisse CXX. Aperuit vir sanctus (sepulcrum) et surrexit magnus sanus; et dixerunt, "Indica nobis cujus es" (Respondit sibi dicens), " Ego sum macc maicc Cais maic Glais qui fui

———

[1] rech*r*eitset, *Ms.*
[2] *sic*; *read* is siedi?
[3] centum viginti pedes in longitudine habens, *V.* 4, c. 62.
[4] The *nominative* campum reflects the

Irish *neuter* mag.
[5] Aigleum shows that Aigle is *neut.* or *masc.*
[6] *read* in modum Dei.
[7] perhaps for *creduli* = 6es bœth.

*fui subulcus* Lugair ríg Iruatæ 7 romgon fíann Maicc Con *in regno*
Co*irpri* Niod fer, isin cetmad blia*dain* atáu cosindiu." Rombaithis P.
7 dochuaid inn a adnacul *iterum*.

[*O' C.* 80.] Secht maicc Draigin, rosbaitsi P., *et elegit ex eis* Macc
Erce, 7 atnói do Epscop Brón for altru*m*. Dororaind Caissiul n-Irre.
[*O' C.* 77.] Luid hi Forraig m*a*cc n-Amalgaid, is hi suidiu robaithes
in mnái torraig 7 a gein.

[*O' C.* 79.] Dodechoid asi*n* tír di Bertlachaib aníar i *m*Bertlachai
sair in inbiur Muadi fri beolu mara. [*O' C.* 80.] An*n*sin donanaic
Brón 7 Macc Rime *et ibi eis scripsit alphabetum* . . . oc raith Rígbairdd.
[*O' C.* 56.] Luid tre crích Ua n-Ailella 7 fothaigis *in* eclaiss sair[1] hi
Tamnuch. [*O' C.* 72, 75.] Luid tar Múed. Ni móu míli itir in port
asan-acca P. inna naimtiu.

26. [*O' C.* 84.] Luid P. iar maig Eni conaccaib Dom*n*ach Mór
Maige Eni. Is andsin mallachais do Duib ar in n-era doratsat na

---

subulcus ríg Lugir ríg Hirotæ; jugulavit me fian maicc Maicc Con
in regno Coirpri Niothfer anno C usque hodie, et babtitzatus est et
resticuit et positus est iterum in sepulcro suo.

[*LA.* 14 b.] Septem filii Dregin, benedíxit illum cum filiis et elegit
unum ex epsis cui nomen erat Macc Ercæ et commendat illum Brono.
Indicavit illi locum. Perrexit ad agrum qui dicitur Foirrgea filiorum
Amolngid, et babtizavit mulierem habentem in utero infantem et
filium in utero.

[*LA.* 15 a.] Et reversus est ad flumen Muaide de Vertrige in
Bertrigam in sinu maris. Et venit apud Bronum et benedixit Macc
Rime et scripserunt elimenta illi . . . juxta fossam Rigbairt. Exiit
trans mortem filiorum Ailello et fundavit ecclesiam (liberam)[1] ibi .i.
Tamnach. [*LA.* 14 b.] Per Muadam venit. Viderunt illum hostem
procul P. et Endeus quasi milia passuum.

26. [*LA.* 15 aa.] Et perrexit ad campum Aine et possuit ecclesiam ibi. Et maledixit flumen quod dicitur Niger, quia postulavit et

---

[1] *Cf.* "ecclesiam liberam," *LA.* 11 d, 13 b, 21 b.

iascairi fair.   Robendach im. do Dróbeiss.[1]   [*O'C.* 22.]   Dobert dano maldachtain for Inbiur Ainge.

[*O'C.* 86.]   Luid iarsin itír Ess Ruaid 7 muir bi crích Conaill du ita indiu Rath Chungai; saidis cli and.   Iss e*d* dochoid iarsin i tír Eoguin m*aicc* Neill for B*er*nais tíri Aeda hi mag n-Itha do domnach mór Maigi Itha.   [*O'C.* 90.]   Is and conacab Domnach mór Maigi Tóchair.   [*O'C.* 84.]   Co bá thrí, *tra*, dochuaid P. tar Sinuinn secht mblia*dna* dóu ic praicept do Chon*n*achtaib.   [*O'C.* 90.]   Issed doluid o Domnach Mór Maigi Tochuir isin mBretaig.   [*O'C.* 92.]   Issed docuaid am maig Dola, f*or*othaigestar secht ndom*naige* and; dochoid iarsin in Ardd Dáilauig 7 isnal-Lei don Bandai airthir.   [*O'C.* 97] I Cúil Rathin for ur na Bandæ anair,[2] is ua damsa 7 duitsiu bias and .i. epscop Coirpri. 95.   *Et fundavit* il-cella i nDáil Araidi.

[*Lismore Life*, 4.]   Isinn inbaidh sin itconnaic Miliuc fís .i. Cothraige do thuidecht cuca 7 lasair theined as a gion, 7 roloiscc a meic 7 a ingena comdar luaithred.

---

nihil illi dabant Sancto; Drobaiscum autem benedixit.   Et male-dixit flumini Oingi.

[*Ibidem*] Etiam intravit in Campum Sereth inter es Ruaid et mare, et fundavit ecclesiam ir-Raith Argi et castrametatus est in campo Sereth.   Et perrexit for Bernas filiorum Conill in Campo Itho et fundavit ibi Ecclesiam Magnam.   Et exiit ad Campum Tochuir et fecit ecclesiam ibi.   Pervenit P. per Sinonam tribus vicibus et septem annos complevit in occidentali plaga.   Et de Campo Tochuir venit in Dulo Ocheni et fecit septem ecclesias ibi et exiit in Ardd Eolorgg, et Lee Bendrigi, et perrexit trans flumen Bandæ.   Cellola Cuile Raithin in Eilniu in quo fuit episcopus.   Et fecit alias cellas multas in Eilniu.

[*LA.* 15 ba.]   Sed alia nocte vidit Miliucc scintillas de ore Succeti ignitas, et inflammatum est corpus filii sui et filiarum, et con-sumpti sunt in cinerem.

---

[1] The *Tripartite* has here: "Is sainred do Dróbeiss *tonnem* cáin and tria ben-dachtain Patraic"; and the *B. of Armagh* has "Drobaiscum, in quo *tenentes*, magni pisces, sive piscium genus effectum est."   In *Eg.* 10 ab : "Ae Drobeiseach cainem do thonemaib Eirend."   Hence, tenentes = tonnem *or* tonem.

[2] *in air, Ms.*

.[*Gloss. of Fiac's Hymn.*] Maraid slicht a choss beos forsin cloich ;
*LB.* 25*b.* Is fairithe in long co ndecha-su innte. [*O'C.* 97.] Iss*ed,*
*tra,* doluid P. *for* fertais Tuama co hU Turtri do Slíab Calland 7
nombathess. [*O'C.* 107.] Issed dochuaid hi crích Mugdorn*n* 7 dorat
gr*á*d n-eps*cuip* fair .ı. *for* Victor 7 forácaib i *n*Domnach Maigen.
[*O'C.* 108.] Luid iarsi*n* do Biliu Thortan, *et fecit.* . . . Aird Brecain.
Oc tascna*m* do Patraic hi cr*í*ch Laigen fíu aidchi ic Dr*u*im Urchailli.

[*O'C.* 110.] Luid im Mag Liphi ; rofothaig cella 7 congbala
hisuidiu, 7 foracaib Uasaili i cill Uasaili, 7 Iserninum 7 mac Tail hi
cella Culind. [*O'C.* 114.] Roorddnestar Fiacc Find hi Slebti ; luid
iar suidiu for Balach Gabra(i)n hi tír n-Ossairgi 7 *for*othaig cella
7 congb*a*la and dú hitá Martartech i*m* Maig Roigne ; 7 robathiss
maccu Natfruich 7 firu Muman olchenai co maigin hitá lec Patraic
indíu.

27. [*O'C.* 66.] " In fail naill adcota da*m* ?" ol P. " Fail," ol int
aing*el,* " muir mór do thuidecht tar hÉri*nn* secht *m*bliadna ria mbráth."
" In faill naill condesta," ol int angel, " F*il*," ol P. " Saxain ná
rothrebut hEri*nn* aro áis nách ar éicin céin mbeosa *for* nim, Nach oén
donair aithrigi in Eirinn ní ría (a) anim an Ifi(u)rn. [*O'C.* 65.] Ar
roptar P. 7 Moissi cosmaili in ilib—1. Rosaccill Dia díblínaib asin

------

[*LA.* 15 ba.] Vestigium pedis illius usque nunc pene adest. . . .
Ecce navis tua parata est, surge et ambula. Venit vero sanctus per
Doim in regiones Tuirtri ad Collunt Patricii et babtizavit filios Tuirtri.
Venit in Maugdornu, et ordinavit Victoricum episcopum, et ecclesiam
ibi magnam fundavit. Finito autem circulo exiit et fecit. . . . Airdd
Breccáin. Et perrexit ad fines Laginiensium ad Druimm hUrchaille.

[*LA.* 15 bb.] Exiit ad Campum Lifi, et posuit ibi ecclesiam et
ordinavit Auxilium et Eserninum et Mactaleum in cellola Cuilinn.
Ordinavit Feccum Album i sleibti ; et erexit se per Belut Gabráin,
et fundavit ecclesiam ir-Roigniu Martorthige ; et babtizavit filios
Nioth Fruich i tír Mumæ super petram Coithrigi hi Caissiul.

27. [*LA.* 15 b.] Hæ sunt tres petitiones Patricii, rogans, Ne super-
vixerit aliquis Hibernensium septem annis ante judicium quia dele-
buntur æquore. Ne barbaræ gentes dominentur nobis in sempiternum.
Ut unusquisque nostrum pœnitentiam agens non claudetur in Inferno.
In quatuor rebus similis fuit Moysi Patricius—1. Anguelum de rubo

tenid.   2. Bía cen dig cen biad o die sathairn Initi co dia sathairn
Cásc fo chosmailius Móissi.   3. Secht fichit bliadan an æs díblínaib.
4. Is inderb an adnacol diblinaib.

[*O'C.* 152.]   Bái im. tríall cumling móir 7 catha etir chóiced
n-Érenn .ı. Ultu 7 Uu Néill 7 Airgialla ic cosnam chuirp Patraic;
Airgiallu 7 Ui Neill ic triall a tabartha do Ardmacha, Ulaid oca astud
occu.   Co ndeochatar co alailiu husce an*n* co tuarcab ind ob friu tria
nert Dé.   O dochóid in lía asind obaind dochuatar na sluaig fo chom-
baig do breith chuirp Patraic.   Issed tarfas do chach díib breith in
chuirp leis dochum a thíri.   Co rusetarscar Dia fon indas sin tria
rath Patraic.   Fri re da aidchi deacc nocho raibi adaig hi Maig Inis
acht soillsi ainglecda.

28. Isin nomad bliadain flatha Teothanes[1] rofaid comarba Petuir
inní Patraic do praicept do Góidelaib.[2]   [*O'C.* 19.]   Is é im. airchindech
róbæ hi Roim, Celestinus i*n* dara fer XL ó Petur.   Rofuid side i*n*di
Paladius huasaldechon ; dafarraid gal*ar* hi tírib Cruithnech *co n*derbalt

---

audivit.   2. Quadraginta diebus et quadraginta noctibus jejunavit.
3. Aetas sua tota centum viginti.   4. Ubi sunt ossa ejus nemo
novit.

[*LA.* 8 ba, 15 bb.]   De reliquiis S. Patricii dira contentio ad bellum usque perveniens inter nepotes Neill et Orientales ex una parte,
et Ultu (qui) corpus Patricii contenderunt.   Inter aliquando propin-
quales et propinquos irarum intrat certamen secundum fretum quoddam quod collum Bovis vocatur.   Misericordia Dei surrexit freti
feritas et pugnare prohibuit.   Freti tumore sepulto (refuso, repulso?)
hostes, *i. e.* Orientales et nepotes Neill contra Ultu, sed felici seducti
sunt fallacia et sanctum corpus rapere æstimabant.   Merito Patricii
misericordia Dei plebem pugnare prohibuit.   Duodecim diebus noctem
inter se non viderunt sed diem semper.

28. [*LA.* 16 a.]   XIII anno Teothosii imperatores a Celestino epis-
copo papa Romæ Patricius episcopus ad doctrinam Scottorum mittitur.
Qui Celestinus XLV. episcopus fuit a Petro apostolo in urbe Roma.
Palladius episcopus primo mittitur, qui martirium passus est apud

---

[1] *LB.* 220.          [2] *Lismore Life,* 8.

de.  ¹ᵃDochum n-Erend dodfetis aiṅgil Dé, ⁊ rofaid comarba Petuir inni Patraic ; Patraic pridchais do Scottaib, pridchad ⁊ batsed.ᵃ

[*O'C*. 37.]  O thanic P. con a chobluch dochum n-Er*enn* foracaib Lom*m*an an inbiur Bói*nn*e i(c) coimét a lungu fri XL aidchi.    Foror-conggart P. fair a ethar do imrum inaig*id* na Bóindi congabud baili itá indiu Ath T*r*uim, dún Feidlimthe m*eic*c Loigairi.    Co ndech*aid* isin maittin Fortchern*d* mac Feidlimthi co fuair Lommán ⁊ a soscela ar a bélaib.    Ingnad lais in forcetal rochual*ai*, rocreit ⁊ robaitsed ó Lommán.    *Ocus* roboi icoitsecht f*r*isin forcetul co tolaid a máthair for a iarair; dorigni failti frisna cleirchiu ar ba di Bretnaib di.    Tánic Fedelmid² féin do accallai*m* Lommáin, ⁊ rocreit ⁊ roedbairt Ath Truimm do Patraic ⁊ do Lommán ⁊ do Fortcernn.

29. [*O'C*. 37.]  Dochóid P. féin ⁊ rofoth*aig* Ath Truim XXV *annis* ría fothugud Airdd Machæ.    Do Bretnaib im. bunad Lommáin .ı. filius Gollit; derfiur do Patraic a máthair.    It é immorro bráthir Lomáin .ı. eps*cop* Muinis hi F*o*rcnidi la Cuircniu³ .ı. hi tuaisciurt Midi

---

Scottos, Patricius ab anguelo Dei, Victor nomine, et a Celestino papa mittitur ; cui Hibernia tota credidit, qui eam pene totam baptizavit.

[*LA*. 16 ab.]  Quando Patricius cum sua sancta navigatione ad Hiberniam pervenit, Lommanum in Hostio Boindeo navim custodire reliquit quadraginta noctibus.    Deinde secundum imperium sui magis-tri in sua navi contrario flumine usque ad Vadum Truimm, in hostio Aireis Feidilmedo filii Loiguiri pervenit.    Mane autem facto Foirt-chernn filius Fedeilmtheo invenit Lommanum evangelium recitantem ; Admiratus doctrinam credidit et a Lommano baptizatus est.    Et mansit cum illo donec mater ejus quærere eum pervenit ; et læta facta est in conspectu ejus, quia Brittonissa erat.    Salutavit autem Fedel-midius Lommanum, statimque credidit et immolavit regionem suam illi et Patricio et Fortcherno.

29. [*LA*. 16 ba.]  Pervenit P. ad illos in vado Ath Truimm et ædifi-cavit ecclesiam cum illis vicesimo quinto anno antequam fundata esset ecclesia Alti Machæ.    Progenies autem Lommani de Brittonibus, id est, filius Gollit ; germana autem Patricii mater ejus.    Germani autem Lommani hii sunt episcopi : Munis hi Forgnidiu la Cuircniu, Broccaid

---

¹ᵃ⁻ᵃ *Fiacc's Hymn.*          ² Feidlimthi, *Ms.*          ³ Cuiccniu, *Ms.*

forsin Eithne indess, Broccaid in Imliuch ech[1] la Ciarraigi Chondacht, Brocán i mBrechmaig la hú Dothrain, Mugenócc hi Cill Dumai Gluind i ndesciurt Breg. In derbchlann im. is dilis do P. o chomfuilidecht 7 ó iris 7 ó bathis 7 ó forcetal; 7 inna huili atcotaiset do thalmuin 7 do ecailsib roedbairset do Patraic *in sempiternum*. *Post aliquantum autem tempus* o rochomaicsegestar etsecht Lommáin roescomlaid Lommán 7 a dalta (.i. Fortchern*n*) do acallai*m* a bráthar .i. Brocada; 7 roaithne a eclais do P. 7 do Fortcern.

[*O'C*. 38.] *Acht* ro(f)rithbruith Fortchern*n* co roairaimed orba athar 7 is heside roerb do Dia 7 do Pat*raic*. Acht adubairt Lomán, "Noċon airamife mo bennachtain-si mani airime abdai*n*e mo ecailse." Aroírachair im. Fortchern*n* iar n-eitsecht Lom*á*in in*n* abdaine ó trib lathib co riacht co Áth Tr*u*im, 7 dorat iarsin a eclais Chathlaido perigrinó. *Hæ sunt oblationes* Fedelmedo filii Laog*airi* *sancto Patricio et Lomano et Fortcherno* .i. Áth Tr*u*im hi cr*i*cha*ib* Laogairi Breg, Imgæ i cr*i*cha*ib* Loigaire Midi.

30. [*O'C*. 83.] Luid P. iarsin hi cr*i*ch Callraigi do Dr*u*im Dara,

---

in Imbliuch equorum apud Ciarrige Connaċt, Broccanus i mBrechmig apud nepotes Dorthim, Mugenoc hi Cill Dumi Gluinn i ndeisciurt Breg. Hæc autem progenies Patricii propria est consanguinitate et fide et baptismate et doctrina; et omnia quæ adepti sunt de terra (et) de ecclesiis Patricio in sempiternum obtullerunt. Post aliquantum autem tempus, adpropinquante Lommani exitu perrexit ipse cum alumpno suo Foirtchernn ad fratrem suum Broccidium salutandum, commendavitque ecclesiam suam Patricio et Foirtchernno.

[*LA*. 16 ba.] Sed recussavit Foirtchernn tenere hereditatem patris sui quam obtulit Deo atque Patricio, nisi Lommanus dixisset, "Non accipies benedictionem meam nisi acciperis principatum ecclesiæ meæ." Tenuit autem post obitum magistri sui tribus diebus usque dum pervenit ad Vadum Truimm, ac deinde statim Cathlaido perigrino distribuit ecclesiam suam. Hæ sunt oblationes Fedelmedo filii Loiguiri sancto Patricio et Lommano et Foirtcherno, id est, Vadum Truimm in finibus Loiguiri Breg, Imgæ in finibus Loiguiri Midi.

30. [*LA*. 17 ab.] Veniens Patricius in finem Calrigi babtizavit

---

[1] ach, *Ms.*

bali itá i ndíu Druim Lías.  Is and robaitsi mac Caerthinn, 7 roedbrad in port sin do P. *in sempiternum.*  Rogab P. iarsin forsind edbairt i nDruim Daro, Druimm Líass i ndíu .ı. di sostaib Patraic and 7 dina líassaib roainmniged.  Forácaib P. Benén and a dalta in abbdaine fri ré fichet blíadan.

[*O'C.* 139.]  Fecht n-aili roboi P. inn a chumsanud i ndeired aidchi oc Tiprait Cernai i tír Tiprat.  Dolluid int angel adochum 7 do-n-íusaig.  *Dixit ei P.,* "Hin fil ní hi cráidind do Dia no in fail a baraind frim?" ol P.  "Nocon fail," ol int aingel, "ocus timarnad duit ó Dia 7 is he comus termuind do chathrach o Dia co Sliab Mis, co Bri n-Airigi, co Dromma Breg masu ed is maith lat.  Ocus dorat Dia hÉirind hüili duit-siu 7 nach sóer bias in hÉriu bid lat-su? "Deo gratias," ol P.  *Respondit P.,* "Modebrod ém," ol P. "ticfat, maicc bethad im diaid-si, 7 is maith limsa honóir dóib ó Día dom' eisi-si isin tír.

31. [*LA.* 18 b.]  D. g. Ailbe i Senchui. altare . . . (*O'C.* 53. Dodechatar co Duma Graid ; is hi suidiu roortne Ailbi . . . i Senchoi, 7 roincossc P. dó altóir.)

[*LA.*]  Machet, Cetchen, Rodán, Mathona.  (*O'C.* 55. Ocus forácaib inti Maichet 7 Cetchen 7 Rodán úasalsacart 7 Mathona síur

---

filium Cairthin, et, postquam babtizavit obtulerunt quintam partem Cáicháin Patricio . . . atrópert flaith 7 aithech inso huile i tosuch iar tabuirt baithis duaib.  Congab Patraic iar n-a idpuirt i nDruimm Daro .ı. Druim Lias.  Fácab Patraic a daltæ n-and, Benignus a ainm et fuit in se xvii annis.

[*LA.* 20 b.]  Quondam itaque P. juxta fontem in orientali Alti-Mache urbis parte ante lucem expectavit et sopor eum prostravit.  Venit angelus ad eum et excitavit eum de somno.  Et dixit P., "Numquid inique gessi nuper in conspectu Altissimi?"  Respondit "angelus," Non, sed constituitur terminus ad refugium urbi Alti Machæ a pinna montis Berbicis usque ad montem Mis, a monte Miss usque ad Bri Erigi, a Bri Erigi usque ad Dorsos Breg certe si volueris. Ac deinde donavit tibi Deus universas Scotorum gentes.  Dixit P., "Gratias ago Deo meo."  Item sanctus dixit, "Quosdam tamen electos prævideo orituros post me, tibi amicos.  Post me idcirco debeo a Deo abundantiæ donationem dimittere Hiberniæ religiossis."

Binén.) [*LA*. a.] Buail. ˙(*O'C*. 82. Fecht do Patraic ... co torchair im Búaill.) [*LA*. b.] Genus m. Eirc, Ep. Maine 7 Geintene in Echianiuch. (*O'C*. 83. Luid P. hi crích Maigi Luirg, co ructha a eich la cenél macc n-Eirc ... acht epscop Maine do muintir Patraic 7 Geintene in Echainuch.) [*LA*.] Domnach Mór Ailmaige, Domnach Mór Maige Ene, Dub, Drobés, Esrúaid. (*O'C*. 84. Domnach Sratha, conacaib Domnach Mór Maigi Ene; is ann sin mallachais do Duib, ... robennach immorro do Drobéiss ... Nách ǽ mór gaibter in Ess-Rúaid ised atberat ind iascairi.) [*LA*.] Muirgus macc Maileduin maicc Scand*ail*. Rath Cungi cli Ardd Fothid. (*O'C*. 86. *Immolavit* Muirgus macc Mailiduin maicc Scandail ri amra do chenél Choirpri a raind do Cholumb Chille ... Luid itir Ess Rúaid 7 muir dú itá Raith Chungai. Rosáith-som clí in Ard Fothaid.) [*LA*.] Domnach Mór Maige Itha. Mudubai macc Orcáin. (*O'C*. 87. Dochoid ... hi mag n-Itha do Domnach Mór Maigi Itha, co faracaib Dudubæ macc Corcain and.)

[*LA*.] Achad Drumman ... Coilboth macc Fergusso maicc Eogin Breccán macc Aido maicc Fera*daig* maicc Eo*gin*, Eogan i Fid Mor. (*O'C*. 89. Achad Drumman ainm in tíre hi fothaigestar. Gabais Cóelboith macc Fergussa maicc Eugain a láim ass, et dixit Patricius nadbiad decleithi la(a)chenél and ... Rotbia limsa failti it (f)arrad ol Aed macc Fergusa.)

[*LA*.] Eogan i Fid Mór. (*O'C*. 87. I Fid Mór is ann conranic Eogan fri Patraic.)

[*LA*.] Doro Carn Sétni. xii filii Eirc. Fergus Mór. Macc Nise, Olcán. (*O'C*. 92. Doluid P. i nDáil Riáta. Is andsin dodechaid Doro ri do Charnn Sétnai ... Olcán quem Patricius babizavit ocus roleg macc Nissi Condiri a salmu ic Patraic. Foranic Patraic failti la da macc déacc Eircc, 7 rorádi Fergus Mór macc Eircc fri Patraicc.)

32. [*LA*.] Epscop Ném i telich ceniúil Oingosso, Muadan martrach 7 presbiter Erclach i Raith Muadain Da Cheinndán i nDomn*uch* Cainri i Cothrugu, Enán i nDruim findich ... xii filii Coilboth Cellg*lass* in Eilniu fri Domnach Mór anair. Láthrach Patraic. Daniel, Slanán. Sarán macc Coilboth Conlae macc C*oilboth* Domnach Comba(i)r la Cenél Fiachrach reges. (*O'C*. 94. Forácaib epscop Ném hi Telaig Cenéoil Oengusa; fundavit Ráith Mudáin, foracaib cruimthir n-Erclach inti; forácaib da Chenn(f)indán i nDomnuch Cáinri hi Cothrugu, Enán i nDruim (F)indich. Forránic dá macc

deacc Cóilbad ar a chiund dú itá Cell glass . . . ocus arbertai congabad
dú itá Lathrach Patraic; is annsin ata Daniel, is occo ata tipra
Patraic, Slan a ainm.　Gabais iarum a laim Saran macc Caelbad
ass . . . arroet immorro Conlæ macc Coilbad Patraic 7 adrobart dó
Domnach Combair 7 forácaib no beitis ríg 7 airig dia chenél co bráth.)

[*LA.*]　Macc Decuil. c. bb. . . . Im*blech* S*escinn*.　Mulu. a . . .
t. s. la. f. a. Ath M. f. b. m.　Enda m. m.　Cair. m. Fergosso. (*Stokes'*
*Tripartite*, p. 78.　Fer muintire dó conaggaib macc Decuil la Colomb
cille; Molúe ailithir di Bretnaib ind Imliuch Sescainn.　Temair
Singite la Firu Asail.　Folamastair Patraic congbail oc Ath Maigne
ind Asal.　Fristuidchid fris Fergus bráthair do Brenain macc Echach
Muin Medoin.　Fristuidchetar fris Fiacha 7 Endai.　Mallacht . . . for
clocha Uisnig . . . condaforslaic Nuadæ ab Aird Macha.)

[*LA.*]　Cru. Munis, presbyter leo et d. s. presbyter Lugach i
cuil air. p. Colo. C. Er. Mel. C. Cre., Lug(ai)d m. Eirc i Fordruim,
C. Cas. c. m. P. Sen-Chiaran S. Lonán m. Senich de g. Cócil. Rigell
ma. Du-Luae Chroibige. (*Stokes' Tripartite*, 82, 74, 76.　Epscop
Munis . . . Seisiur macclerech léu 7 Darerce (soror) germana Patricii
. . . Cruimthir Lugach i Cill Airthir, cruimthir Columb i Cluain
Ernáin, 7 Meldan Cluano Crema, 7 Lugaid macc Eirc i Fordruim 7
Cruimtir Cassan i nDomnach mór Maige Echnach.　In seised Sen-
Chiaran Saigre.　Iss é Lonán macc Senaig, Rigell immorro a máthair.
. . . Do-Lúe Croibigi is hé fil i nDruim Inasclaind.)

Trían m. Féic m. Amal. fr.　Tricheim.　Setne, Leet.　(*O'C.* 130.
Mogaid-ne, ol síat, do Tríun macc Féic maicc Amalgaid .ı. bráthair do
Trichem.　Bennachais Patraic Sétna macc Trena 7 Iarlaidi macc Trena.

33. [*LA.*]　Echu, Cairel, Domungart.　(*OC.* 133. Asbert Patraic
fri hEchaich . . . Do bráthair in Cairell bid rí féin . . . Rosbaithis Patraic
7 robennach in gein bói in a broind .ı. Domangort macc Echach.)

[*LA.* 19.]　Oi Bair.　Fiac, Oingus, Ailill Mór, Conall, Etarsce;
Macc Ercae pater . . . Echuid Guin*ech* macc Oin*gosso* . . . Crim*thann*
m̀. Cen*selaig*. (*O'C.* 113.　Batar intan sin fo ingreim la ríg Laigen
Cremthann m. Censelaig col-lotar for longais . . . Quinque fratres:
Fiacc, Oengus, Ailill Már, Conall, Etarscela; pater eorum Macc Ercae.
In t-Oengus hi sin roort in ríg iartain Cremthan macc Censelaig do
digail a loingsi.)

[*LA.*]　vii. Muchonoc 7 Muchatoc, Erdit Inse F*áil*, A*gustin* I*nseo*
Bi*cce*, Tecán, Diarmit, Naindid, Pol, Fedil*mid*.　Do*m*n*ach* Féic. lx.

Cúl-Maige. Currus. Cnoc Drommo Gablæ. (*O'C.* 112, 144. Forácc-aib morseisser dia muntir leis .ı. Mochatóc Insi, Augustin Insi Bice, Tecán 7 Diarmait 7 Naindid. 7 Pol 7 Fedelmid. Congab iarsuidiu i nDomnach Feic 7 bái and con-torcratar tri fichit fer leiss dia muintir. Annsin dolluid int angel cuice et dixit fris : " Is fri abainn aníar ata du esergi hi Cuil Maige." . . . Conaccai dá ech carpait for a chiund for scur 7 roráidi Sechnall . . . Issi tucait in charpait do breith co Fiacc, ar noteiged Dia Sathairnd Initi co mbith oc Cnucc Dromma Coblai).

[*LA.*] Bríg *filia* Fergni maicc Cob*thig* de Uib Ercan Bile m*acc* Cru*aich* (*O'C.* 110. Luid Brig ingen Fergnai maicc Cobthaig de Uib Ercan con-éicid do Patraic an ancride bái ar a chiunn, Isand tarb-laing Patraic isind tailig dia mbu ainm intan sin Bili Macc Cruaich).

[*LA.*] Cell Auxili Macc Táil. (*O'C.* 110. Forácaib Úsaili i Cill Úsaili 7 Iserninum 7 Macc Táil hi cellaib Culind).

[*LA.*] cumbir, g. t. Pat. d. s. (*O'C.* 95, 98. Arroet Conlæ macc Coilbad Patraic con humolloit 7 adrobart dó Domnach Combir. Secht ndomnaigi do Patraic la uu Tuirtri)[1].

[*LA.*] D. mór C. F. (*O'C.* 112. Congab iarsuidiu i nDomnach Féic. Is hi trichtaib 7 cethrachtaib ataat inna cella dorat do Patraic . . . la Uu Censelaig im Domnach Mór Maige Criathar).

34. [*LA.*] Cruim. C. = Cruimthir Cathbad or Cruimthir Columb, or Cruimthir Collait of *O'C.* 94, 99, 156.

[*LA.*] Dom. m. Maige Sile. (*O'C.* 54. Robói míass chethorchari dib . . . i nDomnach Mór Maige Seolai . . . fota ó Ailfinn síar. Here the Armagh scribe wrote Sile, having seen Bid bendachtha do *sil* a few lines before this.)

[*LA.*] Sendom. la au er. (*O'C.* 59. Ro hedbrad Sendomnach Maigi Ai do Patraic in eternum. The "Hui Ercæ," the cenél macc n-Eirc or cenél maicc Ercæ, or genus Eirc dwelt in Mag n-Ai: *cf. O'C.* 54, 82, and my *Documenta de S. Patricio*, pp. 82, 110.)

[*LA.*] d. f. pp. may be duo Franci prespiteri, or Frainc Patraic dochuatar uad . . . .ı. Bernicius et Hibernicius of *O'C.* 60, or it may refer to the *duæ filiæ principis* "di ingin Loegairi," whose story pre-cedes the previous extract.

---

[1] Here g. t. = genus Tuirtri = Uu Tuirtri, and d. s. = dominicæ septem = secht ndomnaigi. The *LA.* Tripartite differed in sequence from *Eg.* and *Rawl.*

[*LA.*] C. co. vii. d. m. Maige Réto. (I read, *cum comitibus septem*: cf. *O'C.* 112, 114. Foraccaib morṡeisser dia muintir leis . . . Domnach Mór Maigi Reta, bái Patraic and fo domnach.

[*LA.*] Mogin Fedelm. Dubán Dubaed. (*O'C.* 109, 143. Luid iarsuidiu do Náss . . . dú robaithes dí ingin Ailella, Mogain 7 Fedelm. Da bráthair di Ultaib Dubán 7 Dubæd gatait da gerran Patraic.)

[*LA.*] Ingena ríg Long. Britonisa. reliquiæ. ymnus. Berach Bríg. doas. (*O'C.* 138, 143, 146, 147, 148. Fecht nand dodechatar nói n-ingena ríg Langbardd 7 ingen ríg Bretan dian ailithri dochum Patraic . . . Is ed tucad and cóic martir ar tri fichtib ar trib cétaib im reilcib Póil 7. Petair 7 Laurint 7 Stefain et *aliorum plurimorum*, 7 anart and co fuil Crist 7 co folt Maire Ingine . . . Luid Sechnall con a immon do Patraicc . . . Dobretha trí fáscri grotha dó 7 imm ó lánamain irisig .i. Berach 7 Bríg. Doas ind imuin, (ol Sechnall . . .)

35. [*LA.*] Oingus . . . fer nadgair . . . nambas afongair. Muru áth eirnn . . . Lonan m. m. eircc . . . cae. (*O'C.* 116, 120. Am-bói P. oc baitsed Oengussa luid ermted na bachlai tréna thraigid Oengussa. Asbert Patraic cid rombá *naderbartais* frim? Ni rega do chomarba *oeded ngonai*. Issed dochóid Patraic i *Muscraigi mBregoin*. Lá nand bói oc innlat a lám ind áth. Luid iarsuidiu cu Ua Fidgenti condernai Lonán macc maicc Eirgg fleid do Patraic im-mullach Cae fri Carn Feradaig andess.)

[*LA.*] Cuillenn Ailill m. Cathbad m. Lugthig. (*O'C.* 117. Luid iarsin combái ind Ochtur Cuillenn. Rossís fris Ailill macc Cathbad maic Lugdach.)

[*LA.*] Felaimbir i crich Coirpri m. Briuin. dau m. Briuin, tuad clare Coirp. Broccan. Coiman cell raith. ard ted. muin, lombchu. grian. (*O'C.* 119. Folamastar fedlegud hi toeb Clare oc Raith Coirpri 7 Broccan . . . 7 foráccaib fer dia muintir and .i. Cóeman Cell Ráth. Adrochabair dano congbáil i nGrein la Aradau. Bai Patraic la Aradu Cliach oc Tediul . . . Muin 7 Lomchu i Cill Tidil la Patraic.)

[*LA.*] n. m. m. banchuire. dens, cuir. lc. b. oirbri. (*O'C.* 120, 116. *Ille dixit*, "Nipa níe *Nena*[1] acht ataat i ndóiri la *Muscraigi Mitini*. Oc tuidecht ass, dolluid *banchuiri* inna Gréine do gubu

---

[1] I italicize the words of *O'C.* that refer to the words of *LA.*; the word "oirbri" was either misread for *roce-labrai* or stands for Oirbrige, the people and region of Orrery.

tuidechta Patraic uadib.   La nann bái oc innlat a lám ind áth, co
torchair *fiacal* as a chinn . . . 7 Cell Ḟiacla a ainm inna cilli hi fargaib
Patraic ind ḟiacail 7 ɪɪɪɪ dia muintir ꞉ɪ.  *Cuircthe 7 Loscán, Cailech 7
Beoán. rocelebrai* dóib.)

36. [*LA.*]  Fuirg muindech mechar f. forat m. conli. Musc. cel.
imch. dub. gart. lam. trian, carthach nial. nain. m. nise conán sepis.
debita. alump. xɪɪɪɪ duntarich. trian. foto m. fo. xvɪɪɪ.  (*O'C.* 125.
Invenuintur tres fratres illius regionis potentes, Fuircc 7 Munnech 7
Mechar meic Forat maicc Conlai . . . Duodecim vero Munnich filios
sustenuit ad se venire, hoc est, Muscán, Cellachán, Imchath, Dubthach,
Gairtne, Lamnid, Trian, Carthach, Niall, Naindid, Macc Nissi, Coninn
. . . Coninn excusavit causam *sepis* exponendæ . . . Cellachán dixit
quod causa munerum *debendorum* tarde pervenit . . . Carthach dixit
quod credidisset si tantum expectaret *alumnum* suum .ɪ. a aiti.   Con-
darochaill *Dungalach* do sil Failbi Flaind.   Dungalach macc Fælgusa
Ua Nadfroich fir.   Is andsin robennach fleith in méich i Craibecaib ic
epscop *Trian.*   Is andsin doroithiusaig Patraic *Fot macc Deraig* do
feraib Muman xxvɪɪ.)

37. [*TL.* 8.]   Hin Nemth*ur* imorro rogenair 7 in lec forsa rogenair
intí Patraic cech aen dogní luga ṅ-eithig foithi, dofuisim huisce amal
bid oc cained in gúforgaill ; mád fír imorro a luga, tairisid in a
haicned chóir.   Issed rucad cusin mac ndall claireinech dia baitsiud.
Gornias ainm in tṡacairt, 7 nocho raibi usce ocai asa ndénad an
baitsidh, co tarat airrde na cruiche di láim inna náiden tarsin talmain,
co rommid topar uisci ass.   *Lavit faciem* 7 roeroslaicti a roisc dó 7
roerlég in mbathais intí na rofoglaind litri riam.

Doróne Dia firt trédai a(r) Patraic isin maiġin sin .ɪ. in topur

---

37. [*VV.* 2, 3.]   Natus est igitur in Nemthor . . super lapidem
qui adhuc honorifice habetur, omnes enim pejerantes juxta se vident
illum aquam effundere, quasi flentem falsum testimonium ; aliàs vero in
natura sua stat.   Ille autem baptizari portatus est ad alium sanctum
a nativitate cæcum tabulata facie, cui aqua defuit.   Fertur autem
quod Gornias fuerit nomen sacerdotis, qui de manu infantis signum
crucis in terra posuit, et inde erupit fons, et lavit faciem, et aperti
sunt oculi ejus, et relegit baptismum qui nunquam literas didicit.

Tres virtutes fecit simul (fons de terra erupit, et cæcus a nativitate

uisci asin talmain, 7 a roisc don mac dall, 7 airlegend dó uird na baisti
cen aithgne a litri cósin; 7 robaitsid intí Patraic iarsin.  Rofothaiged
imorro eclais forsin topar sin in robaitsed P., 7 is and atá in topar
ocon altóir, 7 techtaid fuath na cruiche am*al* adfiadat ind eolaiġ.

[*TL.* 10.]  *Nutritus est . . . filium.*  Mór di fertaib 7 di
mirbailib dorone Dia tré Patraic in a gillacht, acht aisnefimit uáiti
do ilib dib.  Fecht and bái Patraic i toig a muime, dorala ind aimsir
geimrid col-linad tola 7 lia usci less a muime, co rabutar lestra 7
fointreb in tiġe for snám, 7 co mbaided in tenid.  Patraic imorro
rochí for a muime, amal is bés do [*O'C.* 5] naoden*aib*, ic
tothlug*ud* bíth.  Is annsin rorade a mui*me* fri*s*, "Ni se snim fil forn*n*d;
bói ni ba toisigiu dún anas biad do dénu*m* duit, lasse ní beu cid i*n*
tene."  Patraic, im., an dochluined in*n*a br*iathra*-sa, dorothlaig alaili
locc na ranic ind t-uisci isin tig, 7 rothuim láim isin n-uisci, 7
dorep(*r*)ensat[1] cóic ban*n*a a mér*aib* Patraic; 7 dorónai cóic oibli dib

---

lumen oculorum recepit, qui nunquam literas viderat sacra baptismatis
verba relegit),[2] et postea baptizatus est.  Aedificata est autem
ecclesia super fontem in quo baptizatus est; ipse autem fons est juxta
altare et habet[3] figuram crucis ut periti aiunt.

Nutritus est . . . filium.  Multa signa, multaque mirabilia
in illius pueritia fecit per illum Deus, sed de multis pauca perstringemus.  Quodam tempore cum puer in domo materterae suæ quæ eum
nutrierat moraretur, contigit ut hiemali tempore aquatica inundatio et lues castellum nutricis illius subintraret ita ut domus vasa et
suppellex innatare videretur, et ignem demergeret.  Ille autem flevit
a nutrice sua, ut solet illa ætas, postulans alimentum.  At illa
respondit, "Non hæc, inquit, nostram sollicitant mentem; debemus
curare prius de nostris quam tibi alimenta parare, cum nullus vivus
ignis appareat."  Ille vero hæc audiens, locum quemdam petivit
quem aqua in domo non attigerat,[4] et manu in aquam intincta, et ex
digitis quinque guttulæ profluentes quinque scintillæ apparuerunt, et

---

[1] do repensat, *O'C.*

[2] The words in parenthesis are from
*Vita* 4ta.

[3] et habet, *Vita* 4ta; habens, *VV.*
2, 3.

[4] invaserat, *V.* 4.

focétóir, (7) rolass in tene, 7 nírardraig in t-uisci. Romórad ainm nDé 7 Pátraic de sein.

38. [ *O' C.* 5.] Fecht aile do Patraic ic cluithiu itir a comaistiu, .i. a comaltud, inn aimsir gemrid 7 fuachtu in t(s)ainriud, co torinol[1] lán a utlaig do bissib ega co tucc leis dia thaig co a muime. Is annsin roráid a muine frissom, "Robod ferr dun brosna crinaig do tabairt di ar ngorud fris andas a tucais." Atrubairt-som fria muime, " Creitsiu uair is sochmactu do Día co rolassat ced na bíssi amal crinać." Ocus is deniurad a m(b)dar suidigthi na bissi eg forsin teinith, 7 a ndorat a anáil fáe, rolassaiset fócetoir amal crinach. Romórad ainm nDé 7 Patraic tresan fert sin.

Fecht do Patraic 7 dia fiair .i. Lupait, ic ingaire caorach, co tancatar ind uain co hopunn doc(h)um a mathar, amal is bes doib, do ol lomma. Otcondairc P. 7 a fiur inní sin roreithset co dian dia terpud. [*O' C.* 6.] Dorochair ind ingen[2] 7 roben a cenn fri cloich corbo comfocus bas dí. An doadchuired im. Patraic, atconnairc a fiair como

---

ille ignis conflagravit, et amplius aqua non apparuit. In illo (signo) nomen Dei clarificabatur per illum.

38. [*VV.* 2, 3.] Alio die puer inter alios suæ ætatis æquales ludebat, sed hiems eadem similitudine et frigus abundabat, ille vero glaciei concretæ crustis sinum implens, ad domum in qua fuerat nutrix veniebat et in solum fudit. Cui illa dicebat, "Multum nobis utilius erat nutrimenta ignium copulare, frigore nos urgente, quam ista cumulare." Ad quam ille dixit, " Crede quia[3] possibile est Deo etiam de hoc fomites efficere flammeos"; ac dicto citius ipsa glacie in modum fomitum composita, illoque subditam materiam insufflante, et glacierum partes quasi lignorum aridorum congeries inflammabatur. In isto signo nomen Dei clarificabatur per illum.

Post hoc tempus credita erat illi et sorori suæ Lupitæ cura ovium, ex improviso contigit ut agnorum impetus, sicut sæpe solet, in matres prorumperet lacte volentes satiari. Quo viso ipse et soror ejus cursim properabant[4] disjungere a matribus agnos. Soror ejus cecidit et ad lapidem caput fregit ita ut usque ad mortem propinquaret. Ille

---

[1] *O' C.* seems to have *tormol.*
[2] ind ningen, *O' C.*
[3] quàm of *V.* 2 must be a mistake

of Colgan's in lengthening a contraction.
[4] Cursum properabant, *V.* 4.

comḟocus bas di *in* a ligu, 7 rotogáilsigestar co hadbul, 7 conuargaib
fochetoir in siair, 7 dorat airḋe na *cru*ichi tarsan c*recht* 7 roslan*ai*g cen
nach galar; aráidi nóardraigdis foillechta i*n* gelcrecta and.   Ocus tancat*ar* iarsin imalle dia taig m*ar* nac comairsed olc f*ri*u.

39. Fecht aili do Patraic oc na cáirib co ruc i*n* cu all*ai*d chairic
uaḋ.  Rochairigestar a m*ui*me co mór in*d*.   Dob*er*t in cú *in* cairig sl*án*
arabar*ach* cosi*n* maigin c*et*na; 7 ba hingn*a*d aisig asand in*u*d sin .1. a
déd*ai*b in c*on* all*ta* imun *m*biad ngnáthach.   Ótch*on*dairc di*di*u muime
Patraic co f*or*bred rath nDé an*n* hi f*er*taib 7 hi m*ir*bailib, nócharad si
he co mor, 7 nocon-occobr*a*d sí co ndigsith nach leth cen héso*m*
maraon f*ri*e.

Fecht an*n* luidi a m*ui*me do blegon na (m)bó, luid-so*m* do*no* lea do
ól digi leamn*ach*t*a* Dástaigther[1] tra .1. demon docoid i*n*ti i*m*mon mboin
isin mbuaile, co romarb cóic bu aile.   I*n*tan boi ic cuingi(d) loma
atbert a m*ui*me f*ri*som tódiuscud na mbó.   Dodiussaig-som da*no* na

---

autem revertens, vidit sororem suam morti contiguam, et contristatus
est valde, et statim levans eam vulnus signaculo crucis signavit, et
sanata est nullo dolore remanente, apparentibus tamen cicatricis
vestigiis.   Deinde reversi domum suam simul ingrediuntur tanquam
si nihil mali paterentur.

39. Ex eodem grege cui puer pastor erat lupus ovem rapuit.  Cujus
rei causa nutrix sua ipsum increpabat.  In crastinum eo ingrediente
eadem pascua vidit lupum cum ove, et eam intactam[2] coram ipso
exponit;[3] ecce mira res facta est ut dentes lupi abstineant ab alimento
consueto.   Videns ergo nutrix tantam gratiam in signis faciendis
in eo inardescere, impatienter[4] eum amabat, et sine eo comite nusquam
ire[5] volebat.

Alio tempore, illo perambulante cum ea, premendi scilicet lactis
causa, diabolus unam vaccarum ingreditur vesanam faciens, ut alias
quinque vaccas occideret; (tunc puer potum lactis a nutrice flagitabat[6]), ad quem nutrix aiebat vaccas reviviscere facere.  Vaccas

---

[1] So Stokes' MS.; O'C. could make
out only da or dcos*tar*.

[2] incolumem, *V*. 4.

[3] produxit, *V*. 4.

[4] ardenter, *V*. 4.

[5] so in *V*. 4; nunquam ambulare, 2
and 3.

[6] *V.* 4, as in parenthesis; 2 and 3
have "modicam mensuram lactis sibi
repleri."

bú cum̄dar slána 7 bícais in da, sach̄taigi. Romórad dono ainm
(n)Dé 7 Patraic tresan fert-sin.

40. [ *O' C.* 7.] Boi dono dail mor la Bretnu, luid-som la muime 7 la
oiti don dail.   Dorala *co* nd̄erbailt a oiti isin dail.   Rosoc̄t na huile di
hein 7 rochiset a comnestai 7 rochain a chommam,[1] 7 is *ed* roraidi, "A
gillai, ced ara reilcis in fer roboi cot' imorchur do eccaib?"   In gilla
im. an noc̄etfanad roreith co a aitti 7 dorat a lama imm a bragait, 7
atrubairt *fri,* "Eirig 7 tiadam[2] di ar tig."   Atrarach(t) focetoir la
breitir Patraic.   Dobertis[3] meic in poirt in roalt P. mil dia maithrib
asna miltenaib.   Is annsin atbert a muime fri Patraic, " Cia doberad
cac̄ mac aile mil dia muime ni tabraid-siu damsa.   Rouc P. iarsin
lestar lais (do)chum an uisce,[4] 7 rolín 7 ro sén ind n-usce, co rosóad
im-mil 7 roicc cechgalar 7 cech n-aingces (.i. roboi do cretraib leo)
forsa tarda.[5]   [ *O' C.* 7.] Fecht nand dochoid rec̄tairi rig Bretan do

---

reviviscere fecit, et vesanam revocat ad sua quæ mitis facta .est.
Magnificabatur nomen Deo in eo.

40. Alio die congregata magna multitudine in curia, maritus mater-
teræ ejus qui et ipse nutrivit eum (secum ad curiam perduxit).   Accidit
ut ille moreretur alumnus[6] in curia.   Omnes stupefacti (sunt) hoc casu,
flevere cognati et conjux planxit, dicens, "Quare reliquisti, puer,
portitorem tuum mori?"   Ille autem hoc sentiens ad alumnum suum
cucurrit, cui manus suas circa collum dedit, dicens, "Surge, eamus
(ad domum nostram)."[7]   Qui confestim surrexit ad verbum pueri.

[ *V.* 4, c. 12.]   Contigit ut, sicut in illis regionibus solent, pueri
mel de alveariis campestribus matribus suis asportarent.   Tunc nutrix
dixit ad eum, "ceteri matribus suis pueri mel deferunt, et tu nihil
mihi defers."   At puer quoddam vas arripiens ad fontem perrexit,
quod aqua implens oravit,[8] et convertit in mel; nutrix vero ad morborum sanitatem servavit.[9]

[ *V.* 4, c. 13.]   Quadam die, procuratore regis imperante, exiit

---

[1] *or* commain.
[2] *read* tiagam?
[3] Doberdis, *O'C.*
[4] *or* Cus an nuisce, chanuisce, *O'C.*
[5] tardag, *O'C.*

[6] *i. e.* altor, nutritor.          [ *V.* 4.
[7] The words in parenthesis are from
[8] benedixit (*V.* 6, p. 66) = ro sén.
[9] So, *cretra* = blessed things used for
curing diseases.

fuac*ra* for P*a*traic, 7 for a mui*me* condnicsitís do glan*a*d tellaig ind rígthigi.  Do*c*uaid P. 7 a mui*me*.  Is annsin tainic in t-aingel co P. 7 is *ed* roraid ris, "Dena irnaigti 7 ni ba hécen duit ind opar sin." *Oravit Patricius.*  Roglan iarsin in t-aingel a tellach.  Is ann sin adrubairt P., "Ce noloisc*ter* a fail do chonnad isin tellach-sa nocho mbia luaithne de iarnabar*ach*."

41.  Fecht n-aile luid re*c*taire ríg Breta*n* do chui*n*chid chísa grotha 7 im*me* co mui*me* Patraic.  Ni bi bai léesi ní dorattad hisa chís ; is annsi*n* dorone P. in gr*uth* 7 in*n* im don t*s*nechta co rucad don rig.  Uair rothaselbed iar*om* don rig rosoad i*n*d aicned snechta dorithissi.  Ro-maith iar*um* i*n*d ri*g* a chís do Patraic dogr*és*.

Is hé im. tuirthed tuidechta P*a*traic hi tos*s*ug dochu*m* n-Eirenn.

[*Trip. Life*, p. 16.]  Otconnairc imorro Miliuc gurbo mog hires-sech, ro*c*endaig on triur co fognad dó a oenur, 7 foruigénair-som s*echt* mbliadna fo bés nan Ebraidi.  Ocus is ed roherbad dó ingaire mucc, 7 ba comrorcu dontí ronortaig samlaid, uair ba córu a bith combad ægaire cairech.  Is ed dorala dó iartain co rúndai.

42.  [*O'C.* 18.]  Isé im. airchindech róboi hi Róim Celestinus in

---

puer cum sua nutrice, ut domus regiæ fornacem purgarent.  Venit angelus ad puerum dicens, "Ora, in hac re enim vobis laborare opus non erit."  Angelus enim fornacem mundavit.  Tunc dixit Beatus pater, "Si omnia silvarum ligna in illa fornace comburantur, usque in finem sæculi pulvis ibi non apparebit."

41.  [*V.* 4, c. 14.]  Quodam tempore, regis procurator censum butyri et caseorum a nutrice pueri quæsivit.  Qua respondente nihil tale quid inveniri posse, puer de nive cumulum faciens in caseos et butyrum convertit quæ regi direxit.  Rex autem quæ facta erant agnoscens, casei et butyrum ad propriam reversi sunt naturam.  Ab omni censu pro puero nutricem ejus liberavit.

[*V.* 2, 3.]  Causa hæc erat primi adventus ejus in Scotiam.

[*V.* 2, c. 12.]  Videns autem Miliuc quod esset servus fidelis, emit eum ab aliis ut sibi soli serviret, illique in servitute Hebræo more septem annos exegit.  Credita est vero ei cura suum, non minime autem erravit, qui hunc ita ordinavit quem oportuit esse pastorem ovium.  Quod mystice postea contigit.

42.  [*VV.* 2, 4.]  Nam Celestinus, Papa Urbis Romae, qui tenebat

dara fear xl o Pet*ur*. Rofuid side i*n*di Palladius huasaldecon do praicept do Góidelaib.   O doruacht Palladius co crích Lagen .ı. co Inber Dea, fr*i*starrassair dó Nathi mac. Garrchon.   Robaitsi Palladius huaiti i *n*du sin, 7 rofothaig t*ri* ecail*si*, Cell Fine i farcaib a lib*r*u 7 in chomrair co taisib Poil 7 Petair, 7 in clar i scribad 7 Tech na Róman, 7 Do*m*nach Airte, hi fail Silvist*er* 7 Solonius.   Ic intud do f*or* culu dafarraid gal*ar* hi tírib Cruithn*cc*h co *n*derbailt de.

Isin láu c*é*tna rooirdned Auxilius 7 Eisirnius 7 alaili do muintir P*a*t*raic*.

[*LB*. 26 a; *O'C*. 19.]   Issed doroacht P. co hInber nDeæ hi cr*í*ch Laigen.   Ni fuair failte intib 7 mallachais an inber sin co*n*id etoirthech o sin ille he.

[ *O'C*. 20.]   Sinell im. mac Findchada isé toisech ro*b*hreit Deo i*n* hEiri*nn* tria praicept Patraic ; is aire si*n* dorat P. b*enn*achtai*n* fair 7 for a sil.

-------

sedem Apostolicam, quadragesimus quintus ab Apostolo Petro archidia-conum Palladium in Hiberniam ad prædicandum transmisit.   Palladius in Lageniensium fines pervenit, ubi Nathi filius Garrchon sibi con-trarius erat.   Aliis baptizatis tres ecclesias in eodem pago construxit, unam quæ dicitur Cell fine[1] in qua libros suos reliquit, et capsam cum reliquiis[2] Petri et Pauli et tabulas in quibus scribere solebat; alteram Tech na Roman,[3] tertiam Domnach Ardec[4] in qua sunt sancti viri Sylvester et Salonius et ibi honorantur.   Revertens Pictorum finibus defunctus est.

Auxilius et Serenus et ceteri inferioris gradus ordinati sunt eodem die.

[*V*. 3, 28.]   Tenuit P. quemdam portum qui dicitur Inber Dee in finibus Lagenorum.   Donum de piscibus postulavit sed illi non deder-unt (et sententiam maledictionis protulit),[5] et fluvius ille pisces non habebit in eternum.

[*V*. 2.]   Sinell vero filius Findchatho primus ex gente Scotorum per prædicationem Patricii Deo credidit; propter quod et sibi et semini ejus benedixit.

---

[1] Ecclesia Fine, *V*. 4.
[2] So *V*. 4; campsam reliquiarum, *V*. 2.
[3] Domus Romanorum, *V*. 4.
[4] Dominica Arda, *V*. 4.
[5] So *V*. 6, c. 29.

43. [*O'C.* 23.] C*onid* andsei*n* fosfuair muccaid Díchon baile itá Saball P*átraic* indíu. Dóig leis roptar látroin *nó* meirrlig co ndech*aid* co *n*-ecid dia tig*er*nai; co tanic Díchu co ngreis a choi*n* (rógéir)[1] fó na cléirchiu. Is annsein rogab P. in fers faith*echda*, *Ne tradas* . . .

[*O'C.* 25; *LB.* 26 b.] Dochoid P. co Saball fodess co rop*ri*tchad do Rús mac Trichim, is é síde robói i nDerl*us* fr*i* Dúnlethglaise andess. Ata cathair becc and indíu 7 Brectain a hainm-sium· dú ita E(p)scop Lóairnn, *qui ausus est* . . . *suam.* A mbái di*no* P. hiarn a sét co*n*accai maethóclaig oc ingaire mucc, Mochae a ainm, 7 rop*ri*tchai P. dó 7 rombaitsi 7 romberr 7 dorat soiscela 7 menistir dó. *Ocus* doratt dó da*no* fecht aile bachaill tucad dóib o Dia .i. a cend in ucht Patraic 7 a coss[2] in ucht Mochae. Ocus is í sin in "i*n*d detech Mochae Nóendroma."[3] Ocus dorairgert Mochae mu(i)cc cecha blia*dna* do P. 7 is*ed* ón atberar fós.

---

43. [*VV.* 2, 3.] Et invenit eos subulcus viri cui nomen erat Dichu ubi nunc est Horreum Patrici. Putans eos esse fures aut latrones exiens indicavit domino suo; (venit Dichu) et dimisit canem ferocissimum ut illum devoraret.

[*V.* 2, 31.] Perrexit Patricius ad australem plagam prædicare Rus filio Trichem qui fuit in oppido suo, nomine Derluss in australem plagam. Hodie civitatula est quæ dicitur Mreathan,[4] ubi est episcopus Loarne, qui ausus est . . . suam. In illa igitur via invenit P. adolescentem sues pascentem, nomine Mochoe, et prædicavit ei et baptizavit eum ac totondit, et dedit ei evangelium et ministeir. Alia quoque vice dedit ei baculum, qui missus est inter eos a Deo, caput in sinu Patricii et cauda in sinu Mochoe. Is i sin "inditchech Mochoe Noendroma."[3] Et promisit Mochoe suem per singulos annos Patricio et redditur adhuc.

---

[1] rógéir, *LB.* 26.
[2] *i.e.* cuspis, *V.* 6, c. 37.
[3] Isí sin tra ind eittech, *LB.* That is the flyer or winged thing—"Baculusque *volans* ab Hibernicis nominatur," *V.* 6,

c. 37. For *etech, itchech,* read *ettech* from *ette* gl. *pinna, Z.* 765. Ettech occurs in *LU.* 122 a: "cochline ettech," *Stokes.* Ind ettech = cuspis volans (?).
[4] Inreathan in *V.* 2.

E 2

44. [*LB.* 25 b.] Ticced Victor aingel dia acallaim 7 dia forcetul; cét slechtain cech láithi 7 cét cech n-oidche dognid.

[*O' C.* 51.] Dochoid P.; iarsin do Maig Sléchta, baile ir-rabi ardidal na hEir*end* .i. Cenn Cr*ú*aich cumtachta o ór 7 ó argatt 7 da idal deacc aile cumtachta ó umai *i*mme. O róchomaicsig don*d* ídal conuargaib a láim do chur bachla Íssu fair; 7 nóco rala, acht dorairb*ert* síar don inntiuth for a leith ndeiss, ar is i *n*dess roboi a agad; *ocus* maraid slicht inna bachla in a leith clíu béus, aráide nocho roscaig an bachall a láim Pátraic; 7 rolluicc i*n* talam na dá arracht deacc aili conicci a cinnu 7 atáitt fon indus sin ic comardugud in*d* (f)erta; 7 romallach don demon 7 ro índarb i*n* iffr*inn*.

[*O' C.* 70.] O espartain aidche ndom*n*aig co anteirt día luai*n* ní theiged P. assin maigin i*m* mbíth. Olai̯liu domnuch do P. i*m* maig i*n* húair (f)escuir co rosnig flechud mór isin talmai*n* sin 7 nír sníg isin lucc i rabi P., *sicut in concha et vellere Gedeoni accederat.*

---

44. [*V.* 3, c. 14; *V.* 2.] Venit angelus nomine Victor qui eum visitabat, et colloquio ejus P. fruebatur; centies in die et centies in nocte orabat.

[*VV.* 3, 4.] Divertit autem P. ad Campum Slecht ubi erat idolum ex auro et argento fabricatum, et duodecim dii ærei fabricati hinc et inde erga idolum, cujus nomen vocabatur Cenuerbe. Veniens P. ad campum in quo idolum erat,. elevata manu baculo Jesu idolum jugulare minabatur; dæmon vero timens Patricium lapidem in latus dextrum vertit, et in latere sinistro vestigium baculi adhuc manet, et tamen de manu sancti baculus non recessit;[1] cætera autem duodecim simulacra terra absorbuit usque ad capita, quæ tantum videntur in miraculi memoriam; Dæmon vero venit foras, quem P. jussit abire in infernum.

[*VV.* 3. 4.] Consuetudo erat illi[2] ut a vespere dominicæ noctis usque ad mane secundæ feriæ non ambularet e loco ubi manebat. Quodam dominico die erat in campo ubi vespertina hora pervenit, et gravis pluvia in illam terram defluebat; in loco in quo P. erat pluvia non descendit, sicut olim in concha Gedeonis accidit.

---

[1] de manu sancti non recessit, *V.* 4, c. 53.     [2] *i.e.* ba béss dó, *O' C.* 71.

45. [*O' C.* 72.] Fecht an*n* do aru(ith) Patraic testatar a eich airi. Ní chóimnacuir a fogbail la doiṙci na aidchi.[2] Tuarcaib P. a láim súas. Roin(ṡ)orchaigset a chúicc mer in mag n-uile, am*al* bitis chóic ṡutralla 7 fofritha na eiċ fochétóir.

[*O' C.* 75.] Asbe*rt* Réon, dú i*n*-aicciged Patraic nasluicfed in talum. Atfes do P. aní sin. "Is meisi ém," ol P., "cita-n-accigi." *Ut vidit P. illum* sloicsi in talam sís. "Creitfe," ol sé, "ma num-anaċar." Foceirt i*n* tala*m* súas; co mbui osnaib gaithib; *credidit et baptizatus est.* Focoisled da*n*o súas Roéchred 7 dolléced anúas com-memaid a chen*n* frisinn ailich. Fecht and dolluid dall arcend Patraic; tairpech dondechuid la accobur na ícci; fáithbid fer do muintir P. immbi . . Pa slán iar*um* in dall 7 pa dall in slán.

46. [*O' C.* 88.] "Cid-si delb doguisi," ol P. "Delb inna óclaigi fil fo teigsiu."[1] Dosnailgi P. fo óen bratt. Rigid Eogan a láim suas lia gaisced, "Is cui*m*mse limm inso," ol sé; asaid *protinus illa longitudine.*

---

45. [*VV.* 4. 3.] Tunc auriga sancti amisit equos suos. In tene-brosa nocte[2] eos invenire non poterat. P. manum elevavit, et quinque ejus digiti, quasi quinque lampades,[3] proxima quæque illuminabant, et auriga equos invenit.

[*V.* 4. 66.] Dixit Reon, quia ubicumque videret Patricium terra eum absorberet. Hoc audiens P., ait, "Sed ego prius illum vi-debo." Videns P. magum, terra eum deglutire coepit. Magus dixit, "Parce mihi et credam." Terra eum sursum projecit, et credens bapti-zatus est. Rechrach autem sursum elevatus est atque deorsum dejectus, caput contra saxum illisum est. Quodam die venit ad Patricium quidam cæcus, qui cum festinanter ad Sanctum curreret, quidam clericus de Beati familia deridebat eum . . clericus lumen oculorum perdidit quod cæcus recepit.

46. [*V.* 4, c. 71.] P. dixit, "Cujus formam eligis?" "Illius juvenis de familia tua." P. præcepit ut sub uno vestimento dormi-rent. Eugenius extendit manum suam sursum contra hastam et dixit, "Talis altitudo sufficit mihi"; mira velocitate ad optatam altitudinem crevit.

---

[1] *i.e.* custodis codicum, *V.*6, c.84; de familia tua = dit muintir.

[2] propter tenebras noctis, *V.* 4.
[3] luminaria, *V.* 4.

[*O'C.* 94.] Gaibais iar*um* a láim Sárán ass 7 atrub*art* Conlæ dó Domnach Combair; 7 romb*en*dach P., 7 furácaib nobeitis rig 7 airig di a chenél co brath.

[*O'C.* 103.] T*ri* láa 7 teora aidchi do icon pr*o*ciupt 7 nirpu sia leu oldaas oen uair.

[*O'C.* 106, *LB.* 27a.] Tallsat t*ri*ar indala bocc nobít ic taba*irt* uisci do P., 7 do dechatar dia lugu in éithiuch do Patraic, co romeiglestar in bocc a br*o*ndaib in triir. "Modebrod," ol P. "f*o*rdindet in bocc fesi*n* du in*d*æs."[1] "Ondíu co bráth," ol P., "lilit gabair far clainn 7 far cenel," *quod impletur.*

[*O'C.* 108.] Is an(n) tucsatar Úi Lilaig an neim do P. isna fascraib grotha. Rosén P. iarsin i*n*na fascra *co n*der(g)eni clocha díib. Dochotar Ui Lilaig cóicait marcach i*n*na ndiad. Tintai P. friu *et dixit,* "Sech ni tergaid assin n-ath illei 7 ni regaid i*n*nund; beithi isi*n*nuisce sin co br*á*th." Dodechoid i*n*d uisciu tairsiu fochetóir.

---

[*V.* 6, c. 136.] Saranus manum ejus apprehendens illum de loco ejecit, Colladius autem locum qui dicitur Domnach Combuir ei obtulit; P. igitur illum benedixit, prædicens quod reges de eo exirent et per multas generationes regnarent.

[*V.* 4, c. 72.] Per tres dies totidemque noctes verbum populi non plus unius horæ spatio opinati sunt.

[*V.* 3, c. 70; 4, c. 73.] Tres latrones hircum qui S. Patricio aquam vehebat furati sunt, et furtim devoraverunt, et venerunt perjurare volentes. De ventribus trium virorum fortiter clamavit. Tunc P. ait, "Ipsum animal vestram ostendit[1] impietatem." Dixit P., "Vestra progenies usque in æternum hircinum caput portabit," quod usque in præsentem diem impletur.

[*V.* 4, c. 74.] Quidam vero filii Belial venenum in caseis ei dederunt. P. vero signaculo crucis facto caseos in lapides con*v*ertit. Illi, qui numero quinquaginta fuerant, ascenderunt equos et post eum cucurrerunt. P. vero respiciens retro vidit vadum transeuntes, et dixit, "Neque appropinquare neque reverti poteritis; in flumine usque ad finem sæculi permanebitis." Illi extemplo submersi sunt.

---

[1] Ni dichlend in bocc fén baile itá, *LB.*

47. [*O'C.* 115; *LB.* 28 a; *Lism. Life*, 13.] Luid iar suidiu *for* Bealach Gabran i cr{í}ch Mu*m*an do Chaisiul na Ri{ġ}, co tarla do[1] Oengus mac Natfr*aí*{ġ} .i. ri Muman, 7 nusbeir leis dia thig[2] *con*ice Caissel; 7 cre{í}tis Oengus annsin 7 robaisdeth {é}. In tan tra rob{á}i P. oc bennachad cinn Aengusa, luid ermted[3] na bachlai *tré*na thraigid Oengusso. Atbert P., "N{í} telcfider fuil isin inud-sa ond{í}u co br{á}th,[4] 7 n{í} gonfaither acht oen r{í} do neoch gebus t'inud." Bennachais P. Oengus isin maigin it{á} Lec Patraic ind{í}u, .i. Lecc Cathraigi foran ordnigtea na rig ic Caissel.

48. [*O'C.* 120; *Lism. Life*, 14.] Luid P. hin Urmumain,[5] co ndernai Lon{á}n fleid do P., 7 dechon Mantan do Muintir P. im mulluch Cæ leis ic a fur.[6] Tarraid cliar aesa dana[7] inn{í} Patraic do chuinchid b{í}id, (7) n{í} damdatar erchoi*m*ded. Is ann sin do dechai aaraile moethoclach, Nesan a ainm, 7 molt{á}n *for* a *m*ui*n* do Patraic, conastuc P. dona caintib,[8] co rodasluicc i*n* tala*m* fochetoir.

---

47. [*V.* 3, c. 60.] Tunc venit per Belach Gabran ad regionem[9] Mumunensium, et occurrit ei Oengus filius Natfraich, rex Mumunensium, et adduxit eum secum in habitaculum suum qui dicitur Caissel, et ibi credidit et baptizatus est. Cumque P. caput regis benedixisset, cuspis baculi affixa est pedi regis. P. dixit ad regem "Non effundetur in æternum sanguis omnium regum qui in hoc loco sederint super solium tuum, excepto uno rege." Est autem in loco lapis Patricii qui hucusque hodie dicitur *Lec Coithurgi*, super quo ordinantur omnes reges *Caissill*.

48. [*V.* 3.] Deinde perrexit ad regiones Urmumen et fecit ibi cœnam magnam dechon Mantan. Præco[10] non cessavit graviter ab eo quærens cibum. Tum sanctus vir erubuit[11]; et vir quidam nomine Nesan, qui nunc dicitur Dechon Nesan, obtulit vervecem Patricio, et ille datus est præconi; præco ille cum omni sua familia mortui sunt.

---

[1] docuirither do, *LB.*     [*Lism.*

[2] isin dun, *O'C*; dia thig don d{ú}n,

[3] teit erlund na bachla, *LB*; luid fo{ġ}rain na bacla, *Lism.*

[4] asbert nad mb{í}ad acht oen guine and co brath, *O'C.*

[5] So *LB*; cu Ua Fidenti, *O'C.*

[6] 7 b{á}i fer muintiri do P. oc denum inna fleidi lasin rig.

[7] cl{é}ir æsa ceirdd, *O'C.*

[8] druthaib, *O'C.*

[9] reges, *V.* 3.

[10] cum comitibus suis.

[11] Because, as the Irish texts show, he asked Lon{á}n and Mantan to give food to the aes dana, or cainti, or præcones, and was refused.

49. [*O'C.* 117.] Rossís[1] fris Ailill. Doluid a séitig, "Dootar mucca ar m*acc*," ol sí. *Et dixit* Ailill, "Creitfesa dia tódíuscad mo macc dom." Roradi P. a chn*ama* m*aicc* do thinol, 7 fororchongart for céli nDe dia muintir, .1. Malach Britt, a thodiuscu(d). "Ní digen," ol sé, "*ammus* forsin Coimdid."[2] Fororċongair*t* P. iarsin for Eps*cop* Ibair 7 for Elbi tothiusc*ad* in meicc,[3] 7 rogaid-se*m* in Coimdid leo. Dorodiuscud i*n* macc iar suidiu.[4]

[*O'C.* 129.] Romáidi Foilgi nomairfed Patraic dú i comraicfed fri*s*, i ndigail Chinn Chr*u*aig, ol is eiside r*o*bu dia do Foilgiu. Doċeltatar *tra* a muinter ar Patraic aní romoidi Foil*ge*. Láa ann asbe*rt* Odran a ara fri Patraic, "Ol atú-sa ciana oc araidecht duitsiu, a bobb*a* Pat*raic*, nomleic-siu isin p*r*imsuidi(u) indíu; bat tusu bas ara." Dorigni P. Iarsin dochóid Foilgi co tarat fuasma t*r*ia Odrán ir-richt Patraic. Atbath Foilgi *statim* 7 dochoid i*n*d Iffrind.

---

49. [*V.* 4, c. 78.] Quidam vir Patricio resistebat. Superveniens uxor ejus ait, "Filius noster a grege porcorum devoratus est." Tunc ille dixit, "Credam si filius meus per te a morte suscitetur." P. jussit ossa ejus copulari, dixit autem uni de suis discipulis nomine Malacho, qui erat Britto genere, ut suscitaret eum. Ille autem renuit Deum tentare. P. dixit Episcopis Alveo et Yboro, "Pro defuncto debemus orare." Tunc cum Episcopis oravit Dominum, et puer a morte surrexit.

[*V.* 4, c. 77.] Minando sæpe dicebat Foilge quod ubicumque beatum virum inveniret occideret, ira instigatus quoniam P. idolum, quod ille pro deo colebat, destruxit. Quidam de familia Patricii Sancto non revelarunt quod Folge Patricium interficere minabatur. Quadam vero die dixit Beato viro suus auriga, "Per multas dies tuus auriga sum, hodie esto meus." Patricius officium aurigæ tenuit. Venit autem ille Folge et lancea Odra*n*um transfixit, opinabatur enim quod Patricius in curru sederet. Et statim mortuus est Foilge, et anima ejus portata est in infernum.

---

[1] rosis, *Rawl.*

[2] Non tentabo Dominum, *V.* 6, c. 83·

[3] injunxit Episcopis Albeo et Hibaro quatenus puerum restituerent superis, *V.* 6, c. 83.

[4] *O'C.* adds St. Patrick's words to Malach, "Ni ba árd do chongbail hi talmain, bid tech n-oen fir do tech," *i.e.* (*V.* 6, c. 83) "Domum exiguam habebis in terra, non erit nisi habitatio tantum unius hominis in ecclesia tua."

50. [*O'C.* 130.] Fecht luid P. for sligi Midlúachra[1] do thecht hi tír n-Ul*ad* cu co*m*arnic an*n* fri sáiru batar ic esorgain o*m*mna ibair.[2] Conaccai P. dolluid a fuil tr*i*a na dernanda (.ı. na mogad) icond esórcai*n*. "Ca*n* duibsi," ol P. "Mogaid-ni," ol síat, "do Tríun macc Féic. Ataam i *n*doirsi 7 i mór-*i*mmniud, con ná léicth*er* dún cid aithigud arn iaronn fr*i* líicc corup messu-de dun 7 corup ánsu-de co taet ar fuil trian ar láma." Bendachais P. na iarnda co*m*dar soimmb*er*tu-de; 7 luid dochu*m* ind r*i*g do Ráith Trena, 7 troiscis P. fair. Ní derna Trían ní airi. Sois P. arabárach on dún. Focheird a saili forsin n-ailig bái dou for-sin t-ŝét cor-roemid hi trí ind ail. Setig i*n*d ríg luid i ndegaid Patraic, dogeni aithrigi, slechtais. Bendachais P. a broin*n* 7 in geni .ı. Setna mac Trena, 7 adub*air*t P. rubu chomarba dou iartai*n*. Tr*i*an fadeisin luid do c(h)englad 7 do búalad *i*nna mogad doratsat contan dou. Nosrengat a eich i*n* a charput 7 a ara, col-lotar isin loch ; bid he sein a oscur dedenach.

51. [*O'C.* 138.] Carais i*n*gen Dáre i*n*dní Benen ; dorala galur f*ui*rri

---

50. [*V.* 4, c. 80.] Quodam tempore P. Ultorum regionem adiens invenit quosdam viros, quorum cruentatas manus intendens causam tantæ crudelitatis interrogavit. Illi autem dixerunt, "Nos servi sumus Triani filii Fieci, qui nos non permittit nostra ferramenta acuere ut inde majorem tribulationem habeamus." Ferramenta Sanctus benedixit, et acutissima facta sunt ; deinde ad castellum illius hominis perrexit, et tota illa nocte orans jejunavit. (Sed Trianus unde debuit emolliri durio reffectus est).[3] Sequenti vero die cœpit ingredi viam per quam venerat. (P. sputaculum super lapidem coram illis forte jacentem projecit, qui in tres partes divisus crepuit).[3] Uxor Triani, pœnitentiâ ducta, indulgentiam a Patricio et in Deum credens benedictionem ab eo suscepit quæ postea virum sanctissimum nomine Setna enixa est. Trianus autem præcepit currum præparari volens ire et damnare servos suos, quod eorum culpa P. ad eum devenit. Sedens in curru equi ejus veloci cursu contra aurigæ voluntatem in stagnum cucurrerunt, et ita de vita migravit.

51. [*V.* 4, c. 87.] Filia Dairi Benignum dilexit ; et inde ægro-

---

[1] iter agens in Mud*o*rnia, *V.* 6, c. 132, *i.e.* i Mugd*o*rnib.

[2] cædentes ligna, *V.* 6.

[3] So *V.* 6.

co mbu marb de.    Bert Benén cretra dí o Patraic *et surrexit confestim
viva et postea spiritualiter dilexit eum.*    *Ipsa est* Ercnat ingen Dáre fil
i Tamlachtu Bó.    Fecht and dodechatar noi n-*in*gena rig Lang̔bardd
7 ingen rí(g) Bretan dian ailithri dochum P. Dodechus huádib dochu*m*
P. dus in regtais adochum.

[ *O'C.* 157.]    I*n*na ferta-sa di*no* adcuademar doronai in Choimdiu
er Patraic cia beith nech res nídat morai.[1]    Araide isat úathe do ilib;
ar ni fail[2] *f*oraithmet dóenai[3] conísad a chui*m*nigud.    Ocus ni fil
scr*i*bnid conisad a scríbend inna nderna do fertaib 7 do mírbuilib
isnaib feran*naib* irroacht.

[ *O'C.* 158.]    Iar fothugud di*d*iu eclas n-*im*dai, iar cossecrad
manistr*e*ch 7 iar mbaitsed fer n-Eirend, iar mór enmne 7 iar mórṡoethar,
iar coscrad ídal 7 arracht, iar comai*n*sem rí̇g n-*im*dai na dentais a réir,
7 iar n-oirdned do deichnb*air* ar dib no tri fichtib ar trib cétaibh do
epscopaib 7 iarn ordned do theora mili do ṡacartaib ocus áes cech uird
archena isind eclais; iarn ái*ne* 7 ernaigthi, iar *tr*ocoiri 7 chainua-
raige, iar cendsai 7 ailġine f*ri* m*acc*u bethad, iar seirc Dé 7 coibnesam,

---

tavit ac defuncta est.    Benignus aquam benedictam a Sancto
suscipiens, quam aqua aspergens illico incolumis surrexit, et postea
spiritualiter dilexit eum.    Ipsa est Ercnata filia Dairi quæ est in
Tamlachta Bo.    Quodam tempore filiæ regis Longobardorum, numero
novem et filia regis Britanniæ causa peregrinationis venerunt.    Miserunt
nuntios ad Patricium ut interrogarent si ad ejus præsentiam venirent.

[ *O'C.* 153.]    Hæc ergo quæ denuntiavimus opera, quæ divina
gratia per Patricium ut essent concessit, quamvis audientibus magna
videantur, pauca tamen sunt de multis; (nam non est) recordatio quæ
ea continere potest.    Quis enim scriptor constringere valet singula
quæque signa et miracula quæ in singulis locis confecit?

[ *O'C.* 153; *V.* 3, c. 94.]    Post igitur fundatas ecclesias, post
monasteria consecrata, post homines (Hiberniæ) baptizatos, post
tantam patientiam et tantum laborem, post idula destructa, multis
quoque regibus contemptis; post episcopos ordinatos et ṡacerdotes
et presbyteros, diaconos et reliquos ecclesiaticos ordines constitutos;
post preces[4] et jejunium, post misericordiam et benignitatem, post

---

[1] riora, *O'C.*          [3] do oen *tra, O'C.*
[2] nisaib, *O'C.*         [4] *O'C.* has " præsentiam."

arroet Corp Crist ón epscop, o Thassach ocus roťáid iar sin a spirut
dochum nime.

52. [*LB.* 24.] Patraic dino do Bretnaib Ailcluade a bunudus, Cal-
purn ainm a athar, Fótid ainm a senathar diochan atacomnaic, Concess
ainm a mathar, foruigénair som vii mbliadna fo bés na n-Ebraidi.

[*LB.* 25a.] *Fecht* ann atbath mac aroli mná nochungnad *fri* a
mumi-sium oc blegon a bó. Atbert *tra* mummi *Patraic*, "Tucc latt
do mac isin airge." Dobert a mummi lemn*acht* do Patraic 7 atbert
fris, "Gair chucat th' fer cúmtha co*n*asebi cumaid aræn fritt."
Atbert Pátraic "Tair, a ťir chumtha, conusebem cumaid." Ocus
atracht in mac a bás.

[*LB.* 25 b.] Rochomfogsig *tra* aimser thuaslaicthe *Patraic* a
dóire, ur nochlechtatis na genti særad a mogad isin schtmad bliadain. O
náimráided im. Miliucc indas noastfad intii Patraic rochendaig cumail
co rusnaisc do Patraic hi. O rocuirtha hi tech fo leth aidche na
baindsi, is andsin pritchais Patraic don chumail co ro thoċathitis inn
uile n-aidche oc ernaigthe. Isin matain iarnabaruch atco*n*nairc P. in

---

mansuetudinem et lenitatem, post tantam charitatem, post sacrificium
assumptum ab Episcopo Tassoch migravit ad Dominum.

52. [*Brux.* p. 21.] Patricius Brito natione in Britannis natus
Cualfarno diacono ortus filio Potiti presbyteri, matre etiam conceptus
Concessa nomine, in servitute detentus est sexennium more hebraico.

[*V.* 4, c. 11.] Quadam die contigit ut cujusdam mulieris, quæ
apud nutricem ejus mulgendo vaccas fuerat, filius moreretur. Nutrix
Patricii dixit, "Porta corpus defuncti ad locum ubi vacoas mulgere
solemus." Cum mutrix ejus modicum lactis sancto tradidit, dixit ei,
"Voca ad te sodalem tuum." Puer dixit, "Veni, frater, ut simul de
lacte bibamus." Ille autem qui defunctus erat surrexit incolumis.

[*V.* 2, c. 16; *V.* 4, c. 20.] Interea tempus libertatis ejus appropinquavit, solebant enim gentiles dimittere servos anno septimo
transacto. Cogitans autem Miliuc quomodo eum retineret,[1] voluit
ancillam illi adjungere.[2] In domo separatim nocte nuptiarum collocati sunt, tunc ille ancillæ prædicavit, ut in oratione totam noctem
transigerent. Luce autem orta ipse in fronte ancillæ vestigia cicatricis

---

[1] obtineret, *V.* 2; retinere posset, *V.* 4.     [2] conjungere, *V.* 4.

gelchrecht hi ndreich na cum*aile* 7 roiarfaid di fochann in chrechtai.
Atbert in chumal, "In tan ba-sa in Nemthur i mBretnaib doroch*ar*,
co ru*s*ben mo chend f*ri* cloich *cu* *m*ba foc*us* bas dam. Ótcho*nn*airc mo
br*á*th*air*, .ı. Succet, in crecht, dorat ar*d*e crochi Cr*is*t tairis co mba
hóg*s*lan foch*é*toir." Is *ed* atb*er*t P., "Messi fén do brathair, 7 is me
rot*í*cc." Gn*í*set insin atlugud do Dia 7 tiagait isin dithreb. O robói
P. isin dithr*ub* itchuala guth ind aingil atbered fris, "Is fairithe in
long co ndecha-su innte co hEt*á*il do fogluim na scrept*tra*. Is maith
dogn*í* aine, rage co luath cot' athardai fodein."

53. [*LB.* 25.] Roergabad dino hi creich intii Patraic for a sét
co raba accu fri ré da mís. Roatachsat a tuistidi hé corothairis accu a
sin amach dogrés 7 ní frith uadh. [*Fiac's Hymn.*] Menic atch*í*the hi
f*í*sib dosnicfed arithisi.

[*LB.* 25b.] Ticed im. Victor aingel dia acallaim 7 dia f*or*cetul
im chrabud do dénum.

[*LB.* 26b.] Is annsin ronochtustar D*í*chu a cloidem 7 teit do
marbad Patraic, corfémid cor do chois nó do laim de. Ocus dorat in

---

intendit,[1] atque ei interroganti quæ causa hæc esset, illa respondens
dixit, "Tempore quo eram in Brittania, in patria mea Nemthor, contigit mihi offendere caput lapidi, ut morti contigua jacerem. Hoc
frater meus, cui Succet vocabulum erat, videns, caput meum signaculo
crucis signavit, et statum vulnus sanatum est." At ille ait, "Ego sum
frater tuus qui te sanam feci." Post hæc gratias Deo agentes desertum
petunt. Cum illic demoraretur audit vocem (angeli) dicentem sibi,
"Navis tua parata est ut peteres[2] Italiam ut per scripturam disciplinan-
dus esses. [*Brux.* 22.] Bene jejunas cito iturus ad patriam tuam."

53. [*Brux.* 23.] Iterum capturam ab alienigenis Patricius pertulit et duobus mensibus erat cum illis. Parentes rogarunt illum ut de
reliquo vitæ nunquam ab illis discederet; sed ille non consensit.
Ostensæ sunt ei multæ visiones.

[*V.* 2, c. 14.] Angelus Victoricus solebat eum visitare et
docere eum ordinem orationis.

[*V.* 3, 31.] Hoc videns Dichu surrexit cum gladio et pro-
posuit sanctum interficere, et nec pedem nec manum movere potuit.

---

[1] prospexit, *V.* 4.     [2] peteret in *V.* 2.

feronn sin do P. Rochumtaig P. eclas isin inud sin dianid ainm Saball Patraic indíu.

[*L.B.* 27 a.] *P. dixit*, "A mo Choimdiu, is tú conicc in uli, is at' chum*ach*tu attát, is tú ro*n*fáid il-leth-sa ; malartar *nunc* int écraib-dech-sa fil oc écnach t' anma-su." Déniu rad la bréthir Patraic tuar-gaibset démnu isind æor in drúid, 7 roslécset uadib *fri* lár co roben a chend fri cloich co nderna men 7 luaith de a fiadnaise cháich, co ru*s*gab crith 7 uamun do*f*ula*c*ta na sluaig batar and.

[*LB.* 27 b.] Rolá P. cuairt Lagen 7 rocreitset meic Dúnlaing *tra* don Chóimdid 7 do *Patraic*.

54. [*LB.* 28 a.] Dorat-*sum* inad ardecla*ise* dó P. bale hita in Ferta indiu. O tharnic in recles do chumtach 7 rofás a fér co mór, rucc gilla Dáre a ech maith isin recles dóchum ind feoir díguind. Rothoccraid sin cu mór do P., 7 tanic in gilla iarnabarach isin matain 7 fuair a ech marb isin recles. Dochuaid *tra* in gilla ass cu toirsech 7 roindis do Dáre a ech do mar*bad* don chlerech. *Dixit* Dare in clerech fén do marbad índ. Atbail Dare fo*che*toir lasin mbré*th*ir sin. *Dixit* setig Dáre, "Is é fochund in báis-sea in t-ancride dorigne frisin

---

Et obtulit ei agrum. P. in eo loco erexit ecclesiam quæ usque hodie dicitur Sabul Patric.

[*LA.* 4 ab.] P. dixit, "Domine, qui omnia potes et in tua potestate consistunt, quique me misisti huc ; hic impius qui blas-phemat nomen tuum elevetur nunc foras, et cito moriatur. His dictis elivatus est in æthera magus et iterum dimissus foras desuper, verso ad lapidem cerebro, comminutus et mortuus fuerat coram eis, et valde timuerunt gentiles.

[*V.* 3, c. 58.] Migravit P. ad fines Lageniensium et crediderunt ei filii Dunlinge.

54. [*V.* 3, c. 28.] Locum largitus est ei, in quo ecclesiam ædifi-caret, qui nunc Ferta nominatur, in quo sanctus ædificavit ecclesiam. Duxit eques Daire equum sui optimum in illum locum ut ibi pascere-tur. Multum hoc displicuit (Patricio), crastina vero die veniens eques invenit equum jam mortuum. Reversus tristis ait ad dominum suum, "Christianus ille occidit equum tuum." Dixit Daire, "Oc-cidite eum." Dicto citius mors irruit super Daire. Dixit uxor sua, "Offensio Christiani est causa mortis hujus. Eat quis cito, et

clerech.   Tiagar co luath 7 tabar a riar dó."   Docotar na techta co P.
7 atchotar dó inní forcoemnacair ind.   Senais P. usce 7 dosbeir darsin
ech 7 darsin fer 7 atregut díblinaib a bas.

55. [*LB.* 28 a.]   *Dixit* Dáre fri díis dia muintir, "Berid mo-
chori umai don clerech."   Atbert P. iar tor*acht*u in chori dó, "*Graticum.*"   Iarfaigis Dare dia thimth*er*ib, "Cid atbert in clerech?"
"*Gratiam,*" ol na timtherig.   "Ercid," ol Dáre, "7 tabraid (in çori)
uad *for* cúla."   Iarfaigis Dáre dona timtherib cid atrubairt P.   "In
*Gratiam* cétna," ol siat.   Is ní maith[1] aca *sum* in briathar sin, ol Dáre,
in *gratiam* oc a thabairt do 7 *gratiam* oc a br*eith* uad.

56. [*LB.* 28 b.]   Tanic P. iarsin do Róim co tucc tassi Póil 7
Petair 7 Zepháin 7 Laurint, 7 anart co ʄuil Crist fair.

[*LB.* 29*a*.]   Ba hí-seo riagol a chrabuid .ı. nogebed in uli
ṡalmu con an imnaib 7 cantacib 7 abcolips, 7 .cc. ernaigthi aili cech

---

portentur ei beneficia nostra."   Exierunt duo viri ad Patricium revelantes ei quod factum est.   Benedixit Patricius aquam, et ait illis,
"Aspergite equum et regem[2] de aqua ista."   Et surrexit equus et
rex sanatus est.

55. [*V.* 3, c. 81; *V.* 4, c. 85.]   Misit Daire ministros suos ad
sanctum, portantes cacabum æneum magnum.   Cumque P. accepisset
eum dixit, "*Grazacam.*"   Ministris dixit Daire, "Quid dixit christianus?"   Et illi dixerunt, "*Grazacam* dixit."   Ait Daire, "Ite et
adducite mihi cacabum æneum."   Dixit rex, "Quid dixit christianus?"   Illi dixerunt, "Verbum suum *Crazacam.*"   Et ille respondit,
"*Grazagam,* quando datus, *Grazagam,* quando ablatus,—bonus est
sermo apud illos *Grazagam.*"

56. [*V.* 3, c. 84.]   Post hæc perrexit P. Romam et attulit inde
reliquias Petri et Pauli et Stephani (et Laurentii) et linteamen super
quod fuit sanguis Christi.

[*V.* 3, c. 86.]   Quotidiana ejus vita sic erat: omnes nempe[3]
psalmos cum hymnis et canticis, cum ducentis orationibus, et apoca-

---

[1] is e cétbriathar aici-sium, *Lismore
Life,* p. 17 ; is degbriathar leissiom,
*Tl.* 230.

[2] The *Lismore Life,* p. 17, is more
literal : "Bennuigis P. in t-uisgi 7

raiḋis a tabairt do Daire 7 tar na
heochu.''

[3] "namque," in *V.* 3, is perhaps a
misprint.

lai.  Nophritchad, nohidprad corp Crist 7 a fuil.  Dobered sigen na
crochi dar a agaid co bá cét on trath coraile.   Isin cétna frithaire na
hoidchi nochanad cét salm 7 dogníd cét slechtain, isin (f)rithaire
tan*aise* in us*ciu* uar; in cethrumad (frithaire) for úir luimm 7 cloch
fó chind 7 culchi fliuch imbi.

[*Lismore Life*, p. 6.]  Dorat Dia doib muic n-uir fonaithi;
7 dobreath mil choillidi do Patraic amal Iohain Baptaist.

[*ibi.* p. 9.]  Dorala ri feóchair for Eirinn .ı. Lœgaire.  Is ann
di*diu* bái a sosad 7 a greim rígda i Temraig.

57. [*ibi.*]  Iarsin ispert P. ria Dichoin, "Eirg uaim," ar se, "co
Loeguiri mac Neill co n-ebre mo athiusc[1] fris cu rab flaith 7 eclas isin
tír."  "Dia ndeochus-sa cu Lǽguiri," ol Dichu, "itat ix ngeill damsa
i Temraig; muirbfit*er* mo geill 7 nom-muirfit*her* féin in lín ragat."
"Ternaife-sa fein 7 ternaifeat.do geill," (ol e)sium, "(co a coi)mdid."
"Ge (gu terno no) gingu terno," ol Dichu, "ragat ar do bennachtain."
Luid iarum Dichu co Temraig.   "Is e tra in fer," ol Lœguiri, "ceta-
roch*rei*t don tailcenn ria feru Eirenn; beirid," ol se, "in fer so an

---

lipsim canebat.   Prædicabat, offerebat corpus Christi.  In omni hora[2]
signo crucis Christi centies se signabat.  In prima noctis parte centum
psalmos canebat, et ducentis genuflexionibus genua curvabat in nocte, et
aliam partem noctis in aquis agebat.   Post hoc dormiebat super nudam
terram[3] et lapis sub capite ejus, et tunica pellicea circa lumbos ejus.

[*Brux.* p. 22.]  Abundantiam cibi ex grege porcorum Deus
eis præbuit; mel quoque silvestre ut quondam Ioanni subvenit.

[*V.* 2, ·c. 27.]  Fuit rex ferox imperator in Scotia Leogarius
nomine, cujus sedes erat et sceptrum regale in Temoria.

57. [*V.* 3, c. 35; *V.* 6, c. 38; *V.* 7, c. 49.]  Alio die dixit P.
amico suo Dichu, "Vade ad Laogare filium Neil, et ab eo nomine meo
pete quatenus vellet permittere fidem Christi et ecclesiam per sub-
jectas provincias."   Respondit D., "Si regem adiero, novem obsides
quos a me habet et me cum omnibus comitantibus curabit enecari."
P. ait, "Domum reverteris incolumis et obsides libertati restituentur."
"Sive," inquit D., "revertar, sive non, paratus sum mandato tuo
satisfacere."  Tunc perrexit Dichu ad regem.  Rex propter novam

---

[1] et nuntia mea verba, *V.* 3.          [3] super nudum lapidem, *V.* 3.
[2] omni hora diei, *V.* 21, c. 63.

æntech re gial(lu), tarduiđ biađ saillti doib 7 na tarduïđ di (uisciu)."
Doronad samlaid, dosnanic (ingen) macđacht 7 dobreath drolṁuiġ ḟina
đóib [tria ernaiġt]æ Patraic, 7 [fo]dáil doib 7 dobreth soillsi dóiƀ.
Dosnainic cleirech cu casal lin[imm]e, 7 tall na glasa 7 na slaƀrada dib
7 tuc an eochu ba for lár in lis in a srianuiƀ; 7 rooslaic doirrs(ea) na
Temrach reompa. Leangait iarsin for an eochu 7 ti(agait) co P. i tír
n-Ulad. Atfet iarum Dichu a scél do P. . . . co rissa fein.

58. [*Ibi.* p. 13.] Nir' cian *co* n-erbail Failġi, teit iarsin Demun
i curp Failġe co mbui eter dainiƀ amal b(uđ beo).[1] Teit P. iar céin
mair iarsin co Failġe, 7 rothoiris a ndorus in dunaiđ i muiġ cu roḟia-
fraig do aen do ṁoġuiƀ Failġi cait i mbui Failġi. "Roḟacbas-sa in a
thiġ," ol in moġ. "Raiđ fris," ol P., "tuidecht dom' accalaim."
Teit in moġ ar cenn Failġi, 7 ni fuair đe isin tiġ acht a cnaṁa lomai
cen fuil cen ḟeoil. Tic in moġ co P. cu mbron 7 toirrsi 7 atfet dó
amal doconnuic Failġi. Asbert P., "On lo roġon Failġe mo araid
am' ḟiađnuisi, dochuaiđ a ainim in ithḟern 7 dochoiđ Demun in a churp.

---

ejus ad Christum conversionem curavit illum in carcere concludi
in quo obsides custodiebantar, et cibos salsos et nullum potum eis
dari. Postquam mandatum datum est, quædam virgo speciosa eos
visit, eisque attulit vas vino plenum, orante Patricio, et dedit potum
eis et recreavit eos. Apparuit eis quidam clericus lineo amictu
super indutus et seras et catenas dissolvit, et equos paratos adduxit,
et apertis urbis portis. Quos equos conscendentes iter susceperunt
versus Ultoniam. Dichu autem quæ contigerint Patricio refert . . .
donec ad illum perveniam.

58. [*V.* 3, c. 59.] Statim mortuus est Foilge, et intravit Diabolus in corpus ejus, et habitavit in eo quasi homo inter homines.
Post multum tempus venit P. ad domum Foilge, cumque sedisset
ante januam, interrogavit unum de servis ejus dicens, "ubi est Foilge."
Respondit, "Nunc reliqui eum in domo sua." Dixitque P., "Voca
eum ad me." Cumque intrasset domum, invenit ossa arida Foilge in
domo sua. Reversus cum tristitia nuntiavit hoc Patricio. Dixit P.,
"Ex eo tempore quo jugulavit Foilge aurigam meum coram me ille
positus est in inferno, venitque Diabolus in corpore ejus.

---

[1] Words or parts of words in parenthesis or brackets are suggested by the
Latin version.

# LIFE OF ST. BRIGIT.

59. [*LB.* 62 a.] Rochendach side cumail, Broigsech a ainm.
Rosæntaig Dubthach i comámus di, co mba hallachtu uad. Nir bo tol
dó recc na cumaile etir. (Fecht ann)[1] dolluid Dubthach 7 a c(h)umal
i carput immalle fris sech thegdais araile druad. O ruscló in drúi
fogur in charpait is ed roatbert, "Fég, a gille, cia fil isin carput, ar is
fogur charpait fó rig indso." Atbert in gilla, "Dubthach fil and."
Imchomarcis in drái cia orb halachta in chumal. "O Dhubthach,"
or in chumal. Atbert in drái, "Bid amra in gein (fil in a broinn)."[2]
*Atbert Dubthach*, "Ní léic dam mo śetig cen a creicc na cumaile-si."
Atbert in drái, "Fognife síl do mná-su do śíl na cumaile-si. Ar béraid
in chumal ingin (reil taitnemaich thaitnigfes amal grein etir renna
nime)."[3] Dochoid Dubthach iarsin dia thig 7 a chumal lais.

Dodechutar di epscop do Bretnaib otá Elpa (nó Alba) .i. Mel 7
Melchu *nomina eorum*.[4] Imcomaircis Mel di fochund a torsi. "Fognife
do síl-sa do śíl na cumaile acht tarmnaigfid a śíl dot śíl-so."

---

59. [*V.* 3, c. 1.] Emit ancillam nomine Brocsech. Dormivit
Dubthachus cum ea, quæ concepit ab eo. Sed nolebat vendere
ancillam. Quadam die exierunt ambo in curru vir ille et ancilla secus
domum cujusdam magi. Audiens autem magus sonum currus dixit
servis suis, "Videte quis sedeat in curru, currus enim sub rege sonat."
Servi dixerunt, "Neminem cernimus nisi Dubthachum in curru."
Magus dixit, "O mulier, de quo viro concepisti?" Illa respondit,
"De Dubthacho." Cui ait, "Mirabilis erit conceptus illius." Dubthachus respondit, "Compellit me uxor mea ut hanc famulam vendam."
Magus dixit, "Uxoris tuæ semen semini famulæ serviet." Claram
namque filiam paries quæ sicut sol in vertice cœli lucebit. Reversi
sunt ergo Dubthacus et ancilla in domum suam.

[*ibi.*] Duo episcopi ex Britannia venientes, quorum alter vocabatur
Mel, et alter Melchu. Dixitque Mel ad uxorem, "Quare tristis es?
Famulæ partus excellet semen tuum, tamen progenies illius tuo semini
proficiet."

---

[1] So *Lismore Life*, p. 35.          [3] *Lismore Life*, p. 35.
[2] *Lismore Life*, p. 35.              [4] an anmanna, *Lismore Life*, p. 35.

Tanic araile (file)[1] a crich hUa Meicc Uais; atbert "In
crecfa in chum*ail*?" "Crecfat," or Dubthach; (acht ni rochrecc in
choimpert bái in a bróind).[1]

. 60. [*Lism. Life*, p. 36.] In ad*aig* iarum rainic in fili a thech,
is ann dorala fer noeṁ isin tiġ og at*ach* in Coimded 7 oc errn*aig*ti.
Rofoillsiged dosom lasair 7 col*oma* tenntidi don inad a mbái in cumal.
[*LB.* 62 ab.] Dorogart in draí ríg *Con*aille don fleid; is and *tra* rop
ámm tu*s*meda do mnái in rig. Bói fáith i coimtecht in rig co roiarfacht de cara don rig, cia huair bid maith don rigain tu*s*miud in tṡíl
rigdai. *Dixit propheta*, "In gein notu*s*émtha imbarach la turcbail
ngr*é*ne noforuaisligfed cech tu*s*med[2] in Eir*inn*." Remdechaid da*no*
tu*s*med na rígna in uar[3] sin. Dodechaid in c(h)umal iarnabarach la
tu*r*cabail ngr*é*ne 7 lestar lán do lémn*acht* in a láim; in tan tuc a cois
dar tairsech in taige istech 7 in choss aile amuig is andsin ruc in[4]
ingin. Nigset na bantimthirid· in ingin don lémn*acht* bói illáim a
máthar.

---

[*ibi.*] Venit quidam poeta de Nepotibus Neill, et emit ancillam
Dubthaci, sed non vendidit ille partum quem illa habebat in utero.
Perrexit poeta eum ancilla.

60. [*V.* 3.] Et in illa nocte in qua intravit (poeta) in domum
suam, venit quidam sanctus vir orans Deum per totam noctem. Vide-
batque globum igneum in loco in quo ancilla dormiebat. Magus
ille regem suum invitavit ad cœnam; sed regina erat vicina partui.
Amicus regis interrogabat quemdam prophetam, quandonam[5] oportebat
reginam prolem parere. Magus dixit, "Si die crastino, orto sole
nasceretur neminem in terris haberet æqualem." Sed regina ante
horam genuit filium. Mane autem facto et orto sole venit ancilla
portans vas plenum lacte; et cum posuisset unum pedem trans limen
domus et alterum pedem foris, genuit filiam. De lacte illo quod por-
tabat illa corpus infantis lotum est.

---

[1] The words in parenthesis are from
the *Lismore Life*, and render the Latin
better than does *LB.*

[2] *or* doroiscfed cech ṅgein, *ibi.*

[3] uair, *Lismore Life.*

[4] *better* inn, *as in Lismore Life.*

[5] quoniam, in *V.* 3: cf. "*Cuin* bud
maith sen don riġain tusṁed," *Lismore
Life*, p. 36. .

61. [*LB.* 62 b.]  Rogenair Brig*it* i Ḟochart Murthémni ; ata beos fr*i*sin eclais anairdess in lecc forsa ngena*í*r Brigit.   Rucad in ingen foch*é*toir iarn a breith c*u*sin mac marb na rigna ; o rosiacht anal nà hingine chucca atracht a bas co luath.

62. [*LB.* 62 b ; *Lism. Life,* 36.]  Luid iarsin in dra*í* con a chum*ail* i cr*í*ch *Connacht,* ar do *Chonnacht*aib a mathair, a athair im*orro* don Mumain ;[1] a aittreb la *Connacht*aib.[2]  In araile ló doluid in chumal do bleagun a bo, 7 forfacuib (a hingin[2]) na hoenar na cotlud in a ti̇g.  Atconncat*ar* araili comḟoigsig in tegduis for lasad̉.  In tan tancatar do cabair in taige ni ro artraig in tene, 7 is *ed* atḃertsat, "co mba lán in Spir*ta* Nóib in ingen."   Laithi n-ann deisid in drai con a chum*ail* in araile inad̉ conacatar in cannadas[3] bói for cind na hingine *for* lassad ; o roṡínset a láma chuci ni ro art*r*aig in tene. Tan and roscotail in d*r*a*í* con*u*sacca t*r*iar clerech in étaigib gelaib co roimbretar ola *for* cenn na hingine cu roḟoirḃrigset ord in baitsi on beus gnáthach.  Atbert in tris clerech fr*i*sin d*r*a*í,* "Bid he a hainm na hingine, Noeb Brigit."

---

61. [*V.* 4.]  Villa in qua Brigita nata est Fochart Muirthe*n*ne vocatur ; lapis vero super quam genita Brigita post tergum ipsius sanctuarii constat.   Ipso jam die nativitatis suæ, cum esset Sancta prope infantulum extinctum et subito infantulæ tactu vivus surrexit.

62. [*V.* 3.]  Post hæc magus cum ancilla perrexit ad̉ regionėm Connachtorum, quia de Connachtis erat mater illius, pater vero de Mumuniensibus, et habitavit ibi.   Quadam autem die exiit ancilla ista ad emulgendas vaccas, et reliquit filiam suam solam dormientem in domo.   Tunc domus illa accensa igne apparebat.   Cum appropinquassent omnes domui ut extinguerent ignem, ignis non apparuit, et dixerunt, "Hæc puella plena est Spiritu Sancto."   [*VV.* 3, 4.] Die quadam magus et ancilla sederunt in loco quodam et viderunt pannum contingentem caput puellæ incendio ardere, et, porrigentibus illis manus suas, ignem non viderunt.   Die quadam magus dormiens vidit duos clericos vestibus albis indutos effundere oleum super caput puellæ, ordinem complentes baptismi consueto more.   Unus ex illis dixit ad magum hanc virginem vocare Brigidam.

---

[1] So *Lismore Life,* which is somewhat more literal than *LB.*

[2] So *LB.*

[3] cannadas of *LB.* and *Lismore Ms.* = "pannum" in *VV.* 3, 4.

63. [*Lism. Life*, 37; *LB*. 62 b.] In araili ló roclos guth na naiden oc diucaire, ⁊ iss*ed* roraid, "*Meum erit hoc*, .ı. bid leam so." O rochuala in drai sin iss ed roraid, "Comaillfider inní adbeir in ingen .ı. bid leam an ferann iardain." Ocus iss ed on ro comailled. O rachualatar aitreabthaig an feruinn. Nofrithbruidead (.ı. noobad) biad in druad ⁊ nosceided. Roimraith in drai cid rombui an ingen, co roerb iarsin boin find dia blegun do Brigit; ⁊ erbais banscail n-iressáig dia blegun ; toimleth in ingen noeb sin ⁊ ní sceided. Roalt in ingen noeb-sa com̄ba timthirid, ⁊ cech ní *fri*sa comraiced a lám[1] noforbred ; nosfor‑ bred cech cuccán adchíd.

Accobair do Brigit techt do thórruma a atharda ⁊ rofóid in drai techta co Dubthach. Rogab galar a muime,[2] ⁊ foidis intíi Noem Brigit ⁊ araile ingin immalle fria do thig araile fir do chuinchid dige do chormaimm fair. Dorat era for Brigit, taraill Brigit co topur gur' lin lestar as, co rosoud i mblass chorma, ⁊ dosbeir dia m*umm*i co mba hógslan de fo*chét*oir.

64. [*Lism. Life*, 37.] Nirbo cian iarsin tainic áige uasal do tig

---

63. [*VV*. 3, 4.] Quodam die audita est vox infantis orantis, et respondit, "Meum erit hoc, meum erit hoc." Audiens magus dixit "Prophetia est qua respondit infans, quia hæc loca illius erunt in æternum." Quod completum est. Hoc audientes habitatores regionis. Fastidiebat cibos magi atque vomebat. Hæc magus considerans scrutabatur causam nauseæ, et deinde destinavit vaccam albam puellæ, quam mulgebat aliqua fœmina christiana ; et bibebat sancta puella, et non vomebat. Cum autem crevisset puella sancta, ministrabat in domo, et quodcunque manus ejus tetigissent vel oculus vidisset de cibis, amplius crescebat.

[*V*. 3, 11.] Intravit cogitatio in cor ejus ut rediret ; Magus misit nuncios ad patrem illius. Nutrix ejus dolens misit S. Brigitam et aliam puellam cum ea ad domum cujusdam viri ut postularent potum cervisiæ. Inde nihil sumentes, Brigita declinavit ad puteum et implevit vasculum aqua, et facta est cerevisia optima, et cum gustasset nutrix sua surrexit sana.

64. [*V*. 3.] Non multo post hospes venerabilis venit ad domum

---

[1] al-lám *in Lism.* is phonetic.     [2] a muime bói an indlubra galair, *LB*.

Dubthaig, co ndernad foidi[1] dó co tartad cóic thochta saille do Brigit
da mberbad.[2] Dothoet cú goirt elscothach isin tech, dorat Brigit di
in cóiced tócht; dorat Brigit tócht aile dó. Doiġ lesi ba codlud don
aigid. Tanic Dubthach iarsin, 7 roairim na herranda 7 ni thesta ní
dib. Atchuaid in t-áigid do Dubthach a ndorigne Brigit; ní rocha-
ithset in biad sin uair roptar esinnraic, acht rofodlad do bochtaib in
Choimded. [LB. 63 a; Lism. 38.] Dorothlaig bannscal iressech co
Dubthach co tised Brigit le i Maġ Life, ar bói comthinól senaid Laigen
ann. Rofoillsiged hi fís di araile fir noeb bói isin dáil .i. Muire Ingen
do thecht isin dáil. Teit in bannscal iarnabarach 7 Brigit immalle
fria, 7 intí itchonnairc in fís ised atbert, "Issi seo in Muire itchonnarc-
sa." Robennachsat in uile slóg inní Noem Brigit fo anmaimm Muire.
Iarsin dochuaid B. do torruma[3] a máthar. Is amlaid robui in mathair
7 da bai dec aice 7 si oc tinol ime. In maistred dognith B. rosfodail
in díb cuibrennaib déc in onóir in da apstal déc; 7 rosuidiged in tres
cuibrénn dec cu mba mou hé indás cech cúibrend in onóir Ísu Crist,
ar atbread si, "Bid Crist i persóin cech aiġed."

---

patris sui, cui pater disposuit carnem coquere, dedit filiæ suæ quinque
particulas ad coquendas eas. Ille egressus est foras. Venit canis
avidus in domum et Brigida dedit ei particulam unam; dedit ei
alteram. Illa vero putabat eum hospitem dormire. Postea venit
pater illius et integras particulas invenit. Hospes narravit omnia
quæ vidit; et dixerunt indigni sumus ut hunc cibum manducemus,
sed melius est ut detur pauperibus. [V. 3, c. 14.] Religiosa quædam
vidua in proximo vico habitans postulavit a patre ejus ut Brigida
secum iret ad synodum quæ collecta erat in Campo Liffi. Vir sanctus
in synodo vidit visionem, i.e. Mariam quæ habitat inter vos. Super-
venit vidua cum Brigida, et qui vidit visionem dixit, "Hæc est Maria
quam vidi." Tunc omnes glorificaverunt eam quasi in typo Mariæ.
Post hæc exiit B. ut visitaret[3] matrem suam. Sed mater ejus procul
a domo erat, et duodecim vaccæ cum illa ad colligendum butyrum.
Dividebat B. butyrum in duodecim partes, quasi duodecim Apostolis;
et una fiebat major pars quam Christo dedit, dicens, "Omnis hospes
Christus est."

---

[1] rannais  D.  assil tṡailli  hi  cóic     [2] dia mbruith, LB.
tóchtaib, LB.                                [3] do fiss scel a máthar, LB.

65. [*LB.* 63a; *Lism.* 39.] Tanic in drai 7 a sétig 7 rusc mor leo dia línad do immim. Ni raibe immorro aici-si in erlaime acht torad æn-maisterda. Ferais B. failté friu 7 roinnail a cosa 7 tuc biad dóib. Tuc leathtorad maistirtha aniar. Rofaitbestar la sodain ben in druad 7 is ed atbert. "Línaid bar rúsc," ol B. Is ed nogebed si oc techt in a culid, "A De, a mo Ruri-sea." Roadamraig in drai an firt atchonncatar conid annsin atbert fria Brigit, "In t-imm-sea 7 na bu robligis idpraim-sea duit iat." Atbert B., "Ber-siu na bú 7 tuc damsa soer mu máthair." Atbert in drúi, "Ac sud do máthair soer duit 7 na ba." Robaitsed in drai 7 ba hiressach;[1] rofodail B. iarsin na bu do bochtaib 7 do aidilcnechaib Dé, 7 tanic 7 a máthair lea co tech a h-athar.

Accobrastar iarsin Dubthach a reic nahi Noeb Brigte, uair cacha bagbaitis a lama do chrud 7 biad doberead do bochtaib 7 aidilcnechaib. Luid i carput 7 B. immalle fris. O racantar co dún in rig, luid cusin rig, 7 foracaib a claideb i fail mBrigte isin carput. Dothæt clam co Brigit, dobeir si claideb a bathar dó. Raidid Dubthach frisin

---

65. [*V.* 3, 15.] Venit magus et uxor ejus habens vas magnum ut impleretur butyro. Non enim habebat Brigida nisi mensuræ unius diei et mensuræ remis alterius. Quibus læto animo ministrabat virgo et pedes eorum lavabat, cibumque apponens refecit eos. Protulit modicum butyri. Videns hoc subrisit uxor magi dicens. Virgo ait "Implete vas." Post hæc ingressa penu suum adoravit Dominum. Cum videret magus hoc miraculum, ad Brigidam dixit, "Hoc vas plenum butyro tuum fiat et vaccæ quas mulsisti tuæ sint." B. dixit, "Tuæ vaccæ tecum sint, matrem meam mihi liberam relinque." Magus dixit, "Ecce offero tibi matrem tuam et vaccas." Magus credidit Deo et baptizatus est; B. vero omnia sibi oblata dedit pauperibus, et reversa est cum matre sua ad patrem suum.

Post hæc cogitabat Dubthacus filiam suam vendere, quia omnia quæ videbat pauperibus dabat. Assumpsit eam secum in curru. Cum venissent ad aulam regis, exiit ad regem et reliquit gladium[2] juxta eam (in curru). Venit pauper[3] ad Brigidam et dedit illi gladium

---

[1] hiressech, *Lismore.*        context and Irish show.
[2] *V.* 3 has *currum* erroneously, as the     [3] Leprosus in the Irish texts.

rig, "In cendgaid cumail .i. m'ingen-sa?" *Dixit* Dúnlaing, "Cid ara
reccai t'ingin féin?" *Dixit* Dubthach, "Cacha baġbaitis a láma-si[1]
*furantur.*" "Toot in óg cucainn," ar in rig. Toet Dubthach aracend,
roꞟiafraig do Brigit, cid doroine don claidiub, "Doratus,'" ar B., "don
bocht." Roꞟergaiġ Dubthach. Atbert fria in rí, "Cid ara tucuis in
claideb do bochtaib?" *Dixit* B., "Roꞟitir Mac na hIngine, da mad
lemsa do chumung-sa cot' uli indmas, dobéraind don Choimdid." Do
raid in rí, "Ni comadais dún diblinaib cunnrad na hingine-sea, ar is
uasli a hairilliud fiad Dia innám-ne." Ocus dombert in rí claideb do
Dubthach daracend.

66. Nír 'bo cian ꞁiarsin[2] co tainic araile fer sochenelach co Dubthach do chuinchid a ingine. Ba tol do Dubthach 7 dia macáib
inní sin; Rosopustar tra B. Moidis tra a suil-side fochétoir. Otchon-
nairc Dubthach sin, atbert, "A ingen, geib caille fortchend."

Luid B. 7 araili oga immalle fria do gabail caille co Epscop
Mel. Atracht columa tenntide dia cind.

[*LB.* 64 a; *Lism.* p. 41.] O rachomacsig Sollamain na Cásc

---

patris sui. Dixit Dubthacus ad regem, "Eme filiam meam ut serviat
tibi." Dixitque rex, "Qua causa vendas eam?" Dubthacus dixit,
"Quidquid invenerint manus ejus furantur." Dixit rex, "Illa veniat
ad nos." Exiit Dubthach ad eam, dicens, "Ubi est gladius meus?"
Illa ait, "Ego dedi illum Christo." Iratus (est) pater. Rex vero ait
ad eam, "Cur dedisti gladium pauperibus?" Respondit illa, "Si te
ipsum et illum Dominus meus a me postulasset, si potuissem, vos cum
omnibus quæ habetis darem illi." Tunc rex ait, "Ista filia major est
ad emendum mihi, et major est ad vendendum tibi." Tunc rex tribuit
virgini gladium ut daret patri suo.

66. Non longo post tempore venit quidam vir honorabilis ad
Dubthachum ut peteret filiam suam in conjugem. Et hoc placuit
patri et fratribus; B. vero respuebat eum. Tunc unus oculus ejus
crepuit. Hoc autem videns pater ejus permisit eam velatam esse.

B., acceptis secum puellis, perrexit velamen accipere ad Episcopum Mel. Apparuit columna ignis de vertice Brigidæ.

[*V.* 3, 21.] Cum dies Paschæ appropinquaret, voluit Brigida

---

[1] So *Lismore*, l. 1308.          [2] Garit iarsin, *LB.*

duthracair[1] coirm do dénum dona heclasib immdaib robatar immpe; acht ní rothecht acht æn miach[2] bracha, 7 robui terca arba in inbuid sin. Ni rabatar lestair la muintir Brigte acht da lothar. Doratsat in braich isin dara lothar. Rofodlad iarsin o Brigit in chuirm dona vii n-eclasib dec, co roferastar[3] torad in æn méich bracha iat o Chaplait co Minchaisc. Tanic araile clam co B. do chunchid bo. Doraid B. fris, " Cia de is ferr lett bó do breith leat no th'ícc don chlaime?" Atbert in clam, ba ferr leis a ícc oltas rige in domain dó.

[*Lism.* p. 41.] Araile caillech do muintir Brigte dorala a ngalar, cu romianaig leamnacht;[4] acht ni tharla bó isin recleis ind inbaid sin, cu rolínad leastar lan d'uisce do Brigit co rosoud il-leam-nacht; dorat don chaillig, 7 ba hogslan hi focedair.

[*LB.* 64 b; *Lism.* 41.] Tancadar da dall do Bretnaib, 7 clam ic a remthus, dia n-íc co Brigit. Doraid B., "Bíd imuig colléic." Atbersat na Bretnaig, ar deinmnedaig iat-sein, " Rohíocais dóine dot' cheniul fén 7 ní rofuirigis cenco n-íccai sinne."

---

facere coenam omnibus ecclesiis quæ circa se fuerant; (sed) illa non habuit nisi unum modium, et penuria panis illis temporibus erat. Fecit autem illa cervisiam de illo modio in duabus pelvibus, alia enim vasa non habebat. Divisa est ergo hæc cervisia a Brigida octo et decem ecclesiis, et eis a Coena Domini usque ad clausulam Paschæ abundavit. Ad B. quidam leprosus venit postulans ab ea quamdam vaccam. Illa dixit ei, " Vis ut rogemus Deum ut a lepra sanus fias." Ille respondit, "Hoc mihi omnibus donis melius est."

[*V.* 3, 22.] Una ex puellis Brigidæ dolore ægrotabat, et pusillum lactis postulabat; sed nulla vacca apud eos erat. B. dixit, " Imple phialam aqua et da ægrotanti," et factum est vasculum plenum lacte calido, et sanata est.

[*V.* 3, 23.] Duo Britones cæci, cum leproso qui eis ducatum præbebat, venerunt ad Brigidam quærentes ab ea sanitatem. Quæ dixit eis, " Expectate paulisper." Illi indignati dixerunt, " Infirmos generis tui sanas, nos autem negligis curare."

---

· [1] rop ail, *LB.*·        [3] co rourthastar, *LB.*
[2] criathar, *Lismore.*        [4] leamlacht *in Ms.* ?

67. [*LB.* 63 b; *Lism.* 41.] O rof*or*bad sollamain na Cásc roiarfaig
B. da hingenaib in rabai fuigell occu do lind na Cásc.   Atbertsat na
hóga, "Dobéra Dia."  Is and sin tancatar da íngin[1] istech 7 drolmach[1]
lan do uisci leo.   Doig lee-si *co m*ba coirmm.   Rosoud in t-usce
hi coirmm.   Isan n-aimsir cétna tainic galar sula do Brigit.   O
rochuala Epscop Mel sin, iss ed roraid, "Tiagam aroen do c(h)uingid
leġa cu rotleict*her* fort c(h)enn."   Doraid B., "Ni bud ail damsa
liaiġ corpdai etir, acht araide doġenam anní atb*er*a-sa."   O robatar
oc imthecht, dorochair B. as a carput co tarla a cenn fria cloich cu
rocrechtnaiged cu mor 7 cu rotheiper in fuil.   Rohícta dano don fuil
sin di bannsc*ail* aṁlabrai.   [*Lism.* 42.] Dorala doib iarsin for a sét
in liaiġ ic a rabatar iarraid.

[*LB.* 64 b; *Lism.* 42.] Bói ri Tethba i comfocus doib ic fleid.
Bói lestar cúmdachta ó ilgemmaib il-láim in rig.   Gabais araile fer
anfaitech as a laim, cu torchair 7 co nderna(d) bloga de.   Dogabad
in fer lasin rig.   Dochuaid Escop Mel dia chunchid, 7 ni ḣétas on

---

67. [*V.* 3, 26.] Postquam consummata est septimana Paschæ,
dixit B. puellis suis, "Si defecit cervisia quam paravimus solemnitati
Paschæ."   Responderunt puellæ dicentes, "Deus mittet."   Cum hoc
dixissent, venerunt in domum vas aqua plenum portantes.   Puta(bat)
Brigida quod cerevisia esset.   Conversa est illa aqua in cervisiam.
Eodem tempore B. dolore oculorum cruciabatur.   Hoc audiens Episcopus Mel, misit ad eam, quatenus ambo ad quærendum medicum
pergerent qui curaret eam.   Cui B. dixit, "Corporalem medicum[2]
quærere nolo, sed tamen[3] quod tu vis faciemus."   Cum iter agerent,
cecidit B. de curru suo, et vulneratum est caput ejus lapide, et
sanguis fluebat, de quo sanatæ sunt duæ mulieres mutæ.   Accidit
post hæc ut ille medicus quem quærebant occurreret eis in via.
Dixit, "Illum medicum semper quære qui caput tuum sanavit."

[*V.* 3, 29.] Rex Thebæ procul[4] ab eis fuit in convivio.   Rusticus quidam accessit ut tolleret de mensa regis vas facturae mirabilis,
et cecidit et confractum est.   Rex jussit illum obligari.   Perrexit
Episcopus Mel ut rogaret pro misero, sed rex non dimisit eum; tunc

---

[1] dias ingen, dronglaċh, *Lism.*
[2] medicinam *in V.* 3.
[3] tum, *V.* 3.
[4] *read* non procul, i comfocraib, *Lism.*

ríġ acht a bás; dottaig imorro Mel in lestar mbriste 7 tuc leis co Brigit, 7 rohathnuged.

68. [*LB.* 64 b; *Lism.*, p. 42.] (Ho roson clu ina Brigte sethno Tetba, bai alaili óġ craibdech o totoided ara tessed B. di-acaldaim .ı. Bríg. Luid dano B. 7 atarecht Bríg fadeisne do indlat a coss)[1] 7 in t-uisci doratad ar a cossaib do Brigit roíc araile óiġ robai istiġ a ngalar, 7 (ba ógslán focétuair, 7 ba oen na timthirthite[1]). Ho thuctha am-miassa ar a mbeulu gaibid B. for sirdecsin na méisi. Doraid B., "Atchiu Demon 'na suide forsin méis ar mu belaib." "Masa soch-macht," ar Bríg, "robad maith lemsa a decsiu." "As sochmacht em," ar B., "acht tabair ardi na crucha tar do ṡúilib." Dorat in óġ crois ar a suilib, 7 itchonnairc si in Satan,[2] dochruth lee a delb, 7 a de 7 a lasair as a c(h)raes 7 as a ṡronaib. Roraid B., "Tabair freacra duin, a Diabuil." "Ni chumcaim a chaillech," ar in Demon, "cen t'acallaim, uair coimetai timna Dé, 7 a(t) trócaireach fri bochto in Choimded." "Cest, tra," ar B., "cid dia tangais forsin méis sin?"

---

Mel portans frusta vasis confracti venit ad Brigidam, et restauratum est.

68. [*V.* 3, 30.] Fama Brigidæ illam regionem Thebæ implevit. Erat quædam virgo sancta nomine Briga, quæ misit ad Brigidam rogans ut ad ejus domum veniret. Tunc B. perrexit ad domum illius, et lavit pedes ejus et de illo lavacro pedum sanata est statim quædam virgo quæ in domo jacebat ægrotans, et cum cæteris ministrabat. Cum appositus esset cibus cæpit B. diligenter mensam intueri. B. dixit, "Dæmonem sedentem in mensa nostra aspicio." Dixitque Briga, "Si possibile est volo videre illum." Respondit B., "Non illud est impossibile sed prius signentur oculi tui"; Signatisque oculis vidit inimicum tetra figura, et per fores omnes ejus flamma et fumus exhalabat. Tunc B., dixit ad eum ("Da responsum)[3] nobis, Dæmon." Ille respondit, dicens, "O sancta virgo, non possum non tibi loqui, nec tua jussa contemnere, quia tu præcepta Dei non con-temnis et pauperibus ejus affabilis es." Dixitque B., "Qua do causa huc venisti?" Dæmon respondit, "Quædam virgo est hic apud quam

---

[1] The words in parenthesis are from *Lism. Lives*, p. 325.

[2] "in manach" (*Lism.*, p. 325) is per-

haps a mistake for *in namaid.*

[3] So in *Lism. Lives*, p. 325; loquere nobis, *V.* 3.

"Araile óg craibdech fil sund,"˜ ar Deamon, "7 is˙'na coimitecht atússa ag *fu*rail leisce 7 maindeachtnaige˙ uirre." Adubairt B., "Tabair cros Crist tar dot śuilib." Dorat focetoir, atcondairc an óg an torathar ngranna; rosgab ecla mor in˙óg o atcondairc in Demon. Adubairt B., "Cid fora n-imgaibe in dalta oc á tai lessugud fri re Ciana?" Rohícaď inn oǵ ón Demon.

69. [*Lism.*, p. 43.]   Araile bannscal tuc (dán m̄bec)[1] d'ubluiḃ co, Brigit. Is ann sin (tancatar claim)[2] ic faiǵde uball co Brigit. Doraiḋ B., "Tabair ḋoiḃ na hubla." O'tcuala in bannscal -sin, ruc a rusc uball chuice, 7 is ed roraiḋ, "Duitsi féin tucas-sa na hubla 7 ni do chlaṁaiḃ." Ba tocraḋ do Brigit tairmeasc na halmsaine uimpe, 7 romallach na cronna dia tucad. O rainic in bannscal da tiǵ, ni fuair oen ubull in a ḣithlainn giar ḃọ lán intan rofacuiḃ, 7 batár etairthiǵ o sin immach.

[*LB.* 64 b., *Lism.* 43.]   Doluid B. 7 sloig mora inna comitecht 7 da claṁ ina diaiǵ, cu tarla deabaid etarra; intí tuarcaib dib a laim ar tús araile do ḃualaḋ, rośecca a laṁ uasa 7 rocrap laṁ indalanai. Doronsat aith̄riǵi iarum, 7 ros-íc Brigit.

---

hic habito, et propter ejus pigritiam in ea locum habeo." (" Signa," inquit B., "oculos ejus," signatisque oculis horridum contuetur monstrum);[2] et illa videns monstrum perterrita est. Dixit B., "Vide quem nutrire solebas multis annis." Virgo liberata est a Dæmone.

69. [*V.* 3, 31.]   Quædam mulier munusculum pomorum attulit Brigidæ. In eadem hora venerunt leprosi postulantes ea. B. dixit, "Dividite illis hæc poma." Hoc audiens illa (mulier) rapuit ad se poma, dicens, "Tibi hæc poma attuli et non leprosis." Hoc displicuit Brigidæ, et dixit, "Male agis, prohibens eleemosynam dare, ligna tua fructum non habebunt." Tunc illa foras egressa pomum nullum invenit in horto suo quem plenum pomis reliquerat; et sterilis in æternum permansit.

[*V.* 3, 33; *V.* 4, 35.]   Duo leprosi secuti sunt Brigidam euntem cum turba multa; contigit eis rixari; sed manus illius, qui prius percutiebat socium, incurvata non potuit eam erigere, alterius dextra erecta recurvari arefacta non potuit, riguerunt eorum manus. Pænitentiam tunc egerunt, sanavitque B. manus eorum.

---

[1] So in *Lism. Lives*, p. 326; at p. 43, doraladar claiṁ.

[2] The words in parenthesis are from *Lism. Lives*, p. 325.

[*LB.* 63 b; *Lism.* 43.] Dochuaid B. co araile ecl*ais* i tír
Thethba do chelebrad na Cásc.   Doraid banairchinnech na hecalsa`fri
a hingenaib, d'osaic,[1] Dia Dardáin Cennla, dona senorib 7 dona dainib
fannaib.   Ni frith nech dib don umaloit.   Doraid B., "Dogén-sa in
umaloit."   Cethrar do dainib galair robátar isin recles, .ı. duine
abrachtach,[2] 7 dásachtach, 7 dall, 7 clam.   Ragab B. for ósaic a
cethrar 7 rohíctha.   Fecht ann bói B. i taig for aigidecht.   Dorala
co ndechsat in muinter uili immach, acht æn gilla bec anbfabrachta
7 se balb;[3] 7 ni fitir B. a beith amlaid.   Is ann tancatar oegid do
chuingid bíd.   Atbert B. frisin maccæm cait i raibi eochair na cuil*ne*.
Doraid in gilla, "Rofetar-sa baile ita."   Doraid B., "Erig 7 tabair
dam."   Atracht foch*é*toir 7 rothimthirig dona haigedaib.[4]

70. [*Ibi.*]   Is and dorala comdál fer n-Erenn i Tailltin in airm i

---

[*V.* 3, 35 ; 4, 37.]   B. ad aliam ecclesiam in regione Thebæ
exiit ut ibi celebraret Pascha.   Domina[5] ecclesiæ illius puellis suis in
Die Coenæ Domini dixit, "Quænam ex vobis lavacrum hodie faciet
senibus et infirmis?"   Omnibus nolentibus, Brigida dixit, "Volo ut
ego miseras abluam."   Erant autem quatuor ægrotæ in domo, una
paralytica quæ jacebat immobilis, et energumena, et caeca, et leprosa.
B. coepit lavare (eas quatuor) et sanatæ sunt.   Brigida rogata manebat
in quadam cellula aliquibus diebus.   Casu accidit, ut omnes familiæ
exirent, remansitque B. cum solo puero muto et paralytico ; nesciebat
vero B. quod ille mutus et paralyticus erat.   In eadem hora venerunt
viatores[6] quærentes cibum.   Dixit B. ad puerum, "Nosti ubi est
clavis coquinæ?"[7]   Ille dixit, "Scio."   B. dixit, "Surge et da mihi
eam."   Tunc surrexit, et ministrabat cibum hospitibus illis.

70. [*V.* 3, 38 ; *V.* 4, 39.]   Tunc accidit conventus virorum Hiberniæ in loco qui vocatur Talten, ubi erat Patricius cum Episcoporum

---

[1] d'umaloit (*Lism.*), *i.e.* to humble
themselves to the aged by washing their
feet.

[2] anbfabracta (*Lism.*) means 'para-
lysed' in paragraphs 69, 70, 71, not
'consumptive,' as Mr. Stokes renders it.

[3] acht maccæm cen labra riam 7 cen

lúd i cois nó il-láim dó, *LB.*

[4] 7 dogní timthirecht nan oiged, *LB.*;
"ministrabat largiter secundum morem
Scotorum," *V.* 4.

[5] Abbatissa, *V.* 4.

[6] so *V.* 4 ; laici *in V.* 3.

[7] cellarii, *V.* 4.

mbói Patraic 7 senad Clerech n-Erenn imbi. Dochuatar dino dochum
na dála B. 7 Epscop Mel, 7 fuaradar caingin doilig ar a cinn san
oirechtus, .1. araile ben ruc lenabb ann 7 ised atbert conid la hEpscop
mBrón do muintir Patraic in lenabb; rodíult tra in t-Epscop aní sin.
Tucad in ceist sin co Brigit dia tuaslucud. Roiarfaig B. don bannscail
cia o rochoimprestar in gein. Rofrecair in ben, "Is o Epscop Brón,"
ol si. Dorat B. airde na crochi dar ġin na mná, rolín tra att 7
borrfad a tengaid in a cinn fochétoir. Dorat B. arrde na crochi dar a
bél na nóiden, 7 roiarfaig, "Cia th'athair-siu?" Rofrecair in Nóidiu,
"Duine duthair deroil fil a n-imul in airechta, is é sin m'athairsi."
Co rosærad Epscop Brón.

71. [*Lism.* p. 44.] Is and sin dochuaid fer ar cenn Brigte co
ndiġsed do coisecrad tiġi nua doriġned aige. O roerlaṁaiġ biaḋ do
Brigit, is ed roraiḋ B., re a hingena, "Ni haḋa dúin biaḋ ind ḟir
genntlidi-sea do thomailt, ár roḟaillsiġ Dia damsa na robaisted etir he."

---

et aliorum sanctorum conventu. Perrexerunt ad locum B. et Episcopus
Mel, et in illo concilio maxima quæstio fiebat : quædam autem mulier
dicebat infantem quem genuit esse cujusdam Episcopi de discipulis[1]
Patricii momine Broon; ille autem negabat. Omnes dixerunt quod
hæc. quæstio per Brigidam solvi[2] posset.

Dixit B. ad illam, "De quo viro concepisti infantem hunc?"
Illa respondit, "De Episcopo Broon." B. itaque signans os illius
feminæ signo crucis, statim intumuit caput ejus cum lingua.[3] B.
linguam infantis benedixit dicens, "Quis est pater tuus?" Ille
respondit, "Quidam homo qui sedet in parte concilii ultimus, ac
vilis turpisque, est pater meus." (Episcopus liberatus est.)[4]

71. [*VV.* 3, 40; 4, 43.] Tunc quidam homo[5] invitavit illam
dicens, "Volo introeas ad domum novam consecrandam." Ipso cibum
Brigitæ largiter apponente, B. puellis suis dixit, "Non debemus[6]
cibos viri gentilis comedere, ostendit mihi Dominus quod ille vir
gentilis sit." Tunc compunctus, et baptizatus est ab Episcopo Broon.

---

[1] qui fuit alumnus P., *V.* 4.

[2] so in *V.* 4; finiri, *V.* 3.

[3] co roráith at a cend furi *cum lingua,*
*Lism. Lives,* p. 327.

[4] The words in parenthesis are in *Lism.
Lives,* p. 327.

[5] so *V.* 4; plebeius, *V.* 3.

[6] so *V.* 4; non possumus, *V.* 3.

.O rochuala in fer maith sin ron-gaib congain cridi, 7 robaist Espoc
Bron. Iarsin roforcongair Patraic for Brigit co nach beth dogres gan
fer gráid 'na comuidecht. Is aire rogab Natfraich grada sacairt.

. Isin aimsir cétna tuc fer a mathair for a muin co Brigit, ár ba
hanfabrachta, co roslai for foscad mBrigti ; 7 o tharaill in foscud rob
ogslán acétoir.

72. [*Lism*. p. 44.] In araile aimsir ann adconncatur Patraic
chuca, senad mór maille fris. Doraid Lassair re Brigit, " Cid
dogenam frisin sochaide tangadar chucainn?" '" Cid do biud fil
'ocuib," ol B. " Ni fil," ar Lasair, " acht aen chúra 7 da bairgin déc
7 becán loma." Doraid B., "Atá maith ann ; dogentar proicept
breithre De dun 7 non-sasfaither uad.". Tucad an biad co Brigit dia
.roinn, 7 robennach ; 7 rosasta in da phopul De .ı. samad Brigte 7
samad Patraic ; 7 roba mó cu mor a bfuigeall ina in t-adbar robai ann
ar tús. Araile fer robai for a tarat a ben miscuis, cu tainio co Brigit
do chuinchid eptha co rocharad a ben hé. Robennach B. uisci do 7
is *ed* atbert, " Tabair in t-uisci tar in tech, 7 tar biad, 7 tar dig, 7 tar

---

Sequenti die dixit Patricius ad Brigidam, " Ex hac die non licet tibi
ambulare sine sacerdote semper." Ordinavit autem sacerdotem nomine,
Nathfroich.

. In illis diebus venit ad Brigidam quidam homo,[1] portans matrem
suam paralyticam in suis humeris, et deposuit matrem in[2] umbra
Brigidæ ; et cum illa tetigisset umbram sanata est statim.

72. [*V*. 3, 44.] Quadam die venit Patricius cum turba magna.
Dixerunt ad Brigidam, " Ecquid faciemus, quia non habemus cibos ad
tantam turbam." Dixit B., " Quantum habetis ?" Qui dixerunt,
" Non habemus nisi duodecim panes, et modicum lactis et unam
ovem." Dixit B., " Sufficienter hæc erunt ; recitabuntur nobis Sacræ
Scripturæ, per quas escas obliviscemur." Postea, benedicente Brigida,
illa cibaria administrata sunt, et populi duo, i.e. Patricii et Brigidæ
saturati sunt ; et demiserunt majores reliquias quam antea fuerunt
materiæ. Quidam vir quem uxor sua odio habuit, venit ad Brigidam
rogans, ut invocato Christi nomine uxor sua eum amaret. B. benedixit aquam, et jussit ea, aspergi illa aqua domum, et cibum et potum,

---

. [1] so *V*. 4 ; laicus, *V*..3.     [2] so *V*. 4 ; sub, *V*. 3.

an leapuid an écmais na mná." O doríne amlaid, dorat in ben seirc
ndimóir dósom.

[*LB.* 65 b.; *Lism.* p. 44.] Araile bannscal d'Uib Mac Uais
tainio do faiġde co Brigit; co tard B. a criss di. Tancatar caraid co
Brigit araile sòllum*un* 7 eḋpairt leo. Tancatar merliġ iarsin 7
tallsatar[1] na daṁu roḃatar isin tiġ. Atracht[2] abann Life friu, co
tardsat an éduiġe for aḋarcuib na ndam, cu ra impaset na daim otha
sin cusan inad a ṁbui B. cusna h-etaiġiḃ leo.

73. [*LB.* 63 b; *Lism.* p. 45.] Luid B. do acall*aim* Patraic im
Muig Lemne. Boi oc procept soscela, conid ann sin rochotuil B.
Atbert P., "Cid f*or*archotlais?" Rofill B. a gluni[3] 7 ised atbert,
"Fís itconnarc," ol si. "Indis dún in fís," ol P. "Atchonnarc,"
ol B., "cethra barathra roarsatar inn uli n-indsi, 7 resiu rosiacht a
sílad rofás in buain, 7 tancatar topair gela 7 srotha taitnemacha as na
hetrigiḃ; 7 étaige gela im na síltoiriḃ. At*c*onnarc cethra harathru
aile roarsetar an innsi fo tharsnu, 7 resiu rosiacht in buain roás in

---

et lectum uxore absente. Aspersa est domus illius, et illa mulier
maritum suum nimio amore dilexit.

[*VV.* 3, 4.] Quædam faemina de Nepotibus Guais eleemosynam quærens venit ad Brigidam, cui dedit B. suam zonam.
Venerunt parentes[4] ante diem cujusdam solemnitatis et celebraverunt
festum. Fures autem venerunt et furati sunt boves. Invenerunt
flumen Liffi repletum abundantia aquæ, et alligaverunt vestimenta
sua super capita boum, et reversi sunt boves ad civitatem Brigidæ
portantes spolia.

73. [*V.* 3, 57; *V.* 4, l. 2, c. 27.] Exiit B. cum Patricio ad
aquilonarem partem Hiberniæ. P. verbum Dei prædicabat, sed illa
hora B. obdormivit. Dixit P., "Cur obdormisti?" Hæc genua flexit
dicens, "Somnium vidi." Dixit P., "Narra nobis illud." Dixit B.,
"Ego vidi quatuor aratra arantia hanc insulam, et semininatores
seminaverunt, et statim maturescere coepit, et rivi lactis novi repleverunt sulcos; et seminatores illi erant induti vestibus albis. Vidi
alia aratra, et aratores nigros qui bonam illam messem sciderunt

---

[1] tallsat, *LB.*
[2] tuargaib, *LB.*
[3] roslecht B., *Lismore.*

[4] In the sense of French 'parents,'
as sometimes in Latin.

corca rošilsat fochétoir corbo habaid,' 7 tancatar srotha duba as na
hetrigib." *Dixit* P., "Is maith inní atchonnarcais"; na ceth*r*i harathru
atchonnarcuis, mise sin 7 tussu, sílmait ceithir-libair in t-šoscéla co
síl irse.

[*LB.* 64 b.] Fecht do B. con a ógaib in ' Ard Macha; dolluid
dias secca 7 drolmach¹ usce forru. Tancatar do bennachad do B.
Dorochair in drolmach² dia n-éisi, 7 dochuaid druimm dar druimm
7 ni robris, 7 ni thorchair banda esti. *Dixit* P., " Fodlaid in usce for
Ard Macha 7 for Airtheru."

74. [*LB.* 65 a; *Lism.* p. 45.] Luid B. do thuaslucud chimmeda
bai il-laim oc ríg. Doraid B., "In lece orumsa in cimmid út amach ?"
Atbert in ri, " Cia dobertha-su damsa," ol se, " rige ťer mBreg, ni
thibrinn duit é; acht dobérthar a animmchomét oen óidche fortsu³ dó."
Ìoartraig di*diu* B. díulái⁴ don chimmid 7 atbert fris, "Intan tuaslaic-
fith*er* in slabrad dítt, éla fort' láim ǹdeiss."

[*LB.* 65 a; *Lism.* 46.] Bói dásachtach nooirced na cuitechta.

---

vomere, et zizaniam seminaverunt, et flumina aquarum repleverunt
sulcos." Dixit P., " Veram visionem vidisti." Nos sumus aratores
qui quatuor Evangeliorum aratris seminamus verbum Dei.

[*V.* 3, 62.] Quadam die B. sedebat cum puellis suis in
latere Oppidi Machæ, et vidit duos viros plenum vas⁵ aquæ secum
portantes. Cumque venissent rogaverunt Brigidam ut aquam benedi-
ceret. Contigit ut caderet in terram vas ab eis super latus suum, et
non est fractum, neque effusa est aqua de eo. P. jussit aquam illam
dividi Ecclesiis illius regionis.

74. [*V.* 3, 68; *V.* 4, 1. 2, 39.] Adivit B. ut liberaret virum
qui erat in vinculis apud regem. Dixit B., " Dimitte mihi vinctum."
Rex respondit, " Si mihi dedisses totum Campum Breg non dimitterem
illum"; vix obtinuit B. ut vita unius nocti sconcederetur ei. Ideoque
in principio noctis apparuit B. vincto quæ dixit, " Cum catena de
collo tuo ablata fuerit, declina ab eis in dexteram partem."

[*V.* 3, 65; *V.* 4, 1. 2, c. 35.] Quidam insanus affligebat

---

● ¹ secce 7 dromlach, *Lism.*
² dronglach, *Lism.*
³ erutsa, *Lism.*
⁴ *for* díud lái, at the end of night?

The Latin has "principio noctis," "in
prima vigilia noctis."
⁵ vas ligneum apertum, *V.* 4.

Rosgab uamun mor na hóga batar i fail Brígte.   Adubairt B. fris,
" Pritcha bréthir ṅDé dún."   "Ni chumcaim," or se, " cen umaloit
duit : Car in Coimdid, a chaillech, ⁊ notcarfa cách; airmitnig in
Coimdid ⁊ notairmitnigfe cách; aigthi[1] in Coimdid ⁊ notaigthife[1]
cách."  ·Luid iarum in dásachtach uadib.

75. [*LB.* 64a ; *Lism.* p. 46.] Fecht doġuiḋ a hathair Næṁ Brigte
co ndigsed co riġ Laigen do chuinghiḋ dilsigthe in chlaidiṁ dorat d'a
hathair fecht aile.   Luid B. iarum co Dunlaing.   Dia mbói i ndorus
in duine, tanic mog do mogadaib[2] in ríg do acallaim Brigte, ⁊ is *ed*
atbert fria, "Dia nomsærtha-su don fognam hitú don ríg, ropad am'
cristaide ⁊ rofogenaind duitsiu."   Roráid B., "Condiug-sa sin forsin
rig."   Luid B. iarum isin dún ⁊ conataig da ascaid forsin rig; dilsiugud
in claidib do Dubthach ⁊ a ṡaire don mogaid.   "Cid ara tiber-sa
sin duitsiu," ar an ríġ.   Atbert B., "Mad ail duit, dobérthar rige dot'
macaib ⁊ nem duit féin."   Atbert in rí fri B., "Flaith nime," or se,
" uair nach facimm, ni chunnchimm ; rige tra do mo macu ni-chun-
chimm uair ni beo fén for aird.   Tabair dam fot sægail ⁊ cac*h* buaid

omnes ambulantes per loca.   Comites Sanctæ valde timentes (erant).
Dixit ad illum B., " Prædica mihi verbum Domini."   Insanus dixit,
" Jussa tua implebo : Ama Deum et amabunt te omnes ; honora
Deum, et honorabunt te omnes ; time Deum et timebunt te omnes."
Et cum hæc dixit, fugit.

75. [*V.* 3 c, 90 ; *V.* 4, 1. 2, c. 10.] Quodam tempore B. patrem
suum rogavit ut iret ad regem Laginensium, ut gladium quem ille
rex patri suo ad tempus donaverat, in perpetuum donet.   Exiit igitur
B. ad regem.   Cumque illa sedisset ad portam civitatis, venit ad eam
unus servorum regis, dicens, " Si me absolveris a jugo regis, ego
christianus ero et servus tuus ero."   Dixit B., "Petam pro te."   Tunc
B. vocata est ad regem et dixit illa, " Volo a te ut detur in æternum
gladius patri meo, et ut servum dimittas."   Dixit rex, " Quid dabis
mihi pro his."   Ait B., " Si vis, vitam eternam dabo tibi et semen
tuum reges erunt per sæcula."   Dixit ei rex, "Vitam, quam non
video, non quæro ; de filiis, qui post me erunt, non procuro.   Da mihi
longam vitam, et victoriam in omni bello contra Nepotes Neil ; jugem

---

[1] ataig, notatuiġfea, *Lism.*          [2] tainic mog, *Lism.*

fri hU Neill; uair is menicc coccad etraind." "Dobérthar," ar B.
Ised rocomailed, ár xxx. cath romebad roime ind Eirinn, ⁊ a nai an
Albain.    Tancatar hUi Neill i Laignib iarn a ecaib-sium.    Tucsat
Laigin a c(h)orp dochum in chatha co romebad rompa focedair.

76. [*LB.* 65 a ; *Lism.* p. 46.]    Fecht do B. oc imdécht a muig
Laigen[1] co facca mac légind in a rith secci.  "Cid thégi col-luath
amlaid sin ?" ol B., "Dochum nime," ar in scolaige.  "Duthraccur-
sa dul lett," ol B., "dona ernuigthi leamsa curab reid dam dul."
"A chaillech," ol in scolaige, "guid in Coimdid lem corup soraid
damsa techt dochum Nime, ⁊ guidfed-su Dia letsu corub reid duit ⁊
co ruca hilmíle lett dochum Nime."    Gabais B. pater leis ⁊ ba craibdech ó sin immach.

[*LB.* 65 a ; *Lism.* p. 47.]    Fecht ann tanic isin tech.    Fócerd a
cochall fliuch for bunnsachaib na gréne.    Tan ann tancatar da chlam
do chuinchid almsainc co B.    Ni bói araill isin coitchenn acht oen bó.
Dorat B. dona clamaib in mboin sin.    Dorigne indara clam atlugud

─────────────

enim pugnam habemus contra semen Cuinn."    Dixit B., "Dabuntur
hæc duo."    Post hæc triginta bella in Hibernia gessit et vicit omnia,
octoque certamina prospere in Britannia egit.    Factum est post
mortem ejus Nepotes Neill fines vastare Lagenensium.    Posuerunt
Lagenienses corpus ejus mortuum contra hostes, et illico Nepotes Neill
in fugam versi sunt.

76. [*V.* 3, 78 ; *V.* 4, l. 2, c. 61.]    Quadam die B. ambulabat in
loco campestri, et vidit quemdam juvenem scholasticum currentem
velociter.    Ait illi, "Quo tu curris tam cito ?"    Ille respondit,
dicens, "Ad regnum Dei."    Dixit B., "Utinam merear tecum cur-
rere ; ora pro me ut istud valeam."    Respondit scholasticus, "Tu
roga Deum ut cursus meus non impediatur et ego pro te rogabo ut tu
et mille comites tecum vadant ad regnum Dei."    Orante B. pro eo
factus est religiosissimus usque ad mortem.

[*V.* 3, c. 92 ; *V.* 4, l. 2, c. 52.]    Quadam die venit B. in
domum.    Fócerd a cochall super radium solis.    Duo igitur leprosi ad
B. venerunt quærentes eleemosynam.    Illa quia nihil aliud habebat
quod darot eis, unam vaccam quam habebat dedit eis.    Quorum unus

─────────────

[1] isin Currach, *Lism.*

budi do Dia; dimmdach imorro in clam aile uair ba díumsach.  Doraid
B. frisin clam n-umal, "An-su i foss dús in tibre Dia ní duit, 7 teit
ass in clam díumsach ut con a boin."   Is ann sin tainic araile fer co
mboin lois do B.; dorat B. in mboin sin don chlam umal.  O dochuaid
for sét in clam díumsach foremdid[1] immáin a bó a oenur, co tanic
for cula co B., co mbói ic glamud 7 ic immdergud Brigte, "Ni ar
Dia," or se, "doratais t'idpairt."     Tiagait diblínaib na dá chlam
dochum na Berba iarsin; dofuit isin sruth in clam díumsach coros-
baided; élaid in clam umal con a boin.

77. [*LB.* 65 b; *Lism.* 48 ]   Tanic rigan Laigen 7 slabrad argait
lea do B. an ídpairt, fuath delbi isin dara cínd de.  7 uball argait forsin
cind aile.   Rothaisciset na hóga e cen fis do B., uair ba mór nogata[2]
B. a crod 7 dosbered do bochtaib.   Tanic clam co B., co rotriall B. in
slabrad cen fis dona hógaib 7 co tarut dó.  O ru*s*fetatar na hóga is ed
atbertsat, "Is becc do maith dún do thrócaire-siu fri cách," ol siat,
"7 sind fén ic riachtain lessa bíid 7 étaig."   "Ercid," ar B., "isin

---

gratias egit Deo, alter vero ingratus et superbus extitit.   Dixit B. ad
humilem leprosum, "Tu hic paulisper expecta donec Dominus
aliquid nobis mittat; et exeat leprosus superbus cum sua vacca."
Tunc vir quidam ad Brigidam venit habens vaccam in oblatione.
Exiit leprosus superbus, sed solus non potuit vaccam minare,
tandem reversus est ad B. et multis convitiis insultabat in eam
dicens, "Non ex corde donasti eam, dura es nimium et immitis?"
Deinde duo leprosi exierunt ad quoddam flumen; mersus est ibi
leprosus superbus et absorptus est in profundum; humilis vero evasit
cum sua vacca.

77. [*V.* 3, 50; *V.* 4, l. 2, c. 18.]   Regina quædam ad B. venit
cum donis, in quibus erat argentea catena, quæ habuit in summitate
formam hominis.   Hanc (catenam) puellæ rapuerunt et absconderunt
in thesauris suis, B. vero distribuit omnia pauperibus.   Venit (leprosus) ad B., et illa exiit ad thesaurum puellarum et invenit catenam et
eam dedit pauperi.   Hoc puellæ agnoscentes locutæ sunt dicentes,
" Omnia das pauperibus et nos inopes relinquis."   B. dixit, "Ite et

---

[1] forfeimig, *Lism.*          [2] nogatad, *Lism.*

eclais baili i ndenaim ernaigthi, fogébthai. and bar slabrad." Dochuatar 7 fuaratar na hóga andsin a slabrad.

[*LB.* 64 a ; *Lism.* p. 48.] Tanio ri Lagen do celebrad dia Cásc
dochum Brigte. Iar forba uird in chelebartha luid ass in rí for
sét. Dochoid B. do praind. Asbert Loman, clam Brigte, na tomelad co
tuctha dó gai rig Lagen. Luid techtaire ó B. i ndegaid in rig.

78. [*LB.* 65 b; *Lism.* p. 48.] Tancatar da chlam dian-ícc co
B. Adubairt B. frisin dara clam nige araile. Dorigned amlaid 7 ba
hógslan fochétoir. *Dixit* B. frisin clám slán, "Déna frisin clam
n-aile ósaic 7 nige th'fir chumtha, amal dorigne-sium umaloit duitsiu."
Ronig B. fén in clam. In clam roniged ann for tus is *ed* atbert,
"Anndar[1] liumm," ol se, "is áible tened moidit trem' chroicenn";
déniu ráid imorro robenad-som fochetoir ó chlami ó mullach a chinn
conice a bonnaigib for a anumaloit.

[*LB.* 65 b.] Fecht n-aill do B. ic techt do laim in epscuip co
tárfas di cend buicc isin cailiuch oifrinn. Roopastar B. in cailech.
"Cid," or in fer gráid, "ara n-opai?" Dorogart in t-epscop in
gilla tuc ind imaltoir. "Tabair do choibsena, a gilla," or int-epscop.

---

quærite catenam ubi ego oro in ecclesia, invenietis ibi catenam." Cum
exirent invenerunt illic catenam.

[*V.* 3, 55 ; *V.* 4, 1. 2, c. 24.] Rex quidam venit ad B. ad
solemnitatem celebrandam Paschæ.[2] Cum ibi celebrasset, surrexit ut
iret ad domum suam. B. venit ad mensam. Leprosus cibum respuit
comedere, nisi B. sibi daret hastam regis. B. misit equitem post regem.

78. [*V.* 3, 77 ; *V.* 4, 1. 2, c. 51.] Duo leprosi venerunt ad B. ut
salvi fierent. Dixit B. eis, ut alterutrum se lavarent. Sic factum
est, et statim sanatus est unus. Dixit illi B., "Lava et tu socium
tuum quod voluisti ut tibi faceret." Tunc B. mundavit leprosum.
Qui vero prius sanatus est ait, "Modo sentio scintillas igneas super
humeros meos"; et statim corpus totum ejus lepra percussum est
propter superbiam suam.

[*V.* 3, 94 ; *V.* 4, 1. 2, c. 50.] Quadam die accessit B. ut
Eucharistiam sumeret de manu episcopi et umbram hirci vidit in
calice. B. noluit ex hoc calice bibere. Dixit episcopus, "Cur non
bibis." Dixit episcopus puero qui tenebat calicem, "Da gloriam Deo

---

[1] atar, *Lism.*    [2] Pentecostes, *V.* 3.

" Dochúadus," or in gilla, "i tech na ngabur co tallus pocc ass 7 co nduadus a feoil." Rophend in gilla 7 dorigne athrige.

79. [*Lism.* p. 49.] Fecht ann tancatar áigid co B., at iat uaisli craibdecha.    Is annsin forcongair B. for araili *fiur* dia muintir techt dochum in mara co ndernad iasg*acht*.[1]    Teit in fer 7 a murga lais, 7 tecmaing rón do ; saidid inn in róngai, 7 cenglaid a theit dia láim.    Tairrngid in rón in fer tar in bfairrce co traig mara Breatan.    Rocuired dano in ron for culai 7 a gai ann, cu rolaa in muir he forsin traig ba comfocraib do B.    Tainic iascaire Brigte tar muir iarsin, co bfuair a ron i traig mara.

[*LB.* 65 b; *Lism.* p. 49.]    Fecht ann dorala do bachlach co romarb petta sindaig.    Rohergabad lasin rig.    Roforcongart B. for sinnach n-allaid taidecht asin caillid.    Tanic di*no* co mbói oc clesrad 7 oc espai dona slogaib.    Doluid in sindach slan fon caillid 7 slog Laigen etir echu 7 chona inn a degaid.

80. [*LB.* 65 b ; *Lism.* p. 50.]    Fecht ann robúi methel mor oc B. ic buain.    Snigis fleochad mor i Muig Life, 7 nocar' fer banne in a

confitendo peccatum tuum."    Puer confessus est se in caprario fecisse furtum hirci et comedisse carnem.    Pœnitentiam egit puer.

79. [*V.* 3, 74 ; *V.* 4, l. 2, c. 48.]    Alia die venerunt hospites religiosi ad Brigitam.    Tunc dixit B. cuidam viro de familia sua, " Vade ad mare, si possis afferre aliquid hospitibus."    Ille exivit et assumpsit secum hastam marinam, statim vero occurrit taurus marinus,[2] et misit hastam jaculatam et infixit eam in taurum; funes vero circa manum viri erant obnixi.    Taurus autem traxit secum virum per mare ad Britanniæ litora.    Tunc funis scissus est et vir mansit in litore.    Phoca vero reversus est cum hasta in mare, et venit ad litus loci in quo erat B.    Vir autem ille tentavit navigare et venit, et invenit phocam in litore.

[*V.* 3, 128.]    Quadam die rusticus occidit mansuetam vulpem. Alligatus est, et ad regem perductus.    Ad Brigitam misericordia permotam Dominus misit unam de vulpibus feris, quæ, cum venisset, variis lusit artibus coram omnibus.    Ipsa vulpes ad sylvam incolumis evasit, equitibus canibusque insequentibus.

80. [*V.* 3, 110.]    Alia die messores B. in messem vocavit.    Per totam provinciam pluviis abundanter effusis, sua messis sine pluvia

---

[1] iasgach, *Stokes* ; iascairecht is more usual.          [2] phoca, *V.* 4.

gort-si. Fecht ann tancatar epscuip co B., 7 ní bói aiccesi ní doberad dóib, iar mblegan na bó fa do robliged doridise.

[*LB.* 64 a; *Lism.* p. 50.] Bennachais in dall clar-enech co mba slána a da súil.

[*LB.* 66 a; *Lism.* p. 50.] Fecht ann dorala B. cusin mbaintrebthaig, co rusmarb loeg a bó do B. 7 co roloisc a garmain fói. Dorigne Dia for B. co mba hógslán inn garmain iarnabarach 7 bói in loeg immalle rá máthair.

[*LB.* 64 a; *Lism.* p. 50.] Fecht ann do Epscop Ercc 7 do B. i tír Laigen. Atbert si fri hEpscop Ercc, "Ata cath etir do thuaith-siu innossa 7 a comaithgiu." Adubairt macclerech do muintir Epscuip Eirc, "Ni doig linn," ol se, "conid fír sin." Senais B. a roisc in macclerig. Asbert in macclerech, " Atcíu-sa mo brathre ic a marbad innossa.

[*LB.* 66 a; *Lism.* p. 60.] Tanic gataige chuicce, 7 tall secht multu uathe, iarn a hatuch for tús. Araide ó rohairmed in trét foritha[1] doridisi na muilt.

---

perstitit. Alia die advenientibus episcopis, dum non haberet B. unde eos cibaret, vaccam unam tribus vicibus mulsit.

[*V.* 3, 102.] Benedixit B. cæcum tabulatam faciem[2] habentem, et oculos sanos semper habuit.

[*V.* 3, 113; *V.* 4, l. 2, c. 79.] Alio tempore venit B. ad virginem religiosam; illa fecit vitulum vaccæ suæ occidi, et ligna telæ suæ fecit comburi. Dominus per orationem Brigitæ omnia renovavit. Ligna telæ mane inventa sunt integra, et vitulus ad matrem suam pervenit.

[*V.* 3, 71; *V.* 4, l. 2, c. 42.] Cum quodam die Episcopus Ercus et B. essent in via, dixit illa ad Episcopum Ercum, "Nunc bellum geritur inter tuam gentem et aliam." Unus de discipulis ex familia Sancti Erci non hoc credens, dixit, " Quomodo potes videre?" B. signavit oculos ejus, et ait ille discipulus, "Ecce, videntibus oculis meis, fratres mei decollantur."

[*V.* 3, 103; *V.* 4, l. 2, c. 72.] Quidam alacer ad B. venit, et septem verveces per astutiam ab ea impetravit. Sed dinumerato grege certus numerus inventus est, additis vervecibus.

---

[1] frith na multa, *Lism.* 50.      [2] qui vocabatur cretanus, *V.* 3.

## LIFE OF ST. MARTIN.

81. [*LB.* 59 b.] Martain di*du* do F*ra*ngcaib a chenel ⁊ is o thustidib særaib sochen*élch*aib rogenair, ⁊ is in Etáil roalt. Miltnidecht do
rigaib talmandaib dogníd a athair. Noṡanntaiged *im.* Mártain as a
na*i*dend*acht* fógnam do Dia, ar, intan roptar slana .x. mbliadna dó,
nothegaid don eclais dar sarugud a thusnigthe co mba sechtaretsid e.
In tan *im.* roptar slana .xii. (bliadna) do, duthracair dul i ndithrub;
acht rothairmisc ind lubra a æssi imbe. Araide noimraided a menma
dogrés ina mainistrecha ⁊ ina reclesa. Iarsinni roboi iar*um* rohescongrad ó ríg Róman coromiltnigitis na m*eic* an inad na senmiled, co
romáirned a athair intí Martain don rig, uair ba format lais a mét
rofognad do Dia, rocuibriged da*no* Mártain do miltnigecht talmanda
ind agaid a tholi.

Oen mog *tra* is*ed* robui oc Mártain, ⁊ ba he Martain dognid
umaloit doside im ghait a iallacrand de, ⁊ im nige a chos ⁊ im chumaid
bíd fris ciarbo tigerna he. Ba hinísel di*no*, ⁊ ba cainuairrech ⁊ ba

---

81. [*LA.* 191 b.] Igitur Martinus Abariæ[1] Pannoniæ oppido
oriundus fuit parentibus non infimis, sed intra Italiam alatus[2] est,
Pater ejus miles fuit. A primis fere annis Martinus divinam servi-
tutem spiravit, nam cum esset annorum decem ad Ecclesiam confugit
invitis parentibus, seque catacominum fieri postulavit. Cum esset
annorum duodecim heremum concupivit si ætatis infirmitas non fuisset
impedimento. Animus tamen aut circa monasteria aut circa ecclesias
semper intentus meditabatur. Sed cum edictum esset a regibus ut
veteranorum filii ad militiam scriberentur, prodenté patre qui felicibus
ejus actibus invidebat, captus et catenatus sacramentis militaribus est
alligatus (non tamen sponte).[3]

Uno tamen contentus servo comite, cui tamen versa vice dominus
serviebat, adeo ut plerumque ei et calceamenta ipse detraheret
et ipse tergeret, cibum una caperent, hic tamen sæpius ministraret.
Multa illius circa commilitones suos benignitas fuit, mira caritas,

---

[1] *leg.* Sabariæ.
[2] *leg.* altus.

[3] add "non tamen sponte" from the
same column.

hainmnetach imm a chommiledaib co tabratis cádus 7 onóir do.   Ocus
ni taiscead ní di a thuarustul acht a dæthin bid 7 étaig, acht dobered do
bochtaib 7 aidelcnechaib De, co na tomnide bad mílid acht bad manach.

82. In araile lathe di*no* in aimsir gemrid roﬔair do Martain oc
imdecht imalle re chommíle*t*haib, dorala bocht nocht dó ic díucaire i
ndorus na cat(h)rach Ambianensium.   Rothuic *im*. M., uair ropo lan
he do rath Dé, conid dó rochoimet Dia in bocht dia étiud.   Dorat
iarum in cloidem triasin mbrat roboi imbe, 7 rothidnaic a leth don
bocht, uair ní bui araill aige doberad dó.   In lucht ba bæth *im*.
noﬔaitbitis imbe, uair ba docraid a ecosc il-leth a broitt ; in foirend
*tra* ropo chundla, ba galar leo-side, nach doib fén dorala amlaid sin in
bocht d' étiud.   Isind aidche arcind itc(*h*)*o*nnairc M. in Coimdid Ísu
Crist col-leith a broit-siu*m* imme ; 7 is*ed* roraid ria angliu, " Martinus
adhuc catechumenus hac me contexit (veste)," .ı. M. exarcistid is he
dorat damsa indiu inn etach-sa.   Robaitsed di*no* iarsin M. focetoir,
acht ni roléic a miltnidecht uad.

---

patientia vero atque humilitas ultra humanum modum, ita ut eum
omnes miro affectu venerarentur.   Nihil sibi ex militiæ stipendiis
præter quotidianum victum reservabat, sed opem ferebat misseris,
ægentes alebat, nudos vestiebat, ita usus est, ut jam non miles sed
monachus putaretur.

82. Quodam itaque tempore, media hieme quæ solito asperior
erat, obviam habuit in porta Ambiensium civitatis pauperem nudum
orantem ut sui prætereuntes missererentur.   Intellexit vir Deo plenus
sibi illum (aliis misericordiam non præstantibus) reservari.   Arrepto
itaque ferro mediam clamidem qua indutus erat dividit, partemque
ejus pauperi tribuit, (quia) nihil praeter (chlamidem) habebat.
Interea de circumstantibus inridere nonnulli cæperunt, quia deformis
esse, et truncatus habitus videretur ; multi tamen quibus erat mens
sanior, altius gemescere quod nihil simile tale fecissent cum vestire
pauperem potuissent.   Nocte itaque insecuta[1] vidit Christum clamidis
suæ qua pauperem texerat parte vestitum ; et audivit Iesum dicentem
ad anguelorum multitudinem, " Martinus adhuc catacommenus[2] hac
me veste contexit."   Quo viso beatissimus ad baptismum convolavit,
nec tamen statim militiæ renuntiavit.

---

[1] in secunda, *LA*., *read* insequente.           [2] seċtaretsid.

83. In araile fechtus tancatar barbardhu do indrud *Franc*, dothinoil iarsin Julian Cessar a míledu 7 a múntir, 7 dorat múine 7 ascada
do *cech* æn díb co toracht co M., ar dáig cathaigthe fri barbardu.
Iss*ed* atbert M. *fr*isin rig, " Duitsiu romíltniges-(s)a *cu*sindíu ; do Dia
*im*. míltnigfet o sund immach 7 tabair *tra* t'asc*ada* do neoch mílt-
nigfes deit." *Dixit autem rex*, " Ni *for* c*ra*bud léce do miltnidecht
uait acht ar omun in catha immárach." " Uair atbere-siu sin," ol M.,
" regut-sa immarach cen arm etir na cathaib 7 nomdídnife in Coimdiu
Isu Cr*íst*." (*LB.* 60a.) Rocoimetad iarsin he lasin rig, *cu* rachomailled
inní rogell do. Rofoidset *tra* na barbárdhu iarnabarach techta uadib
dia tabairt fén 7 cech æin, *no* cech neich bud leo do Julián Cesair ar
síth *fr*íu. Cia *tra* diarbó anfollus cu mbad for Mártain dogneth Dia in
mírbuil sin, ar na roelnitís roisc in nóib o básaib na n(d)óine n-ecraib-
dech in a fiadn*ai*se.

84. For*á*caib iarsin M. a míltnidecht talm*a*nda 7 dochuaid co
hEláir epscop Pictauæ co mbúi ré fota acca. Rop áil do Eláir co
ragab*ad* M. gr*a*da deochain. Rofrithbruid (.i. ro obustair) *im*. M.
na grada sin ar inísle, róforcongair Elair fair co mbad exarċistid.

---

83. Interea, inruentibus intra Gallias barbaris, Jualianus Cessar,
coacto in unum exercitu, donativum[1] cœpit erogare militibus, et singuli
citabantur, donec ad Martinum ventum est. " Actenus," inquit ad
Cessarem, " militavi tibi ; patere ut nunc militem Deo, donativum tuum
militaturus accipiat." Tunc vero tyrannus infremuit dicens, eum non
religionis gratia (sed) metu pugnæ quæ postera die erat futura detrec-
tare militiam. " Si hoc," inquit Martinus, " ignaviæ et mihi adscri-
bitur, crastina die ante aciem inermis adstabo in nomine Domini Jesu
Christi securus. Retrudi ergo in custodiam jubetur facturus fidem
dictis. Postera die hostes ligatos de pace misserunt, sua omnia seque
dantes. Unde quis dubitat hanc Martini fuisse victoriam, cui præ-
stitum[2] sit ne vel aliorum mortibus sancti violarentur obtutus.

84. Exinde relicta militia Hilarium Pictavæ episcopum expetiit,
et aliquandiu apud eum commoratus est. Temptavit Hilarius impo-
sito diaconatus officio sibi eum Martinum implicare. Cum restititisset,
indignum se esse vociferans, exorcistam eum esse præcipit. Quam
ille ordinationem, (*LA.* 193) ne dispexisse tamquam humiliorem

---

[1] donatiu*m*, *LA*.    [2] prestiaitum, *LA*.

Ni ro ob di*no* M. in grad sin ar na facistea co mbad de*roil* laiss. Nirba
fota iarsin cu raforchanad M. i fís co ndigsed d'forcetul a thusnigti
robatar hi ngentlidecht. Rocomarleged iarum do d' elud acht co
tísed doridise. Dochuaid *tra* for a *set* conustarla do díb latr*an*daib.
Rot*ri*all in dara latrand a béim ó thuaig, rothairmisc in latrand aile.
Aráide rocúibrigthea a láma Mártain iarn a chúl, 7 doratad in dara
latrand dia lommrad. Rosruc leis cul-loc nderrit, cor-iarfaid dó,
" Cia halt duine thú ?" Atl*e*rt M., " Cristaide," ol se, " misse."
Roiarfaid in latrand, " Indat ómnach ?" *Dixit* M., " Ni rabus-(s)a
riam tan bam luga m' imecla, uair rofetar co fort*ach*taigend Dia dá
cech æn bís i cúmgi 7 i tréblait ; 7 is mo co mór gallragim detsiu fén,
uair isa(t) nem*an*nac[1] o throcaire Dé." Ropritchastar M. bréthir ndé
do annsin, 7 rochreit iarum co mba craibdech in latrand iarsin.

85. Dochuaid iarsin M. *for* a sét, co tárfaid demun do i ndeilb
duine 7 atbert fris, " Cipe leth dechais, a M*ártain*, no cip ed ní dogné
bid adbartnaigthech demon duit." Is e freccra tuc M. fair, " In
Coimdiu is fortachtaigtheoir damsa dog*rés*," ol M., " conid aire sin

---

videretur, non repudiavit. Nec multo post admonitus per soporem
ut parentes quos adhuc gentilitas detinebat religiossa solicitudine
vissitaret. Ex voluntate Hilarii profectus est multis ab eo obstrictus
precibus ut rediret. Perigrinationem illam aggressus est, ac incedit
in latrones. Cumque unus secure elivata in caput ejus librasset,
ictum ferientis dextram sustenuit alter. Vinctis tamen manibus post
tergum uni spoliandus traditur. Qui cum eum ad remotiora duxisset
percontari ab eo coepit quisnam esset. Respondit Christianum se
esse. Quærebat etiam ab eo an timeret. Profetebatur M. nunquam
se tam fuisse securum, quia sciret misericordiam Domini maxime in
tentationibus affuturam ; se magis illi dolere, qui Christi misericordia
esset indignus. Verbumque Dei latroni prædicabat ; latro credidit,
idemque postea relegiossam agens vitam visus est.

85. Igitur M. inde progressus, diabulus in itenere humana
specie adsumpta se ei obvium tulit, et ait ad eum, " Quocumque
ieris, vel quocunque[2] temptaveris, zabalus tibi adversabitur." Tunc

---

[1] Read *nemranrach*, Stokes ; but per-
haps better *neminnraic*, un-worthy ; an-    *nac*, guiltless, *O'D. Sup.* ; so *nem-annac*.
[2] sic ; *read* quodcumque.

nach fil omun[1] neich form." (O) rachuala *im.* diabul iarsin bria*thra*
na firinde rothinastar focétoir 7 dochuaid ar nemní.[2]

Tuc M. iarsin a m*áthair* a gentlidecht; forémdid *im.* a athair.
Dochuaid M. iarsin cosin indsi dianid ainm Gallinaria. Doromailt
annsin etir na lubid árchena ind athaba; acht uair rosairig M. in
mbríg nemnig roguid in Coimdid *cu* ra*h*íccad focétoir.

Rośuidig iarsin manistir dó, 7 nirḟota o Eláir. Ronaccomail
Eláir do M. araile sechtarétsid dia forcetul 7 dia ḟóglaimm a bés.
Robenad in sechtaretsid o crithgal*ar* co mba marb. In tan sin bói M.
fri a mainistir anechtair. In tan tanic dia eclais foḟuair in sechtaretsid marb fri re tredenais. Tarlaic Mártain déra iar*um* 7 roguid in
Coimdid; atracht focétoir in marb a bás, 7 robaitsed, 7 roindis co rucad
an iffernd 7 co rigśuide in bri*th*emon; 7 rochuala na haingliu ic a rad
frisin mBri*th*emain, "Is é so intí ara nguid Mártain." *Dixit Judex,*
"Lécid iar*um* co Mártain he."

86. Tan aile do M. oc imḋecht, co cuala ualla˙troma oc cáined
araile mogad ḟir airmitnig rofo*r*bai a bethaid ó gasti.[3] Teit M. cu*s*in

---

ei M. respondit, "Dominus mihi adjutor est, non timebo quid faciat
mihi homo." Statimque e conspectu ejus inimicus evanuit.

Itaque matrem gentilitatis absolvit errore, patre hin malis
perseverante (*LA.* 193 b). Itaque ad insulam cui Gallinariam
nomen est secessit. Quo tempore elleborum venenatum gramen in
cibum sumpsit; sed cum vim veneni sentiret periculum oratione
repulit, statimque omnis dolor fugatus est.

Sibi monasterium conlocavit haud longe ab oppido Hilarii.
Quidam ei se catacominus injunxit, cupiens sancti institui disciplinis.
Languore correptus vi febrium laborabat. At tum M. forte discesserat. Regressus exanime corpus per triduum invenit. Cum M.
flens orationi incubuisset, mortuus redditus vitæ, statim baptisma
consecutus est, idemque referre erat solitus se ad tribunal Judicis
ductum, deputatumque obscuris locis; (*LA.* 194 a) tunc per duos
Angelos Judici fuisse suggestum, hunc esse pro quo Martinus orasset;
ita per eosdem se jussum reduci Martino redditum.

86. Nec multo post dum agrum cujusdam præteriret clamorem et
luctum excepit turbæ planguentis unum servulum viri honorati, qui

---

[1] amun *in Ms.*    [2] nem*th*ní *in Ms.*    [3] *Better* goisti *or* goistiu, *Stokes.*

marb sin 7 rothoduisc a bás tria et*arg*uide in Choimded. O dorat M.
ní i fertaib 7 inn adamraib rocomécnig(ed) som on phop*ul* do gabail
eps*cop*oti Torindsi. Doratad gráda fair iarsin. Atbertís i*m*. na
heps*cuip* ec*ra*ibdecha co nar. *per*su dingbala don epscopoti hé, uair
ba dochraid ó gnuis 7 ba dodelbda ó trilis. Rofáitbe i*m*. in pop*ul*
cunnail dásacht na f*oir*ni-se; co rohórdned M. in eps*cop*oti iarsin, 7
ni rosfácaib a éirdergud manaig in a eps*cop*oti, ar ba humal inísel
o chride.

Uair nar fulaing tortromad na ndóine oc athigid chucai isin cat(h)-
raig ar medón, rosuidig manistir dá míle ceimend on chat(h)raig—
sruth Ligir don dara tæb di, carrao mór don leth aile, 7 en chonair
innte. LXXX manach ba he a lín; ni bíd nach diles ic neoch díb;
nirbo dilmain do neoch díb creico no cennach do dénam; in f*oir*end
bas óo ic sc*ri*bend, in lucht ba sine ic aurnaigthi, uair ni bói dán aile
innte acht legend 7 scribend nammá; 7 is uathad nech díb téged as a
recles acht mad don ecluis. Immalle tra dathómlitís a pr*ó*ind; nis-

---

sibi laqueo vitam extorsit. Cellam in qua corpus jaciebat ingreditur,
orat, et mox in oratione illius defunctus eregitur. Sub idem fere
tempus ad episcopatum Toronicæ Aecclesiæ cogebatur a populo.
Nonnulli tamen ex episcopis impie repugnabant, dicentes scilicet,
contemtibilem esse personam indignumque Episcopatu hominem vultu
dispicabilem, veste sordidum, crine deformem. Ita a populo sententiæ
sanioris hæc illorum inrita est[1] dementia; (*LA.* 194 b) jam vero
sumpto episcopatu, eadem in vestitu vilitas eadem in corde humilitas
ut non propositum monachi desereret.

Cum inquietudinem se frequentantium ferre non posset, duobus
fere extra civitatem milibus monasterium sibi constituit—ex uno
latere præcissa montis excelsi rupe ambiebatur, reliquam planitiem
Liger fluvius clauserat, una tantum via adiri poterat. Discipli
fere LXXX erant; nemo ibi sibi quicquam proprium habebat; non
emere aut vendere quicquam licebat; operi scriptionis minor ætas
deputabatur, majores orationi vacabant, quia ars ibi, exceptis scrip-
toribus, nulla habebatur; rarus quisquam extra cellulam suam
egressus est, nisi cum ad locum orationis conveniebant. Cibum una

---

[1] *sic LA.* 194 ab, *read* inrisa *or* irrisa.

ibed nech dib fín acht intí nobid i sérg; soċaide díb nohédithe o
chilic.

87. In tan ticed M. as a manistir don cat(h)raig nobristís na
démna a cúibrige 7 nostrialltís foluamain isin áer for uaman Mártain.

[*LB.* 60 b.] Bui di*no* hi comḟocus do M. loc i tégtis doine do
ernaigthe am*al* bid martir amra nabeth in a ṡuide; uair boi altoir fo
anmaimm martírech and. Noḟiarfaiged M. ainmm 7 aimsir a chesta in
martír hísin, 7 ni fuair. Óenis M. isin luc sin co rófoillsigead Dia dó
cid boi and. At*c*onnairc M. intan sin foscud salach dorcha dia chlíí;
cor' ḟiarfaid dó a ainm 7 a airill*iud*. "Latrand me," ol se, "7 for mo
drochairilliud romarbad mé"; conid amlaid sin rodíchuired in chom-
rorcain sin tria Mártain.

Dia mbói M. for a sét iarsin itconnairc corp araile gentlide
nob*er*tha co forbannach dia ádnocul, sloig mora immalle fris, lín-anarta
gela taris 7 goeth oc an imluad. Doig *im.* la Mártain *cu* m(*b*)ad ídal-

---

omnes accipiebant; vinum nemo noverat nisi quem infirmitas cogisset;
plerique camellorum setis vestiebantur.

87. Siquoties venturus ad ecclesiam pedem extra cellulæ suæ
extulerat videres energumenos rugientes, in ære raptos in sublime
suspendi et trepidare appropinquante Martino.[1]

Erat haud longe ab oppido monasterii locus quem falsa hominum opinio velut consepultis ibi martyribus consecraverat; nam et
altare (*LA.* 195 a) ibi a superioribus episcopis constitutem habebatur.
Martinus flagitabat nomen sibi martyris et tempore passionis ostendi,
sed grandi scrupulo permoveri cœpit quod nihil certi constans sibi
majorum memoria tradidisset. Ad locum pergit, oravit ad Dominum
ut quis esset ostenderet. Tum conversus ad lævam vidit prope ad-
sistere umbram sordidam atrocemque;[2] imperat nomen meritumque
loqueretur. Confitetur latronem fuisse ob scelera percussum; atque
ita Martinus populum superstitionis illius absolvit errore.

In sequenti tempore dum iter agoret accidit ut gentilis cujusdam corpus, quod ad sepulcrum cum superstitiosso funere defferebatur,
obvium haberet conspicatusque venientium turbam et quia agente
vento candida[3] lintiamina corpori superjecta volitarent, profanos

---

[1] Suⁱius, p. 277.                    [3] I supply *candida* from three lines
[2] et trucem, *Surius.*              lower down.

adrad dognethea ann. Tuarcaib M. airrdhe croiche Crist in a agaid co-
rofast iat isin luc sin.   O rathuic tra corba corp dia adnocul, tuc
airrde na croiche doridisi 7 roimdigset focétoir, co mba follus comus
cúibrig 7 tuaslacthi oc Mártain indsin.

88.  Crand gíuis noadratís na gente, 7 rop áil do Mártain a thescad,
acht ní rolecset na gente dó.   Atbert óen díb, "Tescfamít-ne fén in
crand-sa, 7 tair-siu foi."   Ropa tol do Mártain sin.   Rocumbriged
tra M. isin luc i mba demin leo in crand do thuitím; rothescsat na
genti in crand co failte; Otconnairc[1] M. in crand oc tuitimm fair,
tuarcaib airrdhe na crochi coimdeta in a agaid cor' srained iarsin in
crand tar ais forsna gentib co rosmarb sochaide dib; 7 rochreidset
andsin sochaide dona gentib do Críst 7 do Mártain triasin firt sin.

89.  Fecht aile didu do M. ic loscud ídaltige 7 ruc in gæth in
lassar cusin tech comfocus.   Signis M. airrde na crochi in agaid na
lasrach, cu rasoad in lassar iarum in agaid na gáithe ciar'ba machtnad.

---

sacrificiorum ritus agi credidit.  Elevato in adversa signo Crucis impe-
ratur turbæ non moveri loco.   Sed cum comperisset exequiarum illam
frequentiam esse, elevato rursum manu dat eis abeundi potestatem
(*LA*. 195 b) Ita eos et cum voluit stare compulit, et (cum)[2] libuit
abire permisit.

88.  Cum fanum antiquissimum diruisset et arborem pynum quæ
fano erat proxima esset adgressus excidere, tum vero gentilium turba
succidi arborem non patiebantur.   Unus ex illis ait, "Succidemus
hanc arborem, tu veni, ruentem excipe."  Martinus se facturum polli-
cetur.   Itaque eo loco vinctus statuitur quo arborem esse casuram
nemo dubitabat; succidere ipsi pinum cum gaudio cœperunt.   Martinus opperiens, cadenti super se arbori, elevata in obviam manu,
salutis signum opposuit; tum vero turbinis modo retroacta ruit ut
rusticos pene prostraverit; et gentiles stupere miraculo et nemo fere
ex gentilium multitudine fuit qui non in Dominum Jesum crediderit.

89. [*LA*. 196 a.]   Sub idem fere tempus cum fano ignem inje-
cisset, in proximam domum, agente vento, flammarum globi ferebantur.
Martinus tectum scandit obviam se advenientibus flammis inferens, tum
vero mirum in modum cerneres contra vim venti ignem retorqueri.

---

[1] itconnairc *in Ms*.          [2] I insert *cum* from *Surius*.

Rop áil do M. cor darcend araile tempail moir a mboi ídaladrad, acht ní rolécset na génti dó. Dodechutar dá aingel fón armgais*ced* co rustaifniset na genti, 7 cor'laud darcend in tempul iarum. Dodechaid M. iarsin do thóruma ingine ánbra*cht*aige ná cumcad cor do chois *nó* do láim di; 7 dorat aláim[1] ,coisecartha in a gin co rosíc foc*é*toir.

Araile fer, Detradius a ainm, notechtad mogaid lán do demnaib. Is*ed* roraid Detradius fria Martain, "Creitfet-sa do Crist madan-indarba-su na demna om' mogaid-si." Dochuaid M. immalle fris 7 roindarb na demna on mogaid, 7 roc(h)reit Detradius foc*é*toir do Crist.

90. [*LB*. 60 b.] Fecht aile do M. ic imdecht *con*acca demun ngra*na* an indliss araile fir maith. F*or*conga*ir* fair co ndigsed asin luc sin, is*ed* tra dochoid isin coic; noithead in tróg hisin 7 nóathc*um*ad cech *én* ticed chucca. Dorat M. *im.* a méra in a gin 7 is*ed* atbered fris, "Ma techta cumachta tesc na méra-sa." Roimgaib tra demun

---

Cum templum opulentissimum superstitione[2] religionis voluisset evertere restitit ei multitudo gentilium. Duo angeli hastati atque scutati se obtulerunt ut rusticam multitudinem fugarent, et templum dirutum est.[3] Descendit ad domum[4] puellæ quæ paralisseos ægritudine tenebatur, omni ex parte præmortua, et oleum cum benedixisset[5] in os puellæ infudit statimque surrexit.

Tetradi cujusdam viri servus dæmonio correptus erat. Spondet Tetradius se, si de puero dæmon fuerit exactus, Christianum fore. Martinus ad domum descendit, et immundum spiritum a puero ejecit, statimque Tetradius Dominum Jesum credidit.

90. [*LA*. 197 a.] Per idem tempus ingressus patrisfamilias cujusdam domum, horribile in atrio domus dæmonium vidit. Cui cum ut discederet imperaret, cocum patrisfamilias[6] arripuit; sevire dentibus miser cœpit et obvios quosque laniare. Digitos ei Martinus in os intulit, "Si habes," inquit, "aliquid potestatis,

---

[1] *read* ola (?).
[2] superstitiose, *Surius.*
[3] dum profanam sedem diruisset, *LA.*, 196 ab.

[4] ad domum, *Surius*; "ut visitaret," *LA.*
[5] consecratum, *Surius.*
[6] quemdam e familia, *Surius.*

méra Mártain am*al* bid iarnn d*er*g noberthá in a cr*ae*s. Roescomla
demun iar*um* tria thep*er*sin a brond 7 rosléic na follechta salcha.
Araile tan rogab cr*ith* 7 uamun mor in cat(h)r*ai*g a mbói M., ar is é
scél rosílad fon cat(h)raig, na barbárdhu do thidecht dia hinnrud:
*forcon*gart M. duine démnach bói isin catͺh)r*ai*g do thabairt chuige,
co roiarfaid de cid dia mbói in scél.    Atbert in duine fris, "x[1]
*demones venerunt nunc in civitatem;* is iad doronsat in doilbed-sa,
dáig *co n*dechta-su asin cat(h)r*ai*g."   Conid aml*aid* sin rosærad in
chathair.

91. Araile tan do M. co ro créchtnaiged co mor, tainic aingel
isind aidche co roglan a cré*ch*ta 7 nos-imbir ongain slanaide fair, co
mba hogslán iarnabarach am*al* na bud créchtnaigthi riam.

Fecht and do M. in a recles tæt demun chuci 7 ad*ar*cc lán do
fuil in a láim, 7 is*ed* atb*er*ed, "Cáitt itá do nert a Martain? Uair
rotmarbu(s)-sa innossa oen dot' m*úi*ntir?"   Dorogart M. a múinntir
cor' iarfaid díb cia romilled on guasacht-sa.   Atbertís nirba nech dona

---

hos devora."   Tum vero, ac si candens ferrum faucibus accipissit,
digitos beati Martini vitabat attinguere. . . . Fluxu ventris dæmon
egressus est fœda relinquens vestigia.   Interea cum de metu[2] atque
impetu barbarorum subito civitatem fama turbasset: dæmoniaticum
ad se exhiberi jubet, imperat ut an verus esset hic nuncius fateretur.
Tum confessus est se[3] .x. dæmones fuisse qui rumorem hunc per
populum dispersissent[4] ut ex illo oppido M. fugaretur.   Ita metu
civitas liberata est.

91. [197 b.] Ipse autem cum cassu quodam multis vulneribus
esset affectus, nocte ei Anguelus vissus est eluere vulnera, et salubri
unguento corporis superlinere livores,[5] atque ita postero die restitutus
est sanitati, ut nihil unquam pertulisse se incommodi putaretur.

[198 a.] Quodam tempore diabolus bovis cruentum in manu
cornu tenens cellulam ejus inrupit, "Ubi est," inquit, "Martine,
virtus tua? Unum de tuis modo interfici."   Tunc ille vocatis fratribus (ab eis petit) quisnam hoc cassu fuisset adfectus.   Neminem
quidem deesse de monachis, sed unum rusticum mercede conductum

---

[1] xui *in Surius.*
[2] motu, *Surius* and *Hornius.*
[3] *i.e.* sedecim.
[4] disseminassent, *Surius.*
[5] membra contingere, *Surius.*

manchuib acht araile fer tírtha[1] dochuaid fón caillid for cend chonnaid ;
co tarut dam robói fón féidm a adairc in a bléin *co n*usmarb focétoir.

92. [*LB*. 61 a.] Fecht aile do M. in a recles tæt demun chuci
*co n*dessid in a fail-sium ; delrad dermair remi, sollsi adbul imbe-sium
fén, os e solusta taitnemach, étach rigda imbe, mínd rig for a cend,
iallacranda orda imbe. Atb*ert* iarsin, " Cid chunntab*air*taige a Martain ? Is messi Crist dodechaid *cu*sna talm*an*daib, 7 rop áil dam
infoillsiug*ud*[2] duitse *for* tús."

Atb*ert* M., " Ni chreitim-sea Crist do thidecht acht isin deilb
7 isin ecosc in[3] rochesair." O rachuala diabul na bria*thra* sin rothin
focétoir am*al* diaid co rolín in recles o bréntaid.

Atchíd *tra* M. ina haingliu ic imacallaim in a fiad*nai*se ; diabul
*im.* cip e deilb i tísad co M., cid in a folaid[4] díles *no* araile fuath
tarmchruta, atcítea o Martain he. Nochluintís *di*no na b*ra*thre esium
7 diabul ic a aithisiugud Mártain o nach cúmcad araile dó.

---

ut vehiculo ligna deferret, ire in silvam nuntiant junctis bobus, bovem
excusso capite inter inguina cornu dejecisse ; nec multo post vitam
reddidit.

92. [199 ab.] Quodam die oranti in cellula diabulus adstetit
præmissa præ se potestate et circumamictus luce porporea, sereno ore,
læta facie, veste regia indutus, diademate redimitus, calceis auro[5]
inlitis. Tum Zabulus dixit, " Martine," inquit, " quid dubitas ?
Christus ego sum discensurus ad terras prius me manifestare tibi volui."

" Ego," inquit Martinus, " Christum nisi in ea forma habituque
venientem[6] quo passus est; non credam." [199 b.] Ad hanc ille
vocem statim ut fumus evanuit, cellulam quoque fœtore complevit.

[198 a.] Constat etiam anguelos ab eo plerumque vissos ita
ut conserto invicem apud eum sermone loquerentur ; diabulum vero
qualibet sub imagine, sive se in propria substantia contineret, sive in
diversas figuras transtulisset, ab eo videbatur. Testabantur etiam
aliqui ex fratribus audiisse se demonem protervis vocibus increpantem
Martinum quia fallere non posset insidiis.

---

[1] drying man, *Stokes* ; *recte* country-
man, rusticus.

[2] *or* m'foillsiug*ud*.

[3] *for* ir-rochesair.

[4] *read* folad ?

[5] auroque, *LA*.

[6] venisse, *Surius*.

93. Araile fer cristaide, Evantius ainm-side, robenad on *crith*-galur, 7 dorogart Martain chuci.  Ba slán in fer sin resíu tísed M. co leth conaire chuci.  Doc(h)uaid in a frithsét M. *co* nasruc laiss dia thig.  Is andsin roben in nathir gilla do muintir ind fir *cétna*, co nderna att dícend di a churp.  Tucad foc*é*toir co M., 7 dorat-som a méra imon crecht co rofaisc, 7 tanic sruth do neim 7 do fuil asin crecht.  Atracht in gilla foc*é*toir 7 sé ógslan, 7 rosubachsat na huli in mírbuil sin, 7 atb*er*tsat na boi fó nim *con*iced indsam*ail* Mártain i fertaib 7 im-mírbulib 7 in adamraib.

94. Fecht do M. ic imdecht, dodechaid imad dermair na ngenti in a frithset.  Tanic araile bannscál 7 a mac le co M., 7 roguid intí Martain co rothoduscad a mac di.  Rofill M. a glúni annsin, 7 dosgni slechtain 7 crosfigill, 7 roguid in Coimdid *co* nduth*r*acht.  Atracht in mac a bás focétoir, 7 rocretset na genti do Cr*ist*.

Fecht aile do M. oc imdecht, dodechaid bó dásachtach in a

---

93. ⌊209 ba.⌉  Cum Evanthius, vir Christianus, gravissima febris ægritudine cœpisset urgeri, Martinum vocavit.  Priusquam medium viæ spatium M. evolveret virtutem advenientis sensit egrotus recepta continuo sanitate.  Venientibus nobis (i.e. Martino et Sulpicio) obviam ipse processit, et redire cupientem magna prece detinuit.  Interim unum e familia puerum lethali ictu serpens percussit, cerneres omnibus venis inflatam cutem ad utris instar.  Quem jam exanimem Evantius ante pedes Sancti intulit.  M. pertractans membra, digitum prope ipsum vulnusculum fixit, et per vulneris[1] foramen virus stipavit cum sanguine et effluxit.  Puer surrexit incolumis, et omnes obstupefacti tantæ rei miraculo fatebantur non esse sub cælo qui Martinum possit imitari.

94. [*LA.* 210 ab.]  Dum vicum quemdam præteriret obvia ei immanis turba gentilium processit.  Mulier quædam corpus exanime filii sui Beato cœpit offerre, dicens, "Restitue mihi filium meum."  Cum genua flexisset, et ubi consummata oratione surrexit, vivificatum parvulum matri reddidit.  Tum vero multitudo omnis Cristum fateri cœperunt.

[212 a.]  Per idem fere tempus a Triberis[2] revertenti fuit[2] obvia vacca quam dæmon agitabat, quæ, relicto grege suo in homines ferebatur.

---

[1] ulceris, *Surius* and *Hornius*.        [2] Treveris, fit, *Surius*.

agaid, 7 foracaib a bú 7 nosféochraiged fria dáinib. Itchonnairc M. demon *for* a drúimm, 7 atb*er*t, "Forassaig on anmanna nemurchoitech." Forassaig demon foc*é*toir la brethir Mártain, 7 ba cennais in bó.

95. Cessair-galar ticed cecha bliadna i tír Seno(n)icca. Roguidset aittrebthaide in tíre f*ur*tacht o Mártain. Roguid M. in Coimdid f*or*ru 7 rosærtha on tedm*m*aim na cessari. Triasin fichit blia*dan tra* boi M. in a bethaid ní thanic in c(h)essair; iarn éc *tra* Martain foc*é*toir tanic in c(h)essair. Follus tra as sin co cáined in doman do bás Martain am*al* nofailtniged dia bethaid.

Araile daine batar i nguasacht mor for Muir Thorrén; uair runguidset Martain rosærtha forc*é*toir dian im*b*ádud.

Fecht do Martain in a recles atconnairc dá demon forsin carraic os in manistir, 7 is*ed* atbertiss, "Eibisa tebricio,"[1] mar bud ed atbertis, "Dena calma a Bricio, Dena calma a Bricio, nert maith a Bricio, do immdergud Martain." Dodechaid Bricio cen fuirech co Mártain 7 roscéid míle aithise fair. Ni roc*um*scaiged *im*. M. de sin acht is*ed* atberead, "Ar rofodamar Ísu intí Iudas dia b*r*ath, cid d*ino* ar nach

---

Vidit Martinus dæmonem dorso illius supersedentem, "Desiste," inquit, "innoxium animal agitare." Apparuit[2] nequam spiritus et abscessit jubente Martino, et bucula ove placidior gregem suum petiit.

95. [216 a.] Pagum quendam in Senonico annis singulis grando vastabat. Incolæ a Martino auxilium poposcerunt. Facta ibi oratione M. regionem liberavit ab ingruenti peste. Per viginti annos quibus postea mansit in corpore grandinem nemo pertulit; eo anno quo ille diffunctus est rursus incubuit rediviva tempestas. Adeo sensit mundus ejus excessum, ut cujus vitâ jure gaudebat ejusdem morte lugeret.

[218 a.] Cum in Terreno mari navigarent quidam viri, extremum vitæ omnibus fuit discrimen; cum clamaverint, "Martine eripe nos," mox cursum cum summa quiete tenuerunt.

[218 b.] Quodam die dum in area quæ tabernaculum ejus ambiebat resedisset vidit .II. dæmones in rupe quæ monasterio supereminet, inde alacres et lætos hujus adhortationis vocem emittere, "Eia te Bricio, Eia te Bricio." Nec mora, Bricio inrupit et evomuit in Martinum mille convicia. M. quidem mente tranquilla commemoratus est, "Si Christus Judam passus est, cur ego non patiar Bricio-

---

[1] *read* Eia te Bricio *bis* (?)   [2] paruit, *Surius.*

H 2

fódemaind-sea Bricio dom athisiugud?" Rogní *tra* Bricio athrige, 7 roslecht fo chossaib Martain 7 dorat M. dilgud dó.

96. Ar it immda ferta 7 mirbuile Martain, is lor bec díb ar desmb*i*recht, ar ni coemnest*àr* an ais*nes* uli acht mine tísed Dia fessin no aingel Dé do nim dian indisse; uair a betha inmedonach 7 a airb*ert* bith cech lathi 7 a menma indfeithmech dogr*é*s i nDia, a abstanait 7 a mesraigetu, a morsæthar hiń ṕ́ińib (7) in ernaigthib nis-fil nech coníc-fad an áis*nes*; ar ni sechmall*ad* nach uair no nach momint aimsire cen ernaigthe no cen léigend. Ba he mét a úmla *con* niged cossa nan óigead 7 co tábrad usce dar a lámu; 7 ni śuided an ińad cumdachta am*al* tśuidit araile hi cathairib. cumdachtaib. Mor in maith corba cendais do Martain o briathraib, *cor* ba cunnaïl o imacallaim, *cor* ba herlàm ic tuaslucad cest. Ocus ba hingnad sin i nduine nárlég litt*ri* no légend in a óitid. Ba hæn som 7 ba hinund dogr*é*s co taitned in failte nemda .ı. ráth Dé, for a gnúis sechtar aicniud duine 7 is e a mét ón cona tómnithea etir comba duine é for mét a ratha 7 a airmiten.

---

nem?" Interea Bricio reductus ad pœnitentiam ad Martini se genua prosternit, et non erat apud Martinum labor difficilis ut ignosceret ei.

96. [199 b.] Quanquam in Martini virtutibus quantula est ista laudatio, sermo claudendus est, non quod omnia quæ fuerant dicenda defecerint; nam etsi facta illius explicari verbis utcumque potuerunt, [200 a.] interiorem vitam illius, cotodianam conversationem, et animum cœlo semper intentum, perseverantiam et temperamentum in absti-nentia et jejuniis, potentiam in orationibus, non si ipse (ut aiunt) Humerus emergeret, posset verbis exponere; nunquam hora ulla, momentumve præteriit quo non aut orationi incumberet aut insisteret lectioni. Credi non potest qua me humilitate susceperit cum me suo convivio dignatus est adhibere, nobis pedes abluit, et aquam manibus nostris obtulit. In ecclesia nemo unquam illum sedere conspexit, sicut quemdam nuper vidi sublimi solio et quasi regio tribunali celsa sede residentem. Credi non potest qua me benignitate susceperit; jam vero in verbis et confabulatione ejus quanta dignitas erat, quam in absolvendis scripturarum questionibus promptus. Quod mirum est homini illiterato ne hanc quidem gratiam defuisse. Unus idemque semper cælestem quodam modo lætitiam vultu præferens extra naturam hominis videbatur.

## LIFE OF ST. BRENTAN.

97. [*Lis.* 30 b.] Bá fer irisech a athair in ṁeic sin .ı. Findloġ; is aṁlaid batur in lanaṁain sin i coibligi dliġthiġ fo riagail Espuic Eirc. Atconnaic máthair Bren*ainn* aislingi resíu rogenair Bren*nann* .ı. lán a hochta d'ór glan do beith aice, 7 a ciche do taitneṁ am*ail* t-ṡnechta. Iar n-indisi na haislingi d'Escop Eirc, adubairt gu ngeinfeth uaithi gein chumachtach ḃud lán ḍo rath in Spirta Nóiḃ.

Araili fer saidḃir bái in aitreiḃ cofada oc taiġ Finnloga, Airdi mac Fidaiġ a ainm. Tainic priṁfaid na hEirenn in tan sin co tech Airrde .ı. Beg mac Dé. Rofiafraiġ Airrde do Bec, "Cid ni is nesa dún innosa?" Adubairt Bec, "Geinfid do rí dilis dingbala féin eadrat 7 muir inocht, 7 biḋ sochaiḋi do ríġaib 7 do ruirechaib aiḋeorus he." Isinn aḋaiġ sin rucsat tricha bó trichait læġ ag Airrde. Iarsin roéirig Airrḍi co moch arnabarach, 7 boi oc iarraid in toiġi a rucad in mac beag, 7 fuair tech Findloġa 7 in naidiu ann, 7 roṡlecht co duthrachtach 'na fiaḋnusi, 7 ros-edbair in *trichait* loilgech con a læġaiḃ ḍó.

---

97. [*Cod. Kilk.* 56 ba.] Ejus pater Findluag nomine erat fidelis, qui cum uxore sua in legitimo matrimonio sub confessione Erci Episcopi vivebat. Mater Brendani, antequam natus ipse esset, vidit visionem, id est, sinum suum auro obrizo plenum et mamillas suas magno radiantes splendore, et hanc visionem narrans Erco episcopo, qui ait, "Homo potentia magnus[1] plenus spiritu sancto ex te nascetur."

Quidam vir dives filius Airde erat in vicina domo. Ad cujus hospicium venit veridicus propheta nomine Beccus. Interrogavit eum ille dives dicens, "Dic nobis aliquid novum bonum quod citius eveniet." Ait propheta, "In hac nocte inter te et mare dominus tuus nascetur, cui semen tuum serviet et multi pro sua sanctitate adorabunt." In illa jam nocte illi diviti triginta vaccæ totidem vitulos parturiverunt. Mane[2] autem ille dives surrexit, et villam ubi puer sit natus quæsivit, et inveniens infantulum humiliter adoravit genibus

---

[1] Sic *Ms. Salmant.* magnæ felicitatis, *Cod. Kilk.*    [2] lucente aurora, *Sal.*

Rogaḃ iarsin an brugaid in mac in a laim, 7 adubairt, "Bid dalta damsa in mac so."

98. An adaig im. ġene Brenainn adconnaic Espoc Eirc Alltraigi Cailli fo æn lasair dermair, ͺ7 timtirecht nan aingiul imon tir immacuairt.   Eirgius Espoc Eirc gu moch araḃarach 7 taìnic gu tech Finnloġa, 7 roġaḃ in mac in a laim, 7 aduḃairt fris [*Lis.* 31 a], " A ᵭuine Dé! gaḃ misi cucat amal ṁanach ndilius ; *et,* cid sochaidi is forḃfæilid friat' ġein, as forḃfail*tiu* mu chridi-si."   Ocus rochí i comurtha fælti 7 ron-baist.   Ruᵭsat a ṁuinter leo hé cu mboi bliadain occa iarsin ic a altrum.

I cind bliadna iar sin ruc Espoc Eirc lais ar amus a ṁuime féin .ı.  Íta ; 7 bai coic bliadna oc Ítta 7 tuc in chaillech graᵭ ndermair dou.   Ocus nobith Brenainn oc sirġaire frisin caillig cech tan atᶜíᵭ hí ; rofiarfaig Ita ᵭe, " Ciᵭ dogní faeilti ᵭuit, a næidi noeṁ," ol sí.   "Tusa," ol sé, "atᶜím oc labra frim choiᵭchi, 7 oġa imᵭa ele amail tusa, 7 siat acum coṁaltram as cech láim dia chéle."[1]

---

flexis, et ei obtulit xxx vaccas cum vitulis suis.   Et accepit puerum in ulnas suas et dixit, " Confiteor te, fili, in alumpnum meum."

98. Sanctus autem Episcopus Ercus in illa nocte in  qua natus est B., vidit regionem illuminatam luce clarissima et angelos circumvolitantes super villam.   Et exurgens mane venit ad domum Findloga, et accipiens eum in ulnis suis ait ei, " Homo Dei vivi ! suscipe me monachum tibi obedientem ; [*C. Kilk.,* 56 bb] quanto gaudio corda hominum de tua nativitate debent gaudere cum angeli lætentur de te, et cor meum magis omnibus de te gaudet."   Lachrymansque baptizavit infantem.   Nutritusque uno anno in domo parentum suorum.

Finitoque anno venit Episcopus Ercus, et duxit eum secum ut aleretur apud Sanctissimam Ytam ; et Yta nutrivit quinque annis et gloriosa Virgo diligebat eum valde.   Et virgo, videns euṁ jocundo frequenter animo, interrogavit eum dicens, " O sancte infans, quid lætificat te ?"   Puerulus dicebat, " Quia te video mihi loqui, et alias tibi similes sanctas virgines semper, et me lætificant tenentes me in manibus suis."

---

[1] The Irish adds that these were angels in the forms of *sanctæ virgines.*

I cinn .v. mbliadne iar sin roleġ oc Espoc Eirc a ṡalma co
gressach, 7 ba fada la hIta beith 'na ecmais. Ni raḃa bó blicht oc
Espoc Eirc ; robói siuṁ tra in araile la occ iarraid bainne for a aidi.
Is iar sin ticeḋ ind aġ allaid ce*cha* lái do Ṡléiḃ Luachra con a læg le, co
mbligthe dosum hi.

99. Is ann sin bói Bríg inn a farrad-sum .ı. derḃṡiur ḋo, 7 ba
derṁair méd a grada lais ; 7 rofegaḋ gnúis a aidi amail ruithen
grene.

[*Lis.* 31 ab.] Dochuaid Eirc do proicept. Luid-sium lais isin
carput 7 ba hæsach deich mblí*adan* Bren*ann* in tan sin. Facabar*som*
a ænar isin charput iar ndul don chlérech don proicipt. Suidius
B. isin carput 7 sé oc gabail a ṡalm a ǽnar. Is ann sin doriacht
ingen mín macachta do cenel rígda 7 sillis fair 7 fegaiḋ a ġnúis
aluinn edrocht, 7 fuabrais léim chuice isin carput, 7 a cluiche do
denaṁ ris.

Is ann aspert-som fria, " Imthiġ dod'tiġ, ciḋ dod-fucc ille ?"
Ocus geiḃiḋ-sium ialla in c(h)arpait 7 gaḃuiḋ for a sraeiġled cu cruaid,
cu raiḃi ic cai 7 occ diucairi cu riacht gu hairm a raiḃe a máthair 7 a
hathair.

---

Post jam quinque annos legebat apud Episcopum Ercum, et erat
S. Ita tristis de absentia sui alumpni. Nec lac nec vacca erat in illo
loco ; quærebat quodam die lac et postulavit ut biberet. Deinde
Dominus fecit cervam cum suo vitulo per multos dies de Monte
Luachra venire, et mulgebatur pro Brendano.

99. Habebat B. germanam nomine Brig, quæ visitans eum effecta
est gratiâ Spiritus Sancti sancta, quam valde amavit ; cujus facies
quasi aspectus lunæ, facies sui magistri Erci quasi globus solis semper
videbatur.

Solebat Ercus ire prædicare. B., cum decem annorum esset, exiit
in curru in comitatu Erci. Descendente viro Dei prædicare, B. mansit
in curru. Sedit B. in curru legens. Vidensque eum pulchra regia
quædam puella speciosum forma volebat ascendere ad illum in curru
et cum eo ludere.

Cui ait, " Revertere ad propinquos tuos, quid huc quaeris, filia ?"
Et accepit flagellum [57 a] et percussit eam fortiter. Quæ flens et
tristis reversa est ad suos.

100. Impoidius iar sin Espoc Eirc 7 gabuid ic a cairiugud-sum cu gér im bual*ad* na hoigi neimelnidi. "Dogen-sa aithrigi inn," ar B., "7 abair-si hí." "Tair isin uam*aid*-sea co maduin," ar Erc, "7 bí at' ænar intí." Oirisid Epscop Eirc i bfarrad na huamad ic eistecht ra Brenainn cen fis dó. Atclos tra fogur gotha Brennain ag gabáil a salm. Is ann sin adconnuic in clérech buidne aingel súas cu nem 7 anuas co talmain immon uamaid co maduin. O sin imach im. nír' chumaing nech gnúis Brennain d' faicsin ar imad na ruithn*ed* ndiada *acht* Finan Cam a ænar, áir ba lán do rath in Spirta Nóib éiside.

101. Araile lá batar oc imthecht foran sligid .ı. Brenann 7 Espoc Eirc ; dorala oen óclach in a cuidechta for an sligid. Teacmuid di*diu* namait batur aigi do, 7 adubairt, [*Lism.* 31 b.] "Muirbfit sud misi innosa." "Eirg ar scath in chairthi cloichi ucut," ar B., "7 sín ar a scath tú." Et tocbuid B. a lama fria Dia 7 dogní ernaigthi, coros(o)ei trea in t-óclach i richt coirthi cloichi. Teacait a namait-sium 7 benuid a cenn de in a richt-som ; et maraid beos in cloch sin arna

---

100. Rediens autem Episcopus increpavit illum de percussione virginis non cognoscentis adhuc malum. Respondit B., "Dic quod vis, et ego poenitentiam implebo." Dixit ei Episcopus, "Mane in illa spelunca usque mane solus." Mansit ergo B. ympnos Deo decantans ; Episcopus prope speluncam contemplando sedit, nesciente Brendano ; et mansit B. psalmos decantans. Et videbat Ercus choros angelicos inter speculum et caelum ascendentes et descendentes per totam noctem. Tantum deinceps vultum pueri Deus claritate illustravit ut in faciem ejus, præter S. Finanum cognomento *Cam*, qui similem sortitus est gratiam, intendere non possent.

101. Alio die cum Ercus Episcopus et Brendanus ambularent in via, accidit ut quemdam militem in comitatu conviatorem haberent. Qui, cum vidisset inimicos suos sibi occurrentes, dixit, "Ecce ad me occidendum veniunt." B. ait, "Vade et esto juxta propinquum lapidem. Elevansque manus suas in oratione benedixit virum et mutavit virum in formam lapidis (et lapidem in formam viri). Venientes inimici occiderunt hostem et amputaverunt caput ejus ; lapisque ille truncus stat adhuc. Ercus ait, "Debetis poenitentiam[1] agere ;

---

[1] 'perviam' seems to be in the *Ms.*, which is perhaps a rendering of *aithrigi*, or return, *conversio*, to God.

dicennad. "Denaiḋ aithrigi," ar Escop Eirc, " uair ceann na cloiche
fil occuiḃ." Dogníat iarum aithrigi ndicra fo riaguil Espuic Eirc
o sin immach.

102. Iar bfogluim im. can*one* petarlaice 7 nuifiadnuissi do Brennain, dob ail dó riagla noeṁ n-Erend d' fogluim. Cedaiġis tra Espoc
Eirc dósum dul d' fogluim na riagla sin ár ro f̈itir gurup o Dhia robui
dósoṁ in comairli sin; 7 adubairt, " Tar doriḋisi cucamsa cu roġaba
tú graḋa uaimsi."

Iar ndul dosom d'agalluim a muime .ı. Ita, is ed aduḃairt in
cedna fris, riagla næṁ n-Eirenn d'f̈ogluim 7 aduḃairt ris, " Na dena
foġluim ag mnaiḃ na ac óguib cu nach derntar hégnach." " Imthiġ,"
ar sí, " 7 teiceṁaid læch duit ar an sligid. Ecmaing da*no* ba hé mac
Lenin in læch sin." Dorala mac Lenín dó, is ann doraiḋ B. fris,
"Dena aithrigi, ar itá Dia ocut' toġairm." Is ann sin rosoei Colmán
mac Lenin cusan Coimḋiḋ, 7 cuṁduiġter eclasa leis focédair.

103. Iar sin rosiact B. crích Connacht fo clú araili fir craibḋiġ bai
ann .ı. Iarlaithe, *et* rosfoglaim-sium na huili riagla aici-sein. *Et*

---

videte modo caput lapideum quod habetis." Et fecerunt poeniten.
tiam[1] sub lege Episcopi Erci usque ad mortem.

102. Cum vero esset ipsi studium maximum in divinis Scripturis
desideravit ad discendas scripturas et sanctorum exempla sanctos
visitare Hiberniæ.[2] Postulata igitur magistri licentia Episcopus Eirc
ait, "Ex Deo est hoc consilium ; revertere ad me post tempus ut
gradum de manibus meis sacerdotalem accipias."

[57 ab.] Postea B. perrexit ad S. Itam nutricem suam, quæ
dixit ei, " Regulas perfectorum patrum Hyberniæ disce; et cave ne
frequenter visites virgines ne blasfemeris." Et ait ei sancta, "Vade,
occurret tibi in via quidam laicus filius Lenin." Vidensque eum B.,
ait ei, "Age poenitentiam, quod te vocat Deus ('do tibi nomen Col-
manum')." Et ille homo vere sanctissimus effectus est, et postea
cellas edificavit.

103. Post vero B. audiens famam sanctitatis S. Iarlaithe in Con-
nachtheorum regione exivit ad eum doctrinæ salutaris pocula hauriens.

---

[1] cognoverunt perviam, in *Ms.*
[2] So *Salm.* ; but. *Cod. Kilk.* has,

videre vitam quorumdam Sanctorum
Hiberniæ.

asbert fria Iarlaithe, "Ní hann-so bias h-eséirgi etir," ar se : "Act cena," ar Iarlaithi, "abuir frim cait i mbia mo eiseirǵi?"    Atbert B. fris, "Dentar carpat leat," ar se, "áris senóir thu ⁊ eirg foran sligid; ocus cipe inad i mebat dá fertais an c(h)arpait, is ann bias h-esseirǵi ⁊ eiséirǵe sochuiḋi immaille frit."    "A meiċ noeim," ar Iarlaithi, "cid uma ḃfolcai ratha diaḋai in Spirta Nóiḃ filet innat? Acht geiḃ misi it' manchaine."    Iarsin tra téit in seanóir isin carput ⁊ ni cian rainic intan romebsat da fertais in c(h)arpait, ⁊ as é aiṁm an inaid sin, Tuaim da Ghualann.

Iar ḃfacbail Iarluithe annsin do Brenann gabais roime for amus Muiǵe hÁi.    Dorala *im.* aingel dó ⁊ ised asbert fris, "Scríḃ," ar se, "briathra in craḃaid uaimsi." Scríḃais B. ann sin occonn aingel ind uili riagail noemḋa ⁊ maraid beous in riagol sin.

104. In tan *im.* batar oc imtecht in muiǵe conaicet in fuat,[1] ⁊ duini marb fair, ⁊ a charait ic á cháiniuḋ.    "Tairisnigid isin Choimḋid," ol B., "⁊ biḋ beo in duine fil ocuiḃ."    Iar ndenum ernaiǵthi co Dia do B., eirǵes int oclaech acedoir, ⁊ berait a muinter

---

B. dixit ei, "Resurrectio tua non erit hic."    Cui Episcopus ait, "Ubi ergo resurrectio mea erit?"    Ait ei B., "Sede in plaustro, quod senex es, et vade in viam illam; et ubicumque rotæ plaustri fractæ[2] fuerint, ibi (resurrectio tua) et resurrectio multorum tecum erit." Tunc Iarlathe ait, "O Brendane juvenis! quare archana[3] Domini in te abscondis? Vere magister noster debes esse." Ascendit in plaustro Episcopus et iter egrediens non longe, fractæ sunt rotæ plaustri in loco cui nomen *Tuaymm da Gualann.*

B. cum benedictione Iarlathi discessit ad alium locum in campo Aii.[4]    Apparuit ei angelus, dicens ei," Scribe a me regulam." Et scripsit ibi B. regulam ab angelo,[5] et illa usque hodie manet.

104. In ipso campo aliquando, B. mortuum vechi ad sepulcrum [57 b] et amicos ejus, tristes circa eum vidit. Quibus ait, "Confidite in Deo, mortuus enim vester vivet." Oravit B. ad Christum, illico jam juvenis surrexit, et universi exultant. Et oculi omnium intende-

---

[1] *i.e.* feretrum; *cf.* accedens ad fere-trum, in the Kilk. Latin text here.
[2] ruptæ, *Sal. Cod.*

[3] divina dona, *Sal. Cod.*
[4] in campo nomine Magae, *Sal. Cod.*
[5] ab eo dictante, *Sal. Cod.*

leo he co bfæilti ndermair. Iar sin tra geibid cach ic a fegad-som cu
mor 7 berait leo hé co rig in muigi; 7 tairgid in rí ferann do in
baile in bud ail do isin maig sin ; 7 mír 'gab uada ár nírb ail leis beith
isin maig soin. Impais co hEspoc Eirc 7 gabais grada uaid.

[*Lis.* 32 a.] "Dorad Dia duit inní rochuingis .i. tír tairngire."
Ba maith lais a menma on aitheasc sin, 7 teit a aenar i Sliab
nDaidche, 7 fegais ind aicen ndermair uad for cech leth, 7 is ann
sin atconnuic-sium an innsi n-aluind n-airegda. Iarsin tra anaid-
sium tredenus annsin; tic aingeal in Coimded dia acallaim 7 atbert
fris, "Múinfet-sa duit an innsi n-áluind atconnacais." Cíís B. ann
sin co dermair leis aitheasc in aingil fris, 7 dogni atlaigthi buidi do
Dia, 7 tic co a muintir. Seolais tra B. ann sin for tongor in mara.
Batar amlaid fria re .v. mbliadan for an aicen.

105. [*Lis.* 33 a.] Conaccatar araili inis 7 si árd, acht cena ní
fuaratar port reid aice; batar cu cenn da lá dec uimpi imma cuairt 7
nír fétsat dula innti frisin re sin. Adconncatar eclais n-innti ; iar
cloistecht doib-sium foguir gotha lochta na hinnsi cotlaid Brenain
cona muintir in a suan spirdalta. Cuirthear clar ciartha doib anúas 7

---

bantur in S. Brendano, adducuntque eum secum ad regem terræ;
qui obtulit ei quemcumque in terra sua locum eligeret; sed B. hoc
renuit non appetens mansionem in illo loco. Reversus est ad Ercum
Episcopum qui fecit eum sacerdotem.

[*Salm.*, p. 765.] " Fiet tibi secundum desiderium tuum."
Quo lætatus dicto suos seorsum relinquens ascendit in montem
*Aidche*, directoque in aquora prospectu insolam vidit amoenissimam.
Post triduanum denique jejunium vox facta est ei, "Tibi insulam
quam vidisti promitto." Fusis diutissime lacrimis de promissione
tanti doni gratias Deo egit, et reversus est ad suos. Ascendit igitur
B. in navem et mari se commisit et coepit navigare. Quinquennio
equora perlustravit.

105. [*Salm.*, p. 765.] Quandam invenerunt insolam nimis autem
altam cujus introitum invenire cupientes per dies xii laboraverunt,
sed minime repererunt; viderunt et autem in ipsa ecclesiam, audierunt-
que humanarum vocum concentum ad quarum dilectabilem melodiam
dormire cœperunt. Missa est ad eos de rupe tabula quædam literis

se scribtha 7 is ed bai ann : "Na denaid soethar frisin innsi-sea do
t(h)iachtain innti, acht an inis iarrthai fogebthai ; 7 eirg dod thír féin,
ár itá sochuidi ann las bud ail h-faicsin."

[*Lis*. 33 b.] Impáis B. doridisi co a thir 7 co a thalmain fein.
Is ann sin dochuatar lucht a thuaithi fein 'na agaid, 7 tucsat máine
7 ascada do amal doberdais do Dia.  Iar bfacbail *im*. in tsæguil do ilib
dib leanait iar sin Crist, 7 dogni-sium ferta 7 mírbuili imda ann sin.
Accaillis iarsin a aidi .ı. Espoc Eirc, tainic iarsin co du a mbui a
muime .ı. Ita ; feraiss Ita foeilti fris, 7 is ed atbert fris, "A meic
inmain, cid dia ndeachadais for longais cen a chomairle friumsa?
Uair in talam ic a tái iarrad ar Dhia nocha nfagbai hí iarsna croicnib
marbaib mochlaigib sin ; acht cena," ar si, "dentar longa crannda lat,
7 is doig is amlaid sin fageba in talam sire." Iarsin tra luid B. i
crích Connacht 7 dognither long mór aice ann sin, 'sí derscaigthech
dermair, 7 teit innti cona muindtir.

106. [*Lis*. 34 b.] Iar rochtain im. doibsium i comfocraib in tiri
atcualatar guth araile senorach ; is amlaid bai in senoir, cen etuch
etir, acht ba lan a chorp uile do clumuib glegealaib amal cholum ;
ferais failte friu 7 ised atbert friu : "A oilithrecha lansæthracha, a

---

inscripta taliter intitulata : "Noli ad intrandam insolam laborare quia
terram tibi promissam adipisceris ; prius repatria, gens enim tua te
videre desiderat."

[*Sal. Kilk*., 62 bb.] Remeans igitur ad terram suam pervenit.
Postea confluunt multi ad eum undique et munera ei obtulerunt in
Christi nomine.  Nonnulli etiam relinquentes hujus res sæculi se jugo
religionis subjiciunt,[1] Christo ubique evangelizato sequentibus signis.
Erco Pontifice visitato, ad Itam nutricem suam perrexit, quæ exul-
tanter et honorifice suscipiens ait, "Quid, dilecte mi, absque meo
temptasti consilio?  Mortuorum pellibus animalium vectus promissam
non adipisceris terram ; invenies autem facta de tabulis nave." Itaque
in Connactiam profectus fabricatam tabulari artificio navem LX cum
discipulis ascendit.

106. [*Salm*., p. 766.] Applicantibus vero ipsis, senior quidam
plumis pro vestibus tectus accedens ad eos salutavit et dixit : "O

---

[1] *i.e.* fecit eos monachos, *K*. ; ad monasterialem vitam vocatis, *S*.

lucht ernaiġit na logu nemda, a beatha bithscith ic ernaidi in tíre-
sea, ernaiġid bican da bar sæthar coleic. Cid nach faicthi-si in
talmain n-airegda-sea ar nar doirtead fuil duini riam, 7 nach
imchubaid do adnacul pectach na drochdaine ann ; a braithre
inmuini hic Crist, facbuid in bar luing cech ní fil ocuib cenmothá
becc n-etuiġ umaib nama." Iar tiachtain im. doibsium for tír pocais
·cach díb a chéle, " Sirid 7 feġaid," ar se, "bruġe parrthais.
Ceileabarthar in teirt leo iar mbein a cluicc, canait atlaiġi buidi
do Dhia 7 a menmana tudmidi ind.

laboriosi peregrini coelestia expectantes, premia o sacro lassi labore
paulisper sustinete. En terram sanctam nullo corruptam sanguine,
ad nullius sepulturam nocentis apertam invenistis ; fratres mei in
Christo, præter indumenta nichil afferatis." Intrantibus vero illis,
omnibus osculatis, " Aspicite," inquit, " terram paradiso similem."
Hora tertia sonante simbalo laudes dicunt divinas fixis in Deum
mentibus.

## ADAMNAN'S LIFE OF ST. COLUMBA.

107. [*LB*. 31 a.] Rogenir Colum cille m*ac* Fedlimid me*ic* Fergusa, a mathair tra Ethne ingen Neic Noee.   Fechtus dósum ic
denam a aicechta ic Gemán conaccatar ingin a ndochum for teichiud
ria n-aroli duniorcnid co torchair in a fadnaise 7 corusmarb in duidlid.
Rofurim C. bréthir n-escaine fair co n-epil fochétoir.

[*LB*. 31 b.] Luid iarum do fógluim ecnai cusin uasal-epscop .i.
co Findén; fechtus ann testa fín on aiffriund.   Bennachais C. in usce
co rosoad hi fín co tartad isin coilech n-aiffrind.

[*LB*. 32 a.] Fecht and foidid-sium a manchu do buain choelaig
i ferund arole óclaig do cúmtach ecl*ai*si.   Rola side isin tal*main* 7
rofás co mba habaid imm Lugnasad iarsin.

[*LB*. 32 a.] Fecht ann dósum i nDoire, dobreth lenam bec-
chuice dia baitsed.   Ni boi t*ra* usce i fochraib do; co tarut-sum sigin

---

107. [*Adamnan*, p. 9.]   Columba nobilibus fuit oriundus genita-
libus patrem habens Fedilmithum filium Ferguso, matrem Ethneam
nomine, cujus pater Latine Filius Navis dici potest, Scotica vero
lingua *Mac Naue* [p. 137].   Cum addiscens apud Gemmanum conver-
saretur accidit ut quidam crudelis filiam fugientem persequeretur, qui
eam super pedis eorûm jugulavit.   C. in ipsum protulit sententiam,
et ille in eadem cecidit horula.

[*Adam*. p. 103.]   Cum apud Vinnianum Episcopum sapientiam
addiscens commaneret, quadam die vinum ad Sacrificii mysterium
minime inveniebatur.   C. aquaticum elementum benedixit, et aqua-
dica natura in vinalem conversa est, et deponit sanctus liquorem
in urceo.

[*Adam*. *L*. 2, *C*. 3.]   Alio in tempore suos misit monachos ut
de alicujus plebei agellulo virgarum fasciculos ad hospitium affer-
rent construendum . . .   Obsequitur prebeius seminando in terra, et
messem in exordio Augusti maturam messuit.

[*Adam*. p. 118.]   Alio in tempore infans ei ad baptizandum
offertur.   In vicinis aqua non insoniebatur locis et proximæ rupis

na crochi darsin carraic bói in a fiadnaise, cor-remuid topar usci esti, 7 cor baitsed in lenam ass iarum.

108. [*LB.* 33 a.]   Laisse mor tanic dosum[1] fechtus in hÍi.   "Tene do nim," ol esium, "tanic innossa for teora cathracha isin Etáil, co rosmarb trí mfle fer cenmotá mná 7 maic 7 ingena.   Tan ann tanic Cainnech uadsom a hÍi.   Dermatis a bachall tair.   In tan doriacht ille fuair a bachall for a chind i fus.   Galar tromm tanic dá thim-thirid-sium, Diarmait a ainm, co n-epil; co nderna-sum ernaigthi leis, 7 co rotódùscad a bás he.   I nDer-maig tuctha ubla serua dosam corusbennach iat comtar millsi.

[*LB.* 32 b.]   Luid C. co Aed Slane co nderna fáitsine dó. Asbert Comgall co ndernad C. hidpairt choirp Crist 7 a fola in a fiadnaise.   Doróine C. umalóit doib imme sin, conid annsin atconnairc Caindech colamain tentide os cind Coluim Cille cein bói icon edpairt.

[*LB.* 33 a.]   Boi aroile duine dia ropritcastar C. co rochreit con a múntir uli don Choimdid.   Roben Demun mac in duine o galar

---

frontem benedixit, de qua consequenter aqua ebulliens fluxit, in qua continuo infantem baptizavit.

108. [*Adam.* p. 56.]   Facies ejus miro superfusa est rubore.   De coelo flamma super civitatem intra Italiæ terminos sitam. effusa est, triaque millia virorum, excepto matrum puerorumque numero, disperierunt.   [*Ad.* p. 129.]   Alio in tempore Cainnichus a portu Ionæ navigare incipiens baculum oblitus est, Ad Oidecham propin-quans baculum ante se invenit.   [*Ad.* p. 144.]   Diormitius ejus minister usque ad mortem ægrotavit, et sanctus pro eo exorans (excitavit eum a morte).   [*Ad.* p. 105.]   Prope Roboris Campum poma benedixit et in dulcedinem versa sunt.

[*Adam.* p. 42.]   Ad Aidum Slane ad se venientem prophetice locutus est.   [*Ad.* 219.]   Hi elegerunt ut C. coram ipsis sacra Eucharistiæ consecraret mysteria ; qui eorum obsecundans jussioni, dum missarum solemnia celebrarentur, Brendenus igneam columnam de vertice Columbæ vidit.

[*Adam.* p. 145.]   Quidam cum tota familia sua, praedicante Columba, credidit.   Ejus filius gravi ægritudine correptus usque ad

---

[1] 'tanic laise mor d'a gnuis,' 33 b, renders the Latin better.

tʰromm, co n-epil de.   Baṭar na gentlide oc ecnach Crist, co nderna C. ernaigthi co Dia, co rothodiuisc in mac a bás.

[*Lis.* 8 a.]   Rogenair isin aidchi-si innocht mac n-uasal n-airmit-nech fiad Dia 7 daine, 7 ˌdoraġa sunn i cinn xxx bleadne, 7 is é foillsiġfes mu liġi-sea 7 toirrnebus mu relec.

---

mortem perductus est.   Magi cœperunt Deo derogare ; et C. precatur Dominum et defunctum erexit.

[*Adam.* p. lxix.]   Hodie, inquit, natus est infans cujus nomen Columba, qui coram Deo et hominibus gloriosus existet, quique post xxx annos abhinc huc veniet, et meum sepulcrum revelabit, et cemiterium designabit.

# INDEX OF WORDS.

adrubrad, indicatum erat, 32.

adubairt, dixit, 21, 28, 38, 81.

æ, salmon, 40.

ægaire, pastor, 49.

æm : nír æm, noluit, 20.

ros-æntaig, dormivit cum ea, 65.

æssi, ætatis, 87.

æsaċ, of the age of, 103.

afrithissi, back, 4.

agad, d. agid, facies, 13, 52.

aicce : -bói a., illa habebat, 86.

áible, np., scintillæ, 84.

aiceċta, gs., addiscendi, 110.

aicen, as., æquora, 107.

aidelcneċaib, dp., pauper, miser, 70, 88.

aiffriund, ds., Sacrificii mysterium, 110.

aige, hospes, g. aiged, d. aigid, np. áigid, dp. aigedaib, hospes, 68, 69, 76, 85.

aigidecht, hospitium, hospitalitas : bói for a., rogata manebat, 20, 76.

aigi alltaige, cervos, 8.

ail, lapis, 57 ; as. ailig, 57.

áil : noċorb a. do, nolebat ; ní hail dam, nolo ; mad a. duit, si vis, dob a. do, rop a. dó, voluit, 3, 9, 81, 95, 97, 105 ; nirb ail leis, non appetebat, 107, 108.

ailgine, lenitatis, 58.

ailit, cervam, 16.

ailithir, pilgrim, 41.

aimsir : in a. gemrid, media bieme, 88.

áine, jejunium, 20, 58, 60.

aingcess, morbum, infirmitatem, dolorem, 48.

ainglecda, angelica, 36.

ainmm, nomen, pl. anmanna, ds. anmaimm ; fo anmaimm, sub typo, 65, 69, 93.

roainmniged, vocatus e., 39 ; ruainmnigthi, vocaretur, 31.

ainmnetaċ, patiens, 88.

airbert bith, conversatio, 100.

aird : for a., to the fore, alive (?), 81.

roairaimed, teneret ; -airamife, accipies ; -airime, acciperis, 38 ; cf. airfemaid.

airccet, argentum, 26.

airċindech, prælatus, papa, episcopus, 36, 49.

airrde, signum, 44, 94.

airdig, erdíg, das., poculum, 9.

airdrenn, siderum, 26.

airecha, prælati, 2.

airechas, ' ordinatio,' 18.

aireċta, concilii, 77.

airegda, amoenus, 107.

airet : an a., while, 18.

airfemaid, accipietis, 27.

airge : locum ubi vaccas mulgere solemus, 59.

airig, np., optimates, 5, 41, 54.

ros-airig, sentiret, 91.

airilliud, meritum, 71, 93 ; also = quod meruit, what one earned and owned, = ' substantia sua,' 3.

roairim, numeravit, 69.

airlegend, relectio, 45.

airm, loco, 76 ; cia a. ubi ?, 25, 76.

rohairmed, dinumeratus e., 86.

airmitnech, np. airmitnig, honorabilis, honorati, 14, 91 ; gloriosus, 112.

airmitnig, honora ; not-airmitnigfe, te honorabit, 81.

airnaigthi, preces, 23.

airnicc : con-a., et invenit ; con-airnechtatatar, invenerunt, 25.

Airte, gs., 50.

aisig, restitutionis, 47.

aislingi, gaf., visio, 101.

aisnefemit, perstringemus, 45.

aisnes, narratio, 100.

aithgne, visio, cognitio, 45.

aithi, gs., ultionis, 9; ns. aithe, gl., talio.

aithigud, acuere, 57.

athise, gp. ar sg., convicia, 99.

aithisiugud, dicere verba dura, 27 ; ic a. increpans, 97, 100.

aithrige, pœnitentiam, 57.

roaithne, commendavit, 38.

aitti, altorem, 48.

aittreb, habitatio, 67.

aittrebthaig, habitatores, aittrebthaide, incolæ, 68, 99.

al-, her, phonetic for a, 68.

alaile, alaili, quidam, quoddam, cæteri, 1, 2, 12, 14, 19, 32.

aláim, his hand, recte ola, 95.

alachta, allachtu, prægnans, 65.

allaid, ferus, 85.

alltaige, feros, 8.

almsaine, *gs.*, eleemosynæ, 75, 82.

alt : cia halt, quisnam, 90.

roalt, nutrivit, crevit, altus e., nutritus e., 27, 48, 68, 87.

roaltatar, nutrierant, 23.

altrum : for a., to be brought up, 33.

am : ropad am cristaide, ero christianus, 81.

amal, as, 12, *et passim.*

aṁlabrai, mutæ, 73.

amlaid sin, tam, 82 ; conid a. sin, ita, 96.

ámm, tempus, 66.

ammus, tentationem, 12, 56 ; for amus, ad, 106.

amra, mirabilis, 65.

amuig, foris, 66.

an, expecta, 82 ; roan, anais, mansit, 4, 30 ; anaid, manet, 107.

anachar : manum-a., si parcas mihi, 53.

roanacht, protexit, 11, 21.

anal, *as.* anáil, sufflatus, 68, 46.

anart, linteamen, 62, 43.

anas, quam, 45.

ánbrachtaige, paralyticæ, 95.

ancride, offensio, 61, 42.

andiarid : co a. turvo oculo, 7.

andgaid, sævus, 12 ; *in L.B.* 29 a, it is angbuid.

aneċtar : fri ... a., outside, ' discesserat,' 91.

anetarcnaid, ignota, 2.

anḟabrachta, anbḟabrachta, paralytica, 76, 78.

anḟaitech, rusticus, 73.

anḟollus, dubium, 89.

aniar : tuc ... aniar, protulit, 70.

animchomét, vita, 80.

anmanna, animal, 98.

-annac : nemannac, indignus, 90.

anndar : a. liumm, sentio, 84.

ánsu-de, the more difficult, ' inde major tribulatio,' 57.

anteirt, *as.*, mane, 17, 52.

anumaloit, superbia, *g.* anhumolloti, 84, 12.

apstulacht, apostolatus, 1.

ar, dixit, ait, 104.

ár, quia, 77, 105.

ár, expugnatio, 7.

arabáraċ in crastinum, sequente die, mane, 47, 57, 102.

araid, anrigam, *d.* aru, 64, 17 ; araideċt, charioteering, 56.

aráide, araide, tamen, sed, 47, 52, 73, 86, 87, 90.

araile, quidam, cujusdam, una e duabus, aut pluribus, 65, 67, 72, 83.

araill, aliud, 82.

árasc, verbum, proverbium, 27.

arathra, arathru ; aratra, 79.

arba, panis, *gs.*, 72.

arbíad, quod venturum esset, 9.

archind : nobith a., antequam essent, 2.

árdraig, r'ardraig, comparuit, apparuit, 8, 46 ; roartraig, 67, 80.

noárdraigtis, apparebant, 47.

ardsollamuin, festivitas, 5.

ari, exequias peragere, 18.

arm : cen a. inermis, 89 ; fon armaib, armati, 23.

armċrith, commotio, 7.

armgaisciud, *ds.* fón armgaisced, hastati et scutati, 22, 95.

aro-áis nách ar éicin, = aut voluntate aut vi, *i.e.* ullo modo, 35.

aroerachair, aroirachair, venit in, tenuit, 28, 38 ; arroerachair, et tenuit, 28.

aroli, cujusdam, 59.

arracht : dá a., duo simulacra, arrachta nan ídal, deos, 52, 2 ; *gp.* arracht, idulorum, 58.

arrad : it a., tecum, 11.

arranic, et invenit, 30.

arroet, accepit, assumpsit, acceperat, 18, 41, 42, 50, 59.

arroétatar, acceperunt, susceperunt, 13, 27.

aridféimḟed, susciperet, 2.

arsaid, senectute, 26.

roarsatar, arabant, 79.

arthiur, *ds̄.*, anterior pars, 2.

asaid, ' crevit,' 53 ; roás, maturescere coepit, 79.

ascaid : dá a., *ap.* ascada, donativum, munera, 81, 89, 108.

roaslag, instigavit, 3.

aspert, dixit, 103.

asráraráćtatar, revixerunt, 15.

assil, particulas, 69.

noastfad, retineret, 59 ; astud, retentio, 36.

at, es, 74.

ata, constat, 67 ; ataam, sumus, 57 ; atáitt, videntur, 52.

atać, *d.* atuć, petere, orare, 66, 86.

roatachset, rogarunt, 60.

no-ataifed, eum incenderet, 5.

atacomnaic, was, 59.

atar : a. lium, sentio, 84.

atareét, perrexit, 74.

atbail, mortuus e., 61.

atbath, mortuus, defunctus e., 23, 24, 32, 56.

atbera, atbere, dicis, 73, 89.

atberad, atbered, dicebat, 60, 96.

atberar, redditur, 51.

atberat, dicunt, 28.

atbert, roatbert, dixit, 62, 65.

atbertsat, dixerunt, locutæ s., 72, 83.

atbertis, dicebant, 92.

atchíu, atcíu, atchím, aspicio, video, 74, 86 ; 102 ; atchí, videt, atćiam, videmus, atchíthe, ostensæ s., 8, 9, 60 ; atćíd, videt, 97, 102 ; atćítea, videbatur, 97.

atclos, was heard, 104.

atcobraim, volo, 26.

atćonnairc, atconnairc, itćonnairc, vidit, prospexit, 32, 59, 69, 93 ; atconnairc, 101.

atćonnarcis, vidisti, 80, 107.

atconncatar, viderunt, 67, 107.

atćuaid, narravit, 69 ; atćotar, revelarunt, 62.

atfét, ait, refert, 15, 65 ; atfes, dictum e., 53.

áth, a ford, 38.

athaba, *as.*, elleborum, 91.

athardai, patriam, 60.

nóathcumad, laniabat, 95.

athigid, frequentare, 92.

athiusc, petitionem, 63 ; dictum, 107.

roathne, non sivit, 22.

rohathnuiged, restoratum e., 74.

athrige, pœnitentia, 85.

atlugud, *g.* atlaigthe (buidi), actio gratiarum, 10, 23, 60, 82.

atnói, illum commendat, 33.

atraćt, surrexit, apparuit, 59, 67, 71, 76, 91 ; = tuargaib, 79.

atraraćt, surrexit, inruit, 6, 12, 48.

atregut, 'surrexerunt,' surgunt, 62.

atrubairt, dixit, 46, 62 ; ótrubairt, his dictis, 4.

atrubart, obtulit, 54.

att, tumor, inflata cutis, 77, 98.

atúsa, atussa, sum, habito, 56, 75.

au, *ap.*, nepotes, 42.

auctair, inventores, 2.

aurnaigthi, oratione, 92.

ba, eram, 60.

baćall, *gf.* baćla, baculus, 52, 111.

bachlać, rusticus, 85.

bæth, foolish, opposed to cundla, 88.

bagbaitis, invenerunt, videbant, 70, 71.

robáided, rosbaided, absorptus e., 5, 83 ; baidfither, extinguetur, manidbaither, nisi extinctus fuerit, 5.

bailiu, *ds.*, locus, 3.

baindsi, nuptiarum, 59.

bainne, *gs.*, lac, 103.

baintrebthaig, 'virginem religiosam,' 86.

bairgin, panes, *dual,* 78.

baisti, *gsf.*, baptismatis, 45.

robaist, baptizavit, 78, 102.

rombaisti, eum baptizavit, 21.

baistter, baister, baptisatur, 20, 21.

robaisted, robaisteth, baptizatus e., 77, 55.

robaithis, robathiss, baptizavit, 33, 35, 43 ; rombaithis, eum baptizavit, 33, 41.

robaitsi, baptizavit, 28, 32, 39, 50 ; rombaitsi, eum baptizavit, 51 ; rosbaitsi, rosbathis, eos baptizavit, 33, 41.

baitsed, baptizabat, 37.

robaitsed, baptizatus e., 70, 91, 111.

robaitside, baptizati s., 13.

baitsed, baitsiud, *ds.* baptizare, 44, 110.

bam, essem, sim, 90.

banairchinneċ, domina, abbatissa, 76.

banċuire, mulieres, feminarum turba, 43.

banne, banda, aqua, guttula, 45, 80, 85.

Bandæ, ġsf., 34.

bannscal, as. banscail, femina, 68, 69, 75.

baraind, as., displeasure, quia 'inique gessi,' 39.

barbárdu, barbaros, 89.

bas, sis, eris, 56.

básaib, mortibus, 89 ; macc báis, impius, 12, opposed to macc bethad, elect us.

bat, sit, 56.

bebuil, ignominia, 8.

becán, modicum, 78.

béim, ictus, 90.

belaib : ar b., juxta, videntibus, in conspectu, coram ; ar mu b., coram me, 6, 9, 10, 11, 74.

belut, a pass = belaċ, 35.

benaid, amputat, strikes off, 104 ; roben, fregit, percussit, incendit (excudit ignem) ; rusben, offendi eum, 46, 5, 60, 98.

robenad, percussus e., correptus e., 84, 91 ; coepit urgeri, 98 ; iar bein, sonato, 109.

robendaċ, benedixit ; rombendaċ, eum benedixit, rosb. eos benedixit ; rotbendaċ, 9, 40, 54, 30, 8, 10 ; robendaċ do, benedixit, 34.

bennaċad dó, eum salutare, 80; oc b., benedicens, 55.

benneċais, benedixit, 86, 110.

robennaċsat, glorificaverunt, 69.

bendaċtha, benedictus, 24.

beo, ero, sim, 81.

beo : cein mbeosa, as long as I live, 35.

beo, vivus, 106 ; ap. beu, 45.

beos, hucusque, 20, 104 ; béus, adhuc, 52 ; béous, usque hodie, 106.

béolu, ore, 32 ; fri b. mara, in sinu maris, 33.

nusbeir leis, adduxit secum, 55.

béraid, pariet, 65.

nobertha, differebatur, 93.

Berba, ġsf., 83.

berbad, coquere, 69.

bernais, bernas, das., a gap, 34.

romberr, eum totondit, 27, 51.

bés, disciplinam, 91 ; beus gnáthaċ, consueto more, 67.

béscna, mos, béscnai, regulam, 2, 13.

beth : ara mb. ut sit; conach b. ut non sit, nab., esset, 16, 78, 93.

beitit erunt, 31 ; nobeitis, (quod) essent, 54.

bethaid, vitam ; maicc bethad, electi, 93, 39.

-rabi, erat, 3, 52.

noco bía, non erit, noco bíat, non erunt, 21, 106.

bican, paulisper, 109.

bice, ġsf., parvæ, 42.

bíid, bith, cibi, alimenti, 45, 55, 83.

bid, erat, esset, 92, 93 ; nobit, qui erat, 54, bith, esse, 49.

bile, d. biliu, arbor, 30, 35.

bís, qui est, 90.

bíssi, crusta (glaciei), 46.

tre bíthu, tre bithu betha, semper, in sæcula, in sempiternum, in æternum, 2, 4, 21, 29.

bíu, vita, 22.

blaistí, gustaveritis, 27.

blegan, blegon, blegun, mulgere, 59, 67, 68, 86.

bliċt : b6 b., milch-cow, 'vacca,' 103.

nobliged, emulgebat, robliged, mulsit, robligis, mulsisti, 22, 70, 86 ; bligthe, mulgebatur, 103.

bléin, asf., inguen, 97.

bloga, fragmenta, 73.

a bobba ! my master ! 56.

bocc, hircus, a. pocc, g. buicc, 54, 84, 85.

boin, ds., vaca, 83.

bolo(d)mairib, dp. fragrant (?), 18.

bonnaigib, soles of feet, 84.

borrfad, tumor, 77.

braich, cerevisiam, g. bracha, 72.

brat, g. broitt, chlamys, habitus, 88.

brath, betrayal, 99.

brathre, ap., fratres, 86.

brattana, magni pisces, 21.

bréccud, deceptio, 12.

brécsith, feigned peace, ' finxit,' 7.

Brectain, *ns.*, 51.

breith, nativitas, 67.

breith, *ds.*, to bear, 19.

breithem, judex, 18.

bréntaid, *d.*, foetor, 97.

bri n-, *as.*, hill (?), 39.

robris, fractum e., it broke, 80; robristis, frangebant, 93.

Britt, Britto genere, 56.

brond, *gs.*; broind, *d.*, venter, *dp.* brondaib, 96, 41, 54.

brosna, *np.*, nutrimenta ignis, 46.

brugaid, dives, 102.

bruge, *ap.*, terram, 109.

bruith, coquere, 69.

bú, vaccas, 70.

buaid, victoriam, 81.

buaid laec, 'principes digni,' 24.

buaile, cow-house (?), 47.

buain, metere, messis, 79, 85 ; caedere, 110.

budi, *gs.*, gratiarum, 83.

rombui : cid r. an ingen, causa (suæ nauseæ), 68.

buidne, choros, 104.

bunudus, natio, 59.

bunnsacaib, radiis, 82.


cabair, protegere, 67.

cacha, quidquid, 71.

cadet, quæ ? 9.

cádus, veneratio, 88.

nochaifed, fleret, 20; ic cai, flens, 103.

cailech, calicem, *d.* cailiuch, *gp.* cailech, 20, 29, 84.

caille, *nags.*, pallium, velamen, vestis, 25, 26, 71.

caillech, o ch. ! puella, virgo, 72, 81.

caillid, *das.*, sylva, 85, 97.

rochain, planxit, 48.

cáined, lugebat, 99.

cáined, fletus, lugere, plangere ; ic cáiniud, tristis, 44, 91, 106 ; cainti, ululationis, 27.

caingin, ' quæstionem,' 77.

caintib, præconibus = druthaib, 55.

cainuairrech, benignus, cainuaraige, benignitatem, 87, 58.

cairdes, *as.*, foedus, 22.

cairich, cairig, ovem, *dp.*, cairib, 47.

rochairigestar, increpabat, 47; cairigiud, increpatio, 104.

cait, cáitt, ubi, 76, 96, 106.

rocaithset, manducaverunt, 69.

can, unde ; can duibsi ? who or whence are you ? 25, 57.

nochanad, canebat, 63 ; canait, dicunt, 109.

cannadus, *as.*, pannus, *bis*, 67.

canone, *gsf.*, canon of Scripture, 105.

Caplait, *ds.*, Coena Domini, 72.

car, ama ; notcarfa, te amabit ; carais, dilexit, -rocarad, amaret, 81, 57, 78.

cara, amicus, 66.

carput, *d.*, plaustrum, 106.

carrac, rupes, 92 ; *da.* carraic, 99, 111.

carreni, *ds.*, plaustrum, 19.

casal, *gsf.*, na caslea, casula, 11.

Cásc., *gsf.*, Paschæ, 71.

cath, *g.* catha, *gp.* cath, bellum, 19, 82, 86.

cathaib : etir na c., ante aciem, 89.

cathaca, consistentes in bello, 22.

cathaigthe, pugnandi, 89.

cathair, cathedram, 39 ; *dp.* cathairib, 100.

cathair, *ns.*, cathrach, *gs.*, urbs, civitas, 39, 96 ; *das.* cathraig, 96 ; *ap.* cathraca, 111.

ce, si, 49.

cech : c. da bliadain, versa vice in alternos annos, 11.

cedaigis, licentiam dedit, 105.

ceirdd, *gs.*, = dana : æs ceirdd, præcones, 55.

ceist, quæstio, 77.

celebrad, *g.* celebartha, celebratio, 76, 84.

noceilebradad, celebrabat, 28.

roceilebráiset dó, dimiserunt eum in pace, 4.

celebarthai, celebrabatur, 5.

doceltatar, non revelarunt, 56.

cenco, sive, 72.

cenel, *g.* ceneóil, ceniúil, 40, 44.

cend : dara c., for her sake, 71.

cend : cor dar c., evertere, 94 ; rolaud dar c., dirutum e., 95.

cend : ar c., ad ; toet ar a c., ivit ad eam ; for a ćiund ; for cend ćonnaid; for wood, 53, 71, 77, 42, 97 ; cind, *ds.*, vertex, summitas, 71, 83 ; cinn : ar a ch., in adventu ejus, ad adventum ejus, ante se, juxta viam ; for a ćind, ante se, 6, 8, 22, 18, 13, 111 ; i cind, post, 112. arcind : isin aidche a., nocte insequente, 88 ; ciunn : ar a ć., before him, = ar a ćinn, 'ante se,' 41, 42.

cenmotá, exceptis, 111.

cennać, emere ; roćendać, roćendaig, emit, 65, 92, 20, 49, 59.

cendgaid, emitis = emis, 71.

cenglaid, 'obnituntur,' 85.

Cheinndán, Chennindán, 40.

cendsai, *as.*, mansuetudo, 58 ; cennais, placida, 99. .

Cenuerbe = Cenn Cruach, 52 ; *g.* Chinn Chruaig, 56.

rocess, roćessair, loboravit, passus e., 20, 97.

cesta, passionis, 93.

cessairi, *gf.*, grando ; cessairgalar, pestis grandinis, 99.

ceta : cetaroćreit, primus credidit, 63.

noćetfanad : an n., sentiens, 48.

cetlaib, psalmis, 18.

cetmad, centesimo, 33.

cethar-threib, *ds.*, quatuor domibus, 20.

cetheor, four, 10.

cethrai, *ds.*, pecoribus, 19.

cethrochoir, cethraćoiri, quadrata ; *ap.* cethroćairi, cethraćori, 32, 24, 30, 42.

cethraćtaib, *dp.*, forties, 42.

rochí, flevit, lacrymatus e., 45, 102 ; roćíset, flevere, 48 ; cíis, fudit lacrymas, 107.

cia, si, 25.

cia can, ubi, 25.

cian : nirbo c. iarsin, non multo post, 68 ; ni c. non longe, 106.

ciana, per multos dies, 56 ; fri ré c. multis diebus, 4.

ciartha, waxed, 107.

cíće, mamillas, 101.

cid, quid, 62, 97.

cid, si sit, etsi, 13.

cid . . no, whether . . or, 16.

cilic, *ds.*, camellorum setis, 93.

cimmid, *g.* cimmeda, vinctus, 80, 84.

noćinged, descendebat, 16.

cinnu, *ap.*, capita, 52.

cipe inad, ubicumque, 106.

císa, *gs.*, census, 49.

roćlaid, fodivit, 29 ; oc claide, facientes fossam, 14.

claideb, *ap.* claidbiu, gladius, 30, 70.

clam, leprosus, 70, 76, 82.

claimi, clami, *ds.*, lepra, 72, 84.

clár, tabulam, 50.

clair-eineć, clarenech, tabulatam faciem habens, 44, 86.

noćlećtatar, solebant, 59.

cleirćiu, clericos, 37, 51.

clesrad, ludendi artes, 85.

clí, *as.*, a stake ; saidis clí, castrametatus e., 40, 33.

cliar, a company, 55.

clíi, laevam, 93 ; clíu, sinistro, 52.

cloćtha, lapideus, 23.

do-ćluined, audiebat, noćluintís, audiebant, roćuala, roćualai, -cuala, audivit, 9, 97, 14, 37, 45 ; raćualatar, audierunt, ótćuolatar, audientes, 23, 68 ; rusclo, audivit ; roclos, audita e., 65, 68 ; cloistećt, audire, 107.

clú, fama, 74, 105.

clud, *ds.*, sepulcro, 22.

cluithiu, *ds.*, ludus, 46 ; *recte* cluichiu.

clumuib, *dp.*, pluma, 108.

nocnited : an-n., suspirans, 4.

cnama, ossa, 56, 64.

co, at : co maigin itá = dú hitá, 35.

con, et, 1, 3, 3, 4, 6, 6, 7, 7, 12, 60, 62, 84, 85, *et passim* ; co tarfas, et visum e., co n-epair, con-erbairt, dicens, co facca, et vidit.

cobluch, *ds.*, navigatio, 37.

cobsaid, firm, 15.

coćall, *as.*, 82.

coccad, pugna, 82.

codail, .1. croicionn, 14.

coelaig, *gs.*, virgarum fasciculus, 110.

coemnactar, potuerunt, 30 ; ni coem- nestar, non possent, 100.

coggarar, vocatur, vocetur ('vocabitur'); roćoggair, vocavit, 6, 7.

cói, fletus, 27.

coibligi, *d.*, matrimonium, 101.

coibnesam, proximorum, 58.

coibsena *ap.*, confessionem, 84.

coic, coquum, 95.

coiced, unam, one of five, 69.

coidći, semper, 102.

coileć, urceus, 110.

coillidi, sylvestre, 63.

Coimded, Domini : in Ch. always with the article, 18.

coimdeta, dominicalis, of the Lord, 94.

roćoimet, reservavit, roćometsat, custo- dierunt, 19 ; cometai, servas, 88, 74 ; rocoimetad, custoditus e., was imprisoned, 81.

coimitećt : na c., apud eum ; coimtećt : i c. indrig, in the house of the king, 75, 66, 78.

cóimnacuir, potuit, 17.

coimpert, *asf.*, partus, 66 ; roćoimprestar, concepit, 77.

coimsam : co c., ut possimus, 27.

cóine, *as.*, ululatus et ploratus, 27.

coire, æneus, 15.

coirmm, cerevisia, 73 ; coenam, 72 ; cuirm, 72.

coisecrad, consecratio, 77.

coisecartha, benedictus, 95.

coitćenn, the convent, 82.

coitsećt ; i c., audiens, 37.

colléic, paulisper, 72.

columna, coloma ; columna, globus (ignis), 66, 71 ; *as.*, colomain, 111.

comadais, congruous, proper, 71.

roćomaicsig, venit ad, appropinquavit, rocomaigsegestar, appropinquavit, 52, 71, 4, 38.

coracomailled, ut impleret ; rocomailled, rócomalled, completum e. ; comaill- fider, implebitur, 3, 68, 89, 68.

comainsem, contemptio, 58.

comairli, consilium, 105.

comairsed : mar nach c. olc friu, tan- quam si nihil mali paterentur, 47.

comaistiu, *ap.*, æquales, 46.

comaithgiu, 'aliam gentem,' bordering tribes, 86.

comaltram, joint nursing, 102.

comaltuḋ, æquales, 45.

comámus : i c. with (?), 65.

comardugud, memoria, 52.

roćomarleicestar, permisit, rocomarleged, permissum e., 12, 90.

comarnic fri, invenit, 57.

combaig, *das.*, certamen, 19, 36.

combair, combir, *gs.*, 41, 42.

comdál, conventus, 76.

rocomécniged, cogebatur, 92.

comeirgi, *d.* comeirgiu, inruere, plaga, 7.

comfoćroib, comfocraib, near, i c., non procul, 15, 85, 73, 108.

comfocus, proximus, 46, 94 ; i c., non procul, non longe, 73, 93.

comfoigsig, *np.*, viciṇi, 67.

roćomfocsig, roćomfoicsećestar, roćo- mocsegestar, appropinquavit, 18, 59.

comfuilidećt, consanguinitas, 38.

commainn, communionem, 18.

commam, conjux, 48.

commílethaib, commilitonibus, 88.

comnestai, cognati, 48.

comól : c. fris, confligere adversus (?), (scarcely, to challenge him to drink), 9.

comraiced fri, tetigisset ; comraicfed fri, inveniret, 68, 56.

comrair, capsam, 50.

comrorcu, error ; *as.* comrorcain, 49, 93.

comśoḋ, convertere, 1.

comtar, so that they were, 111.

comtha, fer c., socius, unus ex nobis, 9, 13 ; fer cúmtha, sodalis, frater, 59, 84.

comus, potestas, 'terminus' potestatis, 94, 39.

conaccaib, et posuit ; conacaib, fundavit, 33, 34.

conacca, conaccai, vidit, conusacca, eos vidit, 57, 67, 95 ; conaicet, conac- catar, viderunt, 106, 107.

cuilne, *gs.*, coquina, 76.

cuimling, contentionis, 19.

cuimse, sufficiens, 53.

cuin, quandonam? 66.

-chunćimm, -ćunnćimm, quæro, 81 ; cuinćid, quærere, petere, 49, 55, 71, 82; roćuingis, desiderasti, 107.

rocuired forcula, reversus e., 85 ; rocuirtha, collocati sunt, 59 ; cuirther, mittitur, 107.

cuitechtai, *ap.*, hospites transeuntes, 12 ; na cuitećta, *ap.*, omnes ambulantes per loca, 80 ; *d.* cuidećta, comitatus, 104.

cúl ; iarna c., post tergum, 90.

culći, tunica pellicea, 63.

culid, *as.*, penu, 70.

cumaćta, potestatem, 95 ; cumaćtać, potens, 101.

cumaid, simul, uná (bibere, cibum capere) ; 59, 87 ; *or* cumaid, bene?

cumaing ; nír ć., non potuit, 104 ; ćumcaim, cumgaim, cuimgim ; ní, nocha ć. *or* c., non possum, 9, 10, 74, 81 ; -cumcad, potuit, posset, 95, 97 ; ćumgaidsit, 'potestis'; co coimsam, ut possimus, 27.

cumdaćta, honorata fuerat (?), 25.

cúmdaćta, facturæ mirabilis, excelsus, sublimis, 73, 100.

cumgi, *d.*, tentatio, 90.

rocumscaiged, motus e., 99.

cumsanud, sopor, 39.

cúmtać, ædificare, constructio, roćumtaig, erexit, cumtaćta, fabricatum, 51, 52, 110 ; cumduiġter, ædificantur, 105.

cumung, power, 71.

cungeuin, 'faciem,' cognovit, 32.

noćungnad frie, ' apud eam fuerat,' was helping, 59.

cunnail 'sententiæ sanioris,' sanior, dignus; *pl.* cundla, quibus mens sanior, 92, 88, 110.

cunnrad, venditio etemptio, 71.

cunntabairtaige, dubitas, 97.

cúra, ovis, 78.

curuć, *ds.*, navis, 13.

Currać, *ds.*, the Curragh, 82.

dæs, was eaten (?), (54).

dæthin, 'quotidianum victum,' sufficiency, 88.

dafarraid, overtook, seized him, 1, 36, 50.

dail, *ns.*, meeting, 48.

Dail (Araidi, Riata), *ds.*, 34, 40.

dall, cæcus, 86.

dalta, alumpnus, 102.

dambér, eum portabo, 27.

damu, boves, 79.

dán, munus, 75, ars, 92.

-dara, unus, uni, uná, one of two, the first, 82, 83, 90, 92.

dara n-, alteram, 27.

dara, daro, of an oak, 38, 39.

daroćaill : co nd. till he broke it (?), 44.

daridisi, again, 9.

dásacht, dementia, 92.

dásachtach, energumena, insanus, 76, 80 ; dásachtaigi, vesanam (vesaniam), 48.

dástaigther, vesana fit, 47 ; read dás(ach)taigther (?).

de, fumus, 74 ; *as.* diaid, 97.

deabaid, rixa, 75.

rodecai, vidit, 3.

decha, eas, 60 ; -dechaid, ivit, 3 ; dechatar, iverunt, 7, 19 ; -dechais, iveris, 6, 90 ; -dechsat, irent, 76 ; deaćadais, ivisti, 108.

déchain, dechon, deochain, diaconus, 21, 28, 89.

dechruth, deformis, dochruth, tetra, 74.

decleithi, good roof (?), 40.

dedenach, ultimus, 57.

dedoil, ón d., diluculo, 8.

deg, certe, 10.

degaid : inna d., eam insequentibus, 85.

deicsiu, intueri, 74.

deimess, *as.*, biceps, scissors, 27.

deinmnećaig, indignati, impatient, 72.

deired, finis, 39.

deisciurt, 38.

deisell, 'cito,' right about (?), 4.

delbe, figuræ hominis, 83 ; *d.* deilb, forma, 97.

delrad, 'potestas,' brightness, 97.

demin leo, non dubitabant, 94.

demon, demun ; dæmon, zabulus, 90 ;
  demna, energumenos, 93.
dena, fac, 13, 49, 84 ; -denaim, facio,
  84 ; denam, faciamus, 9 ; -dentais,
  faciebant, 58 ; denum, parare ; dentar, fiat, 106 ; cu naċ derntar, ut
  non fiat, 105.
déniu rád, dicto citius, statim, 10, 46,
  61, 84.
-denus : tre-denus, 107.
deochus, adiero, 63.
derbċlann, progenies, 38.
derfiur, germana, 37.
derg, candens, 95.
-dergeni, fecit, 54.
-derna fecit, fecit, 57, 58, 111, -dernai,
  55.
-dernad, fecit, 6, 69, faceret, 85, 111.
-dernasat, fecerunt, 14.
dermair, immanis, 98.
dermatis, oblitus e., 111.
dernanda, manus, 57.
deroil, vilis, despectus, humilior, 77, 90.
derrit, remotior, 90.
derscaigtheċ, distinguished, 108.
deisiḋ, sedit, 67 ; destitar, sederunt, 25 ;
  dessid, stetit, 97.
di : ba di Bretnaib di, Britonissa erat, 37.
dia, gs. diei, 17, 84.
diaid : imdiaid, post me, 39.
diberca, 12.
díblinaib, 35, 36.
diċeltair, quod demit ab oculis, 8.
dícend : att d., headless, endless swell-
  ing (?), 98 ; sudden, RC. xii., 157.
diċennad, decapitatio, 105.
díchitel, invocatio, incantatio, 10.
-dichlend, celat, 54.
ro-díċuired, absolutus e., 93.
nomdídnife, me securum faciet, 89.
didiu, didu, itaque, 12, 18, 20.
-digen, faciam, 56.
dig, potum, 78.
-digi, eas, 20 ; -digsed, digsith, eat. iret,
  veniret, 31, 47, 77, 81, 90 ; co ndigsed as, ut discederet, 95.
dí-guind, non-rarus, 61, 15 ; LB. 202 a.
dígbas, diminuit, 22 = airdigbann, O'D.
  Supp.

dí̃is, as., two, 62.
díles, diless, proprius, 21, 38, 92 ; dilis,
  propria, ' immolatum e.,' 38, 23.
dilsiugud, g. dilsigthe, donatio (perpetua,
  in æternum), 81.
dilgud, ignoscere, 100.
dilmain : nírbo d., non licebat, 92.
dimmdach, ingratus, 83.
dimoir, nimiam, 79.
dingbala, digna, 92.
-díngen, faciam, 11.
disciri, instabiles, 19.
dithrub, ds., deserto, convallis, 20, 31.
díucaire : ic d., orans, 68, 88 ; crying,
  103.
diud : indiud lai, ante prandium, 16.
díulái, in principio noctis, in prima vigilia noctis, 80 ; read díud lái.
rodíult, negabat, 77.
díumsach, superbus, 83.
dlighthidi, legitimum, 22 ; df. dligtig (?),
  legitimus, 101.
dluthi, densas, 23.
dó, sibi, 91.
dó : fecht and dó, quadam die erat, 86,
  84 ; do C. a mathair, de C. erat
  mater illius, 67.
do : mog do mogadaib, unus servorum,
  81.
do : bid maith do, oportebat, 66.
doadċuired, revertebat, 46.
dobér, inducam, 9.
dobéra, mittet, 73.
doberad, daret, 86 ; dobered, dabat,
  ponebat, 63, 70, 88 ; dodmberad,
  id dictaret .ı. daret, 2 ; dosberad,
  id dabat, 81 ; dobéraind, darem,
  71 ; dobertha, dedisses, 80 ; dobérthar, dabitur, 11, 81, 82 ; dobertis,
  asportabant, 48.
doberur, elevetur, 21.
dobreth, dedit, attulit, 20, 64.
dobreth, oblatus e., 110 ; dobretha, data
  s., 43.
dosbeir, eum dat, sprinkles it, 62.
docifer, videbitur, 26.
doconnuic, erat, 64.
doċraid, docraid, doċruth, deformis,
  despicabilis, tetra, 92, 88, 74.

doċuadus, ivi, 85 ; doċóid, dochuaid, venit, ivit, 56, 64, 69 ; doċuatar, docotar, iverunt, 108.

docuirether, occurrit, 55.

dodeċaid, dodeċuid, dodeoċaid,· dodechoid, venit, ivit, 6, 8, 21, 32, 40, 54 ; dondeċuid, venit ad eum, 53.

dodeċabair, venistis, 25.

dodeċator, dodeċotar, dodeċatar, dodeċutar, venerunt, perrexerunt, 5, 2, 23, 43, 58, 65, 95.

dodeċus : d. uadaib, miserunt nuntios, 58.

dodelbda, deformis, 92.

dóenai, humana, 58.

dofairċeċnatar, prophetabant, 2.

dofanic, inruit, 15.

dofreccair, respondit, 26.

dofucsat, abstraxerunt, exerunt, 13, 24.

dofuisim, 'effunditur,' 44.

dofuit, cecidit, 83.

dof̓ulaċta, 'valde,' unbearable.

dogebthar, invenitur, 26.

dogén, faciam, 76.

dogenam, faciemus, 10, 26, 73, 78.

dogenath, faciat, 9.

dogeni, rogní, fecit, 57, 100.

dogéntar, fiet, 6, 11, 78 ; dogníther, fit, 108.

dogné, tentaveris, 90.

dogneth, faciat, faceret, 89.

dognethea, agebatur, ageretur, 94.

dogníd, faciebat, fecit, 19, 23, 63, 87.

dogníth, faciebat, 24, 69.

dogníset, egerunt, 10.

dogrés, semper, 87, 100.

dogui-si, eligis, 53.

doig leis, putabat, credidit, 69,73,86,93.

doilig, 'maximam,' difficult, 77.

doirtea, was shed, 109.

dolléced, dejectus e., 53.

dolluid, doluid, venit, ivit, 39, 67.

rodolpset, finxerunt (?), 12 ; doilbed, 96.

doromailt, in cibum sumpsit, 91.

domnaig : aitche d., dominicæ noctis, 17.

donair, fecerit, egerit, 35.

dootar, devoraverunt, 56.

doraid, dixit, 80.

dorairbert, 'vertit,' evertit, 52.

dorairngert, promisit, 51.

dorairngred, was promised, 3.

doraitne, refulsit, 10.

dorala, venit, accidit, contigit, occurrit, obviam fuit, 5, 49, 57, 66, 72, 76, 86, 88.

doratus, dedi, 71 ; doratais, donasti, 83 ; dorat, dedit, distribuit, largitus est, erogavit, intulit, 8, 38, 51, 61, 89, 95 ; dosrat, posuit illas, 27 ; dorath, datum e., 18 ; doratad, datus e., was told off, 90 ; dati, 92 ; doratsat, immolaverunt, dederunt, 30, 13 ; dorattad, daret, 49.

dorcha, atrocem, 93.

dorchai, tenebras, 10.

doréll, ivit, incepit, 6.

doreprensat, profluxerunt, 45.

dorigensat, fecerunt, 27.

dorigni, dorigne, doríne, fecit, egit, 37, 56, 82, 85, 79.

dorigne, fecisti, 61 ; dorigned, factus e., 19, 77, 84.

dorinscan, cœpit, 18.

doriucart, doriugart, dixit, clamavit, 7.

doroaċt do, tenuit (portum), 50.

doroċaid, exegit, 13.

dorochar, cecidi, 60 ; dorochair, cecidit, 9, 46, 73.

dorodiusaig, doroithiusaig, don(d)iusaig (excitavit eum), suscitavit, 32, 44, 39 ; dorodiuscad, suscitatus e., 13, 56.

dorogart, invocavit, vocavit, invitavit, dixit, 10, 14, 66, 84, 96.

dorogní, 23 ; doroine, 71 ; doronai, 23, 30, 58 ; dorone, fecit, 49 ; doronsat, egerunt, 75.

doroiscfed, superaret, excelleret, 66.

dororaind, indicavit, 33.

dorothlaig, petivit, postulavit, 69, 45 ; 3 pl. dorothlaiċset, 27.

doruacht, pervenit, 50.

ḍoruimenatar, estimaverunt, 25.

dorus : a nd. i nd., ante januam, ad portam, in porta, 64, 81, 88 ; doirrsib, 8.

dosnailgi, puts them (?), 'præcepit ut dormirent,' 53 ; = dosrat, 27.

dothæt, dothoet, venit, 69, 70.

dothinoil, collegit in unum, 89.

dothaig, 'portavit' (?), gathers up (?), 74, = do-d-aig, brings it (?).

dóu, dou, ei, 27, 57.

draí, magus, 66, 67.

dreić, fronte, 60.

Drobés, d. Drobéiss, 40.

droćairilliud, scelus, 93.

drolmać, as. drolṁuiġ, vas, vas ligneum apertum, 64, 73, 80.

dromlach, vas, 80.

dromma, dorsos; drommo, dorsi, 39, 42.

dronglach, vas ligneum, 73, 80.

drúi, drui, magus, 9, 11, 27, 70; g. druad, 11, 65; as. druid, 61; np. druid, 5, 23; ap. druide, 2.

druidechta, gs., magic art, 4.

druim dar druim, 'super latus suum,' 80.

drumman, dorsorum, 40.

druthaib, præconibus, 55.

dú, locum, 14.

-duadus, comédi, 85.

Dub, d. Duib, 40, 33.

dubaib, dp., niger, 32.

an-duesta, quod deesset, 31.

dúidecht, ductum (?), 8, read drúidecht?

duidlid, crudelis (?), 110.

dúine, civitatis, 81.

dula, ire, 107.

dumi, gs., dumu, ds., a mound, 29, 38.

dunaid, domus, gs., 64.

duniorcnid, murderer, 110.

dús in, donec, 83.

duthair, turpis, 77.

duthraccur, volo, (velim?); duthracair, voluit, concupivit, 82, 87, 72.

conas-ebi, ut bibat, conus-ebem, ut id bibamus, 59.

ebre : con e. mo aithiusc, et nuntia verba mea, 63.

eccaib : do e. mori, iarna e. post mortem ejus, 48, 82.

-ecid, éicid, indicavit, 3, 42.

roecsat, fuerunt erectæ, 30.

euć, ds., echu, ap., equus, 16, 85.

Eću, g. Ećać, a. Ećaić, 41.

eclas, gp., eclasa, ap., ceila, ecclesia, 58, 105.

ecmaing, it happened, 105.

écmais : ina hé. illa absente; an é. na mná, absente uxore, 17, 79, 103.

écnać, blasphemia, derogare, 61, 112; égnać, 105.

ecnai, gs., sapientia, 110.

ecosc, 'videbatur,' 'habitus,' 88, 97.

écraibdeć, eccraibdeć, impius, 12, 61.

edarguidi, etarguide, precem, oratio, 12, 92.

edbairt, immolatio, 24, 39; edpairt, as., Missa, 111.

roedbart, roedbairt, immolavit, 24, 37; roedbairset, obtulerunt, 38; roedbrad, rohedbrad, oblatus e., 39, 42, 27.

nohédithe, vestiebantur, 93; étiud, 98.

eg, gp., ega, gs., glacies, 46.

éirdergud, vestitum, 'propositum' (?), 92.

eirg, eirgg, vade, revertere, 18, 106.

eirig, surge, 48, 76; eirsed assurgeret, 6, roéirig, surrexit; eirges, surgit, 101, 106.

éithiuć, ds., perjurium, 54.

éla, declina, 80; élaid, evadit, 83; élait, 'evaserint,' 10; d'élud, proficisci, 90; eulais, he went, 14.

roelnitís, violarentur, 89.

Elpa no Alba, Scotland, 65.

elscothać, avidus, 69.

elte, dammulas, 22.

ém, tamen, 39.

eneć, facies, 86.

engać, procax, 6.

énlaithib, avibus, 32.

enmne, patientia, 58.

eoćair, clavis, 14, 76.

eóin, gs., avis, 20.

eolaig, np., periti, 45.

-epil, mortuus e., 111, 112.

epscopoti, gas., episcopatus, 13, 92.

eptha, 'invocationis,' 78.

era, refusal, 'nihil dabant,' 33.

erbais, roerb, obtulit, destinavit, 38, 68.

roherbad, was imposed, 20.

-erbail, erbalt, mortuus est, periit, 64, 1, 12, 36.

erbart : con-e., et dixit, 31.

ercid, ite, 62, 83.

roergabad, rohergabad, captus' e., alligatus e., 60, 85.

Ériu, ds., 39.

erlam, erlum, promptus, 100, 13 ; erlaime, readiness, 70 ; roerlamaig, 'apposuit,' 77.

roerlég, relegit, 44.

erlund, cuspis, 55.

roermid, crepuit, 57.

ermadair : ni e., erravit, she missed, 17.

ermted, cuspis, 55, 43.

ernaidi : ic e., expectans, ernaidid, sustinete, ernaigit, expectant, 109.

noernatis, evadebant, 8.

ernaigthe, orationem, 20.

roeroslaicti, aperti s., 44.

herract, surrexit, insurrexit, 6, 7, 8, 22.

erranda, particulas, 69.

escaine, gs., sententia, curse, 110.

roescarad, intimatum e., per edictum, 5.

roescomlaid, perrexit, 38 ; roescomla, roescomlui, perrexit, egressus e., 30, 96.

rohescongrad, edictum e., 87.

noesed : an-n., gemens lacrymansque, 4.

eserge, resurrectio, 106.

esinnraic, indigni, 69.

esorgain, cædere, 57.

espai : oc e., ludendo variis artibus, 85.

espartain, ds., vespere, vespera, 17, 52.

étaig, gs., étaigib, dp., vestis, 67, 83.

rus-etarscar, eos separavit, 36.

hétas, was got, obtained, 73.

etec, volans (?), 51.

etbar, navim, 37.

etir, at all, 77, 106.

étiud, vestire, 88.

etoirthec, (flumen) 'pisces non habet,' 50 ; sterilis, 75.

etrigib, sulcis, 79.

etsect, exitus, mors ; g. etsecta, eidsecta, 18, 38.

exarcistid, exarcistid, exorcistam, 'catechumenus,' recte exorcista, 88, 89.

facbuid, relinquite, 109.

ros-fácaib, deseruit, rofacbas, reliqui ; facbail, relinquere, 93, 64, 3, 108 ; facabar, is left, 103.

-facimm, video ; -facca, vidit ; faicthi, videtis, -facistea, videretur, 81, 82, 109, 90.

fada : ba f. le, erat tristis, 103.

fáe, sub ea, 46.

rofaid, rofuid, misit, 1, 36, 59 ; romfáid, me misisti, rosfaid, dimisit eam, 61, 16 ; rofuided, missus e., 11 ; fuidis, mittebat, 31.

faigde, postulatio, eleemosynam, quærere, 75, 79.

fail : in f., an est ? in failet, an sunt ? 26 ; filet, qui sunt, 106.

fail : i fail n-, juxta, cum, 70, 81 ; dessid in a f., ei adstitit, 97.

failte, gaudio, lætitia, 94, 100 ; no failtniged, gaudebat, 99.

fairithe, parata, 35, 60.

rofaisc, pertractavit, squeezed, 98.

rofaitbe, rofaitbestar, inrisit, subrisit, 92, 70 ; faithbed, deridebat, nofaitbitis, inridere cœperunt, 53, 88.

faithecda, 'psalmistæ,' prophetica, 51.

fáitsine, as., prophetia, 111.

fannaib, infirmis, 76.

fantaissi, np., fantassia, 25.

farrad : i bf. prope, it' arrad, with thee, 104, 40.

farácaib, faráccaib, -farcaib, -fargaib, reliquit, dimisit, 17, 24, 25, 47, 50.

rofas, crevit, 61, 79.

fáscri grotha, dp. fascraib g., caseus, 43, 54 ; np. fascri, ap. fascra, 55.

rofast, detinuit, 94 ; oc a ostud, eum detinens, 19.

fecoir, feccair, ferox, 2, 63 ; nosfeocraiged fri, ferebatur in, 99.

fect n-aili, quondam, 39.

fectus, quadam die, 110.

fég, vide ; rofég, intuitus e., d'(f)egad, videre, 6, 27, 65 ; fegaid, aspicite, fegais, prospexit, 109, 107 ; nofegad, videbatur, it looked, 103.

nofeidliged permaneret, regnaret, 2 ; fedlugud, manere, 43.

folaid, *ds.*, substantia, 97.

folamadair, ' ordinavit' (?), he resolves? folamastar, resolved, 31, 41, 43.

foluamain, suspendi et trepidare, 93.

fón sliab, ad desertum, 8 ; fon˙ caillid, in sylvam, 85, 97.

for: for crabud, religionis gratia, fora anumaloit, propter superbiam suam, 84.

forácaib, faracaib, reliquit, posuit, 20, 22, 28, 35, 39, 40, 89 ; forfacuib, 67 ; 3 *pl.* foracabsat, 4 ; furácaib, ' prædixit,' he left word about the future, 54.

foraithmet, recordatio, 58.

foranic, forránic, invenit, 3 *pl.* forancatar, 16, 40.

forassaig, desiste, destitit, 99.

roforbai, extorsit, 91.

forba, completio; fororbái, consummavit, roforbad, consummata e.,fororbaide, consumpti s., 84, 3, 73, 27.

forbann, ' morem' (superstitiosum), 3 ; forbannach : co f., cum superstitioso (funere), 93 ; faith f., propheta superstitiosus (?), 2.

forbfæilid, gaudens, 102.

forbred, ' inardescebat,' noforbred, nosforbred, amplius crescebat, 47, 68.

raforĉanad, admonitus e., 90 ; forcetul doctrina, 38, 90, 91.

forciund, *ds.*, finis, 32.

forcoimnacair, forcomnacair, evenerat, factum e., 3, 7, 11, 62.

forcongra, præceptum, 13 ; forcongair for, imperat, dixit ad, 95, 78, 85 ; róforcongair, præcepit, 89 ; forcongart, roforĉongart, roforĉongairt, fororĉongart, fororĉongairt, foroconggart, imperavit, injunxit, dixit, 15, 37, 56, 96.

fordindet, ostendit, 54.

fordosrola, eum contendit, he claimed him, 24.

fordunta, conclausam, 11.

forémdid, ' non potuit,' 83, 91.

foriattaib, clausis, 8.

foritha, frith, inventi s., 86.

format, invidia, 87.

fororbái, perfecit, 3.

forraig, agrum, 33.

forruib, posuit, 19.

conda-forslaic, till he released them (?), 41.

fortachtaigid, adest; fortachtaigtheoir, adjutor, 90 ; fortaĉtfaigi, will help, 12.

foruaisligfe, superabit, noforuaisligfed, ' non haberet equalem,' 5, 66.

foruasnad, turbatus e., 5.

fos, adhuc, 51, i foss, hic, 83.

foscud, umbram, for. f., in umbra, 78, 93.

fot, longitudo, 12, 81 ; *d.* futt, 32 ; nírĭota, non longe a, 91.

fothaigis, 25, 30, 33 ; fothaigestar, 40 ; rofothaig, 29, 32, 35, 37, 50 ; rofothaigestar, 29 ; forothaig, 22, 24, 25, 27, 29, 30, 31, 32, 35 ; forothaigestar, 34, fundavit, plantavit, possuit, fecit ; fothugud, fundatio, 37, 58 ; rofothaiged, ædificata e., 45 ; rofothaig, ' habitavit,' 15 ; plantavit points to wooden structures.

fri, contra, 18.

roĭreccair, frisrogart, respondit, 17, 77 ; friscérat, respondebunt, 2.

fristarrasair, contrarius erat, 50.

fristuidchid, fristuidchetar, contra-ivit, contraiverunt, 41.

frith : ní f. uad, non consensit, 60.

frithaire, ' noctis parte'; ic frithairi, vigilias faciens, waking (the corpse), 18, 63.

rofrithbruid, roĭrithbruith, recusavit, restitit, 38, 89 ; nofrithbruideaĭ, fastidiebat, 68.

frithlurg ; ina f., per eadem vestigia, 4˙

frithsét ; ina f., obviam, *bis*, 98.

fromad, probatio, 8.

fuabrais léim, volebat ascendere, 103.

fuaĉtu, frigus, 46.

rofŭair, *gs.*, solito asperior, 88.

-fuair, invenit, 37, 50, 61, 93 ; conidfuaratar, et viderunt, 13.

fuascur : i f., præcipites, 7.

fuasma : co tarat **f.**, et transfixit, 56.

fuath, figuram, formam, 45, 83, 97.

fuat, fuatt, 'sub sago,' 'feretrum,' 12, 106.

fuigell, judicium, 10.

fuigell, 'quod non deficit,' reliquiæ, 73, 78.

fuiride, parata, 20.

fuireċ, mora, 99.

rofuiriġis ; ní **f.** cenco, 'neglexisti,' 72.

fulaing ; narfulaing, ferre non potuit, 92.

fur : ic a **f.**, preparing it (the cæna) 55.

furail, urging, 75.

rofurim, 'protulit,' placed, 110.

furtaċt, auxilium, 99.

gaibid ; g. for, coepit, she takes to (looking at) ; ragab for, gabais for, coepit, 74, 76, 103, rongab, rosgab ecla mor, perterritus e., 12, 75 ; rosgab, eas cepit, 81.

gabais a láim ass, manum illius apprehendens illum de loco ejecit : opposed to arroet, 54, 40, 41 ; gabais roime, discessit, 106.

-geba, gebus, accipiet, 53 ; geib, sume, 71 ; gaibther, 40 ; dogebad, ligatus e., 73 ; gebtha sumeretur, 5 ; cu rogaba, ut accipias, 105.

rogaib, se immisit, rogabsat, delati s. in, rogab port, in portum delata e., con-gabat, et perrexit ad ; ni geba, non deferretur, 3, 4, 21, 31, 39.

gabais pater, oravit, 82 ; nogebat, canebat, 62, 70 ; gebas, cantaverit, 18.

gabur, *gp.*, gabair, *gs.* hircus, 54, 85.

gaeth, ventus, *gs.* gáithe, *d.* gaithib, 94, 53.

gai, hasta, 84, *v.* rónga, murga.

rogaid, -guid, roguid, doguid, oravit, rogavit, 10, 56, 91, 81 ; guid, roga ; guidfed, rogabo, 82.

gair, voca, rogairset, clamaverunt, 59, 10 ; gairmtir, vocatur, 8.

gairit iarsin, non longo post, 71.

gaisced, hastam, 53.

galar, dolor (oculorum), 73 ; 'gemescere,' grief, 88 ; dainib galair, ægrotis, 76 ; gallragim, doleo, I grieve (for you), 90.

garmain, *as.*, ligna telæ, 86.

gasti, laqueo, 91.

gatait, rapiunt, nogatad, rapiebat, gait, detrahere, gataige, alacer, 43, 83, 87, 86.

gegu . . gengu, sive . . sive non, 63.

geibid, accipit, incipit, 103, 107.

gela, *ap.*, gelaib, *d.*, albus candidus, 67, 93.

gelċreċt, *g.* gelċreċta, vestigia cicatricis, cicatrix, 60, 47.

geill, *np.*, obsides, 63.

rogell, promisit, or pledged himself to, 89.

gemrid, hiemis, 88.

genair, rogenair, rogenir, genita e., natus e., 67, 77, 44, 87, 110 ; geinfeth, nasceretur, 101.

gein, *naf.*, conceptus, infans, homo, 65, 77, 101 ; *g.* gene, nativitas, 102.

rógéir, ferocissimam, 57.

gente, *np.*, gentiles, 94 ; gentlide, *gs.*, gentilis, 93 ; gentlideċt, gentilitas, 90.

gerran, 43.

gille, serve !, *d.* gillu, puer, gillaċt, pueritia, 8, 45, 65.

gin, os, *na.*, gin, gein, *d.*, 26, 77, 95.

gíuis, *gs.*, pinus, 94.

glais, *gs.*, glasa, *ap.*, compes, sera, 14, 64.

glamud, convicium, 83.

glanud, purgare, 49.

glenta, *gp.* glennaib, *dp.*, vallis, convallis, 24, 26.

glúine, *ap.*, genua, 23.

gluin, *gs.*, vitulus, 38.

gnáthaċ, consueto, 47.

gníset, egerunt, 60.

gnúis, vultus, 92.

gói, *ds.*, mendacium, 24.

Góidelaib, Scottis, 36, 50.

goirt, avidus, 69.

rogon, romgon, jugulavit ; gorfaither, vulnerabitur, 33, 64, 55.

gort, messis, 86.

gorud, to warm, 46.

grad : tuc, *g*. dou, diligeb:it eum, 102.

gráda, *nap.*, gradus, ordines, sacerdotium ; fer graid, episcopus, 78, 89, 92, 84 ; gabais grada, factus e., sacerdos, 107.

gradaigther, diligitur, 26.

graigi, *np.*, equi, 7.

greim, 'sceptrum,' 2, 63 ; greimm, advantage, 27.

gréin, solem, 65.

greis : co ng., et dimisit, he set (a dog), 51.

gressaċ : co g., assiduously, 103.

gruth, *gs.*, grotha, caseus, 49.

guasacht, casus, discrimen, 96, 99.

gubu, *ds.*, mourning, 43.

guforgaill, falsi testimonii, 44.

roguid, oravit, roguidset, poposcerunt, 98, 99.

iadaid, stringit ; rohiadad, conclusa e., 21, 11.

iallacrand, *gp.* ; iallacranda, *np.* ; calceamenta, calcei, 87, 97.

iar, juxta ; iar fír, vere ; iarna sét, in via ; iar tír, pedestre itinere, 24, 13, 51, 5.

iarair, *ds.*, quaerere, 37.

roiarfaid, iarfaigis, roiarfaig, roiarfaċt, interrogavit, percontatus e. petiit, 60, 90, 96, 62, 77, 32, 66 ; iarṙthai, ye seek, 108.

iarnabáraċ, sequenti die, crastina die, mane, mane facto, postera die, 8, 61, 66, 86, 89, 96.

iarnn, *ns.*, ferrum ; iaronn, ferramentorum, iarnda, ferramenta, 96, 57.

iarndoe, hynulus, 8.

iarsuidiu, tunc, 56, *passim.*

iascaire, piscator, *np.*, iascairi, 85, 40 ; iasgaireċt, piscatio, 85.

ibair, *gs.*, a yew-tree, 57.

nisibed, non bibebat, 93.

roícais, roicc, rosíc, notícc, sanavit (eam, te), 48, 95, 60 ; rohíocais, sanasti, 72.

rohícad, rahíccad, sanatus e. ; rohíctha, rohícta, sanati s., 75, 91, 73, 76 ; icci, sanationis, 53.

ídal, idolorum, 58 ; ídaladrad, profanus sacrificiorum ritus, 93 ; ídáltige, *gs.*, fani, 94 ; idlaċta, idololatriæ, 41.

idbairt, *as.*, consummatio mysterii eucharistiæ, 111 ; idpairt, donationem, 83 ; nohidprad, offerebat, 63.

iffernd, *g.* iffirnd, ifrinn, infernum, 52, 56. 91.

ilib, multis, 35, 45, 58 ; ilcella, ilmíle, *ap.*, multas cellas, multa milia, 34, 82.

imacallaim, *ds.*, confabulatio, 100 ; imacallma, *gs.*, teċ i., senatus, 12.

imad, turba, 98.

imaltoir, 'calicem,' i. e. ciborium, 84.

imbádud, drowning, 99.

imbáraċ, immáraċ, cras, crastino die, postera die, 9, 66, 89.

nosimbir, superlinit, applies it, 96 ; roimbretar, effundebant, 67.

imchaisin, visionem, 27.

imchlaidbed : oc i., conflinguens, 30.

imcomaircet, interrogant ; imċomaircis, imcomarcis, quaesivit ; imcomarc, interrogatio, 25, 65.

imċomet, comitem, 1.

imċubaid, proper, 109.

imdai, multorum, 58.

imdeċt, ingredi, ambulare, ro-imdigset, abierunt, 82, 95, 94.

imeċtraċ, outer, 22.

imecla, timor, 90 ; roimeclaigsetar, timuerunt, 7.

imgaibe, vitas, vites ; roimgaib vitabat, 75, 95.

imluad, agere, agitare, roimluaig, agebat, 93, 7.

immaig, foris, 6.

immáin, minare, 83.

immalle, una, 92.

immdergud, insultare, 83.

imme, *gs.*, butyri, *d.* immim, 49, 70.

roimpai, ros-impoi, convertit, impáis, reversus e. remeavit, roimpaset, reversi s., 9, 79, 107, 108.

máine, munera, 108.

mainces, mances, monacha, 25, 28.

maindeactnaige, *gs.*, pigritiæ, 75.

romáirned, prodidit, 87.

maistred, *g.* maisterda, maistirtha; 'butyrum,' 'mensuræ,' one churning, 69, 70.

romaith, liberavit, 49.

maith : fir maith, patrisfamilias, 95 ; mor in m. credi non potest, 100 ; ba m. lais a menma, lætatus e., 107.

maithmairc, aruspices, 5.

malartar, 'elevetur,' let him be 're-moved,' 61.

mallachais, romallac, maledixit, rosmallac, maledixit illis, 33, 40, 50, 52, 75, 30 ; mallactha, maledictus, 31.

manac, monachus, 88 ; *ap.*, mancu, 110.

manistir, *as.*, *g.* mainistrec, *ap.* mainistreca, monasterium, 92, 58, 87.

maraid, manet, stat, 19, 104.

marb, mortuus, 91.

rotmarbus, (tibi) interfeci, 96 ; romarb, rusmarb, occidit, 85, 86 ; romarbum, occidamus, 5 ; nomairfed, occideret, 56, romarbad, percussus e., 93, muirbfiter, enecabuntur, nommuirfither, enecabor, 63.

martartec, *g.* martorthige, 35 ; martir, martyr ; *g.* martír, martírec, 93 ; *np.* martir, reliquiæ, 43.

masa, si est, 74 ; masu ed, certe si, 39.

maittin : isin m., mane ; ar m., mane facto, isin m. iarnabaruc, luce orta, 37, 61, 20, 59.

romeiglestar, clamavit (hircus), 54.

meirrlig, *np.*, latro, fur, 3, 51, 79.

memid, illisum e., 53, romebad roime, vicit, 82 ; remuid, ebullivit, broke out, 111, mebsat, mebad, fractæ s., fuerint, 106.

men, pulvis, 61.

menicc, frequens, 82.

menistir, 51.

menma, mens, animus, *np.* menmana, 87, 100, 109.

méur, *ds.*, mer, *ap.* ; méra, *ap.* ; digitus, 29, 17, 95, 96.

mesraigetu, temperamentum, 100.

messi féin, ego sum, 60.

messude, the worse, 57.

methel, messores, 85.

miac, *g.* méic, modius, 72.

romianaig, postulavit, 72.

mias, míass, *g.* méisi, mensa, 2, 42, 74 ; miasa, *nap.*, patinos, 'cibus,' dishes, 74, 24.

rommid, erupit, 44 ; roemid, crepuit, 57.

romídir, iniit consilium, 4.

mil, *as.*, mel, 48.

millsi, *np.*, dulcis, 111.

miltenaib, *dp.*, alvearia sylvestria, 48.

romill, 'tetigit,' 11 ; romilled, (casu) fuisset adfectus, 96.

mílid, *as.*, miles, *ap.* míletu, 88, 89.

míltnidect, miltnigect, militia, 87, 89.

romíltniges, militavi, romíltnigitis, ad militiam describerentur, míltnigfet, militabo ; miltnigfes, militabit.

míncaisc, clausulam Paschæ, 72.

mínd rig, diadema, 97.

mírbuil, *as.*, miraculum, 89.

míscuis, *as.*, odium, 78.

mithig : is m. adest tempus, 1.

moc : commoc, mane, 25.

mogad, *gp.*, 57, 59, 91 ; *das.* mogaid, 31, 95 ; *np.* mogaid-ni, nos servi sumus, 57.

moidit, erumpunt ; moidis, crepuit, 84, 71.

molac, 'molesta,' 2.

moltan, vervex ; multu, *ap.* 86.

momint, momentum, 100.

romórad, clarificabatur, 45.

morimniud, *ds.* tribulatio, 57.

mórsoethar, tantus labor, 58.

muccaid, porcinarius, 3.

muin : for a m., in humeris suis, 78.

romúin, instinxit, 4 ; múinfet, I will teach, 107.

muine, munni, *as.*, rubus, 18.

múine, donativum, 89.

mullac, vertex, cacumen, *d.* mulluc, 12, 22, 55.

murga, hasta marina, 85.

sirid, aspicite, 109; sire, thou seekest, 108.

síthe : fir s̓., dii terreni, 25.

síur, *d.* siair, soror, 22, 25.

slabrad, catena, 80, 83; *ap.* slabrada, 64.

staitairect, robbing, 12.

slánide, salubrem, 96.

sleibti, montium, 26; sléibidib, montanis, 24.

Sléct, *gp.* Slécta, *gs.*, 52.

roslect = rofill a gluni, 'genua flexit,' 79, 7; roslechtfaid, genua flectet, 7; slechtain, genuflexionum, 'genua curvabat,' 19, 63; adoravit genibus flexis, 101; se prostravit, 100.

slesaib, lateribus, 25.

sliabaib, *dp.*, montanis, 26.

slict, vestigium, 19, 52.

sligid, *d.*, via, 105.

roda-sluic, eos absorbuit, 55; rolluic, ea absorbuit, 52; nasluicfed, eum absorberet, sloicsi, eum deglutire cœpit, 53.

rosmactad, dictum est, it was ordered, 6.

snam, vadum, 23.

snigis, rosnig, nírsnig, effusus e., defluebat, non descendit (pluvia), 85, 52, 17.

snim, sollicitudo, 45.

rosóad, rasoad, rosóud, vertit, revertit, convertit, retorquebat, conversus e., 9, 49, 72, 73, 94, 110.

sois, vertit, 57; rosoei, vertit, mutat, 104, 105.

socaide, turbam, plerique, 78, 93.

socenelac, *dp.* socenélcaib, honorabilis, 71, 87.

socmact, possibile, 74; socmactu, possibility, 46.

rosoct, nullum verbum protulit, 4; *with pl. nom :* ros. na huile, stupefacti sunt, 48; rosoctsat, obstupuerunt, 13.

sóer, *as.* freeman, 39.

rosoillsig, refulsit, 5.

soimm, dives, 14.

soimmbertade, 'acutissima,' the more easily plied, 57.

sollomain, solemnítas, 71.

solusta, luce amictus, 97.

roson, 'implevit,' sounded throughout, 74.

sonairt, firmum, 22; rosonairtnig, firmavit, 21.

soraid : corup s., ut non impediatur, 82; soirthiu, expeditior, *Sg.* 15a.

sosad, sossad, *na.*, sedes, domus fundata, 2, 21, 63; *dp.* sostaib, 39.

soscela, soiscela, *ag.*, evangelium, 37, 79, 51.

spirtaldaib, spiritualibus, 8.

rosrained, 'retroacta ruit,' retracta e., 94.

nosrengat, 'cucurrerunt,' run away with, drag him, 57; sreangad .i. tarrang, *O'Clery.*

srianaib : in a s., (equos) paratos, 64.

rosroiglestar, flagellavit, 21.

srónaib, naribus, 74.

srothan, fluminum, 26.

sruth, fluvius, 92.

suan, somnus, 107.

rosubacsat, obstupefacti s., were delighted, 98.

sud : ag sud, ecce offero, 70.

sude, sedes, 29.

rosuidig, rosuidig, posuit, collocavit, constituit, 17, 30, 91, 92; suidigther, imponatur, 19; suidigthi, *np.*, subditi, positi, 46; suidius sedit, 103.

suthain, sempiternum, 22.

sutralla, *np.*, luminaria, lampades, 17, 53.

tabraid, adducite, 62; ni tabraid-siu, non defers, 48; -tibre, mittat, -tabratis, darent, 82, 88; tabairt, *g.* tabarta, exhibere, rapere, 96, 19; tabar, notabar, porteatur, ponatur, 19, 62.

tacermait, sermocinabimur invicem, 6.

tacrad do, disputing with, 15.

tadall, adire, visitatio, 16.

tai, es, 75.

taidect, venire, 85.

rustaifniset, fugarunt eos, 95.

tailaié, tailig, *das.*, altitudo, 14, 42.

tail-cend, asci-ciput, (asciæ-caput), 2, 12.

tair, veni, 94 ; tar doridisi, revertere, 105.

tairéetul, prophesy, 5.

tairgerthairig, sponsum, 27.

tairgid, offert, 107.

tairisid, stat, 44 ; co rothairis, ut non discederet, rothoiris, sedit, 60, 64 ; tairisfet, requiescent, 19.

tairisnigid, confidite, 106.

rothairmesc, rothairmisc, impedivit, sustinuit, 31, 57, 90 ; tairmeasc, prohibitio, 75 ; tairmiscther, is forbidden, 5.

tairmthiasad, peccaret, 31.

tairniud, colligere, 30, opposed to síniud ; to lower (the hands).

tairpeé, festinans, 53 ; tairptheé, *Rawl.*, tairpeé, *LU.* in Windisch's Dict.

tairrngid, ' traxit,' 85.

tairseé, limen, 66.

taissi, taise, tasi, tassi, *nap.*, reliquiæ, ossa, *d.* taisib, 19, 24, 27, 50, 62.

taisced, reservabat, rothaisciset absconderunt in thesauris, 88, 83.

taitnem, radiare, 101 ; taitnemaié, lucentem, claram ; *np.* taitnemaéa, 65, 79 ; *ns.* taitnemaé, fulgens, 97.

thaitnigfes, lucebit, 65 ; taitned, shone, 100.

tallus, furatus sum, 85 ; tall, dissolvit, impetravit, 64, 86 ; tallsat, tallsatar, furati s., 54, 79.

talmandaib, terrenis, 87.

talumcumscugud, terræ motus, 7.

tan, tempus, 90 ; t. and, die quadam ; araile t. interea, 67, 96.

tanac, tangais, venisti, 18, 74 ; dosnanic, eos visit, apparuit eis, 64.

taraét, pervenit ad, 4.

tarblaing, he leaped, 42.

tarduid, date, 64 ; co tartad, dedit, 69 ; tartam amus, temptemus, 12 ; tárat, tarat, dedit, 4, 56 ; tardsat, posuerunt, 79 ; tarda, impositum e., 48.

taraill, tetigit, 78.

tárfaid, obviam se tulit, 90, tarfas do, aestimabat, vidit, 19, 84.

tarla, erat, 72 ; tarla do, -nustarla do, incedit in, occurrit ei, invenit, 30, 55, 85, 90.

tarlaic, fudit, 91.

tarméruta, transformed, 97.

tarmnaigfid, proficiet, 65.

tarnic : o th. in recles do éumtaé, cum ecclesia edificata e., 61.

tarraid, non cessavit, 55 ; tarrasair, manserat, 4, 7, 8; tarraisetar, castrametati s., 31.

tarsnu : fo th., across, 79.

tascnam, perrectio, 35.

rothaselbad, it was shown, 49.

teacait, veniunt, 104.

teé n-oiged, hospitium, 17.

teémuid, occurrit, teéemaid, occurret, 104, 105.

teénaige, ' debes,' 22.

rotheiéestar, evaserunt, 7 ; for teiéiud, fugiens, 110.

teét, ire, abire, iter carpere, 18, 57, 82 ; t. bás, mori, 5.

teéta, habes, 95, teétaid, teétai, habet, 45, 29 ; noteétad, habebat, 95 ; rotheét, habuit, habuerat, 72, 20, 2.

teéta, *nap.*, legati, 62, 89.

teétaire, eques, 84.

tedmmaim, *ds.*, pestis, 99.

tégi, curris, 82 ; nothegaid, confugit, 87 ; téged, teiged, notheiged, egrediebatur, ambulabat, declinabat, ibat, 92, 17, 16, 42 ; tégtis, ibant, 93.

tegdais, *nas.*, domus, habitaculum, 24, 26, 65.

teig, *ds.*, custodia codicum, 53.

teirt, hora tertia, 109.

teisc, *as.*, patinum, 29.

teit, funes, 85.

teit, taet, toet, it, ingreditur, venit, eat, veniat, 91, 57, 71, 83.

teithed : for t. profugus, 24.

telaig, telié, *ds.* ; *as.* teléai, teléa, collis, altitudo, 40, 16.

telcfider, effundetur, 55.

tellach : a t., fornacem, 49.

tellsat, furati s., 30.

tene, flamma, 111.

tenntide, igneus, 66, 71.

theora, *gp, ap.*, tres, 58, 111.

tepersin, *da.*, fluxus, 96 ; rotheiper, fluebat, 73.

terca, penuria, 72.

tergaid : ni t. illei, neque appropinquare poteritis, 54.

termuind, refugii, 39.

terno, revertar, 63 ; ternaife, reverteris, 3 *pl.* ternaifeat, 63.

terpud, disjungere, 46.

tesc, 'devora,' tescfamit, succidemus, rothescsat, succidere coeperunt, tescad, excidere, 95, 94.

-testa, deerat, non inveniebatur, testatar, amissi s., 110, 69, 17.

testus, testem, 1.

tiadam, eamus, 48.

tiagait, petunt, exeunt, 60, 83 ; tiagam, eamus, pergamus, 12, 73 ; tísed, tessed, iret, veniret, 69, 90, 74 ; 3 *pl.* tiasat, 19 ; tiagar, eat quis, 62.

ticed, ticced, venire solebat, 60, 19 ; ticfat, veniam, ticfa, veniet, 3, 2 ; ticfad dosnicfed, reverteretur, 24, 60 ; condnicsitís, ut irent, 49.

tictu, *ds.*, adventus, 2.

tidect, venire, 96, 97.

rothidnaic, tribuit, 88.

timarnad, constitutum e., 39.

timthirid, *nf.* and *dm.* timtherig, *gsm.* ; timthirite, *gpl.* ; timthirib, *dp.*, minister, 68, 62, 74, 111 ; timthirect, ministratio ; rothimthirig, ministrabat, 76.

rothinai, rothin, rothinastar, evanuit, 10, 91, 97.

tincitlidi, *ap.*, incantator, 2.

tindarscan, exorsus e , 9.

tinol, copulare, 56.

tintai, vertit, 54.

tipra, *g.* tiprat, *d.* tiprait, fons, 41, 39.

tírtha : fer t., rusticus, 97.

rothocathitis, transigerent, 59.

tocbuid, elevat, 104.

tóct, particulam, (carnis), 69 ; *adp.* tocta, tóctaib, 69.

tocrad : ba t. do, displicuit, 75 ; rothoccraid, displicuit, 61.

co ruthodiusci, ut suscitet, 13 ; dodiusaig, rothodiuisc, rothoduisc, excitavit, erexit, 92, 111 ; tódíuscad, suscitetur, 56 ; tódiuscud, tothiuscad, suscitare, 56, 47 ; corothoduscad, ut restituat, 98 ; rotóduscad, excitatus e., 111.

rotogáilsigestar, contristatus e., 47.

togairm : oc t., vocans, 105.

toirnebus, designabit, 112.

toirrsi, *g.* torsi, tristitia, 64, 65.

toirsec, tristis, 61.

toisec, præ omnibus, 3.

toisigiu, prius, 45.

tol, voluntas ; ba t. do, placuit ei, 94, 71.

tola, inundatio, 45.

co tolaid, donec venit, 37 ; *v.* doluid.

tollcend, capite-perforata, 2.

rotoltnaig, placuit, 20.

toimleth, bibebat, 68 ; tomelad, comederet, tormaleth, vesceretur, dathómlitis, acciperent cibum, 84, 8, 92 ; tomailt, comedere, 77.

rotomais, pensabat, 22.

tomnide, tómnithea, putabatur, videbatur, 88, 100.

tonac, tunac, *gf.* tonaigi, vestis, 11.

tonnem, *d.* tonemaib, 'tenentes,' magni pisces, 34.

tongor in mara, 'mare,' 107 ; *cf.* dendgur, barrgar, smút gur.

topar, aqua ebulliens, fons, 111, 34.

toract, pertingebat ad, venit ad, 9, 89 ; toractu, *ds.*, reaching, 62.

torathar, monstrum, 75.

torbu, *ns.*, 27 ; profit.

torcair, cecidit, 73, 80 ; 3 *pl.* torcratar, 42.

torinol, implevit, collegit, 46 ; *v.* dothinoil.

torraig, *asf.*, habens in utero infantem.

tortromad, *as.* inquietudo, 92.

tóruma : do th., ire ad domum ut visitaret, 95, 69.

# IRISH MANUSCRIPTS—FAC-SIMILES.

*[Editions limited to 200 copies.]*

THE accurate study and critical investigation of the ancient literary and historic monuments of Ireland have hitherto been impeded by the absence of fac-similes of the oldest and most important Irish Manuscripts.

With a view of supplying this acknowledged want, and of placing beyond risk of destruction the contents of Manuscripts, the Academy has undertaken the publication of carefully collated lithographic or photo-lithographic copies of the oldest Irish texts still extant.

----

*In folio, on toned paper.—Price £3 3s.*

LEABHAR NA H-UIDHRI : a collection of pieces in prose and verse, in the Irish language, transcribed about A. D. 1100 ; the oldest volume now known entirely in the Irish language, and one of the chief surviving native literary monuments—not ecclesiastical—of ancient Ireland ; now for the first time published, from the original in the Library of the Royal Irish Academy, with account of the manuscript, description of its contents, index, and fac-similes in colours.

----

*In Imperial folio, on toned paper.—Price £4 4s. ; or £2 2s. per Part.*
*Parts I. and II. ; or in One Vol., half calf.*

LEABHAR BREAC--the "Speckled Book"—otherwise styled "The Great Book of Dun Doighre": a collection of pieces in Irish and Latin, transcribed towards the close of the fourteenth century; "the oldest and best Irish MS. relating to Church History now preserved."—(*G. Petrie.*) Now first published, from the original MS. in the Academy's Library.

----

*In Imperial folio, on toned paper, with a Photograph of a page of the*
*Original.—Price £6 6s.*

THE BOOK OF LEINSTER, sometime called The Book of "GLENDALOUGH": a collection of pieces in the Irish Language, compiled in part about the middle of the twelfth century. From the original MS. in Trinity College, Dublin, with introduction, analysis of contents, and index, by ROBERT ATKINSON, M. A., LL.D., Professor of Sanskrit and Comparative Grammar in the University of Dublin, Secretary of Council, Royal Irish Academy.

The Book of Leinster is one of the most important of the fragments of Irish literature that have come down to us. In addition to copies of the native prose historic accounts of the Táin Bó Cualnge, the Bórama, &c., it contains a large fragment of an early prose translation of the Historia de Excidio Troiae of Dares Phrygius ; a great number of the poems and prose introductions of the *Dindsenchas* or legendary account of the origin of the names of places in Ireland ; very many historic poems, in which the legendary and traditional accounts of the early history of the country are preserved; Irish genealogies and hagiologies ; and a great number of interesting stories, illustrative of the manners and customs, the modes of thought, and the state of culture, &c., of the people of Ireland just about the period of the Anglo-Norman Invasion.

*In Imperial folio, reproduced by Photo-lithography.—Price £5 5s.*

THE BOOK OF BALLYMOTE : a collection of pieces in the Irish Language, dating from the end of the fourteenth century ; now published in **Photo-lithography** from the original Manuscript in the Library of the Royal Irish Academy. With Introduction, Analysis of Contents, and Index, by ROBERT ATKINSON, M.A., LL.D., Professor of Sanskrit and Comparative Philology in the University of Dublin ; Secretary of Council, Royal Irish Academy.

The Book of Ballymote contains numerous articles of interest to the Scholar and to the Antiquary. The original portion consists of—Genealogical Lists ; Histories and Legends ; a fragment of the Brehon Laws ; a copy of the *Dindsenchas;* Treatises on Grammatical Topics, &c. The other portion contains translations from Latin originals : the Destruction of Troy, the Wandering of Ulysses, the Story of the Æneid, and the Life of Alexander the Great.

## THE IRISH MANUSCRIPT SERIES.

Volume I., octavo.—Part 1.—Containing: (1) Contents of The Book of Fermoy ; (2) The Irish MS. in Rennes ; (3) Mac Firbis on some Bishops of Ireland ; (4) Tain Bo Fraich ; (5) Tochmarc Bec-Fola, &c. Price 5s.

Volume I., quarto.—Part 1.—WHITLEY STOKES, LL.D. : On the Felire of Œngus. Price 14s.

Volume II., octavo.—Part 1.—ROBERT ATKINSON, M.A., LL.D. : Τρί biop-ġaoiτe an baiτ ["The Three Shafts of Death"] of Rev. Geoffrey Keating. The Irish Text, edited with Glossary and Appendix. Price 3s. 6d.

## THE TODD LECTURE SERIES.

Volume I., octavo.—Part 1.—W. M. HENNESSY: Mesca Ulad.

Volume II., octavo.—ROBERT ATKINSON, M.A., LL.D.: The Passions and Homilies from Leabhar Breac. With an Introductory Lecture on Irish Lexicography. (Pages 1 to 958.)

Volume III., octavo.—B. MAC CARTHY, D.D. : The Codex Palatino-Vaticanus, No. 830. Texts, Translations and Indices. (Pages 1 to 450.)

Volume IV., octavo.—REV. EDMUND HOGAN, S.J. : Cath Ruis Na Rig for Bóinn. Text, Translation, Preface, and Indices, &c. (Pages xxxii. + 282.)

Volume V., octavo.—Rev. EDMUND HOGAN, S.J., F.R.U.I., M.R.I.A.: The Latin Lives of the Saints as Aids towards the Translation of Irish Texts and the Production of an Irish Dictionary. (Pages xii. + 140.)

# Royal Irish Academy.

## TODD LECTURE SERIES.

### VOL. VI.

## THE

# IRISH NENNIUS FROM L. NA HUIDRE

### AND

# HOMILIES AND LEGENDS FROM L. BRECC.

### Alphabetical Index of Irish Neuter Substantives.

BY

## EDMUND HOGAN, S.J.,

### F.R.U.I., M.R.I.A.;

*Royal Irish Academy's Todd Professor of the Celtic Languages.*

## DUBLIN:

### PUBLISHED AT THE ACADEMY HOUSE, 19, DAWSON-STREET.

SOLD ALSO BY

### HODGES, FIGGIS, & CO. (LTD.), GRAFTON-ST.;

AND BY WILLIAMS & NORGATE.

LONDON: | EDINBURGH:
14, Henrietta-street, Covent Garden. | 20, South Frederick-street.

### 1895.

DUBLIN:
PRINTED AT THE UNIVERSITY PRESS
BY PONSONBY AND WELDRICK.

# CONTENTS.

# PREFACE.

THE pages 1, 2, 3, and 4 of the *L. na Huidre*, now published for the first time,[1] contain many hitherto unindexed words, and the earliest examples of others that are in the dictionaries.

The two homilies and the four tales from the *L. Brecc* present a great variety of subjects and vocables, in the interpretation of which I had not, I regret to say, the help of any Latin originals. Besides being linguistically interesting, these texts throw some light on Irish matters, such as manners (§§ 82, 87, 94), the habits of herdsmen (§§ 74, 78), attachment to home (§§ 60, 61), expression of great grief (§ 104), dress (§ 80), food (§§ 73, 78, 94), furniture (§ 62), round towers (§ 93), druids (§ 80). The passage on quick travelling (§ 93) is such as we find in Irish sagas; the Celtic description of the duel between the worms may be compared to the account of a combat between two little "fighting fishes" of Siam, published in *The Field* of September 8, 1894, p. 394.

I have chosen *LB.* texts for my Lectures for this reason, that, out of its 280 pages, 180 have been published and that it is desirable to have the whole of one of our great manuscripts edited and translated. Dr. Atkinson has interpreted about 74 pp.; Dr. Wh. Stokes, 55; Dr. Gustav Schirmer, 16; Dr. Kuno Meyer, 15; Dr. B. Mac Carthy, 6; Dr. S. H. O'Grady,[2] 5; Dr. Reeves, 3; O'Curry, 1; and parts of pages have been translated by others. I here give an index to the work of these scholars, which, with my Lectures for 1864 and 1865, will amount to more than three-fourths of *LB.*

---

[1] §§ 11, 12 are published by Dr. Wh. Stokes in *Rev. Celt.* i.

[2] His texts, 15, 24, 25, of *Sylva Gad.* are referred, by a misprint, to *LB.*; they are, I think, from *BB.*

1 a—9 b 1, Atkinson, *Todd Lect.* vol. ii.

9 b–12 b 29, Reeves, R.I.A. Trans. xxiv. (11 a 19–26, 11 a 44–51, 11 b 20–30, 11 b 45–51, 12 a 1–9 by Wh. Stokes, in *Trip. Life*, cxciv., clxxxii., *Lism. Lives*, 359.)

24 b–34 a, *Lives of SS. Patrick and Columcille*, Wh. Stokes' *Mid.-Irish Hom.*, and *Trip. Life* (31 b 41–48, *Lism. Lives*, 357).

34 a–57 a, Atkinson, *Todd Lect.* vol. ii.

59 a 16–66 b, *St. Martin and St. Brigit*, Wh. Stokes in *Rev. Celt.* ii. and *Three Mid.-Ir. Hom.*

66 b–73 a, Atkinson, *Todd Lect.* vol. ii.

74 a 7, *Litany of the B. Virgin*, O'Curry's translation ; text and English and Latin translation by Rev. J. Grene, S.J., text and translation by Wh. Stokes, *Trip. Life*, clxv.

75 a–106 b. *Félire*, by Wh. Stokes (with corrections *Rev. Celt.* vols. ii. iv., p. 95 ; ten full lines "Longarad-hor," *Ms. Mat.* 501).

106 b, Aibind suide, 27 ll. Wh. Stokes, *Rev. Celt.* v. 343.

107 b, 57–108 a 39, Atkinson, *Todd Lect.* vol. ii.

108 a, b 29, On the colours of vestments, translated by O'Curry in Card. Moran's *Essays ;* text and translation, *Trip. Life*, clxxxvii.

108 b, eight last ll., K. Meyer in *Gael. Journal*, No. 51.

109 a–113 a 37, MacCarthy's *Todd Lect.* vol. iii.

133 b–141 b, *Todd Lect.* vol. vi. (§§ 80, 81 *infra*, ed. by Wh. Stokes, in *Rev. Celt.* viii. 360).

160 a–169 b, 39, Atkinson, *Todd Lect.* vol. ii.

170 a 21–180 b, 44, Atkinson, *Todd Lect.* vol. ii.

180 b–181 b, Personal appearance and deaths of the Apostles, Wh. Stokes, *Rev. Celt.* viii. 362.

181 b, 46–184 b, Atkinson, *Todd Lect.* vol. ii.

187 b, some lines on *samain*, Windisch's *Texts*, ii. 215.

187 b 43–200 b 15, Atkinson, *Todd Lect.* vol. ii. (194 a–197 b, ed., with transl. by Mac Carthy in *Irish Eccl. Rec.*).

201 a 1–202 b, 25, Atkinson, *Todd Lect.* vol. ii.

205–219, Kuno Meyer (parts of the Alexander story had been edited by Geisler; Mac Conglinne had been translated in *Frazer's Magazine*, Sept., 1873); *Ir. Texte*, serie 1, Heft 1.

220 a, Petrie's *Tara*, pp. 98–104.

220 b, Wh. Stokes' *Trip. Life*, pp. 546, 574.

221 a–236 b, G. Schirmer's *Kreuzlegenden in L. Brecc.*

236 b, all that column, Wh. Stokes' *Lism. Lives*, 301.

238 ab, Wh. Stokes' *Trip. Life*, 390–401.

241 b, Gildas Lorica, Wh. Stokes' *Med. Tract on Lat. Declension*, p. 136.

242 b 57 to end of column, O'Curry, *Ms. Mat.* 632.

243 a–246 b, Atkinson, *Todd Lect.* vol. ii.

248 a 45–251 a 1, Atkinson, *Todd Lect.* vol. ii.

251 a to fourth last line, Mac Carthy's *Stowe Miss.* 259.

251 a, fourth last line, to 251 b 37, O'Curry, *Ms. Mat.* 613.

251 b 38–253 b, Atkinson, *Todd Lect.* vol. ii.

256 a 44 and 256 b, *Todd Lect.* vol. vi.

257 a–258 a 10, *Todd Lect.* vol. vi.

258 ab–259 b 39, Wh. Stokes, *Rev. Celt.* xx. 22.

261 a, Rule of St. Mochuta, eight stanzas, K. Meyer, in *Gaelic Journal*, March, 1895.

272–277, Betha Chellaig, O'Grady, *Sylva Gadelica*.

Some grammatical peculiarities of our texts are:—"rodún sib, rolín sib," § 107; "ticcid," 2d. pl. addressed to one person, § 78. "Aingliu," §§ 34, 52, "apstalu" etc. for the *dp.* in *aib*[1]; "crístaige" for "cristaide" (*gp.* cristide, *Ml.* 66 b). As to the contractions:—"ámlaid" is in full only at *LB.* 135 a; "immorro" never in full, (immorro, in L. Hymn.); "iter" should be it*ir* (etir of O. Glosses); "Muire" in full, §§ 49, 58 *ter*; ni*n* is perhaps for "ní anse són," *Ml.* 45 d; I find ni*n* before a statement even when a question does not precede; "no," in full, *LB.* 257 a; i*n*a so*n*sa, p. 63, l. 1, may be = ina sos*cela*.

Dilmainius, § 72, I cannot find anywhere; dilmaine = forfeiture, *Laws*, i. 210, 258; "Ezecias" is invariably for Esaias;

---

[1] I have not always corrected this, as it occurs so often.

iach, § 53, is perhaps = ach .i. interiecht galair, an interjection of grief (*Cormac's Gl.* p. 15) ; imdecht do dénam, § 94, is note-worthy ; Luprucan, Luchrupain, §§ 10, 12, are luchurpáin, luchorpáin, luchuirp, abác, in *Laws*, i. 70, 72; *v.* lupracán, fomóir, *Sylva Gad.* ; muincend, § 8, written for the first time (see *Todd Lect.* iv. 240, *LL.* 135, *Nennius*, 55, 234, *Sylva G.* 242) ; (risnad, risna) duthracht, *Index*, cf. lasnad ail, *Irish Hom.* l. 2412 ; slechtain, kneeling, § 88 ; torathor, § 10 (cf. derbairde 7 torathar, *LB.* 152 b, torathraib, *LL.* 136).

The reference *Cn.* is to the tenth-century Latin *Nennius* of Chartres, published by the Abbé Duchesne, in the *Rev. Celt.* xv. 175. The genealogies, ethnography, geography, and other matters,[1] touched on in our texts are not dealt with by me, as extended antiquarian and historical illustrations are expensive luxuries, and would not be appreciated in a lecturer whose only business is to cater for linguistic interests.

I have appended an alphabetical list of neuter substantives in the hope that it may be useful for lexicographical and gram-matical purposes. I have added many to those given in the *Todd Lectures*, vol. iv.; and I may add the following from *Cormac's Glossary*, ed. 1868, adbulbás, 61, dá n-agra, 163, *d.* aithscenmaim, atach n-amra, 62, find n, 90, forcenn n, 160, fuath n-airt, 3, pl. garmand, 90, ian mbille (?), 27, ucht n, 163.

In conclusion, I beg to apologize for inadvertently attribut-ing to Dr. Windisch, in my last volume, the equation bachlach = bondman; and to express my thanks to Mr. John M'Neill for many helps and hints while preparing these lectures.

EDMUND HOGAN.

*April* 19, 1895.

---

[1] For both sides of the questions concerning the " brethren of Jesus," I refer the reader—(*a*) to Professor Mayor's edition of the *Epistle of St. James;* (*b*) to Dr. Franz Trenkle's Commentary on that Epistle. See also at §§ 58, 95, a reference to the books of St. James and St. Matthew.

# THE LU. IRISH NENNIUS,

AND

# HOMILIES AND LEGENDS FROM LB.

———◦◦———

## THE LU. IRISH NENNIUS.

1. . . . . . To]gorma[1] otát Frigiæ macc side Gomer meicc Iafed.

Da macc Magog meicc Iafeth meicc Noi .i. Baath 7 Ibath. Baath macc do-side Fenius Farsaid athair na Scithecda .i. Fenius macc Baath meicc Magog meicc Iafeth meicc Nói rl—.

Ibad dano in macc aile do Magog macc do side Elonius no Alanius. Tri meicc aici-side .i. Armon Negua Hisicón.[2] Coic meicc ic Armón .i. Gothus, Uolegothus, Cebidus,[3] Burgandus, Longu(bardus). Negua dano .iii. meic les .i. Uandalus, Saxus, Bogardus.[4] Hisicón dano .iiii. meicc aice .i. Francus, Romanus, Albanus ota (sic) Albannai in Asia, Britus ó rater Inis Bretan.

———————

1. . . . . . Thogorma from whom are the Phrygians, a son this of Gomer, son of Japhet.

Two sons of Magog, son of Japhet, son of Noah—namely, Baath and Ibath. Baath, a son of his was Fenius Farsaid, father of the Scythians, that is Fenius, son of Baath, son of Magog, son of Japhet, son of Noah, &c.

Ibad again, the second son of Magog, a son of his was Elonius or Alanius. Three sons had the latter, Armon, Negua, Hisicon. Five sons had Armon—namely, Gothus, Uolegothus, Cebidus, Burgundus, Longubardus. Negua again, three sons were his, Wandalus, Saxus, Bogardus. Hisicon again, four sons had he, Francus, Romanus, Albanus, from whom are the Albanians in Asia, Britus, from whom is named the Island of the Britons.

---

[1] To] gormu, MS.
[2] Armenon, Neugo, Hiscion, Cn.
[3] Cebustus and Cebidi, Cn.
[4] Bogarus, Cn.

2. Is and sain rorrannad in domun i trí rannaib .i. Eoraip, Afraic, Asia, i. Sem in Asia, Cam in Afraic, Iafed in Eoraip ; 7 is é cét-fer de sil Iafeth tánic in Eoraip .i. Alanius is uad rater Alania in Eoraip, macc Ibath meicc Magog meicc Iafeth meicc Noi.

Is amlaid tánio Alanius 7 a trí meicc les .i. Armo(n 7) Negua 7 Hisicon conid i fus rochlannaigset na maccu atchuadamar. Saxus[1] macc Negua meicc Alonii meicc Ibath meicc Magog meicc Iafeth meicc Noi, is uad Saxain.

3. Iaban dano macc Iafeth meicc Noi, iiii. meicc aca-side .i. Elisa, Tarsis, Cethim, Dodanim.

Tarsis, is uad 7 Celtecdai. Cethim, is uád Cethei ; uadib-side ainmnigther cathir na Ciprecda .i. Citheum. Dodanim dano, uád-sidc Ródii ; is uádib-sidi rofodlait[2] inse Mara Torren co n-a cenelaib écsamlaib 7 co (n-a) mberlaib. Is iat sain .xu. prim-ch(enel)a clainni Iaféd co n-a fochenelaib ; roselbsat feranna imda isin n-Asia o Sléib

---

2. It was then[3] that the world was divided into three divisions, Europe, Africa, Asia—Shem in Asia, Ham in Africa, Japhet in Europe. And the first man of the seed of Japhet that came into Europe was Alanius (it is from him that Alania in Europe is named), son of Ibath, son of Magog, son of Japhet, son of Noah.

Thus came Alanius, bringing his three sons along with him, to wit, Armon, Negua, and Hisicon, and it is here that they engendered the sons we have related. Saxus, son of Negua, son of Alanius, son of Ibath, son of Magog, son of Japhet, son of Noah, from him are the Saxons.

3. Javan again, son of Japhet, son of Noah, four sons had he— namely, Elisa, Tharsis, Cethim, Dodanim. Tharsis, from him are . . . . . . and the Celts. Cethim, from him are the Cethei. From these is named the city of the Cyprians, Citheum. Dodanim again, from him the Rhodians. By these were shared the Isles of the Torrenian Sea, with their divers races and their languages.

The foregoing are the fifteen chief races of the children of Japhet, with their under-races. They held many lands in Asia,

---

[1] Saxo, Cn.

[2] Here the passive in -it appears for the first time.

[3] Paragraph iv. of the Irish Nennius, p. 3, is substantially the same as §§ 2 and 1 of our text.

Imai[1] 7 o Sleib Tuir co Sruth Tanai 7 connici *in* Scithia ; 7 roṡelbsat *inn* Eoraip uli *con*nici *inn* acían muridi fui*n*eta Insi Bretan 7 *in*n Espain ulide.

4. (De) chlannaib Iafeth m*eic*o Noi *con*nici so *co n*-a prím-chene-laib 7 *co n*-a ṅgabalaib 7 a ferannaib et*er* Asia 7 Eoraip.

De clannaib Cam m*eic*c Noi so sis ifecht-sa.

Cam 7 Oliua a ben, iiii. m*eic*c leo .i. Chus 7 Mesram, Futh 7 Cannan. Chus uad-s*id*e Chusi ; Ethiopia a hai[n]m-s*id*e *in*diu. Mes-ram, is uad Egiptus ; Futh, is uad Afraicdai (*no* Libei[2]) Futhei a n-ain*m*-s*id*e fecht aile riam, 7 is uad r(at*er*) sruth Fuith. Cannan, is uad Cannannai ; is he a ferann-s*id*e ro-gabsat m*eic*c Isr*ae*l iartai*n* iár dílgend na Cannanna 7 iar n-a n-inn(arba).

5. Cus m*acc* Cam .uii. m*eic*c les .i. Saba, is ua(d) Sabei. Ebila, uad-

---

from the mountain of Imarus, and from the mountain of Tor, to the stream of Tanaus, and as far as Scythia, and they held Europe all as far as the western marine ocean, the island of the Britons and all Spain.

4. Thus far of the clans of Japhet, son of Noah, with their chief races, and with their conquests[3] and their lands, both Asia and Europe.

Of the clans[4] of Cham, son of Noah, this below this turn.

Cham, and Oliva his wife, four sons were theirs, Chusand, Mesraim, Phut, and Chanaan. Chus, from him is Chusi ; its name to-day is Ethiopia. Mesraim, from him is Egypt. Phut, from him are the Africans (or Libyans). Phutei, their name formerly, and from him is called the stream of Phut.

Canaan, from him are the Canaanites. It was their land that the sons of Israel took afterwards, after overthrowing the Canaan-ites, and expelling them.

5. Cuss, son of Cham, seven sons were his—namely, Seba, from him are the Sabei ; Hevila, from him the Getuli, who are in the

---

[1] Imari, *Facsim.*
[2] *Written over* afraicdai.
[3] *Or* holdings, conquests = gabálaib,

*gl.* captionibus ; *or*, for gablaib, off-shoots ; síl gel gablas, *Fél.* p 63
[4] *Or* children.

side Getuli filet i ndithruib[1] na hAfraice. Sabatha, is uadh Sabatheni; Astabarí imurgu a n-ainm indiu.

Recma, Sabata, Acha, Nebroth is leiside rocumtaiged in Babiloin ar thús cia rocumtaiged la Nín macc Beil iártain in tan rogab ríge Asár. Babilonia .i. confusio .i. cumasc iarsin-ni rocumaiscthea na berla isind luc sain; 7 is la Nebroth rocumtaiged Arach, ainm aile di Edisa; 7 is leis rocumtaiged Achad 7 Cabann, 7 is é a hainm-side indiu Seleucia ond ríg Seleucio ro-ráded; imMaig Sennar atat sin ule.

6. Is de síl Nebroith Asúr ótat Asardai iar fairind, nó is de síl Sém meicc Noi in tAsur .i. Asur macc Sém meicc Noi, 7 is and rogenair imMaig Sennár 7 is leis rocumtaiged Ninues 7 Thala 7 Resen .i. cathir mor (fil) eter Ninues 7 Thala. Dá macc ic Recma macc Chus meicc Cam meicc Noi .i. Saba 7 Dadam. Saba macc Recma Persin scríbthair a ainm; Saba[2] macc Chus Persainech scríbthair a ainm-(side).

---

desert of Africa; Sabatha, from him are the Sabutheni, but Astabari is their name to-day; Regma, Sabathacha, Nebroth [Nemrod]. By the latter Babylon was first built, though it was afterwards built by Nin, son of Bel, when he took the kingship of Asar. Babylonia, i.e. confusio, i.e. confusion, from the fact that the languages were confused in that place. And it was by Nimrod that Arach was founded; another name for it is Edisa. And by him was (were) founded Achad and Chalanne, and the name of the latter to-day is Seleucia, from King Seleucus it was called. In the plain of Senaar are all these.

6. Of the seed of Nimrod is Asur,[3] from whom are the Assyrians, according to some, or else of the seed of Shem,[4] son of Noah, is this Asur, that is to say, Asur, son of Shem, son of Noah. And where he was born was in the plain of Senaar, and by him were founded Nineveh, and Chale, and Resen, a large city which is between Nineveh and Chale. Two sons had Regma, son of Chus, son of Cham, son of Noah, namely, Saba and Dadam. Saba, son of Rechma, Persin his name is written. Saba, son of Chus; Persainech his name is written.

---

[1] Leg., dithriub (?).
[2] Leg., Dadam (?).
[3] See Gen. x.
[4] So Paralip. i. 1.

7. Clanna Mesram m*eicc* Cam m*eicc* Noi .i. L[udim], Anami*m*,
Labaim, Népthann, Pet[rusim], Chesloim. Is uadib si*n* ro-genatar
na Filisti*n*nai 7 Capturim 7 ciniuda imda aile 7 nitat achinti indiu ar
rocloen(ait)[1] (an) anmand.

De chlannaib Cannan m*eicc* Cam m*eicc* Noi so sis.

8. Cannan m*acc* Cam, m*eicc* Noi, xi m*acc* les .i. Sidon, Cetheus,
Iebuseus, Amnorreuus, Eutheus, Gergesius, Aracheus, Sineus, Arca-
dius, Samarius, Amatheuus. Sidon is uád a*i*nmnig(th*er*) in chathir .i.
Sidon isind Ḟoenici; Arachius is les rac*u*mtaiged Arachas .i. cathir
fil ar agid Tripolim i fail Slebe Leuain. Aradius, is uad atat Aradai, is
iat-s*i*de roselbsatar Ninnis[2] dianid ai*n*m Aradum, mui*n*cend[3] c*u*mung
etar . . . Samarius, is uad atat Samari is leis rocumtaiged Samaria
.i. c(athir).

De clannaib Se*m* m*eicc* Noi so sis.

9. Sem m*acc* Nói, Olla a ben-s*i*de, is dia sil s*i*de na Hebraide uli.
U. m*eicc* aici .i. Elam, is uad Elamitae, toisig P*er*sidis Siriae iat-s*i*de.

---

7. The descendants of Mesram, son of Cam, son of Noah [are as
follows], viz. Ludim, Anamim, Laabim, Nephthuim, Petrusim,
Chasluim. From those sprang the Philistines and Captorim, and
many other nations, and they are not recognizable to-day, for
their names have been corrupted.[4] Of the descendants of Chanaan,
son of Cham, son of Noah, this below.

8. Chanaan, son of Cham, son of Noah, eleven sons were his,
viz. Sidon, Hetheus, Jebuseus, Amorrhæus, Hethæus, Gergesius,
Aracus, Sinæus, Aradius, Samaræus, Amathæus. Sidon, from him
is named the city Sidon in Phenicia. Aracæus, by him was founded
Arachas, a city which is over against Tripoli, near Mount Lebanon.
Aradius, from him are the Aradians. It is these that possessed the
island which is called Aradus, (there is) a narrow strait between (that
island and the mainland). Samarius, from him are the Samarians·
By him was founded Samaria (*i.e.* a city).

9. Shem, son of Noah; Olla, his wife. Of the seed of these are
all the Hebrews. Five sons he had—namely, Alam, from him

---

[1] *Or*, recloen*set*, recloen*ta*.
[2] inn inis (?).
[3] *muincend* appears for 1st time in mss.

[4] Have deteriorated, in-iqua facta
sunt; claonad = decline, fail, fall away,
*Exod.* 23; *Hebr.* 12.

Asur, is uád atat Asardai iar fír, 7 is leis ro cumtaiged Ninues 7 Thala
7 Resen .i. cathir mór fil eter Ninue 7 Thala. Arafaxat, is uad Caldei.
Lidi, uád atá Lidia; Sáram is uad atá Siria, is i ba hard-chathir-side
Damascus. Arafaxat macc Sem[1] meicc Nói, macc do-side Sela, macc
do-side Eber, is uad ainmnigter Ebraide .i. (ó) Eber macc Sala meicc
Arafaxat meicc Sem meicc Noi.

10. Dá macc ic Éber .i. Fálec 7 Iactan .i. Falec .i. diuisio .i. fodail
.i. ar is na amsir rofodlait na berlai. Iactan macc Eber .xiii. meicc
aci .i. Elmodad, Saleph, Asarmo, Iare, Aduram, Aduzal, Decla, Ebul,
Abimæl, Saba, Ofir, Euila, Iobab. Atat .iiii. xl. cenela día síl sin
isind Indía, 7 is iat gabait ule feranna na (h)Indiæ .i. othá in sruth
aníar conníci inn acían.

Clanna Saram meicc Sem meicc Noi .i. Us, is uad atat Traconitidi
7 is les rocumthaiged in Damaisc, eter Pasilisitian 7 Cœlensiria átá a
ferand-side; Ul, is uád atát Armiannai; Gether, is uád atat Arcannai;

---

are the Elamites; rulers of Syrian-Persia these. Assur, from him
are the Assyrians in truth, and by him were founded Nineveh and
Chale, and Resen, that is, a great city that is between Nineveh and
Chale. Arphaxad, from him are the Chaldees. Lud, from him
is Lydia. Saram, from him is Syria. Its capital was Damascus.
Arphaxad, son of Shem, son of Noah, a son to him was Sala; a son
to the latter was Heber; from him are named the Hebrews, to wit,
from Heber, son of Sala, son of Arphaxad, son of Shem, son of Noah.

10. Two sons had Heber, Phaleg and Jactan. Phaleg, that is
*divisio*, division, for in his time were divided the languages. Jactan
son of Heber, thirteen sons he had, namely, Elmodad, Saleph, Asar-
moth, Jare, Aduram, Uzal, Decla, Ebul, Abimael, Saba, Oppir, Hevila,
Jobab. There are forty-four races of the seed of these in India, and
it is they that occupy all the lands of India, to wit, from the river
eastwards to the ocean.

The descendants of Saram, son of Shem, son of Noah [are as follows],
viz.:—Us, from him are the people of Thraconitis, and by him was
founded Damascus; between Pasilisitia and Coele-Syria is the land of
these. Hul, from him are the Armenians; Gether, from him are the

---

[1] *gs.* Seim, *LB.* 113.

Mes, is uád atat Meones; sil Samar meicc Sem meicc Noi dóib sein ule 7 isin Asia atat.

11. De senchas na Torothor .i. na Luprucan 7 na Fomorach insó sis (or Lucrupan, *c* being over *p* and *p* over *c*).

Fechtas ro boí Nói in tabernacuil in a chotlud ar n-ól fína 7 is hé lomnocht, co tánic a macc adochom .i. Cam co n-aca amal ro bái, 7 co nderna gári imbi, 7 co ro innis día bráthrib .i. do Iáfeth 7 do Sém; 7 dodeochatar-side 7 a cúl rempo ar n[a] aictís féli a n-athar, 7 doratsat a étach taris.

12. Atracht Noí iar sin as a chotlud 7 rofallsiged do, Cam día fochaitbiud; [romallach Cam] iar sin 7 robennach in dís n-aile. Conid hé Cám de-side cet duni romallachad iar n[d]ilind, 7 conid he comarba[1] Cáin iár n[d]ilind 7 conid huád rogenatar Luchrupain 7 Fomóraig 7 Goborchind 7 cech ecosc dodelbda archena fil for doinib, 7 conid air[e sin] tucad dilgend for clannaib Cam 7 tucad a ferand do maccaib Israel i comarda na mallachtan cétna. Conid hé sen bunad

Arcannians; Mes, from him are the Maeonians. Of the seed of Aram, son of Shem, son of Noah, are all these, and in Asia they are.

11. Of the history of the Monsters,[2] that is of the Luprucans and of the Fomorians, this below.

Once that Noah was in a tent asleep, having drunk wine, and he naked, and his son came towards him, namely Cham, and saw how he was, and laughed at him, and told his brothers, Japheth and Shem; and these went back foremost, that they might not see their father's shame, and they put his clothing over him.

12. Noah rose thereafter out of his sleep, and it was made known to him that Cham had been mocking him. [He cursed Cham] thereupon, and blessed the other two. And Cham was thus the first person that was cursed after the Deluge, and he was the heir of Cain after the Deluge, and from him sprang the Luchrupans, and Fomorians, and Goatheads, and every unshapely form in general that there is on men. And it is therefore that overthrow was brought on the descendants of Cham, and that their land was given to the sons of Israel in fulfilment[3] of the same curse. And that is the origin of the Torothors,

---

[1] *Read* comarda Cáin (?).

[2] Cf. *LU.* fol. 33; torathar = mon-

strum, *Todd Lect.* v. p. 75.

[3] Lit., "token."

na Torothor 7 ni de síl Cai*n* doib, amal adfíadat na Goedil, ar no r*i*
mair ní día sil-*side* iar n[d]ilind; ar ropé fochond na dilend do bádud
clann Cáin 7 robátea cid clanna Sed ule immalle friu *acht* Nóé co*na*
m*a*ccaib 7 co*na* cethri mná*i*b, amal i*n*nises Moisi m*a*cc Ammra i*n*si*n*
Genis ind recta, 7 Dia féin dorat in recht sai*n* do Moisi i Sléib Sína 7
is e roscríb coná laim fei*n*.

13. Is iat so sís airich na haesi tanaisi iar li*n*i genelaig Sem.

| | | | |
|---|---|---|---|
| .s.[1] Noi, | . . . . | ael.[2] |
| .s. Sem, | . . . . | ac.[3] |
| .s. Arfaxat, | . . . . | cccxxxix. |
| .s. Sala, | . . . . | acccxxxiii.[4] |
| .s. Heber, | . . . . | cccclxiiii. |
| .s. Falec, | . . . . | ccxxxix. |
| .s. Reu, | . . . . | ccxxxix. |
| .s. Saruc, | . . . . | ccxxx. |
| .s. Nachor, | . . . . | clxxuii. |
| .s. Tara, | . . . . | lxx. |

and they are not of the seed of Cain as the Gaels relate, for there lived
not ought of his seed after the Deluge, for it was the purpose of the
Deluge to drown the descendants of Cain, and all the descendants of
Seth were also drowned along with them, but Noah with his sons and
with their four wives, as Moses, son of Amram, tells in Genesis of the
Law; and it was God Himself that gave that Law to Moses on Mount
Sinai, and it is He that wrote it with His own hand.

13. These are the chiefs of the second age according to the line of
the genealogy of Shem :—

| The age of Noah, | . . . | 950 [years.] |
|---|---|---|
| ,, Shem, | . . . | 600 ,, |
| ,, Arphaxad, | . . | 438 ,, |
| ,, Sala, | . . . | 433 ,, |
| ,, Heber, | . . . | 464 ,, |
| ,, Phaleg, | . . . | 239 ,, |
| ,, Reu, | . . . | 239 ,, |
| ,, Sarug, | . . . | 230 ,, |
| ,, Nachor, | . . . | 167 ,, |
| ,, Thare, | . . . | 70 ,, |

---

[1] .s. = saegul, age (?).
[2] e = inverted e, or *sampi* = 900 (?).
[3] c = x = 600 (?).
[4] a, mistake for c (?).

Tara .iii. m*eicc* les .i. Abraam, Nachor, Arán. M*acc* dond Arán sin
Lóth; robatar da*no* dí ingin aci .i. Melcha 7 Iascha, di ingin Aráin
m*eicc* Thara, sethracha do Lóth; 7 is i*n*und Iascha 7 Sarra; 7 adbath
Aran rena athair .i. re Tara, 7 is he sei*n* cet m*acc* atbath rana athair
iár n[d]ilind, 7 is and atbath i*n* Úr Caldeor[um], am*al* atb*er* i*n* fili
Goedelach si*n*. Cet m*acc* as . . .

14. Abraam 7 Nachor tucsat da mnai .i. Sarra 7 Melcha, dí íngin
a mbráthar fein .i. dí ingin Áraí*n* m*eicc* Tára. Tuc ém Abram Sarra
dianid co*mainm* Iascha. Tuc im*murgu* Nachor Melcha; ruc Melcha
uiii m*a*ccu do Nachor; ít he so a n-(a)nmand-si*de*—Hus, Buz, Camuel,
Chaseth, Azau, Feldas, Iadilafach, Bathuel; is uad si*de* rogenair Lauan
(f*ilius*) 7 Rabecca (f*ilia*). Hus (n*ó* Chus) m*acc* Nachoir, is uád Iob. 7 is
dia sil B . . .[1] Balam in drúi. Camuel da*no* athai[r] Sirorum eside.
Carat-ben Nachar .i. Noma, is iside mathair Tabe. 7 . . . 7 Thuas 7
Muachai. Dend ais t[anaisi] *con*nici so anuás. Den tres ais so sis[2] . . .

---

Thare, three sons were his, Abraham, Nachor, Aran. A son to
that Aran was Lot. He had also two daughters, Melcha and Jescha.
The two daughters of Aran, son of Thare, sisters to Lot, and Jescha and
Sarah are the same. And Aran died before his father, before Thare,
and that is the first son that died before his father after the Deluge.
And where he died was Ur of the Chaldees. As that Gaelic poet says:—

"The first son who . . . . ."

14. Abraham and Nachor married two wives (respectively), Sarah
and Melcha, their own brother's two daughters, the two daughters of
Aran, son of Thare. Abraham indeed wedded Sarah, whose other
name[3] is Jescha. Nachor wedded Milcha. Milcha bore eight sons to
Nachor. These are their names:—Huz, Buz, Kemuel, Cased, Azau,
Pheldas, Jidlaph, Bathuel. From the latter was born Laban (filius),
and Rebecca (filia). Hus (or Chus), son of Nachor, from him is Job,
and of the seed of Buz is Balaam the druid. Camuel again, this is
the father of the Syrians. The friend-wife of Nachor, *i.e.* Noma, this
is the mother of Tabee and [Gaham],[4] and Thahash and Maacha. Of
the second age down to this. Of the third age, this below [this time].

---

[1] Read " B(alam .i.) Balam in
drúi" (?).
[2] Supply " ifechtsa " (?).

[3] *Or*, cognomen.
[4] Cf. *Gen.* xxii. 24, where *caratben*
is rendered by *leannan*, concubina.

15. In tres æs in domai*n* is e so [lín a bliadan] fil inti, dcccxlú
.i. o gen Ab[raam] co gabáil ríge do D*auid* i tír . . .

                    (caetera desunt).

[p. 3]

16. Acht cena, ol se, a rí failsigfit-sea fírin*n*e duit-siu ; 7 iarfaigim
dona druidib ar thús cid ata i foluch fond e*r*lar-sa in ar fiadnaise.  Ro
ráidset na drúid nochon éta*m*mar, ol siat.  Ro fetar-sa, ol se ; atá loch
us*ci* and, fe*g*tar 7 clait*er*.  Ro claided 7 fr*i*th i*n* loch a*n*d.  A fathe
in*d* ríg, ol i*n* m*a*cc, abraid cid *a*tá im-medon ind locha.  Ní(f)eta*m*ar,
or siat.  Ro fetar-sa, ol se, atát da clar-chiste mora and i n-agid t'agid
7 tucthar as ; 7 tucad ás.

A druide, ol in m*a*cc, abraid cid atá etir na clar-lestraib út ; 7 ni
etatar.  Ro fetar-sa, ol se, atá seol-brat and, 7 tuctar as ; 7 frith in
seol ti*m*marcte[1] etir na da chlár-chiste.  Abraid a éolcho, ol in m*a*cc, cid
atá i*m*-medon i*n*d étaig út ; 7 ni ror(f)ecratar, ar ni rot(h)u(i)csatar.

---

15. The third age of the world, this is [the number of years (?)],
that there are in it, 945, to wit, from the birth of Abraham to the taking
of Kingship by David in the land of  . . . . .


16. " However," quoth he, " O king, I will reveal truth to thee.
And first I ask of the druids, What is in hiding under this floor in
our presence ?"  The druids said, " We know not," quoth they.  "I
know," quoth he, "there is a pool of water in it.  Let it be examined
and dug".  It was dug and the pool was found in it.  " Prophets of
the king," quoth the boy. " say what is in the middle of the pool."
" We know not," quoth they.  " I know," quoth he.  " There are
two great wooden chests in it before thy face,[2] and let them be taken
out of it."  And they were taken out of it.

" Druids," quoth the boy, " say what is between those wooden
vessels."  And they knew not.  " I know," quoth he.  " There is a
sail-cloth within, and let it be taken out."  And the sail was found
gathered up between the two wooden chests.  " Say, ye wise ones,"
quoth the boy, " what is in the middle of that cloth."  And they
answered not, for they understood not.

---

[1] *Leg.*, timmarte (?).                    [2] *Leg.* in-agid t' aigthe (?)

17. Atat dá crúim and, ol se, .i. cruim derg 7 cruim gel, scailter in t-étach; roscailed in seol-brat, robatar na di chruim inn cotlud and. Roráid in macc, fégait(h)-si in dignet innose na bíasta. Atraracht cách díb co araile co rabe cechtarde ic sroiniud araile, 7 co rabatar ic imletrad 7 ic imithi, 7 no innarbad in chruim díb araile co medón in t[s]iuil 7 in fecht n-aill co a imel.

Dorónsat fa thrí fon innas-(s)in. In chruim rúad tra ba fand ar thús 7 ro-innarbad co himel ind étaig. In chruim taitnemach immurgu ba fand fo déoid 7 roteich isin loch, 7 rotinastar in seol fo chétoir. Ro íarfaig in macc dona druidib, innisid, ar se, cid follsiges in t-inguad so. Ni etamar, ar siat.

Dogen-sa, ar in macc, a follsigud dond ríg.

18. Is é in loch flathius in domuin uile, is é in seól do (f)lathius-(s)a a rí. Is iat na dá chruim na da nert .i. do nert-su co mBretnaib 7 nert Saxan.

Do nert-su in chruim ruad, is i ro-innarbad ar thús don flathius;

---

17. "There are two worms[1] in it," quoth he; "a red worm and a white worm. Let the cloth be loosened." The sail-cloth was opened. The two worms were asleep in it. The boy said:—"Look ye, what the reptiles will now do!" Each of them started towards the other, till they were on either side overthrowing each other,[2] and till they were tearing and eating each other in turn, and one worm of them was driving the other to the middle of the sail, and another time to its edge.

They behaved thrice in that way. It was the red worm that was weak at first, and that was driven to the edge of the cloth. It was the bright worm, however, that was weak at last, and it fled into the pool, and immediately the sail vanished. The boy asked the druids:—"Tell," quoth he, "what this marvel portends." "We know not," quoth they. "I will interpret," quoth the boy; "its portent to the king."[3]

18. "The pool is the sovereignty of the whole world. The sail is thy sovereignty, O king. The two worms are the two powers, thy power with the Britons, and the power of the Saxons.

"Thy power, the red worm, it is, that was first driven from the

---

[1] cruim now means "maggot."
[2] *Or* dragging each other.
[3] Lit., "I will make its manifestation to the king."

nert Sachsan im*murgu in* c(h)rui*m* gel rogab in seól uile *acht* bec .i. ro
gab *i*nnis Bretan *acht* bec, co ro n-i̇nnarba nert Bretan fo deoid íat.

Tusu im*murgu*, a rí Bretan, eirg asin dún-sa ar ni chæmais a
chumtac(h), 7 sir innis Bretan 7 fógeba do dun fadéin.  Ro ráid in rí,
cía do chomai(n)m-so, ol se.  Ro (f)recair in gilla, Ambróis, ol se, mo
ai*n*m-se is é sein in t-Ambrois Gleotic rí Bretan.

19. Can do cen*e*l, ol i*n* rí.  *Con*sul Romanach m'athair-se, ol se, 7
bíd hé só mo dún.  Roleic Gorthig*ernd* in dun do Ambróis 7 rige
iarthair Inse Bre*tan* uile, 7 tanic cona druidib co túascert Inse Bre*tan*
.i. cosin ferand dianid ai*n*m Gunnis, 7 rochumtaig dún and .i. Caer
Gorthigernd.

20.            De chathaigecht Gorthemir.

Iartai*n tra* atraracht Gorthemir coscrach ma*cc* Gortegern cona
brathair in agíd Egist 7 Orsa, 7 rochathaigsetar Bretai*n* mar oen ris
co hamnas, co ro-i*n*narbsat Saxono co hinis Teneth ; 7 rogabsat Bretai*n*

---

sovereignty ; the power of the Saxons, the white worm, which took
the whole sail but a little, *i.e.* took the Island of the Britons but a
little, till at last the power of the Britons drove them out.

" Thou, however, King of the Britons, go out of this castle, for
thou mayest not keep it,[1] and seek[2] the island of the Britons, and
thou shalt find thy own castle."  The king said :—" What is thy
name ?" quoth he.  The lad answered :—" Ambrose," quoth he, " is
my name."  (This is Ambrose Gleotic, King of the Britons.)

19. " Whence is thy race ? " quoth the king.  " My father was a
Roman Consul," quoth he, " and this shall be my castle."  Gortigern
left the castle to Ambrose, and the kingship of the west of the
island of Britons all, and came with his druids to the north of
the island of Britons, even to the land called Gunnis, and built a
castle there, to wit, Caer Gortigern.

Of the war of Gorthemir.

20. Thereafter arose Gorthemir, the triumphant, son of Gortigern,
with his brother, against Hengist and Horsa, and the Britons made
war along with him fiercely, till they drove the Saxons to the island

---

[1] Will not be able to protect it.        [2] Search, visit (travel (?) ).

forro fo thrí in n-insi co toracht cobair chucu asin Germáin, 7 rochathaigsetar fri Bretnu cach la.   Tan ba leo, tan aile ba forro; 7 dorat Gorthemir cetri catha doib .i. cath for brú Derguint, 7 cath for
brú Rethenegabáil, 7 is and dorochair Ors 7 Catigernd macc Gortigern;
7 cath for bru mara Icht, 7 taifnitir Saxain co a loṅgaib, 7 cath for
bruaig Epifort.   Marb immurgu Gorthemir íar n-amsir bic 7 atrubairt
fri Bretnu, garr ría n' ec, a adnacul for bru in mara 7 ni ticfaitis Gaill
etir in n-insi íartain.   Ni dernsatar Bretain sin.

Atraracht nert Saxan iar sin ar ba cara doib Gorthigern a los a mna.

21.  Dorala immurgu iár n-éc Gorthemir 7 iar sid Egist 7 Gorti-
ger(n) doronsat Saxain mebuil for Bretnu .i. Bretain 7 Saxain do
thinol in oen baile, amal bid do ṡid, .i. Égist 7 Gorthigern fá chomlin
cen armaib ic [c]echtarnai.   Acht tucsat Saxain scena etarru 7 am-
mælanu,[1] 7 romarbsat na Bretnu bátar and sin acht Gorthigernd a

---

of Thanet.   And the Britons took from them thrice the island, till help
came to them out of Germany, and they warred with the Britons daily.
At one time it was in their favour, at another time it was against them.
And Gorthemir gave four battles to them—a battle on the bank of Der-
gunt, and a battle on the bank of Rethenegabal, and it is there that Horsa
fell, and Catigern, son of Gortigern; and a battle on the shore of the
Ictian Sea, and the Saxons are chased to their ships; and a battle on
the brink of Epifort.   Gorthemir, however, died after a short time,
and he said to the Britons, shortly before his death, to bury him
on the edge of the sea, and the foreigners would not come at all into
the island thereafter.   The Britons did not do that.   The power of
the Saxons rose after that, for Gortigern was a friend to them on
account of his wife.

21.  It befel, however, after the death of Gorthemir, and after
the peace of Hengist and Gortigern, that the Saxons played a
treachery on the Britons, to wit, the Britons and the Saxons to
be gathered into one place, as it were, to make peace.   Hengist and
Gortigern (to be) with equal numbers, neither side having arms.
But the Saxons brought knives between them and their sandals,[2]
and slew the Britons that were there, save Gortigern alone, and

---

[1] dá maelán argit im a cossa, LU. fo. 26 b.   [2] ficones in Latin, Nen.

oenur, 7 rochenglatar Gorthigern, 7 dórat trian a feraind [do] dar
cend a mna .i. Alsaxum 7 Sutsaxum 7 Nitilsaxum.

22. Noforcanad immurgu German inni Gorthigernd co roleced a
mnai .i. a ingin.  Rotheigh 7 rofolaig riá German co clérchib Bretan
isind [f]erund dianid ainm Gorthigernian ; 7 dochuaid German co
clérchib Bretan 7 ro boi .xl, lathi 7 aidche and ; 7 dochuaid doridisi
Gorthigerng for teched na clerech co a dún, 7 dochoid German inna
díaid, 7 robátar trí lá 7 trí aidhchi in aine and sin, 7 roloisc tene do
nim inní Gorthigern and sin cona uile muintir.

Atberat araile is do dercuiniud atbath for fain(n)iul al-luc il-luc.
Atberat dano araile is talam rosluic ind adaig ro losced a dún.

23. Robatar immurgu tri meicc oca .i. Gorthigernd, is eside ro cha-
thaig fri Saxanu, Catigern [7] Pascent, is do-side dorat Ambróis rí
Bretan Boguelt 7 Gorthigerniain iár n-éc a athar Faustus noem .i.

---

they bound Gortigern, and gave a third of their land to him on
account of his wife—namely, Essex, and Sussex, and Middlesex.

22. German, however, was admonishing Gortigern to give up
his wife, *i.e.* his [own] daughter.  He fled and hid from German,
and the clerics of the Britons, in the land which is called Gorthigernian, and German went with the clerics of the Britons, and was
there forty days and nights.  And Gortigern again went in flight
from the clerics to the castle, and German went after him, and
they were three days and three nights fasting there, and a fire
from heaven burned Gortigern then with all his household.

Others say that it is of great grief[1] he died, wandering from place
to place.

Others, too, say that it was the earth that swallowed him the
night his castle was burned.

23. He had, however, three sons—namely, Gortigern[2] (it is he
warred against the Saxons), Catigern, and Pascent.  It is to this one
(last-named) that Ambrose, King of the Britons, gave Boguelt and
Gorthigernian after the death of his father, holy Faustus, that is [to]
his daughter's son.  And it was German baptized him, and reared him,

---

¹ *Or* despair.                    ² *Read* Gortimer.

macc a ingine 7 Germán rombaist 7 ronail 7 roforcan; 7 techtaid cathraig for bru srotha Rém.[1] Nemnus asbert so.

24. Fermǽl fil innosa for ferund Gorthigern meicc Teudubri, meicc Pascent, meicc Guodicater, meicc Morut, meicc Eldat, meicc Eldoc, meicc Paul, meicc Meprit, meicc Briacat, meicc Pascent, meicc Gorthigern, meicc Guitail, meicc Guittolin, meicc Glou.

Bonus 7 Paulus 7 Mauron trí meicc Glou; is e-side dorone Caer Gleu (o over e) .i. Glusester for bru Sabrinne. Dochuaid German día thír. Patraic tra ind inbaid sin i ndáire in Herind oc Miliuc, isind amsir sin rofolded Pledias dochum nErend do preciupt doib. Dochoid Patraic d[f]oglaim fades, co roleg in canoin la German. Roinnarbad Pledias a Hérind 7 tánic co rofogain do Dia i Fordun isin Mairne.

25. Tanic Patraic dochum nÉrend iár foglaim 7 robaist firu Herend.

O Adam co bathis fer nÉrend .um. ccc. xxx.; ferta tra Patraic do innisin dúib-si, a f̃iru Herend, is usce dó loch insin.

---

and taught him. And he possesses a city on the bank of the river Rem. It is Nennius who said this.

24. Fermael is now the name of the land of Gorthigern, son of, &c.

Bonus, and Paulus, and Mauron were the three sons of Glou. It is he who built Caer Gleu (Glou), *i.e.* Gloucester on the bank of the Severn. German went to his country.

Palrick (was) at that time in bondage in Ireland under Mileuc. It was in that period that Palladius was sent to Ireland to preach to them. Patrick went south to study, and he read the Canon[2] under German. Palladius was banished from Ireland, and came and served God in Fordun in the Mairne.

25. Patrick came to Ireland after (his) study, and baptized the men of Ireland.

From Adam to the baptism of the men of Ireland, 5330 (years). To tell to you, men of Ireland, the miracles of Patrick, that is (bringing) water to a lake.

---

[1] *Or* Réin.   o over *e*.   [2] i.e. the Scriptures (or Canon Law (?)).

Rogab *tra* nert Saxan for Bretnu iar n-éc Gorthigern 7 rogab Octa m*acc* Egist rige *forr*u.　Aráide nocathaiget Artúr 7 Bret*ain* ríu co calma 7 dorat dá cath déc doib .i. *in* cet-chath i n-Inbiur Gléir, in tan*aise* 7 in tres 7 i*n* ceth*ramad* 7 i*n* coiced f*or* brú Dubglassi, in sesed f*or* bru Basa; in uii. i Caill Calidoi*n* .i. Cait Coit Cledeb, in uiii. in Les Gui*n*neai*n*.

26. Is and si*n* ro-i*m*marchuir Artúr deilb Maire f*or* a gúalai*n*d, 7 roteichsetar na págáin. [In] ix. i Cathraig ind Leomai*n*, [in] x. in Robroit; xii. is and s*ide* ro marb lám Artuir .xl. ar ocht cétaib in oen ló 7 ba les coscor intib uile.　No-chuinchitis im*murgu* na Saxain ó Germain f*or*tacta doib 7 rígi f*orr*o co h-Ida,[1] is e-s*ide* cét-ri rogab uádib ifós Inbene Ro*í*c .i. fri Umbra atúaid.　Ida m*acc* Euba, Eanfleth ingen Eduni toisech riam robaisted do Saxanaib in Inis Bretan.

———————

The power of the Saxons overcame the Britons after the death of Gortigern, and Octa, son of Hengist, took kingship over them. Nevertheless, Arthur and the Britons warred against them bravely, and gave twelve battles to them, to wit, the first battle in Inber Gléir; the second, and the third, and the fourth, and the fifth, on the bank of Dubglais; the sixth, on the bank of Bassa; the seventh, in the forest of Calidon, *i.e.* Cait Coit Cledeb; the eighth, in Les Guinneain.

26. It is there that Arthur bore the image of Mary on his shoulder, and the pagans fled; the ninth, in the city of the Lion;[2] the tenth, in Robroit;[3] the twelfth, it was in this that Arthur's hand slew eight hundred and forty in one day, and his was the victory in them all.

The Saxons, however, besought help to themselves from Germany, and (offered) the kingship over themselves to Ida.　This is the first king who took (kingship) from among them on this side of Inbene Roic, *i.e.* by the Humber from the north.　Ida (was) son of Euba; Eanfleth, daughter of Edwin, the first ever that was baptized of the Saxons in the island of Britons.

———————

[1] co dia, MS.
[2] Caer Leon.
[3] the 11th "in Monte Bregion," omitted here.

## HOMILIES FROM LEABHAR BREAC.

### Instruction on the Sacraments.

27. [*LB.* 257*a*]. Isu Cr*ist* Ma*cc* Rig ni*m*e 7 talm*an*, in Tres P*er*su na Tr*i*nóti is c*o*moesa 7 is cutruma fr*i*sin Ath*air* 7 fr*i*sin Spir*ut* Nóeb, i*n* Fír-Dia 7 i*n* Fírduine, i*nt* Uasalsacurt 7 i*nt* Ard-Eps*cop* roédpá(i)r he fén f*or* altoir na crochi do ċendach 7 do fuaslucud i*n* chinedu doen*n*a—is ó roedpair isi*n* oídche ria n-a c(h)ésad a ḟuil 7 a feoil, 7 dorat dia apst*a*laib[1] dia caithium. Ocus f*or*ácaib oc na hapst*a*laib[1] sin 7 icon ecl*ais* uile cu f*or*ba i*n* tsaegail gnáthugud dénma na hedp*ar*ta *cet*na do ċuimniug*ud* na c*é*t-edp*ar*ta dia rothairb*ir* he fén fr*i* croich 7 bás ar umalóit don Ath*air* némda do ċomallud a tholi.

28. Is hé in édpairt a raibe lánbuideċus Dé 7 féthnugud a ḟergi fr*i* síl n-Ádaim escai*n*te. Ar is í*n*nte robui f*or*bair[2] umalóti 7 iní*s*le, f*or*-

27. Jesus Christ, the Son of the King of Heaven and Earth, the Third Person of the Trinity, is coeval and coequal with the Father and the Holy Ghost, true God and true Man, the High Priest and High Bishop, who offered Himself on the altar of the cross to redeem and ransom the human race; it is He who, on the night before His crucifixion, offered up His blood and body, and gave them to His apostles to partake thereof. And He left with those Apostles, and with His whole Church, to the end of time, the custom[3] of making the same oblation to commemorate the first oblation when He subjected Himself to the cross and to death in obedience to the Heavenly Father, and to fulfil His will.

28. This is the oblation in which is the full satisfying[4] of God and the appeasing of His anger against the accurst seed of Adam; for in it was the full-growth of humility and lowliness, the full-

---

[1] hapstalu, ms.
[2] f*or*bair, ms., as forair, forbarach, in *AG. Cf.* forbart, forbartach, forbíur, Z.; forbairt 7 bisech, *AG.*
[3] *Or* rite, "an bfuil gnáthuġad an uisge choisreagtha arsaid"? is the use of holy water ancient? *Donlevy,* 442.
[4] *Or* propitiation, "buidech, *gl.* contentus"; buidechas now means "thanks."

bair d*ei*rci 7 cridirċisechta, 7 lán-chomaiditiu f*ri* trógi i*n* chi*n*eda
doenna cu coitcend.

29. Cech tan t*ra* chúimniges 7 cretess ce*ch* díne iar n-araile, 7
ce*ch* dui*n*e arnuair i*n* c*é*t-epairt si*n*, 7 in tan tairisniges ín*n*te, is andsi*n*
trémdíriges¹ doc(h)um ni*m*e; 7 is and is tarba dó césad Cr*ist*, 7 is
and ċesas dosam co toduchtach² he, ocus is and si*n* soerthar he ar
feirg ṅDé 7 ar ċum*ach*tu in diabuil 7 ar a p*e*cdaib fén.   Ar am*al* bói
i*n* nathair umaide ic ma*c*cu Israel f*or* slaitt et*a*ruas, darér am*al* rothecaisc Dia dolb i*n* tan tuctha plaga na nath*r*ach f*orr*u isi*n* díthrub.
ocus cech oen nobenad f*ri*a nathair occu ó sin amach ní erchoitiged
dó o rosdéchad f*or*sa(n) nathraig n-umaide.   Is amlaid di*diu* cipe
c(h)retius 7 chuimnigius am*al* robói Cr*ist* hi ċroich, ní erchoitiget
ṅemi 7 aslaige démnu ní dó.   Ar cia robensat remi he, slanaigfit(h)*ir*
t*ri*a forḟethium in chésta 7 t*ri*a ḟairisium and.

---

growth of charity and heart-pity, and perfect sympathy³ for the
wretchedness of the human race in general.

29. Whenever, then, each generation after another, and every
person in turn, remembers and believes that first oblation, and when
he trusts in it, then it leads him⁴ towards heaven, and it is then the
passion of Christ is an advantage to him, and then He suffers for him
profitably,⁵ and then he is saved from the anger of God, and from the
power of the devil, and from his own sins.   For as the children of
Israel had the brazen serpent aloft⁶ on a rod, as God had instructed
them (to do) when the plagues of serpents were brought upon
them in the desert, and everyone of them who was thenceforth
stricken by a serpent was not hurt by it⁷ when he looked at the
brazen serpent.   Thus, also, whoso believes and remembers how Christ
was on the cross, the poisons and allurements of demons harm him
not in anything.   For though they (may) have struck him before, he
will be healed by contemplating the passion and dwelling on it.⁸

---

¹ *Or* trém*i*díriges (?).

² Perhaps = tothachtach; *cf*. tothacht,
purport, importance, flower (of army),
*AG*.

³ comaiditiu, co-profession (?), fellow-
feeling: *cf*. a mbráthirsi do aiditin
frisna bochtaib, *LB*. 248 b.

⁴ trimedirgedar, *gl*. transfert, *Ml*. 54 a.

⁵ It seems = tothachtach, tádḃachtach.

⁶ eadarḃuas, "swinging in the air,
whirling aloft over head," of *O'D.'s
Suppl*., does not suit here.

⁷ Lit., "it did not harm him," non
ei nocebat.

⁸ *For* airisium, thairisium; *or* a ḟaire-
sium, in watching it.

30. Is aire *imorro*, isí in edpairt *c*etna dognith*er* ocainde .i. oc athcuímníug*ud* mar darónad hi fén i*s*in chesad, *c*ona beth *ter*c men-mnaigi *nó* fai*n*di irsi oc na dóinib dédinch*aib* na tarraid i*n* césad.   Ar diamad sigean *nó* comartha *aile*,[1] ind écmais in fírchuirp 7 na firfola, *c*etna t*r*ia nde*r*ntá[2] int athcúimniug*ud* sin i*n*díu, ni thairisnigfitís in lucht dedenach isi*n* c*ét* edpairt dia særad, uair nach in a áimsir *nó* i*n* a frecnar*c*us doronad, mi*n*e beth occu fen i*n* an aimsir frecnairc i*n* edpairt i*n*and ci*n*cop isin deilb chetna.

31. Ocus (is) aire nach ead ón ar na bud aduathmar lasna hirisechu a ċaithem 7 na rothubtís amirsig f*r*iu fuil 7 feoil duine do chathium, 7 *cum*ad logmairite a cretium cin a chetfanugud i*n* a deilb fen.   Uair amal ba logmar thall cretem Diad*acht*a Cr*ist* a ndeilb d*e*roil a Doen-nach*t*n, is am*laid* is logmar i*n*díu a chretem a ndeilb bairgi*n*e.   Ar am*al*

---

30. Wherefore, then, it is the same oblation that is made by us, remembering how it was made in the crucifixion, so that there be not lack of mindfulness[3] or weakness of belief in the people of later times that the passion has not remained.[4]   For were there other sign or token, in the absence of the same true body and true blood, through which that commemoration was made to-day, the people of later times would not trust in that first oblation for their salvation since it was not in their time and presence it was made, unless they them-selves in their present time had the same oblation, though it be not in the same form.

31. And it is for this reason that it is not so,[5] in order that the partaking thereof might not be deemed terror-causing by the faithful, and lest infidels should charge them with partaking of the blood and flesh of a man, and that all the more precious[6] might be their belief without perceiving Him in His own form.   For as it was precious of old to believe in the Godhead of Christ in the lowly form of His Humanity, so is it a precious thing to-day to believe in Him, in the

---

[1] íí in MS
[2] nd*é*nta(r) *or* ndénta (?).
[3] mindedness ; *cf.* huand-fairsing-menmnaigi ; *gl.* magnanimitate.
[4] *Or* continued; *cf.* tarraid, doruaraid, doruarathatar, *gl.* remanserunt, *Z*. 456, 457.   I think " ni tharraid in animm asin curp " (*Pass. and Hom.* l. 8117),

= the soul did abide or stay out of the body.
[5] i.e. in the same form.
[6] *Or* meritorious, valuable ; luach saothair, "reward," *Revelations*, xxii. is maith in lóg dobeir Dia, "great is the reward God gives," *LB*. 108 a; this compar. is not in dictionaries.

roedpair in Rígsacart coitchend, .i. Isu Cri*st* fodessin, i*n* edpairt sin
artus darcend in *chi*n*e*du doen*n*a, is aml*aid* édpra*s* cec*h* sacart dia síl
ap*er*sai*n* 7 a n*er*t briathar, in edp*airt* si*n*.  Ni hinand dorér am*al*
dori*n*de-sium ro*m*pu, 7 am*al* ròthecaisc doib *con*adernatís ; acht iar fír
ċena di*diu* is esium fén .i. Isu Cri*st* i*n* Sacart cín*n*te oc bendachad
7 oc noe*m*ad na nemaicside na hedp*ar*ta cech lathi cia beth i*n* sacart
*ele* co *h*aicside oc timthire*ch*t fri*a* laim.

32. Is e t*ra* i*n* maigiste*r* eolach 7 i*n* fírliaig rothecaisc do ċách
cu*r*roc*h*tad[1] i*n* sasad slanaigthe si*n* i*n*agaid erchoti 7 ne*m*i na nathrach,
7 dia chalmugud 7 dia bethugud 7 dia thódiuscad a talm*ain* 7 dia
thocbail f*or* nem.  *a*Ar ni theit nech f*or* nem*a* ac*h*t intí tanic de .i.
Cri*st* co*n* a ballaib .i. Cri*st* co cech oen caithes a chorp 7 a fuil, no
ren-a duthr*ach*t a ċaithem dia fagbad.[2]

33. Fath *aile* ar-arfacbad acai*n*d in sásad si*n*, ardaig comad
oenchorp in ecl*ais* uile do Cri*st* iar n-oentaid aicenta oenchuirp t*ri*

---

form of bread.  For as the universal Royal Priest, Jesus Christ
Himself at first offered up that sacrifice for mankind, so every priest
of His race, by the virtue and power of words offers up that oblation.
Not the same is what[3] He did before them, and what He instructed
them to do ; but yet indeed in truth it is Jesus Christ Himself, the real
Priest, who, though invisible, is blessing and sanctifying the oblation
every day, though the other priest be ministering as his deputy.[4]

32. Now He is the learned master and true physician who directed
every one to approach[5] that food of salvation (as a remedy) against the
hurt and poison of the serpent, and to be encouraged and quickened,
and to be raised from earth and lifted to heaven.  For no one goes to
heaven but only He who came from it, that is, Christ with His members,
*i. e.* Christ, with everyone that partakes of his body and blood, or ha
an earnest desire to partake thereof if he could get (it).

33. Another cause for which that food has been left with us (is),
that the whole church might be one body to Christ, after the natural

---

[1] *It seems* cor-roc*h*tad in MS. ; *read*
cur*r*ochaithed *or* cor-roched.

[a-a] This is inserted in the margin.

[2] fadbad written first, and a circlet
put under the *d* so as to form *g.*

[3] *Lit.*, is as He did.

[4] fri láim in rig (a viceroy), repre-
senting the king, *AG.* p. 777.

[5] *Or* partake of = corrochaithed.

[6] *Or rather*, refreshed, nourished.

an ċaithem doib uli a firchuirp-sium 7 a fírfola, am*al* is oen[1] eturru
fén 7 f*ri*s-(s)ium iar n-oeniris 7 iar n-oenduthracht m*en*man. Is hi
di*diu* in edp*air*t sin edpairt is anorchu 7 is diliu la Dia 7 la m*uint*ir
nime dona hulib edp*a*rtaib; ar is logmaire lais hi i*n*at na huli séotu
7 máine orda 7 airg(d)ide, 7 is mó chendsaiges hé f*ri* dóinib domai*n*.
Is hi di*d*u is cend 7 is clethi[2] inan uli n-ádmat 7 n-édpart; ar
ardfíugra 7 foiscthe 7 sígne iatsum uli, is hi *im.* a hoenur i*n* phóind 7
in fírinde. Ar cia brig *nó* cia n*ert* slánaigthe no glanaid *no* fuaslaicthe
anma *no* fethnaigthe fergi Dé nobiad hi fuil na rethi 7 na mbocc 7
na .ix. n-ócdam treothu fen, mine betís oc inchosc 7 ic follsiugud na
fíredp*art*-sa rotholtnanaig[3] do Dia oc Abel 7 oc Noe, 7 oc Abraham dia
roedpair a m*ac*[4] forsan áltoir iarn a chuibrech? figair sin i*n* Ath*air*
Nemda do edpairt a Mac* *for* altoir na crochi.

34. Is hi di*du* in edpairt-si rotucad t*ri*asi*n* mbairgin 7 t*ri*asin fín

---

union of one body, through their partaking, all of them, of His true
body and His true blood, as there is union among themselves and with
Him, in one faith and one will of souls. Now that oblation is of all
oblations the most honourable and agreeable in the sight of God and
of the court of heaven; for it is more precious in His view than all
jewels and gold and silver treasures, and it most (of all) propitiates[5]
Him towards the people of the world. It is it that is the head and
chief of all material things[6] and oblations, for (mere) types and shadows
and symbols were all these; but this alone is the reality[7] and the
truth. For, what virtue or power of saving or purifying or redeeming
the soul, or of appeasing the anger of God, was in the blood of the rams
or the goats or the nine young oxen, by themselves, if they were not
indicating and (fore)showing the real oblations which pleased God on
the part of Abel, Noah, and of Abraham when he offered up his son on
the altar after having bound him, a figure that (last one is) of the
Heavenly Father who offered up His Son on the altar of the cross.

34. This therefore is the oblation which was given through the

---

[1] *For* oentu (?).
[2] bud c*e*nn bud cleithe, *AG. v.* cleithe.
[3] *Sic*, read rotholtanaig (?).
[4] mc .i. mac, MS. * *or* Meic.
[5] *Lit.*, makes Him mild.

[6] ádmat = ὕλη = wood, raw material.
[7] The important, the weighty thing,
from "pondus" (?); poind, use, advantage, *AG.*; a whit, *O'D. Suppl.*,
does not suit here.

redpair[1] melcisedéch thall; isé so in fíruan cáscda *tr*íasa rosoerait *pr*imgene *m*ac n-Is*r*ael. Is i-so *in* máind nemda forsa fácbadar 7 forsa fag(b)ar cech mmlais; is i-so in bó d*er*g threblí*ad*nach[2] isa fuil rohesréti tar macu Isr*a*el dia coisec*r*ad 7 dia mbendach*ad*. In tan *tr*a bend*a*ch-th*ar* 7 noemth*ar* in glanrún sin ch*u*irp C*r*i*st*, bíd Ísu C*r*i*st* in tan sin fo*r*sin altoir *con* aing*l*iu 7 archaing*l*iu *im*me. Ar *n*i hé in sacart iar fír dogní *in* édp*air*t sin it*er*, cid he atcíth*er* icon timthirecht, *acht* Ísu C*r*i*st* fen d*u*gní com*s*ód 7 bendach*ad* ina b*a*irgi*n*e 7 in fína a fíraicned a ch*u*irp 7 a f(h)ola fén i*n* tan chan*a*s in sacart na b*r*i*athr*a roċan C*r*i*st* in tan doríg*n*e artús in edpa(i)rt-sin.

35. Ar is e C*r*i*st* is sacart 7 is edp*a*irt and; ar is iat treda bís ocan edp*air*t sin cuirp C*r*i*st* 7 a fola .i. in sacart cohacside icon timthirechtt i f*i*adn*ai*o cháich co coitcend, ocus aingil 7 árchaingil nime ic a f*or*gell 7 in a fiadnaib aige fri laim Crist, ocus C*r*i*st* fén oc comsod 7 ic ben-

---

bread and wine, which Melchisedech offered of yore; this is the true Paschal Lamb, by which the first-born of the children of Israel were saved. This is the heavenly manna in which is left[3] and in which is found every taste; this is the three-year-old red cow, whose[4] blood was sprinkled over the children of Israel to consecrate and bless them. Now, when that pure mystery of the body of Christ is blessed and sanctified, Jesus Christ is at that time on the altar with the angels and archangels of heaven around Him. For it is not truly the priest who performs that oblation at all, though it be he that is beheld ministering, but Jesus Christ Himself who works the conversion and blessing of the bread and wine into the true nature of His own body and blood, when the priest says the words which Christ said when He first made that oblation.

35. For Christ is (both) Priest and Oblation there; for there are three things at the oblation of Christ's body and blood, to wit, the priest visibly ministering in presence of all in general, and the angels and archangels of heaven witnessing it, and as witnesses for him as minister of Christ, and Christ Himself changing, and blessing, and

---

[1] *Sic.*

[2] colpach thrí mblia*d*an, *Gen.* 15, 9; colpach bainnean dergb*u*íde, *Numbers* 19; *LB.* unites both.

[3] *Or* they found.

[4] *cf.* isa ferg, whose anger, *Molloy's Catech.* p. 71; *read* is a fuil *in* our *te*.*t.*

dachad 7 ic coisecrad na bairgine 7 in fína co ndenand-sum a chorp 7 a
fuil féin díbsin.

36. [*LB.* 257*b*]. Mairg cride tra, mine thairmisce morecin de, na
ticc don eclais in uair dénma na hédpart(a)-sa hi comdail Isu Crist 7
muintire nime do accáine a pecaid 7 do aircisecht friu 7 d'iarraid
fortachta¹ dia anmain.    Mairc is loind 7 is escaid documm na cobfledi
deroile truallnide 7 is anescaid dochumm na fledi hi fil betha bithbuan
7 slánti suthain dogrés.    Mairc nach congbann hé fen a sognímaib 7 i
sobésaib for cind na hedparta-sa, dia fegad in aimsir a dénma 7 dia
caithem con aithrigi ndic(h)ra 7 toirsi menman.

37. Cech duine tra risnad ail in bethu suthain cuitiged in
edpa(i)rt-si 7 caithed in sásad némda co hirisech 7 co trathaigtech 7
co haithrigech.    Ar cech oen chaithes hé con aithrigi 7 déraib 7 con
anath cretmi 7 con a airmitin in a chride, bid aittreb 7 bid tempul
coisecartha do Dia hé ; bid malairt bithbuan imorro hí dá cech oen
noscaithfe co heccomadais .i. cen aithrigi dia pecdaib 7 cen colma

---

consecrating the bread and wine, so that he makes His body and blood
of them.

36. Woe indeed to a heart,² if great necessity does not hinder
him from it, that comes not to the church at the hour of performing
this oblation to meet³ Jesus Christ and the family of heaven, to
bewail his sins⁴ and to (obtain) mercy for them, and to ask help for
his soul.    Woe (to him) who is eager and ready for the insignificant
and defiled feast, and is slow (to come) to the banquet in which is
life everlasting and perennial health for ever.    Woe to him who does
not keep himself in good deeds and practices (as a preparation) for this
oblation, to behold it at the time of the performance thereof, and to
partake of it with fervent repentance and sorrow of soul.

37. Every person, then, who desires life perennial, let him take
part in this oblation, and partake of the heavenly food faithfully, oppor-
tunely, penitentially.    For everyone who partakes of it with penance
and tears, and with steadiness of faith, and with reverence for it in
his heart, will be the abode and consecrated temple of God ; but it
(the Eucharist) will be lasting destruction to every one who shall

---

¹ fortsa, in ms.                          ³ *Or* with.
² *put for* man.                          ⁴ ' sin ' in text.

aice conid fírċorp 7 fírfuil in tSlainíccedu ċaithes, 7 cen anoir ndles-
tenaig dó in a ċride *acht* a gabail amal ce*ch* mbiad arché*na*.

38. Cid ingnad *tra* la nech in comṡód mírbulla si*n* i*na* bairgi*ne* 7
in fina hi fírchorp 7 hi fírf(h)uil Cr*ist*, creted[1] aráisin cen amarcus 7
cen et*a*raisi dontí na hep*ert* gói riam .i. do Cr*ist* fén rodemnig com*e*nic
si*n*. Creit *tra co*nid ulichum*ach*t*ach hé, cúmníg na mírbuli mora *aili*
dorígne ce(n) nach n-ádbar : i(n)t aer uli do ṡoud an usci oc tabairt
na dílend, na flesca ina nathr*ach*aib 7 na nathr*ach*a i flesca isi*n* Egipt,
i(n)t usci hi fuil 7 in fuil in usqi, in luaithriud i loscandaib, Muir
R*uad* do dlugi, S*ru*th Iordanen do thirmugud, int usqi asi*n* carraicc,
7 na mirbuli ile archena dorígne i Petarlaicc 7 i*n* Núfiadn*aise* ar maith
fr*i* dóinib.

39. Ar i*n*d uli mírbuil dorígne Dia ó thús do*m*ain is ar desmbireċt
dorigne iat .i. intí dorói*ne* na mírbuli móra *eli* co fétfad comsód a
chuirp 7 a fola i*m* mbairgin 7 hi fín.

---

partake of it unworthily, that is, without repentance of his sins, and
without having a firm conviction[2] that it is the true body and true
blood of the Saviour that he partakes of, and without due honour to
Him in his heart, merely taking it as any other food.

38. Now, though wonderful may seem to anyone that marvellous
conversion of the bread and the wine into the true body and true blood
of Christ, he should believe, for all that, without doubt and without hesitation,[3] Him who never uttered a falsehood, to wit, Christ
Himself who frequently affirmed that. Believe, then, that He is all-
powerful; remember the other great wonders He did without any
(natural) cause, turning the whole air into water bringing on the
Deluge; the wands into serpents and the serpents into wands in Egypt;
water into blood, and blood into water; dust into frogs; the dividing
of the Red Sea; the drying-up of the River Jordan; the water out of
the rock; and the many other wonders which He performed in the Old
Law and in the New Testament for the benefit of men.

39. For every miracle God worked from the beginning of the
world, it is for an example He did them, to wit (to show) that He who
did the other great wonders could convert His body and blood into

---

[1] credet, in MS.  [2] *Lit.*, hardness, *O'Clery.*  [3] *Or* unfaithfulness.

Tabrat *tra* dian óid a mírbuli gnáithce[1] cech lathi .i. mar chomṡodus
ar desmb*ireċt* in sílne usqide i ḟeoil 7 i cnámu nan anmanda 7 mar
ṡous *tra* in talum fén i*n* an*m*andaib 7 i torthib 7 i cnámaib, 7 na cnámu
i torthaib 7 i*n*t usqi i clochaib 7 i tin*e*d*ib 7 iat-sein i*n* usqi ; ocus *am*al
ṡous torthi in tal*main* 7 na ċínd i feoil 7 i fuil 7 i cnámaib nan anmanda.

40. Intí di*du* dogní na comṡóti mírbulla si*n* i corpaib *ele* do fula*n*g
in betha ercr*a*daig, ní hecen roingnad de cia doneth comṡód a chuirp
fén do ḟágbail na be*th*ad suthain*e* dúin*n*e triasan sásad suthai*n* sin.
Ar is esi*n* in sílne nemda triasa fo*r*bair gort nan irisech 7 triasa
n-érechat a talmain il-ló bratha, triasa soerfait*er* 7 triasa sasfait*er* iat
ar thromd*acht* 7 emeltus in chuirp truallnide, ar thruaigi 7 ar imnedu
ifi*r*n*n, 7 triasa fúigbet in fírbe*th*aid 7 in fírgloir i cutr*u*mus fr*i* haingliu nime. Intí *tra* rosbe*n*nach na .v. bairgena cu ras*á*sta .v. míle
dib, 7 c*u* ralínta .xii. cliab dia fúidlib ;[2] 7 intí dosgní co gnáthach *cet*

---

bread and wine. Let them therefore observe the usual wonders of
every day, that is, how He converts the liquid little seed into the
flesh and bones of animals, and how He turns the earth itself into
animals, and fruits, and bones, and bones into fruits, and water into
stones and fires, and those same things into water, and how he turns
the fruits into earth, and, in addition, into the flesh and blood and
bones of animals.

40. He then who works these marvellous conversions (of things)
into other bodies to support the perishable world, there need not be
great wonder at it, if He should produce a change of His body to
procure lasting life for us through that perennial food. For He is the
celestial seedling by which grows the field-crop of the faithful, and by
which they shall rise from the earth on the day of judgment, by which
they shall be freed from and refreshed against the heaviness and weari-
ness of the corrupt body, against the wretchedness and miseries of hell,
and by which they shall obtain true life and true glory on an equality
with the angels of heaven. He who blessed the five loaves, so that five
thousand were full-fed by them, and that twelve baskets were filled by
the remnants thereof; He who usually makes a hundred grains out of

---

[1] *sic, for* gnáithche, gnáthcha (?).
[2] fúiglib, ᴍs., as if connected with
"fúigbe," "fácbáil." Stokes gives

"fuid*e*ll," from *LU.* 114, and
"fuidlech," from *S. na R.* ; fuideal,
*O'R.* ; mostly "fuig*o*ll," in *LB.*

*gráine* don oen *gráine* 7 *in* gort uli fa deoid triasin mbe*nn*achtain tuc
Ísu Cr*ist* i tús domain fo*r*sin tal*main* con a torthib—is e rosbe*nn*ach
*gráine* glangríbdai a chuirp 7 a f(h)ola fén co rof(h)as gort saidbir de
dianad lán domun uli o thurcabail co fui*n*ed triasa sástar ind uli iri-
sechu o thús núïadn*uise* co dé brátha.

41. Ni messu di*diu* a bec i*n*as a mor i*n* chuirp-si Cr*ist*, 7 ní mó is
airbern[1] a rand oltás a thoitt, ar ata ulídetaid 7 toitt chómlan chuirp
Cr*ist in* cech errandus dé ; ocus ata lánbrig 7 lánn*ert* legis 7 slánaigthe
cech dui*n*e i*n*ntib. Ni ferr, di*diu*, *nó* ní messa, o dui*n*e, sech araile in
glanrúin sin chuirp Cr*ist* 7 a fhola ; ar ní thic do p*e*cad dui*n*e a
corbad-si *no* a holcugud ; ní re maithes t*r*a nach dui*n*e *no* ar a nóime
fásus a maith-si 7 a noemad ; ar is íse maithiges 7 noemas cách it*er*
thuaith 7 ecl*ais*. Ísu Cr*ist*, Mac Ríg nime 7 tal*man*, i*n* dúilem triasa
nd*e*rnta ar tús ind uli dúl, 7 in fírliaig coitchend triasa slánaigth*er*

---

one grain, and in fine the whole harvest through the blessing which
Jesus Christ at the beginning of the world gave to the earth with its
fruits—He is the same who blessed the pure[2] grains of His body and
blood, so that from it grew a rich harvest from which the whole world
was filled from the rising to the setting (of the sun), by which all the
faithful are fed from the beginning of the New Law to the day of
doom.

41. Not inferior is the little part to the great part[3] of this body of
Christ; neither is its part less than its totality, for the perfect whole
and entire of the body of Christ is in each particle thereof; and the
full virtue and power of the healing and saving of every man abides
in them. Not better, then, nor worse, one than another,[4] O man,
that pure mystery of the body of Christ and of His blood, for man's
sin cannot defile it or make it bad; it is not by the goodness of any
man, or on account of his holiness, that its good and sanctification
grows greater, since it is it that makes good and sanctifies every one,
both lay and clerical. Jesus Christ, the Son of the King of Heaven
and Earth, the Creator by whom was made every creature, and the

---

[1] *So in* MS.; *for* airberu (?) ; it may
mean "bulkier" (*airbire*, armful, *O'R.*)

[2] *gríbdai* = swift, quick; *grib* has
many meanings, which do not suit here.

[3] The small particle and the large one.

[4] The meaning seems to be, from what
follows, that when this "pure mystery"
is celebrated by a sinner it is not less
worthy than when it is celebrated by a
holy man

cech oen gabus a forcetul 7 a chomairle, is he forácaib oc cách in glanrúin-si na báiste dia nglanud 7 dia noemad. Ár intan genes nech ó a thustidib collaide tria oelscugud[1] collaide mac do senadam escainti[2] he ón mud sin 7 do diabul; intan tra baistigther he donither duine nua glan dé 7 fírmac Dé.

42. *Ocus* amal ric a less *imorro* in náidiu iarna túsmiud biad do fulang a bethad, is amlaid sin recar a less iarsin athgene(m)ain sásad chuirp Crist 7 a fola dia congbail immon mbethaid spiritalda frith isin bathis. In crismad didiu is e forpthiugud na baiste acht ní forpthi hí ina ecmais. Oenfecht *imorro* dlegar in baisted .i. in aithgen, amal is ænfecht bís in cét-gein, 7 amal is ænf(h)echt nocésad Crist; ar ni dígbaither rath na baiste co bás. Glanaid tra in aithrigi cech salchar thinoilter iarsin mbaithis.

43. Cech oen tra risnad ail leges a anmma 7 comsód cusin Coimdid,

---

true universal Physician by whom is healed everyone that receives His teaching and counsel. He it is that left to all men this mystery[3] of baptism to purify and sanctify them. For when one is born of corporal parents, through concupiscence of the flesh, a son to the accurst Old Adam and to the devil he is in that way; but when he is baptized, a new and pure man and true son of God is made of him.

42. And as, indeed, the child after birth needs food to support its life, so after regeneration the food of the body and blood of Christ is needed to keep (him) up as regards the spiritual life which was got in baptism. Confirmation,[4] again, is the perfecting of baptism, and[5] it is not perfect without it. Once only baptism, that is regeneration, is required,[6] as it is once this first birth takes place, and as once Christ was crucified; for the grace of baptism is not taken away[7] till death. Penance also clears away every defilement that is contracted after baptism.

43. Whosoever wishes for the healing of his soul, and conversion

---

[1] oelscothugud (?), elscothach, *Todd Lect.* v.

[2] escaineti, with dot under last *e*.

[3] It seems to mean "sacrament" here; the Greek Fathers called a sacrament "mysterion."

[4] Stapleton, in *Catechismus Hib.*

*Latinus*, p. 107, says:—"Goirthear don sacrament a Laidin 'Confirmatio' goirthear dhe Chrisma (focal gréagach) chiallaigeas ola no unga."

[5] Lit., but.

[6] *Or* is lawful.

[7] *Or* diminished.

denad a fóisitin¹ co hinisiul 7 co haith*r*igech ; 7 glanaid in foisitiu¹ si*n*
7 irnaigthe na hecla*i*si am*ail* baithis.   Am*al* is teidm millti in chuirp
i*n* galar, is am*laid* is teidm malarta na hanma i*n* peccad ; 7 am*al* atat
lega fr*í* teídm in chuirp is am*laid* sin at*a*t lega fri téidm na hanma.
Mar thaisbenait di*diu* crecḣta² in chuirp do legaib in chuirp is amlaid
si*n* taisbentair crechta na han*m*a.   Am*al* i(s) slán intí a mbí n*e*im
iarna sceith, is am*laid* sin is nuaglan i*n* animm iarsin foeisitiu³ 7 tria
i*n*disi na peccad, tria aith*r*ige 7 t*r*ia hirnaigti na hecla*i*s*e*, 7 tria
foemud dó beth ó sin amach fo riagail ecla*i*si Dé.

44. *Idon* am*al* ticc mac do riarugud a athar 7 laigid i*n* a fiadnaise,
7 nochtaid hé dia sroigled conusfagaib a chendsa desin, is am*laid* sin
fogabar síd Dé triasin fóesitin.   Uair for*á*caib Cr*ist* oca aps*t*alaib⁴ 7
ocin eclais co d*e*riud in domain comus fuaslacthi 7 cuibrig cáich .i.
logtha n*ó* nemlogtha dá cech oen pecdach.   Ar am*al* marus i comus

---

to the Lord, should make his confession humbly and penitently ; and
that confession and the prayer of the Church purify like baptism.   As
sickness is a disease that destroys the body, so sin is a disease that
ruins the soul ; and as there are physicians for the disease of the body,
so are there physicians for the malady of the soul.   As, then, they
show the wounds of the body to the physicians of the body, so the
wounds of the soul are exhibited.   As he in whom there is a poison is
well after vomiting⁵ it, so is the soul renewed and pure after confession, and through the declaration of sins, by penance and by the
prayer of the Church, and by his undertaking⁶ to be thenceforward
under the rule of the Church of God.

44. That is, as a son comes to submit to his father, and lays himself
down in his presence, and bares himself to be scourged, and so obtains
gentle mercy from him, thus the peace of God is got by confession
For Christ left to his Apostles, and to the Church, to the end of the
world, the power of loosing and binding all men, that is, of forgiving
or not forgiving every single sinner.   For as there remains in the

---

¹ fóisitiu 7 foisiuti, in MS.
² *Leg.* créchta.
³ *Sic*, for fóisitin.
⁴ ap*s*talu, MS.
⁵ In a diary of an officer of an old

Irish family, who was in foreign service
in the 18th century, I found at regular
intervals, " p–k–d," I learned from his
son that it meant "went to confession."
⁶ *Or* consenting.

na heclaisi glanruin na baiste 7 glanrúin a chuirp 7 a fola, is amlaid sin ata lee comus logtha 7 cuibrig na peccad [258 a].

45. Is mor 7 is anorach didiu icon eclais glanruin na hongaine ar búi oc Crist 7 oca apstolu in gnathugud sin .i. ongad na ndoine ngalair ar daig a slanaigthi amal fogabur isin tsoscela; erailid didiu Iacop apstol, cicip¹ tan bes bráthair in enerti, na sacairt 7 na senóri do thinol chuci dia ongad, 7 do guide Dé fair im slanti chorpda do mad ferrdi ; 7 lanlogthar a phecda do acht co nderna a fóisitin² co díchra 7 co haithrigech, 7 rl.

ON SOME ARTICLES OF THE CREED.

46 [LB. 256 a.] Cach duine ris na dúthracht síd 7 cendsa in Choimmded dfagbail 7 slanugud a anma, ised dlegar de ar tús, cretem 7 aichentus in Choimded aice co léir; ar ni torba dó nachmait dogena cen in cretem sin aice. Int Ardrig Ulichumachtach tra robui riam rena duilib cen tosach, 7 dorigne na huli dul cen adbar, 7 follomnaigius

---

power of the Church the sacrament of baptism, and the sacrament of (His) body and blood, so she possesses the power of loosing and binding sins.

45. Great and honourable, indeed, in the Church is the pure mystery of unction; for Christ and His Apostles had that practice, that is, (of) anointing sick people for the sake of healing them, as is found in that word (or passage) where James the Apostle enjoins that, whensoever a brother is in infirmity, the priests and elders gather to him to anoint him, and to pray to God over him for the cure of his body, if it should be the better (for him), and (that) his sins be fully forgiven him, provided he makes his confession fervently and peni- tently, &c.

46. Every man who has a desire to find the peace and meekness of the Lord, and the salvation of his soul, is bound, first of all, to have faith in, and knowledge of, the Lord, and (that) fully; for of no profit to him is any good he shall do without having that faith. Now the Almighty High-King, who existed ever before His creatures, without a beginning, and made all creatures without

---

¹ Leg. cip-tan, as cip-indus.      ² foisitiu, MS.

iat, ⁊ dianad¹ lan nem ⁊ tal*am*, is amlaid ata co*n*id Triar ⁊ co*n*id Oen .i. Triar examu*il* he iar P*er*sann*ai*b .i. int Athar nemda as bunad ⁊ is top*ur* na Diad*ach*ta. Oen Mac di*du* i*n* Athar sin is comæsa ⁊ is cutru*m*a fr*is* fén o cech mud. In Spir*ut* Noem di*du*, isa tæniud ⁊ isa dira*m*, fil on Athair ⁊ o*n* Ma*cc* i slán-chutru*m*a friu.

47. Ar intí is Ath*air* ni Ma*cc* no Spir*ut*; ocus intí is Ma*cc* ní hAthair no Spir*ut*; ocus intí i(s) Spir*ut* ni hAthair nó Ma*cc* hé. Is Oen Dia arai in Tr*i*ar sin ⁊ ni *tri* Dee; Oen Dúilem ⁊ ni *tri* Dúilim, Oen Tig*er*na ⁊ ni tri Tig*er*nada. Ar is i*n*and Aicniud Diada doib, is inand Toil ⁊ Cum*ach*ta ⁊ is inand sosad atá accu. Ar att*at* imalle i*n* cech dú, ⁊ isat inunda a gni*m*a; ar is imalle dorónsat ⁊ follamnaigit i*n*d uli dul. Ni sine di*du* nech araile dib, uair róbat*ur* a tr*i*ur ria nduilib ⁊ ria n-aimsiraib, cen tús cen ti*n*dsce*t*ul fon mbith, am*al* na bia cr*i*ch na f*or*cend forru.

---

(pre-existing) material, and rules them, and of whom heaven and earth are full, it is thus He is, that He is Three (Persons), and that He is One, *i.e.* the Trinity distinct as to Persons, to wit, the Heavenly Father who is the origin and foundation of the Godhead. Then the only Son of that Father is coeval and equal to Him in every way. The Holy Ghost also, whose (is the) descent (on the Apostles) and the multitude (of gifts), is from the Father and the Son in full equality with them.

47. For He who is Father is not Son or (Holy) Ghost; and He who is Son is not Father or (Holy) Ghost; and He who is Holy Ghost is not Father or Son. However, these Three Persons are one God, and not three Gods; one Creator, and not three Creators; one Lord, and not three Lords. For They have one and the same Divine Nature; They have the same Will and Power; and They have the same abode. For They are together in every place, and Their acts are the same, since it is together They made and govern every creature. Not older, indeed, is one than another of Them, since the Three Persons existed before creatures, and before times, without beginning, without commencement in the world, as They will have no limit nor end.

---

¹ dia nadlan, MS.

48. In T(ara) Persu di*du* don Triur[1] sin .i. in M*acc* robói ria
nduilib 7 ria n-aim*s*eraib *im*mdaib tanic do fuaslucad síl Adaim hi
comóentaid in Athar 7 in Spir*to* Noim. Is é tanic do némdaib 7 iar
n-aimseraib *im*mdaíb do fuaslucad 7 do slanug*ad* in chi*n*edu doenna
roboi ˙co*n*ice sin fo daire 7 fo˙malairt diabuil; co rogab Doenn*acht*,
*in* oentaid P*er*sai*n*ne *fri* Deacht, *con*id Dia 7 Duine o sin ille hé,
g*er*bá Dia namá *con*ice sin, am*al* is Dia namá cha*í*dche i*n*t Athair
7 i*n* Spir*ut* N*ó*em.

49. Ar am*al* tairises ce*ch* duine o anmain dligthig 7 ó churp i*n*
tan teit hi flaith Dé, is amlaid sin tairiseas anosa Ísu Crist o thanic
locc[2] suthain a Diad*acht*a 7 o thanic aimser a Doenn*acht*a.

Rocoimp*red* di*di*u hi mbroi*n*d Muire Óigi cen chomoentaid ferda[3]
a*cht* tr*i*a rath 7 bend*acht*u in Spir*to* Nóib. Rogenir iar*um*[4] .ix. mísaib
cen scailiud ball cen oslucad brond. Roboi co fola(ch) it*er* dóinib

---

48. Now the Second Person of that Trinity, that is the Son, who
was before creatures and before all[5] ages, came to redeem the seed of
Adam, in union with the Father and the Holy Ghost. He it is that
came from the celestial (regions), and after many ages, to deliver and
save the human race, which was till then under the bondage and
destroying[6] influence of the devil; and He assumed human nature,
in unity of Person to the Divinity, so that He is God and Man
thenceforth, though He was God only till then, as the Father is
God, and the Holy Ghost is God, only (and) ever.

49. For as man consists of a rational soul and a body when he
enters the kingdom of God,[7] so now Jesus Christ consists at present
since the eternal abode of his Godhead has come,[8] and since came the
time of His humanity.

Now He was conceived in the womb of Mary the Virgin without
co-operation of man, but by the grace and blessing of the Holy Ghost.
He was born after nine months without loosening of the members,
without opening of womb. He was hidden among men, promoting

---

[1] trur, *Facsimile*.
[2] (o) locc (?).
[3] ferrda; ᴍs.; ferda, *Ml.* 44 a.
[4] *Or*, iar*um* (iar).
[5] Lit., many.

[6] *Or* malairt .i. drochordugud, *O'Dav*.
[7] *i.e.* into the world (?).
[8] Something seems to have been
omitted: *leg.* o thanic o locc, since He
came from the eternal abode.

oc aslach maithiusa 7 ic toirmesc uile 7 oc scarad síl Adaim *fri* diabul
7 *fri* hiff*er*n, 7 ic a tocu¹ fia(d) Dia dochu*m* na gloire suthai*n*e fil a
nim ; ic dénum *f*ert 7 mirbuli, ic slanugud cecha tedmai, ic tóduscad
marb ; ic fulang bochta 7 daidbri*us*a, ítad 7 ocorais,² dímiada 7
tarcasail, aithise 7 écnaig 7 cecha doccumla arcena, ar dáig soccumla
do beith duin*n*e tr*i*a bithu. [256 b].

50. Rothairb*ir* did*iu* hé fén dia cuibriuch 7 dia sroigled, dia
crochad 7 dia cesad, di ar fuaslucud-ne a gin Diabuil 7 di ar saerad
ar péin If*ir*n*n*, 7 co fagmais-ne, iar scarad fr*isin* domaṅ, i*n* mbethaid
suthain tria n-a bas-sum.

Dochuaid did*iu* a ani*m*m, iar scarad *fri* a chorp ar cend na fir*e*n 7
nan irisech batar a muich 7 a ndorchaib If*ir*n*n*, (i)teged ce*ch* oen
*con*ice sin 7 noragad i*n* cined doen*n*a mi*n*e cesta Cr*ist* dar a cend·
Tanic iarsin in ani*m*m doc*um* a cuirp con-era*cht* o marbaib iar mbeith
tredenu*s* i*n* a adnocul, ar is dia hai*n*e rocrochad 7 roadn*acht*, *con*id
aire si*n* dlegair brón 7 abstanugad in*n*ti.

goodness, and preventing evil, and withdrawing the seed of Adam from
the devil and from hell, and raising them before God to the glory everlasting which is in heaven ; performing miracles and wonders, healing
every disease, raising the dead ; suffering poverty and penury, thirst
and hunger, disrespect and contempt, insult and blasphemy and every
distress, in order that we might have happiness for ever.

50. He also submitted Himself to be bound, and scourged, to be
crucified and put to death on a cross, in order to deliver us from the
jaws of the devil, and save us from the pain of hell, and that we might
obtain, after severance from the world, life everlasting through His
death.

Now His soul went, after severance from His body, for the just and
the faithful who were in the gloom and darkness of hell (into which)
everyone went till then, and into which the (whole) human race would
go if Christ had not been crucified for their sakes. After that, the
soul came towards its body, and He rose from the dead after having
been three days in His grave, for it is on Friday He was crucified and
buried, wherefore sorrow and abstinence are of obligation on that
(day).

---

¹ = tocbáil, *or* togu, electing.          ² A mark like *c* is over the first *o*.

51. Dia domnaig *immorro* atracht a bás 7 tanic co a desciplu 7 co a aps*tal*u dia comdídnad[1] 7 do čalmugud an irsi, dia *forcetul* 7 dia mbendach*ad*. Dia dardain fresgabala *imorro* dočoid *for* Nem i fiad-*naise* a apstal 7 a descip*ul* arčena; *con*id an*n* ata *fri* deis Dé Ath*ar* a ngloir 7 an airechus diaisneti uas ai*n*gliu 7 arčaingliu, i*n* ardčomas nime 7 talm*an*, i cutru*mus* glori 7 cuma*ch*tu fr*is*in Ath*air* 7 frisin Spirut Noem, Fír-Dui*ne* *tra* ciasa Fír-Dia, mog ciasa Tigerna, duil ciasa Duilem intí fil isi*n* gloir sin.

52. Ticfa t*ra* int Árdríg[2] sin do nemdaib il-lo Bratha con aingliu 7 arčaingl*iu*, co noemu 7 firenu do br*eth*emn*us* for cech n-oen duine fo leth do rér a deggním *nó* a drochgním. Atr*aes*et *imorro* a talm*ain* 7 aithbeoaigfith*er*[3] i*n* la sin na huli atbathutar o th*us* domain 7 atbelat co f*or*cend. Biaid i*n* domu*n* uli o thurcabail co fui*ned* 7 o thalma*in* co nem t*ri*a oen-lasa(i)r then*ti*di isin ló sin. Beiti[4] na pecdaig ic gúl 7 éi*g*ium, ic coí 7 ic toirsi sechnón na lasrach sin, uair ni hirchoitigfe

---

51. On Sunday, however, He rose from death, and came to His disciples and Apostles to comfort them and encourage their faith, to instruct and bless them. It was on the Thursday of Ascension He went to heaven in presence of both His Apostles and disciples, and He is there on the right hand of God the Father in glory and pre-eminence inexpressible above angels and archangels, in supreme power over heaven and earth, in equality of glory and power with the Father and the Holy Ghost; true Man, however, although true God, servant although Lord, creature although Creator, is He who is in that glory.

52. And that High King will come from the heavenly (regions), on the day of judgment, with angels and archangels, with saints and the just, for judgment on everyone severally according to his good deeds or his bad deeds. There shall rise indeed from the earth and be revivi-fied on that day all those that have died from the beginning of the world or shall die to the end (thereof). The whole world from the rising to the setting (of the sun), and from earth to heaven shall be in one fiery blaze on that day. Sinners shall be weeping and crying, lamenting and grieving throughout that flame whilst it will not at all

---

[1] comdignad, MS.
[2] ardrig, MS.
[3] Or, *ir*.

[4] Also in 53; usually beit, *or* betit; perhaps it is the *relat.* 3 pl., and means, "and they shall be, the sinners," &c.

it*ir* dona fírenu. Tinoilfith*er* t*ra* m*uinter* nime 7 talm*an* 7 if*ir*n *in* oen airecht *in* Duilem*an* 7 in Bret*h*eman ; na p*ec*daig *im*. dia c(h)lí .i. in lucht in cra*é*is 7 *in* adaltrais 7 in esindracuis, lu*ch*t na fergi 7 na miscen 7 in formait 7 in chosnuma, lu*ch*t na snímche 7 na toirsi sægulda, lu*ch*t in bocasaig 7 i*n* díumais.

53. Cuirfith*ir* uli in slog si*n* imalle f*ri* Diabul *con* a drochm*uin*tir, 7 iadfaider f*or*aib *in* carcair muichnig mallachtnaig, cen sollsi cen áib*n*es, cen biad cen dig cen étach cen bec na mor na maithiusa, *acht* sírdorcha 7 sírthorsi, sírgul 7 síregium, gorta 7 occ*ur*as t*ri*a bithu sír; 7 demnu oc a sroigled co dí*con*dirclech, 7 tene bithbuan ic a sírloscad. Beti t*ra* na p*ec*daig t*ri*a bithu oc fulang na diglasin, cen ċobair cen ċomdídnad.[1] Ba mian leo di*diu* bas d'fagbail 7 ni fagbait t*ri*a bithu. Mairg tra robói i*c* a breith 7 ic a altrom do diabul *in* neich[2] for a tabar ind iach[3] sin ; ar is doilig f*or*bailtius l*æ*i *nó* aidċe f*ri* hecla na mor-dígla sin.

---

hurt the righteous.    Well, the people of heaven and earth and hell shall be gathered in one assembly of the Creator and Judge ; the sinners on his left, that is, the gluttons and adulterers and unjust, those given to anger and hatred and envy and contention, the people of wordly solicitude and sorrow, the disdainful and the proud.

53. All that multitude shall be together sent to the devil with his wicked attendants, and they shall be shut up in a dismal accursed prison, without light, without joy, without food, without drink, without raiment, without little or much of happiness ; (nothing) but perpetual darkness and everlasting distress, perpetual weeping, perpetual crying, hunger and famine through everlasting ages ; and demons scourging them unmercifully, and perennial fire burning them for ever.    Now sinners shall be for ever suffering that punishment, without help and without comfort.    They would wish to die, but they never die.    Woe to him who has been born[4] of and nursed by the devil, the one[5] of whom that groan is uttered, for difficult is joy of day or night in presence of the fear of that great vengeance.

---

[1] chomdignad, MS.

[2] Something seems omitted *before* in neich ; *or*, in neach = noch, the person who.

[3] = ilach (?) ; cf. an iachtaite *gl.* ingemiscentes, *Ml.* 63 d.

[4] *Or* taken and reared.

[5] "the one" is in appos. with "him."

54. Bértar *imorro* na fíreoin 7 lu*cht* na haithrige *co n*gloir 7 anoir
do síraitreb fla*tha* nime in oentaid aingel 7 arċaingel noem 7 firén *in*
domai*n* i frecnarcus na Noem T*r*inóite, Ath*a*ir 7 M*a*cc 7 Spirut N*oeb* ;
cen nach n-esbuid *for* doman, *acht* sírsollsi 7 síroibnius 7 síd suthai*n*
cen ecla bais *no* ifi*r*nn. Mairg *tra* recus a atharthir ndúthaig ar in
oilith*ir* n-andilis ; mairc recus tír na mbeó ar thír na marb 7 ar i*n*ar-
bach[1] n-aduathmar ; mairc recus tír na slanti 7 na fálti ar thír i*n*
galair, parthus nan oirer ar in díthrub n-essuthach ngortach n-acco-
rach. Mairc recus tír na hainmne 7 na noime 7 na sobés ar thír in
chuil 7 in chorbuid[2] 7 na sainti, 7 cech peccaid.[3]

55. Mairc re*cus* tír i*n* ratha 7 na mbend*acht*an ar tír na malla*cht*an
7 na hescaine. Mairc re*cus* tír na firinde 7 na fírs(h)ollsi 7 i*n*d indra-
cuis 7 na célli 7 na comairle ar glend na daille 7 na dorċba, in
meraigthi[4] 7 in aneolais, n(a) me*racht*a 7 na burba 7 in buaidertha.

---

54. But the righteous and the penitent will be borne with glory
and honour to the lasting abode of the kingdom of heaven, in union
with the holy angels and archangels, and the just of the world, in the
presence of the Holy Trinity, Father, and Son, and Holy Ghost, without any want in the world, (nothing) but perpetual light and perennial
joy, and lasting peace, without fear of death or hell.

Woe to him who barters his proper paternal land for a strange
land not his own. Woe to him who barters the land of the living for
the land of the dead[2] and for horrible exile.[5] Woe to him who barters
the land of health and joy for the land of disease; the paradise of
delights for the unfruitful, barren, hungry wilderness. Woe to him
who barters the land of patience and holiness and good manners for
the land of crime and wickedness, and concupiscence and every sin.

55. Woe to him who barters the land of grace and blessings for
the country of the maledictions and cursing. Woe to him who barters
the land of truth and true light, and integrity and sense and counsel,
for the valley of blindness and darkness, of error and ignorance, of

---

[1] *For* ind*a*rpe, *or*, indarbad.
[2] mac an chorbaid, son of wickedness,
*Ps.* 89.
[3] pecdaid, MS.
[4] mearaigthe, "reprobate," *Titus*, i. 16.
[5] *Or* ruin; *ionarbach*, destroyer, *O'R.*

D 2

Mairg recus tír na humla 7 (in)grada 7 in gairdechais 7 na reithinche
7 na suthaine ar tír na sroigell 7 na heisurruma 7 in fuatha 7 in broin
7 in di(u)muis. Mairg recus tir an chaird(i)usa 7 chumsanaid 7 na
céol suthaine ar thír in t-snechta 7 in oigrid[1] 7 na tennte ndorcháite
7 na carraige 7 na nuall nechech nertach.[2] Mairg recus tír na sir-
failte . . . 7 na hainmne ar tir na heicne . . . in chrais 7 na feirge 7
in miruin bæ(g)laig michairdig.[3]

56. Mairc charus na dobésa 7 miscniges na sobésa 7 na coengníma.
Mairc ris nad ferr fognam dia námait .i. do diabul inas dia Duilem 7
dia charait tairise .i. do Dia. Mairc risnad ferr beith in doccomul 7 i
muich ifirnn ; foirb didiu tabraid da bar n-óid aurcra 7 ecobsaidecht in
tsoegail, ocus na plaga 7 na dígla dofulachta filet an ifernn. Cuim-
nigid didiu a ndernsabar fen do malairt 7 do sárugud in Choimded, 7

---

folly, and imbecility, and disturbance. Woe to him who barters the
land of humility and love and gladness and serenity and stability,
for the land of scourgings and disobedience[4] and hatred and sorrow
and pride. Woe to him who barters the land of friendliness and
repose and eternal songs, for the land of snow and ice, and dismal
fires, and of the rock (?), and of lamentations. Woe to him who barters
the land of lasting joy and forbearance for the land of violence, of
gluttony and anger, of dangerous unfriendly grudge (?).

56. Woe to him who loves evil ways and hates good morals and
good deeds. Woe to him who prefers serving his enemy, the devil, to
(serving) his Creator and constant friend, that is, God. Woe to him
who prefers being in the misery and gloom of hell. I beseech you[5]
bear in mind the perishableness and instability of the world, and the
torments and punishments insufferable which are in hell. Remember
also what yourselves have done of injury and offence to the Lord, and
make (acts of) fervent sorrow and penance, with bitterness of heart

---

[1] oigride, MS.

[2] n-echech n-ertach (?) ; these two
words are obscure to me.

[3] From "buaidertha" to this is
written in the margin ; some words are
not legible ; carraige, roughness, from
carrach (?).

[4] urraim, reverentia, *Stapleton's Irish
Catech.*, p. 8; easurramach, disobedient,
apostate, *Donlevy*, 464.

[5] I supply (iarraim d'athchuinge),
foraib ; is *foirb* = finally (?).

dénaid torsi 7 ait(h)rigi ndíchra co ngorti cride 7 deraib; ocus dénaid
aine 7 abstanait iar craes, 7 génus iar ndruis, 7 condircle 7 almsana
iar saint 7 esindracus 7 iar ngait (uair ní cead do neoch in gait do
dénam na do chaithium), 7 cendsa 7 cainnduthracht 7 bráthirsi tairise
iar feirg 7 miscais, cen debaid cen duinorcain fri námait nó carait;
ocus frithaire légind nó umalóti iar laxu 7 emeltus 7 torsi; aithrigi
iar torsi collaide; faísitiu 7 aithrigi (iar) maidmigi; becdacht 7 inísle
iar mormenmain 7 diumas.

57. Bíd grád 7 uaman in Choimded in bar cridib, a sirluad 7 a
s(h)írimrad in bar menmain 7 in bar mbeolu; saint 7 mian na sollsi cen
dorchu, na slanti cen galar, in tsída cen chocad, na nóime cen chorbud,
na firinne cen cheilg, na bethad cen bás, na glóri díoesi cen scithlim
cen erchra, in oentaid aingel 7 arcaingel Mec Dé Bíi.

---

and (with) tears, and practise fasting and abstinence, after gluttony,
and (observe) chastity after lust, and compassion and alms after covet-
ousness and dishonesty and robbery (for it is permitted to no one to
commit robbery or to partake of the things stolen); and abiding gentle-
ness and good-will and brotherliness after anger and hatred, without
quarrel or manslaughter against enemy or friend, and (practise)
watchfulness in reading or humble duty after slackness and sloth and
discouragement; penitence after bodily depression;[1] confession and
repentance after vainglory; littleness and lowliness (of conceit) after
highmindedness and pride.

57. Let the love and fear of the Lord be in your hearts, and the
constant mention and thought of Him in your hearts and on your lips.
(Let there be in your hearts) the desire and longing for the light
without darkness, the health without sickness, the peace without war,
holiness without wickedness, for truth without deceit, life without
death, glory ever young without evanescence or decay, in unity of
the angels and archangels of the Son of the Living God.

---

[1] an uair bíos mo chroide fa thuirse, dum anxiaretur cor meum, Ps. 61.·

## INCIPIT DO SCELAIB NA SOSCEL I*N*SO.

58 [*LB.* p. 133 b.] Ar it t*ri* soscela legth*ar* 7 chant*ar* *in* ecl*a*isib crístaidib[1] adaig notlac, isesside[2] adaig ir-rogenir[3] Isu Cr*ist* Slan*í*cc*id* síl Adam.   Lucas suiscel(ach)[4] *imorro in* súi *in* súi *for*pthi, pr*í*mdalta Póil aps*tail*,[5] ise ro*tracht*astar na di soscela toisechu díb.   Eóin m*a*ccan im*orro* brunn*a*dalta Cr*ist* budesi*n* ise roscr*i*b in sos*cel*a dedi*n*ach díb ; is do*n*a sos*cel*aib si*n* rocachnad su*n*d iarfír.

[a]Is fír t*ra* c*on*id in aimsir Octaui*n* Aug*uist*[6] tancat*ar* na tircl*i*anta si*n* 7 is an*n* rogenir Isu Cr*ist*.   Ar i*n*tan robás oc tabach i*n* chisa Césarda fo*n* uile do*m*un, is an*n* ta*n*ic Ioseph 7 Muire o Nazareth Galílee co Bethil Íuda[7] .i. co cat(h)*r*aig D*abi*d[8] m*ei*c Iese ; ar ropo

---

## THE BEGINNING OF THE STORIES OF THE GOSPELS.

58. For they are three Gospels that are read and sung in Christian churches on Christmas night.   This is (the) night in which was born Jesus Christ the Saviour of the seed of Adam.   Luke, the Evangelist, indeed, the sage, the perfect sage, and chief pupil of the Apostle Paul, it is he that wrote[9] the two first Gospels[10] of them.   But John, the youth, bosom-fosterling[11] of Christ Himself, it is he wrote the last of them ; it is of (from) those gospels has been sung[12] here truly.

True it is, indeed, that it was in the time of Octavius Augustus those prophesied[13] things came, and it is then was born Christ.   For when they were a-levying the Cæsarian tribute through all the world, then came Joseph and Mary from Nazareth of Galilee to Bethil of

---

[1] na crístaigib, of MS., *should be* na crístaide, *or* cristaidib.

[2] isesside, MS. ; perhaps it should be is*i*side, referring to *adaig.*

[3] *Or,* i*n*rogenir.

[4] So in full, *LB.* 166 a. 5.

[5] asp*ail*, MS.

[6] *gs.,* "Octauin Auguist," in full, *LB.,* p. 97, 13 ll. from bottom cf page.

[7] The accent seems to be sometimes over *I*, sometimes over *u.*

[8] *Or,* D*aui*d.  I cannot find the nom. or gen. in full at pp. 128–130, or any-where in *LB.*

[9] = *roscrib* of next sentence ; rothra*c*-tastar fair = he treated, wrote, spoke of.

[10] *i. e.* of the Masses of Christmas night ; the Gospel of the third Mass is from St. John.

[11] *Leg.* bruinne dalta Christ, John of the bosom, fosterling of Christ (?).

[12] I read *ro-canad ;* or *ro-chachna*(t), I will sing, or second. redup. fut., he would sing.

[13] don terchantu, *gl.* prophetato, *Ml.* 53.

[a-a] *From* [a] *to* [a] comes before "Incipit do scelaib . . . sund iar fír."

do síl Dabid do Ioseph 7 do Muire, 7 nir-gabad in cís d'ícc uadaib an
inad aile¹ acht in an atharda dilis budesin.ᵃ  Tanic didiu Ioseph 7
Muire o Nazareth Galile co Bethil Iúda hi cumma cáich 7 a múinnter
.i. Abion 7 Semion 7 Iacop glúinech, tri meic Íoseph insin ; 7 is e int
Iacop glúinech roindis na scéla o gein Muiri co gein Crist, 7 o gen
Crist co a crochad ; Ocus is aire sin atberair brathair Crist fris .i. ar a
beth comulcach fri Crist, ar ba cosmail an ulcha diblinib.  In fath
tan(ais)e arandubrad brathair Crist fri Iacob ngluinech .i. ar a beth
na mac do Iosep ; id est pater Christi, is e int Iacop gluinech-sin
rogab apdaine Ierusalem daréis Crist i tír Israeil, 7 mac sethar do
Muire he, is e romarbsat na hIúdaide iarsin.

    59.  Tanic didiu Muire ann 7 sí alachta on Spirut Noem in tan-sin ;
7 tancatar ann maroen fria na .v. óga bitís na comlenmain cen

---

Judah, i.e. to the city of David, son of Jesse, for of the seed of
David were Joseph and Mary, and it was not allowed² (them) to
pay their tribute in another place save in their own proper fatherland.

    And so Joseph and Mary came from Nazareth of Galilee to
Bethlehem of Juda, like the others, and their family, i.e. Abion
and Simeon, and James of the Knees, the three sons of Joseph
these, and it is James of the Knees that told the narrative from
Mary's birth³ to Christ's birth, and from Christ's birth to his
crucifixion.  And it is for this that he is called Christ's brother,
for his being like-bearded to Christ, for the beards of both were
alike.  The second reason why James of the Knees was called
Christ's brother (was) for his being a son to Joseph (i. e. pater
Christi).  And it is that James of the Knees that took the abbacy
of Jerusalem after Christ in the land of Israel, and he was a sister's
son to Mary ; it is he that the Jews slew afterwards.

    59.  Mary, too, came thither, being pregnant from the Holy
Ghost at that time ; and thither came along with her the five

---

¹ aile in full here, is often .ii. in
texts of LB.
    ² was not received ; cf. res non capiunt
jacturam, non recipiunt dilationem ;
accipio, I allow it, Horace.
    ³ The Apocryphal "Gospel of the

Birth of Mary is an epitome of the
"Protevangelium of James" ;  the
"Book of the Birth of Christ" is sup-
posed to have been nearly the same as
the Protevangelium of St. James ; see
"Bible de Vence," vol. xix., p. 264.

*ctar*scarud fr*i*a tria bithu.   Hité inso an*m*anda nan óg *si*n .i. Sepur, Supstan*n*a, Babecca, Ratiel, Agizabeth.   Cid di*diu* 'ma táinio M*u*iri con a hógaib an*n*?   Nin*n*sa, do erned in chísa Cesarda ; ar ní bói isi*n* uli do*m*an d'fir *nó* do mnái d'óc *no* do sin na bic*ca*d uili in cís sin. Ocus atb*er*t Iose*ph* in tan itchual*a* na callaireda oc tabaċ in c(h)íssa, comad cóir i*n* cís d'ícc a cínd ċruid 7 in*d*mais 7 fer*ain*d, bíd 7 etaíg 7 nan uli nech bítis oc neoch [134a], ba hecen in cís d'ícc aistib. Otchuala *im.*   Iose*ph* in cís oc a thabuch roerig *con* á mu*n*tir do *er*ned i*n* chisa ; Moabitus *imorro* cet ain*m* Iose*ph.*

60.   Lotar doċum na Bethile 7 doċornian co cathr*aig* Da*u*id.   Is andsin ba scíth in Óg. .i. M*u*iri, ar nirfet marcachus na hi*m*decht do dénam ; ar ba facus a hinbuid di i*n* tan si*n*.   Fácbaith*er* iar*um* M*u*iri isin dún si*n* 7 Iacop 7 Semion 'na farrad, 7 na .v. óga ucut.   Luid iar*um* Iose*ph* 7 Abíon rémpu co Bethil Iúda do *er*niud in chísa 7 d'iarr*ai*d tige leptha.   In tan t*ra* rosiacht Iose*ph* medon na cath*r*ach

---

virgins that used to be in her train for ever without being parted from her.   These are the names of those virgins—Sephar, Susanna, Rebecca, Rachel, Agizabeth.   Why, then, came Mary with her virgins thither?   It is not hard to tell, to pay the Cæsarian tribute; for there was not in the whole world, of man or woman, young or old, but paid, every one, that tribute.   And Joseph said, when he heard the criers collecting the tribute, that it would be right to pay the tribute in respect of cattle and treasure, and land, food and clothing, and all the things one possessed, out of which the tribute had to be paid.   When Joseph heard of the tribute being levied he set out with his family to pay the tribute.   Moabitus was the first name of Joseph.

60.   They went towards Bethlehem and Ephratah the city of David.[1]   It is there that the Virgin Mary was weary, for she could not ride or go (on foot), for her time was near to her then.   Then Mary is left in that fortress, and James and Simeon along with her, and those five virgins.   Joseph and Abion then went on to Bethlehem of Judah to pay the tribute, and to seek a lodging-house.   Now, when Joseph reached the middle of the city, he sat down on a large

---

[1] Bethlehem and Sion were called cities of David: is Cornian another name for Bethlehem, is ıt Horoman of   *Isaias*, xv. ?   *Perhaps for* dochornian *we should read* dochotar ; *cf.* et tu Bethelehem Ephrata, *Mich.* 5.

rosuid *for* cloich moir an*n*, ocus rogab mifrigi 7 maithnechus mor
Ios*eph* tri*a* falti 7 oirmiti*n*, 7 boi iar*um* oc tathair na deoraidecta cu
mor, 7 is*sed* atb*er*t:—" Ar cid saidb*ir* indeorad," ol se, "is bocht
ad*er*air fris.   Mad bocht im. is miscnech eisonorach 7 bid tarcaisne*r*h
beth*ir* fair.   Aithrech limsa in*d*iu mo deoraide*cht* uatsi a Bethil
Iúda," ol Ios*eph*.   " Is tria bocta 7 dáidbre docuadus uait.   Olc i*n* tír
ir-rubusa cusi*n*diu," ol se, (.i. tír na Galilee); olc a biad 7 a dói*n*e 7 a
doen*nacht*, ocus olcc na cat(h)*r*acha comaigtbi fri haittreb indtib, ar ni
mor la nech a menma et*o*rru o rosoith*er* cucu oenfe*cht*."

61.  Cid di*diu acht* gabaid oc tathair na deoraide*cht*a co mor 7 oc
formolad a ath*ar*da bun*aid* budessi*n*, *con*id ead atb*er*t, " Is fe*cht*nach 7
is fírén ce*ch* oen na bia *for* deoraidecht," ol se.   Luid Ioseph iarsi*n*
d'iarr*aid* tige leptha for*ut*[1] na Bethile, *con*id ann itchondairc-siu*m*

---

stone there, and great weakness[2] and heaviness (?)[3] came upon Joseph
through joy and reverence, and he was afterwards dispraising the
state of exile greatly, and this is what he said—" For though the
exile be wealthy," quoth he, " he is called poor.   If, however, he be
poor, he is hated and without honour, and he will bear the name
of contemptible.   I reget to-day my exile from thee, Bethlehem of
Judah," said Joseph.   " It is through poverty and indigence I went
from thee.   Ill is the land where I have been until to-day," said he
(*i.e.* the land of Galilee), " ill its food, and its folk, and its humanity,[4]
and bad (are) the neighbouring[5] cities for dwelling in them, for one
has not much spirit[6] among them when once he is turned towards
them.

61.  So then he begins dispraising exile greatly, and much-praising
his own original[7] fatherland, and said thus:—" Happy and righteous[8]
is everyone who will not be in exile," said he.   After that Joseph
went in search of lodgings across Bethlehem, and there saw a certain

---

[1] *Or* fia*r*ut, fiarlait in maige, "throughout the plain," *Wars of the G. & G.* 76.

[2] *Cf.* in sentuine mifrith, *Cormac's
Gl.* p. 37; but *Stokes' Bodl. Cormac*, p. 34,
has *móir* in place of *mifrith*.

[3] *Cf.* ocbail maithnech, gola troga
maithneca, *infra*, § 104, maindeacht-
naige, pigritia, *Todd Lect.* v.

[4] doendacht, *gl.* humanitas.

[5] *Read* comaithgi; *cf.* comaithgiu
" aliam gentem," *Todd Lect.* v. p. 86,
where it seems to mean "neighbours."

[6] *Lit.*, mens, animus.

[7] real, *cf.* a bunad, really, *Frags. of
Ir. Ann.* 208.

[8] If I may use the modern word " all
right" = *go folláin* or *go maith*, it would
suit here better than righteous.

aroile oentech mbec do lethimel sechtarċáich amuig 7 se na oenur cin tech cin treb na farrad .i. arocul becc deroil cumang cendisel.

Luid iarum d'fegad in tige 7 atbert, "Is doig lium," ol se, "is arocul oiged inso, 7 is imchubaid dúinne beth ann 7 is usati don Ógi tusmiud ann, ar is fata o sessib doine 7 o forcongur na popul he."

62. Is amlaid tra bói in tech sin 7 cóir[1] uama bice ann .i. echlasc[2] a m(b)íd assan 7 ócdam la tigerna in tigi, 7 en-stol bec cruind for lár in tigi; is fair nosuid(it)is na hoegid. "Airisium sund a meic," ol Ioseph, "fodáig na hÓigi uaisle ata co scíth ċucaind, ocus bi-sin súnd oca hernaide co ndechsaind-si isin cathraig dús in fuigbind[3] ínte nech dia mbad áil ní dom' eladain tar cend chota na hoidċe anocht."

Intan tra bói Ioseph oc triall dul d'iarraid in bíd, is ann itċuala guth in ċallari 7 in fir furfocra tria ferannaib na cathrach imach

---

small single house on the outskirts out beyond the rest, being alone without house or dwelling in its neighbourhood, a little, tiny, narrow low-roofed cabin.

He went thereupon to look at the house, and said, "It seems to me," quoth he, "that this is a guests' cabin, and it is fitting for us to be in, and it is easier for the Virgin to bring forth in it, since it is far from thoughts[4] of men and from the summoning of the people."

62. In this wise then was that house, having on it the aspect[5] of a little cave, i.e. a stall,[6] in which used to be an ass and a young ox, belonging to the master of the house, and one little round stool on the floor of the house, on which the guests used to sit. "Let us stay here, son," said Joseph, "for the sake of the exalted Virgin who is coming wearily towards us, and be thou here awaiting her, and I might go into the city to know if I might find in it one to whom aught of my craft may be pleasing in exchange for this night's supper."

While then Joseph was setting out to go seek for food, then he heard the voice of the crier and man of proclamation through the open

---

[1] Arrangement, *O'Don. Suppl.*

[2] *Read* echlann (?).

[3] fuidbind, MS.

[4] *séis*, gl. cogitationes; or "songs,"

or = *séselbe*, din, outcry.

[5] arrangement, *O'D. Suppl.*

[6] echlasc, "horserod' will not suit here; at § 63 it is called *crú.*

*con*did ead atb*er*t, "A firu Ebraide 7 a m*a*cu Isr*ae*l*d*a, ticid uli d'érned in chísa Cesarda; uair ata Cirinus rig na Siria 7 oi(r)riga na rig Rómanach oc dul anossa i cind tr*i*ll do Róim, 7 is *ed* atb*er*t, in uli chís do breth co Róim dochum Octaui*n* Aug*uist*; ocus tic*id* uli [134b] d'*é*rned in chísa am*laid*-so .i. bar n-ua, b*ar* clan*n*a 7 b*ar* cum*al*a 7 b*ar* m*ei*c 7 b*ar* mogaid 7 b*ar* cineda; 7 taispenaid b*ar* n-ór 7 b*ar* n-i*n*dmus 7 b*ar* n-indile, b*ar* nglóir 7 b*ar* n-etaigi, 7 tic*id* uli ámla*id* si*n*, 7 tabraid f*or* breth i*n*d ríg 7 i*n* tig*er*na iat; 7 tic*ed* cách dorér a aessi an*n* it*er* óc 7 sen."

63. Ocus is aire thuctha uli iat an*n*, ar ní bói nech dibsi*n* cen čís fóleth dorér a oesi fair. Ocus atb*er*t int irfuacarthid[1] c*e*tna, "C*ec*h nech díčelas f*or*sin rig c*ec*h ní bess aice bent*ar* uad c*ec*h ní chelas 7 c*ec*h ní eli bias do(n) tšægul[2] aice." Ámlaid bói Ios*eph* i*n* tan si*n* 7 se na šessa*m* i *n*dorus i*n* tigi, 7 itčuala an irfuacc*r*a arís 7 atb*er*t, "Is lór

---

places[3] of the city, outward, who said thus, "Hebrew men and children of Israel, come ye all to pay the Cæsarian tribute; for Cyrinus, King of Syria, and the under-kings of the Roman kings are going now after a short time to Rome; and this is what he says, that all the tribute is to be brought to Rome to Octavius Augustus; and come ye all to pay the tribute in this wise, namely, your grandsons, your children, and your bondmaids, and your sons, and your slaves, and your tribes; and show ye your gold, and your treasure, and your cattle, your finery,[4] and your clothes; and come all in that way, and give them up to the judgment[5] of the king and lord; and let each come according to his age, both young and old."

63. And this is why they were all brought thither, because there was not one who was not under a distinct tax according to his age. And the same herald said, "Everyone that hides away from the King whatsoever he may have, let everything he conceals be taken from him, and whatever else he shall have in the world."[6]

Thus was Joseph at that time standing in front of the house, and he heard the proclamation again, and said, "It is enough thou pro-

---

[1] irfuacarthig, MS.
[2] do*n* tšægul (?).
[3] *Lit.*, lands.

[4] *Lit.*, glory, decus, ornatus.
[5] at his disposal.
[6] of the world, or worldly goods (?).

fuaccrai, a duine," ol se, " ár cech oen oca mbia dosbera uada cena cen
imresain.    Mesi fen cettús díb ní fil ní ocam acht mo threlma særsi 7
ragat dúibsi iat mad maith lib, 7 ticid d'fégad mo thige leptha, ar ni
tech iter fil ocumm, acht araile uaim becc co crú assaine innte, 7 ni
mó na re bochtaib tróga bud chubaid beth innte."    Ocus boi oc tathair
a thegdaisi comór.

64. Lotar lucht in tobaig iarum d'fégad in tigi 7 ni facutar do
threlmaib ann acht mad oen stól becc 7 nír leosum cid e-sen acht la fer
in tigi leptha, 7 trelma soersi Ioseph.    " Berid-si lib," ol Ioseph, " mad
maith lib iat."    " Ni maith itir," ol siat, " 7 ni mor cinco maith libsi
sin," ol Ióseph, " is estib sin dogebim-si biad becc dam péin[1] 7 don Óig
rohaithned dímm i tir Israelda ; 7 dogebim-si biad becc doib com-mo
múintir trempu-sin, 7 berid-si lib ina cin fén iat."

65. Iar tra in croind sin rucsat lucht in tobaig leo he tarcend Ioseph

----

claimest, man," said he, " for every one that shall have (anything)
will give it up without resistance.    Myself first among them ; nought
have I but my implements of trade, and they shall go to you[2] if you
will ; and come to see my lodging, for it is not a house at all that I
have, but a certain little cave with a she ass's stall in it, and not
more than two wretched poor people would it be fit to be in it."    And
he was greatly dispraising his dwelling.

64. The tax-gatherers then went to view the house, and they saw not
of furniture there save one little stool, and even that was not theirs,
but belonged to the lodging-house keeper, and Joseph's implements of
trade.    " Take them with you," said Joseph, " if you wish them."
" We do not at all," said they.    " And no wonder that you do not
wish that," quoth Joseph, " it is from them that I get a little food for
myself and for the Virgin who was entrusted to me in this land of
Israel, and that I get a little food for my family[3] through them (the
tools) ; and take them (sc. the children), in their own discharge."[4]

65. After that discussion[5] the tax-gatherers took him (Abion ?) in

----

[1] Mr. J. M'Neill tells me that " dam
péin" is now used in the spoken
language of Connacht.

[2] Note the plural addressing one person.

[3] I read " becc dom-muintir."    The
text has " for them with my family."

[4] cin = liability, Laws, i. 90, 238.

[5] cronuig duine críonna, " argue
sapientem," Prov. 9 ; cruinnim, wrangle,
O'Brien.

cona chlainn 7 tarcend Muiri con a hógaib.    Ocus iar mbreith in chísa
amlaid sin tanic Ioseph co dorus in tigi, 7 bói oc fégud na sliged uada,
7 ba homun lais á muinter do breith do lucht in tobaig leo.    Is ann sin
at connairce Ioseph a muintir[1] chuice .i. Muiri con a hógaib 7 Iacob
glúinech dia leth clíí 7 Semión dia deiss 7 na hoga na diaid[2].    Iar
torachtain doib amlaid sin, (atbert Ioseph)[3] fri Semión, " Is fata atathi
á muinter maith," ol se.    Atbert Semión, " Ni sind rofuirig acht in
óg," ol se, "ar tanic a hinbuid budesta[4] 7 is toirsech hi 7 cech uair
tanic rempi dia haimsir, indarlind doberad a tusmed uasal fil iná broind,
7 is demin co mbera anocht, 7 déntar in uli frichnam ocainde fria."

66.  Tanic iarsin Muiri isin tech, 7 atbert Ióseph fri Semión,
" Taba(i)r usce lat," ol se, " 7 indail cossa na hÓige, 7 tabair biad
di ; sir iarsin 7 cennaig cech ní bus áil di, 7 is demin lind co mbera in
tusmed nua nertadbul[5] fil ina broind anocht ; 7 ni frith remi a macsámla

---

place  of Joseph  with  his children,  and in  respect  of Mary with her
virgins.   And after the  tribute was  thus taken, Joseph  came to the
door of the house, and was looking out on the roads, and he feared that
his family  would  be carried  of by the  tax-gatherers.    It is then that
Joseph saw his family come towards him, Mary with her virgins, and
James of the Knees on her left side, and Simeon on her right, and the
virgins behind her.    They having so arrived, Joseph said to Simeon,
" You are long (a-coming), good friends," quoth he ; Simeon said, " It
is not we that delayed, but the Virgin," said he, "for her time has come
now,  and she is  weary,  and every  hour of her time,  that she came
forward, it seemed to us that she would bring forth the illustrious
Offspring that is in her womb ; and it is certain that she will bring
forth to-night, and let all service be done by us for her."

66. Thereupon Mary came into the house, and Joseph said to
Simeon, " Fetch water," quoth he, " and wash the Virgin's feet, and
give her food ; seek then and buy everything that will please her, and
certain we are, that she will bring forth to-night the new, very
powerful Offspring that is in her womb ; and there has not been found

---

[1] muinter, MS.

[2] dedaig, MS., read degaid.

[3] These words seem to have been omitted.

[4] bud2a.

[5] nuantadbul, with curved line over nt ; I find two other compounds of nert : nertlia, LB. 216 a, nertflaith, Fél. Ind.

7 ni fuiġbither¹ dia ési ; 7 nifitir nech nach in gen sin slanaiges in ciniud dóenna.

Ocht Kl. enair do sunnrad in adaig sin arai lathi mís gréni, ocus [135a] .xiii. esca, 7 domnach arai láthi sechtmaine. *Ocus* iar ndul do Muiri isin tech rogab for hernaigthi 7 for crosfigill 7 a haiged suas fri nem focetoir. Annsin atbert Semion fria athair, "Atchimm in ó(i)g oc labra," ol se,' "7 ni faicim cia frisi labair." "Fri hainglib nime," ol Ioseph.

67. Is ann atchonnairc Ioseph Muiri oc cái 7 oc toirsi truim 7 atc(h)onnairc focetoir hi oc suba 7 oc failti dermáir. "Cid sin a óg," ol Ioseph, "tan latt suba 7 fálti tan aile toirsi 7 dobrón ?" Dofrecair sí dó, "Da phopul atchimm," ol si, "7 indar(a) popul dib oc cói 7 oc dograi 7 i(n) popul eli co subach forbailid." "Ata dethbir saine sin," ol Joseph, .i. "popul nan Iúdaide sin diarobi andán Crist do c(h)rochad 7 a descipuil do díscailiud iarsin ; is iat boi oc dógrai iarom. Popul

---

before Him His like, and shall not be found after Him, and no one knows but it is this Child that saves the human race.

The eighth day before the Kalends of January precisely was that night according to the day of the solar month, and thirteenth of the moon, and Sunday according to the day of the week. And Mary, having gone into the house, immediately began to pray and to make crosfigil, her face upwards to heaven². Then said Simeon to his father : " I see the Virgin speaking," quoth he, " and I see not to whom she speaks." " To the angels of heaven," said Joseph.

67. Then Joseph saw Mary weeping and in heavy dolour, and saw her forthwith rejoicing and in great joy. " What is that, Virgin," said Joseph, " that at one time thou hast jubilation and joy, at another time dolours and sorrow?" She answered him : " Two peoples that I see," said she, " one people of them weeping and sorrowing, and the other people glad and overjoyed." " That has a special suitableness,"³ said Joseph, *i.e.* " those are the the people of the Jews who are destined to crucify Christ, and to scatter His disciples afterwards ; it is they, then, that are grieving. The people of the Gentiles, again, is the other

---

¹ fuidbither, MS.

² with arms stretched out in the form of a cross and face raised to heaven ;

crosfigill does not point to "prostration" here.

³ *Or*, there is reason of difference.

na ngéndti di*diu* in pop*ul* ele bit sén oc fálti 7 oc suba, ar is doib robói
a ńdán Cri*st* do ċretium iarsin."

Atbe*rt* Iose*ph* annsin, " Eirg it' lepaid a Óg," ol se, " 7 cotail
in*n*te, 7 tábr*ad* Semió*n* olai fót' ċosaib, 7 dena cúmsanad ámlaid si*n* co
ruca Dia breith f*ort*."

68. Bat*ar* aml*aid* si*n fri* hed ŕota do*n* aiḋche, c*on*id a*n*nsin roi*n*dis
Iacob Glui*n*ech di dérca 7 diamra 7 de*ri*ti C͊*ist*, 7 ni do mirbuilib
na geni coi*m*detta ; 7 ni mó i*n*dat aingil *nó* asp*uil nó* Dia budesi*n*
bud chóir dia n-in*n*disi ar a*n* uaisle 7 ar a noe*m*dac*ht* .i. na mirbuli
suaċhi*n*nti roboi 7 bias 7 ata su*n*d arċena. Cid *tra acht* intan bói i*n*
Óg oc breiṫ a m*eic* bat*ar* na huile dúl i*n* a tost 7 i*n* étri͘ce cin chor
ci*n* chumscugu*d* oc frithailem a ńDúilemu*n*. Ar ní bói isna huli
dúl(aib) ní na tuc aichne f*orsin* Dúilem *acht* na hIúdai*d*e amairsecha
nama.

Iarsi*n* i*n*tan bói Ióse*ph* i *n*dorus i*n* tigi 7 Mui*r*i isi*n* tig tanic foceŕoir
solus-nél taitne*meac*h do nim anuas co *m*bui ós ci*n*d na huama 7 *n*a

---

people ; they are rejoicing and exulting, for it was to them it was
destined to believe in Christ thereafter." Joseph said then : " Go into
thy bed, Virgin," quoth he, " and sleep therein ; and let Simeon put oil
under thy feet, and rest so, till God brings birth to thee.[1]

68. They were thus for a long space of the night, at which time
James of the Knees told her the charities and the mysteries and the
secrets of Christ, and somewhat of the miracles of the divine Offspring ;
and not more than[2] angels or apostles, or God Himself, would be fit to
tell them, on account of their height and holiness, the manifest miracles
in general that have been and shall be and are now. But when the
Virgin was bringing forth her Son, all the elements were silent and
motionless[3] without stirring, without shaking, doing homage[4] to their
Creator, for there was not in all created things aught that was not
aware of[5] the Creator but the unbelieving Jews alone.

Thereafter while Joseph was in front of the house, and Mary
within the house, there came at once a shining light-cloud down from
heaven until it was over the cave and the city, as it were the sun that

---

[1] Co ruca Dia bre(i)th fair, *LB.* 5 a,
means "till God brings judgment on him."

[2] *i.e.* none but.

[3] *tric*, nimble, *Coney's Dictionary ;*

*go tric*, often, *O'Brien's Dictionary.*

[4] ministering to.

[5] did not recognise ; *cf.* dorat ind
ingen aichni fair, *LU.* 126 a.

cat(h)rach amal bud hí in grian co turcbad for lár na cat(h)rach 7 na
huama.  Is annsin ruc Muiri a mac 7 dorónta na huli mírbuli atrubramar
remainn.  Ar ní thanic do neoch a nꝼaisnés nach a n-innisi, 7 cia
thissad ni bud dímain do.

69.  Is annsin rolínad in úaim do boltnugud dermáir amal bid o
u(n)gain 7 o ꝼín 7 o ꝼírchumra in betha uli rolínta in uama[1] cor
sássta iad uli desin frí ꝛe ꝼota co nꝼacus in rétlu dermáir derscaigthech
os cind na huamad o matain co fescor, 7 ni facus a macsamla riam na
iarom na bud chutruma fria.  Rochóraig tra Muiri a mac in a lige
iarsin co mbrétib lín gil imbe .i. hi crú ind assain 7 ind ócdaim, ar ni
frith inad ele do isin tig óiged.  Ocus tucsat na dúile indligtecha
annsin aichne fora nDuilemain, uair batar oca lige 7 oc(a) adrad .i.
int assan 7 int ócdam, 7 se amedon etorru.  Is annsin rocomallad
and-epert in fáid noem ochéin .i. Ezecias mac Amois.

---

was rising[2] over the middle of the city and cave.  It is then that
Mary brought forth her Son, and all the miracles were worked that
we have already mentioned.  For it has not come to anyone[3] to tell
or to recount them, and if it had come, it were not in vain for him.

69.  Then was filled the cave with a very great fragrance as is
(exhaled) from a (precious) ointment,[4] and from wine, and from the
true-perfume[5] of the whole world; the cave was filled (with it), so
that all were satisfied therefrom for a long time; and the very great
and conspicuous star was seen above the cave from morning till even-
ing, and its like was not seen before or after, nor (aught) that was
equal to it.  Mary set her Son to rest thereafter with (swaddling)
clothes of white linen about Him in the stall of the ass and the
young ox, for no other place was found for Him in the guest-house.[6]
And the irrational creatures then recognised their Creator, for they
were licking Him and adoring Him, both the ass and the young ox,
He being in the middle between them.  Then was fulfilled what
the prophet said of old, namely, Esaias, son of Amos.

---

[1] Read rolinad ind uaim, if uama be
not another form of the nominative; or,
rolínta na huama, the caves were filled.

[2] Or, appearing.

[3] ní thánic le nech = no one could.

[4] Cf ar n-a lionad do bolad na huin-
nemeinte, John xii. 3; goirthear unga
de, "dicitur unctio," Stapleton's Catech.,
p. 133.

[5] Or, fresh perfume; cf. fíruisce.

[6] Cf. do brig nach raib áit aca sa tig
ósta, Luke ii. 7.

Ocus iar tairesin a ligi 7 a adartha dona hiumentib gabaid Mu*i*ri a m*a*c in a hucht iarsi*n* [135 b] 7 ba hoġslán hi ó churp 7 o anm*a*in, ar ni rabut*a*r hidain na assaite f*u*rri, 7 nico rabi doig na tendius i corp na hi colai*n*d di *acht* am*a*l tíssad sollsi grene t*ri*a gloi*n*e cen chneit cen galar cen erc(h)oit.

70. Dochoid iarsi*n* Ios*eph* isin uamaid 7 it*c*(h)onairc Mu*i*ri 7 a m*a*c in a hucht 7 si oc tabairt a ciche do ; ar batar di*diu* si*n*i aice-si oc siled am*a*l tep*er*sain ḟíru*sci*.  Tanic di*diu* Ios*eph* 7 Sémio*n* ina degaid, 7 se suilb*ir*¹ for*b*ailid ; 7 atb*ert* Ios*eph*, "Erig a me*i*c," ol se, "7 fég lat i*n*ni dia rabadais d'iarr*aid* .i. in Sláníccid an ucht Muire a m*á*th*a*r fén ; 7 fer falti f*ri*s, 7 dena subaigi 7 som*en*main fris."  *Ocus* rof*er*sat² a ṅdís falti f*ri*si*n* mac an*n*sin.  Tanic *tra* matan in lái iarnabarach iarsi*n*, 7 is an*n*sin rocómslanaig*ed* cec*h* firt 7 cec*h* mirbuil, cec*h* tairchetul 7 cec*h* fatsi*n*e doronta i Pet*a*rlaic

---

And when the animals had offered³ their licking and worship, Mary takes her Son in her bosom then, and she was perfectly healthy in body and mind, for she had no pains or birth-pangs,⁴ and there was not ache⁵ or soreness for her in body or in flesh, but as the sun's light would pass through glass, without sigh, without sickness, without harm.

70. Joseph went afterwards into the cave, and saw Mary, and her Son on her bosom ; she giving her breast to Him, for she had indeed paps flowing like the gushing of spring-water.

Joseph came then, and Simeon, glad and overjoyed, after him ; and Joseph said :—" Go, son," quoth he, " and behold Him for whom thou wert seeking, the Saviour, on the breast of Mary His own mother, and welcome Him, and be merry and cheerful to Him." And they two then bade welcome to the Son.

Afterwards came the morning of the next day, and then was fulfilled every miracle and every wonder, every prediction and every prophecy that was made in the Old Law and in the New Testament

---

¹ go soilbir, gladly, *Com. Prayer*, p. 38.
² ros*er*sat, MS.
³ do thairgsin, "to present, proff*e*r," *O'Begley's Dict.* ; or, having made.

⁴ *Cf.* idain and no-t-assáitither, *Sylva Gad.* i. p. 315.
⁵ doig chinn, head-ache, *O'Begley's Dictionary*, 532.

7 i Nuafiadn*uise* i*m*daig na geni coi*m*deta; 7 is bec dia mírbulib 7 dia i*n*gantaib i*n*dist*er* su*n*d.    Boi t*r*a Ios*eph* co subach f*or*bailid oc mol*ad* 7 oc adamrug*ud*[1] na geni coi*m*detta am*al* si*n*.    Atbe*r*t Ios*eph* iarsi*n*, "Is fer da*m*sa  dul isi*n*  cath*r*aig  do  ćennach  bíd don óig 7 dom m*ui*ntir, ar is soll*am*ain uasal anorach hi nim 7 hi tal*m*ain i(n)t-šollamai*n*-si, uair is i*n*diu rogenir Tig*er*na na ndoi*n*e 7 nan ai*n*gel 7 na ńdoe 7 nan uli dul arćena.

71. Indíu tanic isi*n* domun intí t*r*ia-sa-r-mairn*ed*[2] in do*m*un.

Indiu ro-fan*n*aig*ed* cum*ach*ta diabuil 7 ro-cómlanaig*ed* cum*ach*tu na heclai*s*i nemda 7 talm*an*ta.

Indíu ro-scailed sollsi i*n* ecnai 7 i*n* eolais don p*o*op*ul* Isra*el*da boi i*n* dorcha *m*eolais 7 anecna.

Indiu glormaraigth*er* 7 anoraigth*er* na fáide noemda ar comall*ad* a fatsi*n*e.

---

concerning[3] the Divine Child, and it is little of His miracles and wonders that is related here.    Joseph was exultant and very joyous, praising  and  exalting  the  Divine  Child  thus.    Afterwards  Joseph said :—"I  had  better  go  into  the  city  to  buy  food  for  the  virgin and for my family, for this festival is a noble and honourable festival in heaven  and  on earth, for to-day was born the Lord of men and angels,  and  gods,  and  all  other  creatures  besides.

71. To-day came into the world He through whom the world has abided (?)[4]

To-day the power of the devil was weakened, and the power of the church, heavenly and earthly, was strengthened.[5]

To-day was dispersed the light of wisdom and knowledge to the Israelite people who were in the darkness of ignorance and un-wisdom.

To-day are glorified and honoured the holy prophets, their prophecy being fulfilled.

---

[1] adadamrug, MS.

[2] I read triasa-r-mair; the *n after* mair, and *before* in, seems a case of anticipating  dittography; *is* mairnim = pr*o*d*o* = betray, produce (?).

[3] *Or,* on account of.

[4] *Or,* was  judged  (mairnim *for* "baírnim, I judge," *O'R.*)

[5] *Or,* was made complete, *from* com-lánaigim *or* com*i*slánaigi*m*.

Indiu ro-suidiged sásad oirmitnech nan aingel iter sássad dereoil na ndoine hi crú assaine 7 oc-daim.

Indiu doratsat na hanmunda indligthecha cen tucsi aichne for a nduilemain, ar is soc(h)etfadach cech duil illeth fria duilem.

Indiu ro-artraig in rétlu rígda dona tri druidib ar tus, co tancatar le for sét¹ do adrad Ísu.

Indiu thuccad apdaine 7 rigi na cathrach nemda do duine .i. do Crist macc De bíí.

72. Indiu rogiallsat aingil nime do doínib in talman, ar rogab ri o doinib rigi for ainglib.

Indiu thuccad dilmainius aigthide² co cairdemail iter da rigda³ in Choimded .i. iter nem 7 talam.

Indiu ro-hoslaiced dorus na cathrach némda condat obela oslaicthe doirsi nime don chined doenna dia inottacht 7 dia aitreb.

---

To-day was seated the venerated food of the angels, amid the mean food of men in the stall of a she-ass and a young ox.

To-day the irrational animals without intelligence have recognised their Creator; for every separate creature is intelligent towards its Creator.[4]

To-day first appeared the kingly star to the three druids, who came with it on their way to adore Jesus.

To-day has been given the supremacy and kingship of the heavenly city to a man, *i.e.* to Christ, Son of the Living God.

72. To-day the angels of heaven have submitted to the men of earth; for a king from [among] men has taken kingship over the angels.

To-day has been made an awful law[5] amicably between the two realms of the Lord, between heaven and earth.

To-day have been opened the door of the Heavenly City, so that the doors of heaven are wide opened to the human race to enter and dwell therein.

---

¹ f. s., MS.
² aigthige, MS.
³ Perhaps some word, as tech, cathaír, tegdais, should come before *rigda*.

⁴ *Or*, very sensible of its Creator('s presence).
⁵ compact, contract (?), *cf.* dílmain, *gl.* legitimus, Z.

E 2

Indiu cuirfither debtha 7 drocb-cetfada as in domun.   Ar thanic faid na fírinne suthaine 7 in fir-śith ind .i. Crist macc De bíí.

Indiu rofess fír-grad in chineda doenna oc in athair nemda in tan rogab [intara] persa na diadachtu doennacht dia forithin uair in doire oc diabul atbathutar hi cin 7 in imarbus Adaim 7 Eua cusindiu.

### 73. [136 a]  Do Scelaib na mBuachalla inso.

Boi tra Ioseph amlaid sin co fota oc cómrad fria a maccu .i. Iacob Glunech 7 Semion 7 Abión 7 oc molad Crist 7 oc tairchetul cecha maithiusa iarum.   Ocus atbert Ioseph doridisi, " Is ferr dam-sa," ol se, " dul do chennach bíd bicc don óig.   Luid iarum comboi for srátib 7 clochanaib na Bethile co bloid[1] do ló.   Amal boi and conacca araile budin moir chuice ocus iat oc comrád fri araile.   Drutid Ioseph friú annsin comboi oc coistecht friu 7 boi didiu oc fochmarcc bíd dia chennach uadib.   Issed atbertatar-som, " Ro-śirsium, ol siat, " in

---

To-day shall quarrels and evil sentiments be driven out of the world.   For the Prophet of the Eternal Truth and the True Peace has come into it, Christ the Son of the Living God.

To-day the true love of mankind has been recognised[2] by the Heavenly Father, when the Second Person of the Godhead assumed humanity to succour them, for in bondage under the devil they died for the fault and transgression of Adam and Eve till this day.

### 73. [136a.]  Of the Tidings of the Shepherds this.

Now Joseph was for a long time thus discoursing to his sons, James of the Knees, and Simeon, and Abion, and praising Christ, and foretelling every good thing thereafter.   And Joseph said again :— ·"It is better for me," quoth he, "to go to buy a little food for the Virgin."   He went then and was on the streets and causeways of Bethlehem till part[3] of day.   As he was there, he saw a certain large band come towards him talking to one another.   Joseph draws near to them then, till he was listening to them, and he was seeking too to buy food from them.   This is what they said :—" We have searched,"

---

[1] Cf. blog don lo sin, "part of that day," O'D. Sup. v. blod.

[2] Better perhaps this :—To-day the

Eternal Father's true love of the human race was known . . .

[3] Break of day (?).

ca*thr*aig uli ⁊ n[i]fagmait in*n*te [intíí][1] iarrmait.   Tiagu*m* did*iu* asi*n*
ca*thr*aig amach," ol siat, " ⁊ siru*m* fós i*n* m*b*iad sechtar cha*thr*aig
amuig."   Is an*n*sin atb*er*t Ios*eph* friu, " I*n* fil loim*m* ocaib oc a
creicc," ol se.   " Ni fil it*ir*," ol siat.   " In filet uigi *nó* cáissi lib ?"
ol Ios*eph*.

74.  "A dui*n*e maith," ol siat, " cid *i*matai dún*n*[2] ni do chennaigecht
tanc*u*mar ⁊ ni he si*n* ní fil foir*n*[3] *acht* scél mirbulda i*n*gnath fil
ocai*n*d," ol siat, " atau*m*m oc a iarr*aid* ⁊ ni fagmait he ar is mirbulda
⁊ is ingnathach he," ol siat.   "Masa i*n*gnath he, is e *for*coemnacair
do b*eth* ocu*m*-sa am thig," ol Ios*eph*.   *Ocus* atbert friu iar*um* " Cia
ꞅib can do*d*echubar ?"   "Sinde," ol siat, " oegaireda ca*thr*ach na
Bethile ⁊ bamar arér im-mullach thuir i*n* oirth*iur* muigi na Bethile "
.i. míle ćeme*n*d on Bethil sair (.i. cnocc mór ádbul eside, ocus is
an*n*sin chomracit oegaireda na Bethile uli oc coimet a cethra *for*
co*n*aib ⁊ gadaigib[4] ⁊ biastaib eli ; ocus i*n* aídchib ba gnath leo beth

---

said they, "the whole city and we do not find in it Him whom we
seek.   Let us go then forth out of the city," said they, " and let us
also search if He may be outside the city without."   Then Joseph
said to them :—" Have ye milk for sale ?" said he.   " We have none
at all," said they.   "Have ye eggs or cheese ?" said Joseph.

74.  " Good man," said they, " why do you come to us ?   It is not
to trade that we have come, and it is not that that concerns us, but a
marvellous strange piece of news we have," said they ; " we are seeking Him, and we do not find Him, for He is wonderful and strange,'
said they.   " If He is indeed wonderful, it is He that happens to
be with me in my house," said Joseph ; and he said to them then :
" Who are ye, and whence have ye come ?"   " We," said they, " are
the shepherds of the city of Bethlehem, and we were last night on
the top of a tower[5] in the east of the plain of Bethlehem " (a thousand paces east from Bethlehem, a very great hill this, and there
the shepherds of Bethlehem all come together, keeping their cattle
from dogs, and thieves, and other beasts, and in the nights it was

---

[1] *Cf.* ní fuaramar innte intíí atámm
d'iarraid, *infra*, § 76.

[2] Seems = *cid notai* of L. macc
n-Uisnig, &c.; or, is *oc techt* omitted
or understood after *imatai* (?).

[3] What ails, troubles us : *cf.* cadé
atá ort (?).

[4] *Sic for* gadaidib (?).

[5] i.e. of an eminence, as appears from
the context.

an*n*). "Cid di*diu acht* bamar an*n*si*n*," ol siat, "oc coi*m*et ar cethr*a*
7 si*n*d uli a n-oen inad; drém uai*n*n na cotlud, drém oc faire, dré*m* oc
scélaig*echt* di-araile, dré*m*m oc cantai*n* chiúil 7 cán*n*tairecht,[1] dré*m*m
eli oc rébrad 7 oc ullán 7 oc dordan, dré*m*m eli oc fetan*acht* 7 oc
staraid*echt*.[2] Bamar tra co *m*binnius mor am*laid* si*n*. Iar n-érgi i*n*
ésca chucai*n*d, am*al* bamar an*n* a medón óidche co *f*acu*m*ar aroli nél-
solus anair cec*h* n̄díriuch co ro-s̄ollsig uli muige na Bethile. Is
am*laid* iaru*m* bói i*n* nél si*n* co ndeilb alaind taitnemaig oiregda anoraig
i*n*a m̄edón. 7 bat*ar* beos hilcheola examla isi(n) *n*íul si*n* 7 ba
bi*n*nithi*r* cec*h* ceol a céli díb.

75. "Iar tor*ach*tain *tra* na sollsi de*r*maire sin chucai*n*d rogab grái*n*
7 ecla sind tucs*um* ar n-aigthi f*r*i lár uli. *C*oni*d* an*n*si*n* atbe*r*t i*n* guth
ai*n*gelta asi(n) *n*eól, 'Na bíd' ol se, 'ua*m̄*un na i*m*mecla f*o*raib uair is
aire tanuc-sa d' i*n*nisi*n* scél duib-si 7 don uli phop*ul* .i. scél do na
f*r*ith *s*et na sam*ail* o thus domain cus anocht. Uair is indíu rogénir

---

usual with them to be there). "Well, then, we were there," said
they, "guarding our cattle, and all of us in one place—some of us
asleep, some watching, some story-telling to one another, some sing-
ing songs and ditties, another lot sporting, and boasting,[3] and hum-
ming, another set whistling and telling tales. Thus we were with
much merriment[4] in that fashion. After the rising of the moon
towards us, as we were there at midnight, we saw a certain cloud-
light from the east coming straight until it lighted all the plains of
Bethlehem. Thus, then, was that cloud, having a comely, shining, conspicuous, venerable form in its midst, and there were many different
kinds of music in that cloud, and each kind of music thereof was as
sweet as another.

75. "That very great light having reached us, horror and fear
seized us, and we placed our faces all against the ground. Where-
upon an angelic voice said from the cloud:—'Be ye not,' said he, 'in
dread or fear, since for this have I come, to tell tidings to you and to
the whole people, tidings to which its equal or like has not been
found from the beginning of the world till to-night. For to-day was

---

[1] *Or*, can*n*taireċt(a).
[2] staraig*echt*, MS.
[3] *Cf.* fulla, a lie, skipping; fullán,

ornament, *O'R.* ul(l)aċ, sport, *O'Begley's
Dict.* uallach, sportiveness, *Coney's Dict.*
[4] *Or*, sweetness, harmony.

*in* slanicc*id* Hisu C*rist* ma*cc* De b*íí* i cat*hr*aig D*au*id i mBethil Iuda d'
*fo*rithi*n in* chineda doe*n*na atbathut*ar in* Adam .i. Dia na *n*dee 7 nem
na *n*dó*ine* 7 n*ert* na n*ert,* duine os na dó*ini*b, rig os na rigaib, milid
c*enn*ais cen feirg cen uabar cen mor*d*ataid.[1]   'Ercid chuice,' ol se,
' 7 fogebthai he 7 bréti[2] becca l*í*n gil i*m*e 7 se hi cr*ú* i*n* assa*i*n.'   Ocus
*in* tan tar*n*ic dó si*n* do ráda, is a*n*n atb*e*rt i*n* slog ai*n*gelta, boi mar
ae*n* fr*is, in* ceol sirre*ch*t*ach*[3] s*í*r-bind.   Gloria *in* excelsis D*e*o 7 in t*err*a
pax omi*n*ibus bone uoluntatis tue.   Laudamus te,[4] . . ."

76. Bat*ar* tra na hoegaireda oc *in*disi*n* na scél si*n* do Ios*eph.*   7
atb*e*rtsat[5] "Ro-*s*irsium-ne *in* cat*hr*aig," ol siat, " 7 ni *f*uaru*m*ar in*n*te
int*íí* atá*m*m d'iarr*aid.*"   Atb*e*rt Ios*eph* friu-so*m* "N*í* celtar *fo*raib-si
*in*n*í* ro*f*aillsig Dia d*ú*ib.   Ticc*id* anosa 7 fegaid bar n-iarr*aid,*" ol se.
"Mó*n*genar deit," ol na hoegaireda, " ár is duit ro-faillsiged Dia ar tús
.i. *in* maith is mó táni*c* 7 ticfa."   Luid iar*um* Íos*eph* rempu co dorus
*in* tige.   Tiagait tra na hóegaireda i*n*a dédaig isi*n* tech co *f*álti moir

---

born the Saviour Jesus Christ, Son of the Living God, in the city of
David, in Bethlehem of Juda, to succour mankind who died in Adam,
God of gods and Heaven of men, and Power of powers, Man over men,
King over kings, gentle Soldier without wrath, without pride, without
pomp.   Go ye to Him,' said he, 'and ye will find Him with little
(swaddling) clothes of white linen about Him, in the ass's manger.'
And when he had done saying that, then uttered the angelic host that
was along with him the melodious ever-sweet song, *Gloria*, &c."

76. The shepherds were telling those tidings to Joseph, and they
said: "We have searched the city," said they, "and we have not
found in it Him whom we are seeking."   Joseph said to them: "Let
not that which God has manifested for you be hidden from you.
Come now, behold your search," said he.   "Hail to thee," said the
shepherds, "for to thee first has been manifested God; that is the
greatest good that has come and that will come."   Then Joseph
went before them to the door of the house.   The shepherds go after

---

[1] mordataig, MS.

[2] *Cf.* breidín, frieze.

[3] ceol sirechtach, plaintive *fairy
music*! (*Man. & Cust.* iii. 361); .i. binn,
*O'Don. Suppl.*

[4] The rest of the Latin *Gloria* follows
down to "*in gloria Dei Patris.   Amen.*"

[5] atb*e*rtsat*ar*, MS.

leo. Tairiss*id* Ios*eph* amuig dia n-ési 7 tuc a aiged suas *for* nem. *co n*-ep*ert*, "A Dé móir! is mor i*n* mírbuil-si; andar li*n*d ni robi fis na geni coimdetta oc nech aile *acht* ocai*n*d fén; ocus co cúalut*ar* na hoegaireda hí 7 siat míle céim*e*nd on Bethil[1] sair."

77. Atb*er*t Semíon "Na hi*n*gantaig," ol se, "ní diaclui*n*fe tú i*m* dala i*n* me*i*c-si *acht* creit cofír ċena in ní atb*e*rim-si f*r*itt co *m*ba garit co ĩndfat fir domai*n* a ḟerta 7 a mirbuile fair." Am*al* bat*ar* sel fota oci*n* chomrád si*n* .i. Semío*n* 7 Iós*eph*, is and tancat*ar* na hoegair*e*da amaċ on chroes-ċró 7 atb*er*tsat, "Atċonncu*m*ar-ni mac i*n* Ath*ar* némda," ol siat. "Ci*n*dus si*n*?" ol Ios*eph*.

> "Áille i*n*a tal*am*, ol siat,
> Amra i*n*a nem,
> Soillsi i*n*a grian,
> Glai*n*e i*n*at srotha,
> Millse i*n*a mil,

---

him into the house with much rejoicing. Joseph tarries without, behind them, and lifted his face up to heaven, saying: "O great God, great is this miracle! We thought that none other but ourselves had knowledge of the Divine birth,[2] and yet[3] the shepherds heard it, they being a thousand paces from Bethlehem eastwards.

77. Simeon said: "Wonder not," said he, "at anything of what thou shalt hear about this Child, but only believe truly what I tell thee, that it will be a short (time) till the men of the world will recognize His miracles and His marvels." As they were for a long time in that conversation, Simeon and Joseph, then came the shepherds out from the stall,[4] and said: "We have seen the Son of the Heavenly Father," said they. "How is that?" said Joseph:—

> "Fairer than earth," said they,
> More wonderful than heaven,
> Brighter than sun,
> Clearer than streams,
> Sweeter than honey,

---

[1] Bethib, MS.

[2] *Or*, "offspring."

[3] *Or*, "and (it is strange) that . . .'"

[4] *Cf.* "a chorp do sáthaḋ a gcród cearc," to wriggle his body into a hen-roost, *O'Begley*, p. 670.

Mo ina domun
Ardi ina treda nime
Coemi inat aingil
Soeri ina'n saegal
Leth(n)i[1] ina'n doman a labra
Ferr ina'n bith
Dile inat na dúli
Ni roich súil he
*Et* ni thuill[2] i cluass*aib*.
Nir ġab 7 ni géba in domun a samail."

78. *Ocus* atb*er*tsat*ar*, "Rophocsam-ni a chosa," ol siat, "7 roligsium a láma 7 rodéchs*um* a gnúis 7 doroine firta 7 mirbuileda mora in ar fiad-nais*e* ; ocus moṅgenar det-siu a Ios*eph*," ol siat, " ar ni tuc*ad* do duine riam remut 7 ní tharga do neoch tar th'esi cádus mar in cadus tuccad

---

Greater than the universe,
Higher than heaven's hosts,[3]
Comelier than angels,
Nobler than the world,
Wider than the universe His speech,
Better than the world,
More precious than creatures,
Eye does not reach Him,
And He finds not room in ears,[4]
The world has not found and shall not find His like."

78. And they said: "We have kissed His feet," said they, "and we have licked His hands, and we have beheld His face, and He has done miracles and great wonders in our presence; and good luck to thee, Joseph," said they, "for there has not been given to a man ever before thee, nor shall there come to anyone after thee, a dignity like

---

[1] lethi, ms.

[2] tuillim, I fit, find room, *O'D. Sup.*

[3] *Or*, flocks; *or*, three things of heaven (?).

[4] ionnas narthuilledar annsna hion-nadaib, so that there was not room to receive them, *Mark*, ii.; tuill, contain, *Bible Foclóir*. In Ml. 30 c. 17, feib du-nd-alla indib = as fits or finds room in them; Ascoli's "congruit" will not suit here; the Eng. "fit" has a wider meaning.

deitt, 7 tab*air*-si a s*e(i)*rcc dúi*n*ne," ol siat, " ar is buidech sínd *conice*
so. ar do chetaigis dún fégad na hetrochta diadai Cid di*diu* is ail duib,"
ol Ios*eph*. [137 a] "Ní *anse són*, toide*cht* det-siu li*n*d," ol siat, " do
ól f̃ína 7 do bi*n*dius 7 do oirfitiud; uair is indíu ata fled mor oc ar táisech
dúi*n*ne .i. táissech na n-oeg̀aired. Is*ed tra* is gnáth do-side flead mor
do denu*m* ce*ch*a bli*adn*a do*n*a hoeg*air*ib in ocht kl. en*air* do s̀undrad do
gnith*er* in fled si*n*." " Ni rag *imorro*," ol Ios*eph*, " ar ni bud cóir
dam-sa sin .i. M*uir*i 7 a m*acc* do f̃ácbail cen biad cen lind occu; *acht*
chena ata mo m*en*ma 7 mo cride mar oen f*ri*b," ol Ios*eph* " 7 b*er*id
bend*acht*ain." " Uair na*ch* ticc*id*-si li*n*de, ol na hóeg*air*eda, " cech ní
bus ferr bias ocai*n*de doria chucut-sa he .i. cáisi nua 7 loi*m*m 7 coróin
do spínib 7 fín 7 fír-cruith-necht 7 uigi cerc 7 lossa 7 luibérad olchena,
7 cid mar f*ri*sin mac mbecc atai is maræn f*ri*nne fós bia."

79. Isaire did*u* is dona haegairib artús atchess in Slanícid .i. ar is

---

the dignity which has been conferred on thee; and give us a love
for Him,"[1] said they, " for we are contented so far, since thou hast
permitted us to behold the Divine brightness."

"What is it, then, that ye wish?" said Joseph. " It is not
difficult to say :[2] thy coming with us," said they, "to drink wine,
and to amuse and enjoy yourself, for to-day our chief has a great
banquet for us, that is, the chief of the shepherds. It is, indeed,
customary for him to prepare a great feast every year for the shepherds; on the eighth of the Kalends of January precisely that feast is
held." " I will not go, however," said Joseph, "as that would not
be right for me, forsooth, to leave Mary and her Child without their
having food and drink; but, indeed, my soul and heart are with
you," said Joseph, "and take my blessing (with you)." " Since
thou comest[3] not with us," said the shepherds, " every best thing we
shall have shall reach you, to wit, fresh cheese and milk and a crown
of thorns,[4] and wine, and good wheat and honey, and hen-eggs, and
vegetables, and herbs likewise; and even as thou art towards the
little babe, so also shalt thou be with us."

79. Now, the reason the Saviour was first seen by the shepherds

---

[1] *Lit.*, his love.
[2] In full; "ní anse són,' *Ml.* 45 d.
[3] *Lit.*, ye come.
[4] This is curious.

iat bói cen cotlad oc *fri*thaire 7 oc h*í*dnaide *s*ollsi in l*á*i. Is*ed* di*du*
dof*orn*e *si*n : secip nech dianad ail in betha marthanach d'*f*agbail is*ed*
is techta do beth cen cotlad *in* aimsir na haid*c*e oc *fri*thaire na sollsi
suthaine .i. gn*ú*si D*é* uli*c*uma*ch*taig. Luidset na h*ó*e*g*aireda[1] ass iar*um.*
Boi di*diu* Ios*eph* 7 M*ui*ri 7 Cr*ist* isin tig *ó*iged *á*ml*ai*d sin 7 tuctha t*ra*
na biada sin uli ona hoegairib doib am*al* atrubr*a*mar rom*ain*d.

### INC*I*PIT DO SCELAIB NA N*D*RUAD.

**80.** Bat*ar* an*n* di*diu* f*ri* re aile f*ó*s. Am*al* boi Ios*eph* an*n* 7 s*é* i
ndorus in tigi in a *s*ess*om* in aroli laa *n*-and *con*-facca t*ra* budin moir
*c*uici anoir ce*ch* nd*í*riuch ; *con*id an*n* atb*er*t I*ó*s*eph* f*ri* Sem*í*on, "C*ú*i*ch*
iatsi*n* cucai*n*d a m*ei*c," ol se, " d*ó*ig c*om*ad a c*é*in noth*í*stais." Ta*n*ic
t*ra* Ios*eph* ina f*ri*thaigid 7 atb*er*t f*ri* Sem*í*on, "I*n*dar lium, a meic,"
ol se, "is celmai*n*e druad 7 is methmer*c*urd*ach*t dogniat, uair ni b*er*ait
oe*n* *c*oisceim cen f*é*gad suas 7 attat oc tac*c*ra 7 oc comr*á*d f*ri* araile

---

is because they were without sleep, a-watching and waiting for the
light of day. This is what that denotes—whoso wishes to obtain
everlasting life ought to be without sleep in the night-time a-watching
for eternal light, that is, the countenance of Almighty God. The
shepherds then went away. And Joseph, and Mary, and Christ,
were in the guest-house like that, and all these viands were given
to them by the shepherds as we have previously stated.

### (HERE) BEGINS ABOUT THE STORIES OF THE MAGI.

**80.** They (Joseph, Mary, and Christ) were there some time longer.
As Joseph was there standing in front of the house on a certain day,
he saw a great band of people coming towards him from the east
straight onwards, and then Joseph said to Simeon, "Who are those
that are coming towards us, my son?" said he, "methinks that it
may be from afar they might have come." Now, Joseph came
towards them, and he said to Simeon, "I fancy, my son," said he,
"that it is the omen art[2] of Druids, and it is soothsaying[3] they are
practising, for they take not a single step without looking up, and

---

[1] *Or*, hoegairi.
[2] c*é*l, "omen," ba c*é*l olc d*o*som, *Frags. of I. Ann.*, 200.
[3] Is "methmerchurdacht" a mistake for maithmar*c*dacht, and had the scribe Mercury in his head?

etorru fén ; 7 indar lium," ol se, "isat doine echtarchenélaig iat 7 is a crichaib cianaib tancutar, uair ni hinand delba nó dath nó ecosc doib 7 diar ndóinib-ne.   Ar it lénti gela fairsiunga 7 inair corccra comdatha filet leosom, 7 cochaill fota forruamanda foraib, 7 bróca brecca bernacha leo amal ríg no taisech dian écosc."

81. Batar tra triar loech hi tossuch na búdni sin .i. oclach álaind oirmitnech dibsen 7 se ulcach liath oisinech, Melcisar a ainm-side, isé thuc in n-ór¹ do Crist.  Oclach ele ulchach cu folt ndónd n-imlebar fair, Balcisar a ainm-side, is é dorat in tuis do Crist.  Oclach aile didiu find cen ulcha lais, Hiespar a ainm-side is é dorat an mirr do Crist. Anmunda n-aill tra dona rígaib-si, .i. Malcus, Patifaxat, Casper. Malcus didiu .i. Melcisar, Patifaxat, .i. Balcisar, Casper .i. Hiespar.

82. Atbert Ioseph [137 b], "Is maith imthigit," ol se, "7 siat nemscithach cid a cein tecait."  Iar sin tra doriachtatar cusin inad i

---

they are discussing and communing one with another among themselves ; and as it seems to me," said he, "they are people of a strange race, and it is from foreign regions they have come, as they have not the same forms or colour or look as our people have.   For white and wide are their tunics, and purple and even-coloured² are their mantles, and they have long reddish hoods, and speckled and gapped shoes,³ like a king or chieftain, by their appearance."

81. Now, there were three warriors in front of that band, to wit, a handsome and venerable man,⁴ bearded, grey, and fawnlike,⁵ named Melcisar,⁶ it is he that gave the gold to Christ ; another man, bearded, with very long brown hair, named Balcisar,⁶ it is he that gave the incense to Christ; another man, also fair, without beard, named Hiespar,⁶ it is he that gave the myrrh to Christ.   Other names for these kings were Malcus, Patifaxat, Caspar; that is, Malcus was Melcisar, Patifaxat was Balcisar, Caspar was Hiespar.

82. Said Joseph, "It is well they march on," said he, "and they are unfatigued though it is from afar they come."   After that then

---

¹ in hór, MS.

² like-coloured?

³ So O'Curry: are bróca bernacha = bernbróca (LL. 70 b) = trousers, "divided skirt" (?): cf. Zim. Kelt Stud. iii. 85 ; pointed shoes, Stokes, Harl.

Notes and Glosses, p. 361.

⁴ oclach = "miles," Todd Lect., V.

⁵ oclach, "juvenis" of Z., will not suit with liath.

⁶ Melchior, Balthasar, Gaspar, Bollandists, Maii, t. 1. pp. 7, 8.

mboi Ioseph 7 a mac .i. Semion.  Lotar didiu sech Ioseph dochum in
tige.  Luid Ioseph leo 7 atbert con-epert " Cúich sib," ol se, " apraid
frium ar Dia, 7 cia leth tegthi dochum in tige cen cetugud dam?"
"Ar tóissech 7 ar tigerna docóid remaind don tégdais bic-se 7 in a diaid
dúinne," ol siat.  " Can didiu asa tancabar fen?" ol Ioseph.  "Anair,"
ol siat, "a hoirthiur hIndia 7 a tírib Arabia 7 a tírib Kallacda[1] 7 arolib
tírib examla oirthir betha," ol siat.  " Cid ima tancabar?" ol Ioseph.
" Ní ansa són" ol siat .i. "rí nan Iudaide 7 rí in domain uli rogenir
isin tír-si, 7 tancamar dia iarraid 7 dia adrad 7 dia fégad," ol siat.
" Can asa tuicebair-si sin? ol Ioseph.  Ní ansa són," ol siat, "a beth
in ar senlebraib[2] 7 in ar senscribennaib o ré in c(het)fir uainn cusindiu
.i. Secip tan atcifemis retlaind a macsámla so ós cind ar tíre dul lee
secip conair nodicsed, ar ba comartha ríg in domain hi.  Ar is don rig
sin ata hi taircetul 7 fatsine sinn fen 7 in cined dóenna do slánugud

---

they came to the place where Joseph was, and his son, that is Simeon.
They, however, went past Joseph to the house.  Joseph went with
them, and he said and said, " Who are ye? " said he, " tell me, for
God's sake, and whither[3] go ye to the house without my leave ? "  " Our
leader and lord went before us to this little dwelling, and after him we
go," said they.  " Whence then have ye come?" said Joseph.  " From
the east," said they, " from the eastern part of India, and from the
lands of Arabia and from Callatian[4] lands and various other regions of
the east of the world," said they.  " Wherefore have ye come," said
Joseph.  " That is not difficult to tell," said they, " to wit, the King
of the Jews and the King of the whole world was born in this land,
and we have come to seek Him, and to adore Him, and to contemplate
Him," said they.  " Whence did ye understand that?", said Joseph.
" Not hard to tell is that," said they, " (on account of) its being in
our old books and old writings from the time of the first man of us till
to-day, that whatever be the time we should behold a star like this
over our land (we were) to go with it what way soever it would go,
as it was a sign of the King of the world.  For it is by that King, it
stands in prediction and prophecy, that we ourselves and the human

---

[1] A line is drawn across the second *l*.
It seems to mean " Chaldeans."

[2] sennlebraib, MS.

[3] Or, what way.

[4] Probably Galatian, as painters re-
present the three as a Persian, an
Ethiopian, and a Greek; the name is
not in the geographical poem, *LL.* 135.

iar n-a gein foce*to*ir." "Cid fodera¹ duib," ol Iose*ph*, "cen dul hin
Ier*usa*lem da iarr*aid*, ar isi ardc(h)ath*ir in* tire-si hi 7 is in*n*te ata tempul
i*n* Choi*m*ded, 7 is in*n*te fos bis c*ó*mn*ai*de r*í*g nan Iudaide .i. Hiruaith."

83. "Do*ċ*uamar *ċ*ena;" ol siat, "7 i*n*tan ra*n*c*a*mar in cat*h*r*a*ig i*s*
an*n* do*ċ*uaid i*n* retla rig*d*a uain*n* 7 ni f*a*camar ite*r* h*í*, 7 do*ċ*uamar
isi*n* tech i robi i*n* rig .i. Hiruath, cori*n*disimar do, r*í* nan I*ú*d*ai*de do*̇*
gene*mai*n i*n* a th*í*r 7 a retla rig*d*a do beth re*m*ai*n*d o airth*iur* domai*n*
coni*ċ*e so, 7 a dula uai*n*d an*n*so. Ocus bamar oc a f(h)iarfaigid don
rig 7 don p*opul* I*ú*d*ai*de archena caitt i*n* rogenir he, 7 atbertsat
natfetat*ar*." Is an*n*sin roti*n*olit co H*i*ruath a uli dr*ú*di 7 ecnaide 7
luc*h*t a f*e*ssa 7 a eolais, co rofiarfaig² d*í*b cait h(i)rabi³ i fatsi*n*e occu r*í*
nan I*ú*d*i*de do gene*mai*n. Atb*e*rtsat uli "Isin (m)*Be*th*i*l I*ú*da," ol siat,
"amal atb*e*rt in Spir*ut* Noe*m* tria gin i*n* rig .i. D*au*id me*i*c I*é*se ' De
diversario in spelonca nasci Christum in Bethelem.' " Ocus atb*e*rt f*ó*s

---

race are to be saved after His birth immediately." "What causes you
not to go into Jerusalem to seek Him, as it is the capital city of this
land, and in it is the Temple of the Lord, and there also is the abode
of the King of the Jews, to wit, of Herod."

83. "We have gone (thither) already," said they, "and when we
reached the city, then the star departed from us, and we did not
see it at all, and we went into the house in which King Herod was,
and told him the King of the Jews was born in his territory, and that
His royal star was before us from the east of the world up to this, and
it went from us here. And we were inquiring of the king and of the
Jewish people likewise the place in which He was born, and they said
they did not know." Then were gathered to Herod all his magi and
sages, and his folk of learning and knowledge, and he asked of them
the place where they had in prophecy that the King of the Jews was
to be born. They all said, "In Bethlehem of Juda," said they, "as
the Holy Ghost declared by the mouth of King David⁴ son of Jesse,".
"From an inn in a cave Christ shall be born in Bethlehem."

---

¹ *f*, with *o* over it, is usually *for* or
*fro*; here it doubtless stands for *fodera*.
*Cf.* cid fodera duit cen, what causes
you not to?

² fiarfaid, MS.

· ³ hr. *in* MS.

⁴ David says merely: "Ecce inve-
nimus eam in Ephrata (i.e. Bethlehem)";
but Michæas has: "Et tu Bethlehem
Ephrata purvulus es in millibus Juda;
ex te mihi egredietur qui sit dominator
in Israel."

cend nan áuctor 7 na fátha .i. Isu fodesin in a soscela "*Tu Bethelem terra Iúda nequaquam minima es in princip(ib)us Iúda, ex te enim exiet dux qui regat populum meum Israel.*" Is tu, a Bethil Iuda, talam 7 tír Iúda meic Iacoip, isat mor 7 isat adamra itir cat(h)racha tíre Iúda uli, 7 is innut genfit(h)ir in tóisech 7 in ríg follamnaigfes in popul (n)Israelta."

84. "Gabaid iarum annsin crith mor 7 omun mor intíí Hiruath 7 atbert, "Ca hinad ele a ngenfed mac rig nan Iúdaide acht am thig-se." Atbertsat didiu na drúdi, "Mac rig in domain uli is e rogenir ann." Batar tra annsin imráti mora 7 smuantigthi iumda for menmain in rig Hiruaith. Rogairmed iarsin doridise ecnaide in popuil Iúdaide chuci co mboi oca athfiarfaigid [138a] díb co frichnamach cáitt i rabi i taircetul no i faitsine a genemain in rig ucut. Atbertsa(t) uli "a mBethil Iúda," ol siat.

85. Is ann atbert Hiruath frisna drúidib tancutar do adrad Crist, "Ercid," ol se, "co Bethil Iúda 7 dia fagbathi Crist innte ticcid chucumsa doridise con-dechsum fen dia adrad; ocus berid," ol se, "mo

---

And again the head of authors and prophets, Jesus himself, said on His own behalf[1]: "Thou Bethlehem of Juda, land and country of Juda son of Jacob, thou art great and thou art wonderful amongst the towns of the land of all Judea, and it is in thee shall be born the leader and king who shall rule the Israelite people."

84. Then and there great trembling and fear seizes the aforesaid Herod, and he said, "What place else should the Son of the King of the Jews be born in but in my house?" Then said the magi, "The Son of the King of the world is he who has been born." Then indeed there were great deliberations and many considerations in the mind of King Herod. Then again were summoned to him the wise men of the Jewish people, and he again inquired of them deligently where in prediction and prophecy was (to be) the birth of that king. They all said, "in Bethlehem of Juda," said they.

85. Thereupon Herod said to the magi who had came to adore Christ, "Go," said he, "to Bethlehem of Juda, and if ye find Christ therein, come back to me that I may[2] myself go to adore Him; and take," said

---

[1] His words are: "Nonne Scriptura dicit quia ex semine David et de Bethlehem castello ubi erat David venit Christus?" The words of our text are those of the priests and scribes, Matt. ii. 6.

[2] *Lit.*, we may go.

mínd rígda do Crist" (.i. mínd ríg di ór na hAraibe 7 se lán do lecaib
lógmaraib 7 do carrmoclaib cumdaigthi. Ocus ba he in mínd sin nobid
um cend Hiruaith fén cech dia). "Ocus beríd lib in fáinne rígda-sa
dó co ngéim nderscagthi ann dona frith s(ét) na samail do-gemaib in
domain riam. Ise thuccad damsa o ríg na Pers, 7 tábraid-si don ríg
sin he 7 in tan ticfathi doridisi ragut sa fén dia adrad, con ascadaib
ele lium dó bus ferr oldát sin."

86. "Tucsam lind didiu na hascada sin," ol na drúdi, "7 tancumar
asin cathraig amach 7 tarfas dún focetoir annsin ar rétla rígdai fen, 7
ba fálti mor linde esein; 7 tanic iarsin co fil os cínd in tigi-se 7 os a
mullach, 7 docóid isin tech in ar fiadnaise, 7 ni léci-se didiu dún dula
in a diaid."

Cubaid didiu in ní forcoemnacair annsin .i. na drúdi 7 na ríga in
oenpersain do adrad ríg na fírinde 7 áugtair na fátsine ar tús re cach.
Arái tra cérbat drúdi ar fátsine 7 ar thaircetul batar riga iat ar ordan

---

he, "my royal diadem to Christ" (i.e. a king's diadem of the gold of
Arabia, full of precious stones and ornate carbuncles ; and that was the
diadem which was on the head of Herod himself every day). "And take
also this royal ring to Him with a brilliant gem in it, for which equal
or like has never been found of the gems of the world. It was given
to me by the king of the Persians, and give ye it to that King ; and
when ye shall come back, I shall go myself to adore Him, bringing
with me other gifts for Him which shall be better than those."

86. "We have brought then those presents," said the magi, "and
we came out of the city, and immediately our royal star was shown
to us and that was a great joy to us ; and then it came on till it is over
this house and over its top, and it entered the house in our presence,
and thou forsooth dost not let us go after it."

Fitting indeed was the thing that happened there, that is, the magi
and kings in one person[1] adoring the King of truth and the Author of
prophecy, at first (and) before all (others). However, though they
were magi by reason of prophesying and prediction, kings were they
for dignity and pre-eminence and strength and power. But the reason

---

[1] as one man, or together (?).

7 oirechus 7 n*ert* 7 treisi.  A*cht* is aire atberthá drúidi díb ar i*n* tairćetul 7 ar in fatsine dorónsat i*m* dála na geni coimdetta, 7 co*n*id roindis in ce*ch* tír otha tír na hI*n*dia 7 tir Arabía 7 Silla*ch*acda[1] co tír Iúda co rogenir i*n* Slanniccid .i. m*a*c rig *in* domai*n* isi*n* inbuid sin Di scel*aib* na nDr*u*ad co*n*icesin 7 dia tairćetlaib in ce*ch* tír i*n* aroli o airth*iur* domai*n* co tír Iúda 7 co B*eth*il.

87. Ocus di*diu* batar oc a ćetug*ud* do Ios*eph* dula isi*n* tech. Atb*er*t t*r*a Ios*eph* friu-som, " Ni tairmisceb-sa u*m*aib," ol se, "i*n*ni ro-fallsig Dia dúib budén." Ba maith t*r*a la Ióseph fiss na scél si*n* do beth oc cách cu coitchend 7 a fállsiug*ad* doib. " B*er*-siu bend*a*ch*t*ain," ol siat, " 7 ragmait-ne co faicem i*n* Slanicc*id* 7 Dia na ndóine." Lot*a*r iarsi*n* isin tech 7 robennachsat do Muiri 7 is*ed* roraidset iar*um*, " *Ave tu benedicta gratia plena*, Dia lat, isat ben*n*achda 7 isat lán do rath." Lot*a*r iarsi*n* cusin croesćró co *m*bat*a*r oc fégad Cr*ist* an*n*. Iar ndul t*r*a dona drúdib isi*n* tech, atb*er*t Ios*eph* fr*i* Semion, " Erig na ndiaid a

---

they were called magi was on account of the prediction and prophecy they made concerning the Lord's birth, and as they told in every land from the land of India, and the land of Arabia, and the Cilicians,[2] to the country of Juda, that the Saviour was born, *i.e.* the Son of the King of the world, at that time. Of the tidings of the Magi hitherto, and of their predictions in every land (from one) to another, from the east quarter of the world to the land of Juda and to Bethlehem.

87. And then they were asking Joseph's permission to enter the house. Now, Joseph said to them, " I will not hinder you," said he, " (as to) what God himself has revealed to you." Joseph indeed was glad that all people in general had a knowledge of those tidings and that it was manifested to them. " God bless thee,"[3] said they, " and we will go to see the Saviour and God of men." They then entered the house and saluted Mary, and said then, " *Ave tu benedicta, gratia plena*, Hail, thou art blessed and thou art full of grace." They then went to the crib, and were contemplating Christ in it. After the magi had gone into the house, said Joseph to Simeon, " Go after them,

---

[1] *Or*, K*a*lla*ch*acda, K*a*llacda.
[2] *Or*, Galatians.
[3] *Lit.*, bear a blessing. It occurs

at § 94, in this text, and seems to mean " Thank you," or something similar.

meic," ol se, "7 feith co glic iat co faicea 7 co finda cid dogniat frisin mac, ar ni dú damsa fethium no findigecht forru.

88. Luid Sémion na ndiaid co mboi oca fegad. Is ann sin batar na drúdi 7 an aigthi for lar oc prostráit 7 oc slechtain[1] do Mac Dé. Ba machtad la Semion in bés batar-som do denam, co-rinnis Semión do Ioseph he. "Fég fós," ol Ióseph, "cid dogniat?" Roerigset iarsin 7 rooslaicset dian ascadaib 7 tucsat do C(h)rist iat. "Cid inní tucsat do?" ol Ióseph. [138 b]. "Ni ansa," ol Semión, ".i. ór 7 túis 7 mírr 7 na bascada thuc Hiruath doib."

Atbert didiu Iacop gluinech, .i. brathair Crist fesin, co tucsat na drúdi ascada imda ele do Crist .i. corcair derscaigtech co sollsi némdibaide 7 margrent thaitnemach 7 coróin de feor úr cen sergad tria bithu acht blath gelcorcera forri dogrés 7 fige thrébraid fos forri do feraib

---

my son," said he, "and watch them cautiously, that thou mayest see and know what they do to the Child; for it is not proper for me to watch and look closely[2] at them."

88. Simeon went after them and was looking at them. Then the magi were with their faces on the ground in prostration and lying down before the Son of God. Wonderful to Simeon seemed the rite they were performing, and he mentioned it to Joseph. "See still," said Joseph, "what they are doing." They rose up after that, and they opened out (some) of their presents and gave them to Christ. "What is the thing they gave him?" said Joseph. "I can tell you," said Simeon, "gold and incense and myrrh, and the presents Herod gave them."

Then James of the Knees, i. e. the brother of Christ himself, said that the magi gave many other presents to Christ, i. e. remarkable purple of imperishable light and a bright pearl, and a garland of fresh grass which never withers, but has a pure purple blossom for ever, and a through-braided wreath[3] of various fresh grasses with blossoms of

---

[1] prostrait = slechtain here.

[2] findaim, know, learn, find out; perhaps we get a glimpse of Irish manners here.

[3] fige, web, woof, Wind. Dict.; trebraid, cf. trebrigedar, gl. continuare potest, Z. 980; tarbsleini trebraid, LL. 70b; luireach threabraide, léine threabnaide, Todd Lect. iv. pp. 80, 68; luirech threbraid, Tog. Troi. 2, 999, thoroughly braided or knit (?); tréntrebraid, stout, Cog. G. re G., 158.

úra examla co mblath*aib* corc*c*ra *fo*raib am*al* bid *in* uair sin robénta[1]
iat ; ocus línan(a)rt[2] nua glégel do*na* fr*í*th s(et) na sam*ail*.  Ba he
di*diu* met a taitnemchi co fact*í*s na dó*í*ne na sáignena oc ergi de am*al*
rind ṅgrianta no am*al* crithre do rigthenid *in* tan is moo a bruth.
Tucsat iar*um* flescc rigda co ṅgemaib do gloine[3] 7 do leccaib lógmara
do*na* fr*í*th s(et) na sam*ail in* ellach dénma na ṅdúl riam o thus do*main*
có a d*e*riud *acht* mine fil firmám*ent*úm, ar imad rétland 7 lecc lógmar
in*n*te fó ćuma gr*e*ne 7 ésca.

89.  Roscen*n*tis di*diu* toidlenacha[4] mongthen*n*techa[5] estib amal rind
ngrianta co leġdais ruisc doenna r*em*pu ar thaitnemchi.  Ocus tucsat asccad*a* ele dona (f)ríth sam*ail* for bith.[6]  Is an*n* sin atb*e*rt
Semíon, "Is *m*aith na dóine," ol se, "7 is ben*n*aigthi an asccad*a*,
7 rospócsat cossa na nóiden *con* ascc*a*daib do.  Nídat in*a*nn tr*a* 7 na
hóeg*ai*re*d*a, ar ni thucsat asccad*a* dó.  Ocus in lu*ch*t tucsat asccad*a*

purple on them as if it were that moment they were cut, and a large
linen cloth new and pure bright, for which equal or like was not found.
Such indeed was the greatness of its brightness that people saw light-
nings rising from it as a sunlike star or as sparks from a great[7] fire
when its glow is greatest.  They then gave a royal wand with gems of
glass and precious stones for which equal or like has never been found
in the junction of the making[8] of creatures from the beginning of the
world to its end, unless it be the firmament by reason of the multitude
of stars and precious stones in it, like[9] the sun and moon.

89.  There darted out of them indeed great fiery meteors,[10] like a
sunlike star, so that human eyes melted before them on account of the
brilliance.  And they gave other gifts for which the like was not
found in the world.  Then said Simeon, "Good are the men," quoth
he, " and blessed are their gifts, and they kissed the feet of the infant,
with offerings to him.  They are not indeed the same as the shepherds,
for these gave no presents to him.  And the folk who gave presents

---

[1] Accent over *n* or *t* in MS.

[2] línanart, *Stowe Mis.*, 63 b ; anart,
*gl.* linteum magnum, *B. of Arm.*

[3] *Or*, co ṅgemaib gloin(i)di ; gloindi
dó 7, in MS.

[4] *Sic, read* taidlecha (?).

[5] *Cf.* retlu mongtheindtech, § 92,
*infra.*

[6] for bith = ar bith, "at all."

[7] *Lit.*, "royal fire"; *rig* seems an
intensitive here.

[8] *Or*, in the whole framework of
creation.

[9] *Lit.*, after the way or fashion of.

[10] *cf.* toidlech, taiḋlech, glänzend,
glanz, *Wind. Dict.*

bid toss*ach* maithiusa moir doib, ar dobérat a síl asc*cada* tr*i*a bith*u*."
Ba fír si*n* tra, ar ba he si*n* tossach na ngén*n*ti do cretiu*m* do Cri*st*;
7 ba hiatsi*n* ce*t*-asc*c*ada na ngén*n*ti do Dia 7 a prímiti[1] ar tús.

90. Andsin atb*ert* Iose*ph* fri Semíon, "Fég latt co glicc cid
dogníat anossa." "Ataut," ol Semío*n*, " oc adr*ad* 7 oc imacalla*im*
fr*i*si*n* m*a*c. Atcluním a nglor 7 nítfetur-sa cid ċanaid." "Oc
anorug*ud* i*n* me*i*c atat uli," ol Ióse*ph*. Iarsin ta*n*catar na drúdi
amach 7 atb*ert*sat fr*i* Iose*ph*, "A f̈ir f̈íreoin f*or*pthi," ol siat, "is
maith i*n* turcharthi[2] fil ocut, dia mbeth a f̈is ocut .i. m*a*c rig nime
7 talm*an* do beth oca altr*am* lat, ar is mó a fis dúinne i*n*ti fil ocut
i*n*das duit fen; uair is e i*n* m*a*c fil i*n* tf̈ail Dia na n̈dee 7 tig*er*na na
tig*er*nad 7 dentaid na n̈dúl 7 nan ai*n*gel 7 nan arċaingel :—

> Is he n*er*t Dé 7 lám Dé,
> Is e dess Dé 7 ecna Dé,

---

it shall be a beginning of great blessing to them, for their seed will
give[3] presents for ever." That was true indeed, for that was the
beginning of the Gentiles to believe in Christ, and these were the first
gifts of the Gentiles to God and their primitæ at first.

90. Then said Joseph to Simeon, " Watch carefully what they are
doing now." " They are," said Simeon, " worshipping, and conversing
with the child ; I hear their voice, and I know not what it is they say."
" They are all doing honour to the child," said Joseph. After that
the magi came out and said to Joseph : " O just and perfect man," said
they, " good is the treasure[4] thou hast if thou didst know it, to wit, the
Son of the King of the world is being nursed by thee, since we have
more knowledge of Him who is with thee than thou hast; for the
Babe who is near thee is the God of gods, and Lord of lords and Creator
of the elements and of the angels and archangels :—

91. " He is the strength of God and the hand of God ;
He is the right-hand of God and the wisdom of God,

---

[1] primiti*n*, in MS. ; but *np.* prímiti
in Z.

[2] Or, i*n* turcharthi (?) ; turchar,
turchairt, wealth, O'R.

[3] cf. is mo as beannaigtl̈e ní do
thabhairt ná do ghlacadh, *Acts* 20, 35.

[4] Dorala slíab óir dóib. Is maith in
turchurtha so, ar a muintir; turcḧairthi
ingnad; tír turchartig, *Merugud Uilix*,
pp. 2, 36.

Is e tacmong na ndúl 7 faircseoir in betha,

Is e bás 7 crith 7 atach na ndúl,

Is e brithem 7 liaig 7 comarci na ndúl,

Is e gairfes 7 scailfes dee na ngennti,

Is e aircfes ifernn 7 faindeochas nert 7 cumachta diabuil,

Is e brisfes guilbend in báis,

Is e scailfess diabulcumachta iffirnn imnedaig con a olcaib adétchib.

Is do fogenait uli treba 7 cineda in uli domain.

Is e didiu brithem 7 sássad nan aingel, 7 [139 a] betha múnntire nime 7 luirec imdegla na bethad suthaine cin crich cin forcend, 7 cathbarr coróni na cat(h)rach nemda.

92. Is annsin atbert Ioseph, "Can iter as arthuicebair-si toircetul geni Crist?" "Do(t)huicsium," or siat, "as ar senscribennaib 7 as

He is the comprehension[1] of creatures, the beholder of the (whole) world,

He is the death and terror and refuge of creatures;

He is the judge and physician and protection of creatures,

He it is who shall summon and scatter the gods of the Gentiles;

He it is who shall straiten[2] hell and weaken the strength and power of the devil;

He it is that shall break the sting[3] of death;

He it is that shall scatter the diabolical power of distressful hell with its detestable evils;

He it is whom all the tribes and nations of the whole world shall serve;

He is also the judge and the nourishment of angels, and the life of the family of heaven, and the breast-plate of protection of eternal life without end, without limit, and the helmet of the crown[4] of the heavenly city."

92. Then Joseph said, "Whence at all did ye understand the prediction of Christ's birth?" "We understood it," said they, "from our

---

[1] *i.e.* He compasseth (?); tacmungad, *gl.* contingebat (?) does not suit here; rather tacmuc, comprehension, ima thacmong, around him of *AG*.

[2] airc .i. dócumail no éigen, *O'Clery;*

or for *oircfes,* who shall smite, devastabit.

[3] *Lit.,* beak; *cf.* "O death, where is thy sting?" 1 *Cor.* xv.

[4] *i.e.* head (?). I do not understand this figure.

ar senḟátsine fén bat*ar* ochéin anall ocaind oc tairċetul Cr*ist*. Uair atai-si oca iarfaigid ci*n*dus douice*m*-ni dala geni Cr*ist* i*n*nisfimit deit uli o thus co d*er*ed am*al* roḟacsat ar n-aithre 7 ar senaithre ocai*n*d o amsir m*ac*[1] n-Abrahá*im* anall· cusi*n*díu.    Cid di*diu*," ol siat,[2] " *acht in* tan bamar-ne oc coi*m*et na ḟátsine 7 i*n* chomartha rofacbad ocai*n*d i*n* aroli lou i K*al*ai*n*d en*air* sai*n*drúd, 7 si*n*d oc légud na fátsi*n*e co ḟacumar foc*et*oir in comartha rofácbad ocai*n*d .i. rétlu mor 7 si*n* mongthei*n*dtech etr*ai*nd 7 nem.    Ba maith *tra* lin*n*e si*n* 7 niḟaicc*ad*[3] nech ele hi *acht* si*n*d fesi*n* a(r)n oenur.[4]    Tuaruscbail *tra* na rétlai*n*de si*n* no a delb no a dath ni ċumai*n*g nech a tabairt *acht* mi*n*a thucc*ad* ai*n*gel Dé.    Ar ba moo a sollsi na sollsi gréne ; ocus ón ló tuarcaib dun i*n* rétlu sin ba hulli 7 ba huaisle a sollsi na sollsi nan uli rén*d* 7 rétlan*n* olċena, 7 ba he mét a sollsi comba lán nem 7 talam di.

---

own old writings and from our ancient prophecy, which were from long ago in our possession predicting Christ.    Since thou art asking how we understand all about the birth of Christ, we will tell thee all from beginning to end as our fathers and our forefathers foretold[6] to us from the time of the sons of Abraham of yore till this day. What then," said they,[5] "but while we were guarding the prophecy and token which they left with us, one day on the calends of January precisely, and while we were reading the prophecy, we saw at once the sign which was foretold,[6] *i.e.* a great star hairy and fiery[7] between us and heaven.    We were indeed overjoyed at it, and no one did see it but ourselves alone.    A description of that star, or its forms and colour, no one can give it, unless an angel of God were to give it. For greater was its light than a sun's light ; and from the day that star appeared to us, greater and nobler was its light than the light of all the constellations and stars together, and such was the greatness of its light that heaven and earth was full of it.

---

[1] *mn*, with a line over *m*.
[2] ol se, MS.
[3] *Or*, ni ḟaicc*end*, *or* ḟaicc*a*.
[4] an oenur, MS.
[5] said he, *ms*.

[6] Lit., left with us, or foretold, "furacaib, prædixit," *Todd Lect.* v. 128.
[7] " stella cincinnata or cincinnita," a comet, " stella comata."

93. Tancamair-ne foce*t*oir i*n* a diaid, 7 tánic si remai*n*d co tait-nemach tóidlenach, 7 nírba siúblach utmall ama*l* retlanda ele, *acht* tanic co cert cobsaid remai*n*d cen dul anú*n*d *nó* amach it*ir*.    Ni dernad 7 ni di*n*gent*ar* mirbuil bud mo na i*n* rétlu do beth ama*l* si*n* 7˙ a taide*ch*t o(t)ha oirth*iur* hI*n*dia co tír Iuda; ar ni bói nech ele oc a stiúra*d acht* cuma*ch*t*a* Dia iarfír.   Tanic iar*um* uidi na xii. mís fr*i* xii. laa, 7 did*iu* ba hardi i*n*a cloicthech hi remai*n*d.   Coibes tra˳ a corp 7 corp ésca; mou a sollsi i*n*a sollsi gréne.   Ocus is aml*aid* thancu*m*ar-ni na diaid 7 sind f*or* echa*ib* diana,'' ol na drúdi fr*i* Ios*eph*. ``Anman*n* immorro nan ech si*n* .i. Droman*n* Daríí, Madian, Effan, 7 is iat na he(i)ch si*n* ber*e*ss udi mís isi*n* oenlo ; *con*id udi xii. mis deside o(t)ha hI*n*dia co tír˙Iuda.  Cid fil an*n acht* tánic in rétlu remai*n*d *con*ice so,'' ol siat, ``co *n*desid for mull*ach* i*n* tige i fil i*n* Slanicc*id*,

---

93.  "We came at once after it ; it came before us brightly and radiantly[1], and it was not slowly moving and unsteady, as other stars, but it came right and firmly before us without going in[2] and out at all. There has not been worked, there will not be performed a miracle which would be greater than the star being like that and its coming from the east quarter of India to the land of Juda ; for there was no one else guiding it save the power of God, in truth.   It came then a journey of twelve months *plus* twelve days, and indeed it was higher[3] than a bell-house before us.   Equal (in size) was its body and the body of the moon,[4] greater its light than the light of the sun.   And thus came we after it and we were on fleet horses," said the Magi to Joseph. Now the names of those horses were Dromann Darii, Madian (and) Effan, and those are the horses that perform[5] a month's journey in the single day, and it is a journey of twelve months thence from India to the land of Juda.   Well then the star came on before us up to this," said they, "and stood[6] over the top of the house in which the Saviour is, and there is no one that should see it but would love

---

[1] = toidlech of *Wind. Dict.* (?).

[2] anonn, over, to the other side, *Coney's Dict.*

[3] Or, taller ; it was a comet.

[4] *Cf.* Rédle ingantach do athruccad,

robe a méd 7 a soillsi co ndebratar na daoine rab esga hí, *Chron. Scot.* p. 28.

[5] Lit., bear ; carry (people) (?).

[6] Lit., sat.

7 ni fil nech atcithsed hi nách tibred grad derscaigthech do Dia ar nóime 7 ar mirbuldacht a caingne.

94. Is annsin atbert Ioseph, "Caide bar n-anmanna-si fen?" ol se. "Niansa són; Melcisar mo ainm-si," ol in fer ulcach liath; is e dorat in n-ór do Crist. "Balcisár mo ainm-si," ol in fer ulchach dúbdónn, is e tuc in túis. "Hiespár didiu mo ainm-si," ol in fer ócc amulchach, is e thuc in mírr. Atbert tra Ioseph friu, "Uair tucabar aichne forin nduilem 7 se na nóidin, ticcid liumsa anossa do thomailt bíd 7 lenna, 7 bíd anoċt oҫumsa 7 ceinnechutsa¹ fín lógmar 7 cruithnecht ilblasta 7 biada examla díb; uair roċretsibar in fírdia 7 rothídnaicsibar asccada uaisle oirmitnecha do." "Imdecht do dénam," ol siat, "uair do sáss² ċena sind don fleid nemda, 7 is óibne duinn indas duitsiu." "Is maith in flead dóenna maroen frisin fleid ndiada," ol Ióseph. "Ni airisfem sunn anocht," ol siat, "7 ni ragam do [139b] Ierusalem cia rogellsamm dula ind, ar bid fatite Hiruath uaind, ar tanic int

---

God supremely on account of the holiness and the marvellousness of His action."³

94. Then said Joseph : "What are your own names?" said he. "That is not difficult (to tell), Melcisar is my name," said the bearded, grey-haired man. It is he that gave the gold to Christ. "Balcisár is my name," said the bearded, dark brown-haired man. It is he gave.the incense. "Hiespár indeed is my name" said the young beard-less man. It is he gave the myrrh. Said Joseph to them, "Since ye have recognised the Creator, He being a babe, come with me now to partake of food and drink, and abide to-night with me, and I will purchase for you precious wine and many-flavoured wheat and various viands; for ye believed the true God, and ye gave noble and honour-able gifts to Him." "(We) must go" said they, "as he has fed us already with the heavenly banquet, and it is more delightful⁴ to us than to thee." "Good is the human feast in addition to the divine feast," said Joseph. "We will not tarry here to-night," said they, "we will not go to Jerusalem, though we promised to go thither, for

---

¹ A *t* is over the *u*. (?) I read cein-nechut-sa; modern ceinneochad-sa. *Cf. John* vi. 5; *Deuter.* ii. 6.

² *Sic; read* do sássad, do sássta (?).

³ *Or,* dealing; caingen, *gl.* negotium,

also case (claims ?).

⁴ *Cf.* gur ceud aoibne ifreann, "that hell is a hundred times more delightful," *Tribes of Ireland,* p. 64.

aingel cucaind arér dia rada frind dula *for* sligid ele diar tig, 7 is*ed* di*diu* dogénum ;[1] 7 ber-siu bend*ach*tu," ol siat, "uair isat f*c*r toga 7 cadusa moir do Dia."

95. Lot*ar* iar*um for* slig*id* ele dia tig am*al* atb*er*t in*t* ai(n)gel fr*i*u. Is exam*ail*[2] *tra* in*n*isit na sc*r*ibenna scela na ndruad. Ised atb*er*t Iacop Gl*ú*in*e*ch is osc*é*la nam*a*certa,[3] "Is morfessiur al-lín na ndruad 7 hi cin*d* ix. lá tancatar iarsi*n* co B*eth*il Iúda." Is*ed* di*diu* atb*er*t Matha m*a*c Alphei i*n* a sosc*e*la et in *Libro de Infancia Marie* .i. isin libur a n-in*d*ister gein Muiri *co*nid hi cin*d* xii. lá tancat*ar*. Ocus atb*er*ait na *t*r*a*chtaireda diada *co*nid *t*ri rig[4] iat 7 *t*ri xx.c. long *i*malle fr*i*u, 7 di*diu* al-longa do loscud do Hir*ua*th ar na[5] dechsat dia acall*aim* oc impód doib. Indist*er* di*diu* beos co tu*c*sat asc*c*a*d*a d*e*rmáire do M*ui*ri 7 do Ios*eph* fr*i* taeb a tuc*s*at do Cr*is*t 7 rl.

---

Herod is to be shunned[6] by us, as the angel came to us last night to tell us to go by another way to our home, and that indeed is to be done, and receive thou (our) blessing, as thou art a man of election and of great honour with God."

95. They then went another way to their home, as the angel had said to them. Variously, indeed, do writers tell the tidings of the magi. This is what James of the Knees says in his Gospel of the Children (?),[7] "Seven is the number of the magi, and in nine days afterwards they came to Bethlehem." This is what Matthew, son of Alphaeus, said in his Gospel and *in Libro de Infantia Mariæ*,[8] *i.e.* in the book in which is narrated the birth of Mary, that it is after twelve days they came. And the sacred commentators say they were three kings, and (that there were) a hundred and three score ships with them, and that their ships were burned by Herod, in order that they should come to converse with him in returning. It is also narrated that they gave very great presents to Mary and Joseph, besides what they gave to Christ, &c.

---

[1] dodénum, MS.

[2] *Or*, examla (?).

[3] A line over *mc*, as in "m*a*craide," eight lines lower down.

[4] rigda, MS.

[5] *Ma* put for *no*, as I think.

[6] fate, "caution," *Cormac* ; faitech,

*gl.* cautus, *SG.* 51 a.

[7] *Perhaps* macraide, of the children.

[8] It is said to have been written in Hebrew by St. Matthew, and translated in Latin by St. Jerome, who considered it apocryphal, see "La Sainte Bible," by De Vence, vol. xix., 182, 652.

OIDED NA MACRAIDE INSO.

96. Hiruath imorro mac Antipatir meic Hiruaith Ascalonta do Indecdaib a athair 7 do Araibecdaib a máthair; ocus is e tra ba rí in tan sin for maccu Israel fri laim Octauin Auguist. Ar roboi i fátsine Moysi meic Amra 7 Ezecias meic Amois 7 na faide arc(h)ena co m(b)ad for macu Israel nobiad rigi 7 flaithius Hiruaith co rogened Crist. Ut Iacob (ait),[1] "Non a(u)feretur scept(rum) de Iuda nec dux de femoribus ejus donec ueniat qui mit(t)endus est, ipse erit expectacia gentium."

Ba fír ón uair tri huird batar occasom o Móysi mac Amra anall co gein Crist. Ar toidec(h)t do Móysi asin doire Egeptacda 7 ar mbeth doib .cccc. bliadan isin doire in Egipt .i. o gellad do Abram co tidecht esti. Iar tuidecht tra doib a hEgipt iudice batar forru co Dauid mac Iesé .i. u bliadna ar .ccc. sin uli; O Dauid iarom cusin

---

THE FATE OF THE CHILDREN THIS.

96. Now Herod, son of Antipater, son of Herod, the Ascalonite of the Indians[2] was his father, and of the Arabs was his mother, and he it was who was at that time king over the children of Israel as deputy of Octavianus Augustus. For it was in the prophecy of Moses, son of Amra and of Esaias, son of Amos, and of the other prophets, that over the children of Israel should be the rule and sway of Herod till[3] Christ would be born. As Jacob says, "The sceptre shall not be taken from Juda,"[4] &c.

That was true, for they had three orders[5] (of rulers) from Moses, son of Amra of yore, to the birth of Christ. When Moses had come out of Egyptian bondage, and after they had been 400 years in bondage in Egypt, to wit, from the promise to Abraham till coming out of it.[6] Now, after their coming from Egypt, judges were over them till David, son of Jesse, that was 305 years altogether. From

---

[1] ut Moyses, MS.
[2] Idumeans.
[3] The text seems corrupt; one would expect "in aimsir."

[4] Gen. xlix.
[5] Or, series, epochs.
[6] bondage in Egypt; cf. the "Chronologia brevior," at the end of the Vulgate.

doire mBabil*o*nda riga bat*ar* fo*rr*u f*ris*in re si*n* .i. ix. (m)bl*iadna*
lxx. 7 ccc. bat*ar* isi*n* doire.    Toisig tra 7 *pontifices* bat*ar* occu o
ndoire Babilonta co tor*acht* Pompéiss C*r*asus .i. i*n* cet c*ó*nsal Rómanach
do thogail Ier*u*sale*im* 7 o Íuil Cesair tanic sen.    Ar ba heside di*diu*
rogab ·ard*r*igi in d*o*ma*in* artus do Romanch*aib* am*al* atrubramar
r*o*ma*ind.*

97.  Luid t*r*a Pompeius[1] C*r*asus o Íuil Cesair do thogail Ier*u*sale*i*m
cordoer*ad* co mor lu*cht* na cat(h)*r*ach 7 corheln*ed* 7 corsalchad in
tempul 7 cormarb*ad* 7 cordoer*ad* dronga d*e*rmaire don p(h)op*ul*
Iuda*i*de lais.    Is e t*r*a ba toiss*ech* for m*a*cu Isr*a*el i*n* tan si*n* .i.
Al*a*xa*n*der m*a*c Fallic do t(h)*r*ei*b* Matias *no* Mannases, 7 roba
táissech eside f*ri* re cian amal atb*er*ait na sc*ri*benna.    Arái si*n* t*r*a
nírf*et* Poimp i*n* cat(h)raig do lott am*al* rob ail lais ; ar boi do
beod*acht* 7 d'imad loech Al*a*xa*n*der m*a*c Fallic co *n*arf*et* Poimp
briss*ed* fair.    *Ocus* luid iar*um* Poi*m*p co Róim do chosait nan Iúda*i*de

---

David, then, to the Babylonian captivity, it is kings were over them
during that time, that is, 379 years they were in captivity.  They
then had leaders[2] and pontiffs from the Babylonian captivity till
the arrival of Pompeius Magnus,[3] the first Roman consul, and he
attacked (and took) Jerusalem, and it was from Julius Cæsar he
came.  For he (Cæsar), first of the Romans, assumed the high kingship
of the world, as we said before.

97. So Pompey the Great went from Julius Cæsar to assault
Jerusalem, and the people of the city were much enslaved, and the
Temple was polluted and defiled, and great numbers of the Jewish
people were slain, and (others) enslaved by him.  The ruler over the
children of Israel at that time was Alexander, son of Phaleg,[4] of the
tribe of Mattatheas or Manasses ; he was ruler for a long time, as
writers say.  However, Pompey was not able to injure the city as he
desired to do, for Alexander, son of Phaleg, was of such activity, and
had such a number of soldiers, that Pompey could not defeat him.
And afterwards Pompey went to Rome to accuse the Jews to Julius

---

[1] Pompens, MS. ; *cf.* p. 128 b, co
toracht Pompens Crasus i*n* ce*t*na c*ó*nsal
románach.

[2] "Duces Hebræorum," of whom
Zorobabel was the first, and Johannes

Hyrcanus the last.

[3] "Crassus" in MS.  Pompey took
Jerusalem, B.C. 63.  *Josephus*, lib. 14,
c. 4.

[4] son Johannes Hircanus.

fri híuil Césair 7 feirg moir fair. il-leth friu. Ba marb tra Iuil
Césair iarsin 7 gabais Octáuin rigi in domain iarom. Ocus is e so
senchas Hiruaith iar fír.

98. Hiruath Ascolonta .i. do Índecdaib do .i. sacart eside asin
Asculóin móir; boi tra mac oca [140a] side .i. Antipater a ainm.
Ecmaing didiu co tancatar slataige do Indecdaib fon cat(h)raig 7
fon tempul co roircset iarum Hiruath .i. in sacart con a tempul ar
ba he coimétaid in tempuil he; 7 rucsat iarsin a mac a ndóire leo .i.
Antipater 7 se ina gilla bicc¹ ann. Boi tra in mac amal sin co fota
d'aimsir marœn frisna slataigib, ar ni boi oc a athair ní doberad
taracend co roailset na slataigi ina mbésaib fen he co cian d'aimsir.

Cid didiu acht Alaxander mac Fallicc oca mboi toisigecht mac
n-Israel, dá mac aice .i. Aristobul 7 Hircan. Ecmaing tra isin
aimsir sin Antipater mac Hiruaith Ascolonta do beth ina fír saidbir
beoda hi tír Íuda. Luid iarum Hircan mac Alaxander cuci co
ndernsat caratrad do beth do oendán i cend Aristobuil meic Alaxandir

---

Cæsar, and (to cause) great anger in him in regard to them. And
Julius Cæsar died afterwards, and Octavianus assumed the kingship
of the world after that. And this is the History of Herod according
to truth.

98. Herod, the Ascalonite, was an Idumœan and a priest from
Great Ascalon, and he had a son named Antipater. Now, it happened that robbers of Idumæans² came through the city and through
the temple, and slew Herod the priest at³ his temple, for he was the
guardian of the temple, and they took away his son Antipater into
captivity, he being a little boy. And thus the boy was for a length of
time with the robbers, as his father had not a thing to give (as ransom)
for him, and they reared him in their own ways for a long time.

Well, then, Alexander, son of Phaleg, who had the leadership of
the children of Israel, had two sons, Aristobúlus and Hyrcanus.
Antipater, however, son of Herod the Ascalonite, happened at that
time to be a wealthy, energetic man in the land of Juda. And
Hyrcanus, son of Alexander, went to him, and they made a (league
of) friendship to be in alliance⁴ against Aristobulus, son of Alexander,

---

¹ Leg. biucc (?).
² i.e. Idumæan robbers.
³ with his temple (?).
⁴ Lit., in one business.

.i. a brath*aír* fesin.  O rabtar- o*en*tadaig d'énlaim i ce*n*d Aristobuil
.i. An*ti*pate*r* 7 H*i*rcán róf*or*uaisligèt*ar* foc*et*oir Aristobuil m*a*c Alaxandir ar dochotar *con* a cloi*n*d a muin*i*gin rig Róman, c*or*gabad laiside
Aristobuil m*a*c Al*a*x*andir* 7 ructha he cu Róim il-laim *con* a cloi*n*d
7 tucad i*n* rigi do H*i*rcàn t*ri*a n*er*t An*ti*pat*ir* 7 t*ri*ana diúmas; 7
gabais H*i*rcán iarum n*er*t mor 7 cum*ach*ta *for* cuid do thír Íuda.

99.  Boi t*ra* An*ti*pate*r* an*n*si*n* fo cum*ach*ta H*i*rcáin m*ei*c Al*a*x*andir*.
I*n*t An*ti*pate*r* sin t*ra*, boi ben do Arabecdaib aice .i. Cispriatis a hainm,
co ruc sí da m*a*c dó .i. Fariceus 7 Herodis an an*man*da.  Iar céin
máir t*ra* ba marb An*ti*pate*r*, 7 i*n* uilec*um*ach*t*a boi eci o H*i*rcán tuc do
Hir*uath*, dia m*a*c fen hi, 7 boi in carat*ra*d c*et*na it*er* H*i*rcán 7 Hir*uath*
m*a*c An*ti*pat*ir*.  Is an*n*si*n* tuc Hir*uath* ingin Aristop*uil* m*ei*c H*i*rcáin
do mnái, uair Aristop*ul* m*a*c Al*a*x*andir* derbráthair H*i*rcai*n* eside, ni
hì a ingen side tuc Hir*uath* it*ir* ach*t* ingen Aristop*uil* m*ei*c H*i*rcáin
fesi*n*.  Bat*ar* t*ra* re cian am*al* sin, ecmai*n*g t*ra* i*n* aroli d'aimsir cath

---

his own brother.   When they, that is, Antipater and Hyrcanus, were
united with one hand[1] against Aristobulus, they at once overcame
Aristobulus, son of Alexander, for they went with their clann, relying
on the King of the Romans, and by him was seized Aristobulus, son of
Alexander, and he was taken to Rome as a prisoner with his children,
and the kingdom was given to Hyrcanus through the power of
Alexander and his influence,[2] and Hyrcanus afterwards assumed great
power and dominion over a part of the land of Juda.

99.  Well, Antipater was then under the power of Hyrcanus, son
of Alexander.   That Antipater had an Arab wife named Cispriatis,[3]
and she bore him two sons, Pheroras[4] and Herod were their names.

After a long time, Antipater died, and the whole power he had
from Hyrcanus he gave to Herod his own son, and the same friendship
was between Hyrcanus and Herod, son of Antipater.   Then Herod
took to wife the daughter of Aristobulus, son of Hyrcanus; since
Aristobulus, son of Alexander, (was) brother of Hyrcanus, it was not
his daughter that Herod took at all, but the daughter of Aristobulus,
son of Hyrcanus himself.   They were thus a long while; there took

---

[1] with one heart and hand.
[2] generally "pride."
[3] Cypros, *Joseph. Antiq.*, l. 14, c. 7, 3.
[4] *Or*, Phasael, *ibi*.

itir H*i*rcán m*a*c Al*a*x*andir* 7 ri nan Araib*e*cda cor-g*aba*d H*i*rcán and
7 co rucsat i m*b*roit leo he.    Gabais tr*a* Hir*uath* m*a*c An*t*ip*a*t*i*r foc*é*toir
rigi f*or* m*a*cu Israel.

100.  Acind t*r*ill iars*i*n rolecset na hAthenin*n*estu H*i*rcán uadib
iar mbén a ćluas de.   Iar toide*ch*t do Hircán tr*a* co tír Íúda rosfua-
bair arís a rígi do gabail.   Rogab Hir*uath* he 7 romarb iar*um* 7 gab*ai*s
fen rigi f*or* m*a*cu Isr*a*el tr*i*a ćeilg 7 elathai*n*.  Is e di*diu* rop errig o
Romanchaib f*or* tír Íuda 7 f*or* cloind Isr*a*el in tan sin .i. Caseus c*ó*nsal
R*ó*manach, is e boi oc tab*a*irt rigi m*a*c n-Israel 7 nan Íud*ai*d*e* do
Hir*uath* tr*í*a ćeilg amal atrubr*a*mar ro*maind*; 7 is e rig déd*i*nach boi˙
do m*a*cu Isr*a*el.   .i. H*i*rcan m*a*c Al*a*x*andir* mei*c* Fallicc.

Boi tr*a* Hir*uath* m*a*c An*t*ip*a*t*i*r mei*c* Hir*u*aith Ascalonta do hIndec-
daib i rigi f*or* macu Israel an*n*sin; ocus ba he c*e*trig e*c*tr*a*nd m*a*c
n-Isr*a*el he am*a*l atrubr*a*mar ro*maind*.   Secht mbl*i*a*dn*a ria ngen Cr*is*t

---

place, however, at a certain time, a battle between Hyrcanus, son of
Alexander, and the king of the Arabs,[1] and Hyrcanus was taken
prisoner in it, and they took him into captivity.   Then Herod, son of
Antipater, at once assumed rule over the children of Israel.

100.  At the end of a short space of time afterwards the Athenians
released Hyrcanus after having cut off his ears.[2]   After Hyrcanus had
arrived in the land of Juda he attempted again to assume his kingship.
Herod took him and killed (him), and assumed himself kingship over
the children of Israel by fraud and art.   This is the man, indeed, who
was a consul (appointed)[3] by the Romans over the land of Juda, and
over the children of Israel at that time, to wit, Cassius, Roman consul,
and he was giving the kingship of the children of Israel and of the
Jews to Herod through craft, as we have previously said, and he was
the last king who was of the children of Israel, I mean Hyrcanus, son
of Alexander, son of Phaleg.

Now Herod, son of Antipater, son of Herod the Ascalonite, the
Idumæan, was then ruling over the children of Israel, and he was
the first foreign king of the children of Israel, as we have said previously.   Seven years before the birth of Christ, Herod assumed the

---

[1] "the Arabs," *supra;* "Parthians,"    bit off Hyrcanus' ears, *Jos. Wars,*
says Josephus.                            i. 13.
[2] Antigonus, son of Aristobulus,    [3] viceroy, ruler.

rosgab Hir*uath* rigi 7 in .uii. bl*iadain* .xx. dia flathus tancat*ar* na drúdi co Cr*ist* 7 co Hir*uath*.   In tan *tra* ba doig la Hir*uath* na drúdi do thor*ach*tain ċuci 7 scela Cr*ist* leo indus co romarbad-s*om* Cr*ist* iarsi*n*, is hisi*n* aimsir tancat*ar* tech*t*a o ríg Róman .i. Octauin Aúg*ust* *for* cend Hir*uaith* meic Ant*i*pat*i*r dia br*eth* co Róim dia damn*ad* iarna ċosáit [140 b] dona hIudaidib ar iu*m*ad a chol 7 a ċorp*aid* 7 a indirge 7 a ecóra i*n* a flat*h*us.   Uair ba hangid ecraibdech a c(h)*r*ide colach i*m*on pop*ul* n-echtra*n*d, co*n*id aire si*n* rucc*ad* s*om* co Róim iarna ċosait.

101.  Luid Hir*uath* iar*um* co Róim co rusdítne fen co glicc góesach[1] 7 co hecnaid eolach i fiad*nuise* ríg Róman *co* *n*arba cintach he, *ach*t ba he in popul *for*sa mboi ba cintach an*n*.   *Con*id an*n*si*n* tuc Octáui*n* Áugust a ċathbarr ríg fen dó 7 i*n* uli onoir 7 cádus 7 cum*ach*ta 7 rigi dermáir *for* cloi*n*d Isr*ael* ; 7 bói bl*iadain* ina farr*ad*, iter dul 7 tide*cht*, co ta*n*ic uada iarsi*n* hi cind bl*iadna* beos *con* asccad*a*ib im*d*aib co tor*acht*

---

government, and the twenty-seventh year of his rule the Magi came to Christ and to Herod.   When, however, Herod thought that the Druids would come to him and bring tidings of Christ, that he might kill Christ afterwards, that is the time that messengers came from the King of the Romans, Octavianus Augustus, to Herod, son of Anti-pater, to bring him to Rome, to condemn him after he had been accused by the Jews for the great number of his crimes, and of his wickedness, and injustice, and iniquity[2] in his government.   For cruel[3] and impious was his criminal heart towards the foreign folk, and on that account he was taken to Rome after being accused.

101.  Herod went then to Rome, and defended himself cleverly, acutely, wisely, and knowingly in presence of the King of the Romans, so that he was not (found) guilty, but the people over whom he was were (found) guilty.   And then Octavianus Augustus gave him his own king's helmet and conferred on him all honour and dignity and power, and great sway over the children of Israel ; and he was a year with him, between going and coming, and he came away after that at the end of a year[4] also, with many presents, and arrived again at

---

[1] góeth—góes—góesach.

[2] corbaḋ, iniquity, *Psalms* lxxxix., cxxv.

[3] *Or*, wicked.

[4] At the end of a year seems super-fluous here.

fo oċt Kl. en*air* co hIer*u*salem doridise i cínd bl*iadna*.   *C*onid ead si*n* rosfuirig he cen i*n* m*a*craid do marbad foc*eto*ir, co *m*boi iar*um* oc cúim- niug*ud* na ndruad dia i*n*disi*n* do rí nan Iud*ai*de do gene*m*ain.   *C*oni*d* hi co*m*airle doroi*n*e iar*um*ʼ .i. na huli nóiden ba comoesi do Cr*is*t do marb*ad*, ar ba doig lais Crist do marb*ad* et*o*rru.

102.  Cuirid t*ra* Hir*u*ath iarsi*n* a amuis 7 a theglach co Bethil Íuda 7 cosin fi*ch*it mag filet imon mBethil :—co mag Inbais m*ei*c Iobais *m*e*i*c Sem  meic Noei, co mag Falleirg m*ei*c Eochais m*ei*c Canai*n* m*ei*c Cáim m*ei*c Noei,[1] co mag Samech m*ei*c Falcheir*aid* m*ei*c Enóc m*ei*c Cannain, co m*ag* Araid m*ei*c Canai*n* m*ei*c Caim, co m*ag* n-Arcis m*ei*c Can*nain*, co m*ag* n-Arma*n*d m*ei*c Can*nain*, co m*ag* nGoba m*ei*c Can*nain*, co m*ag* Sióin m*ei*c Can*nain*, co m*ag* Lais m*ei*c Cuir, co m*ag* Foromon m*ei*c Forchuis, co m*ag* Lerua m*ei*c Curbis, co m*ag* n-Áis m*ei*c Lerua, co m*ag* Hin*n*fin, co m*ag* nGadotragaden, co m*ag* Treoit forsa *m*bitís treoit[2] na Bethile, co m*ag* ñGenges m*ei*c Can*nain*, co m*ag* Samech[3] m*ei*c Falcui*n*d m*ei*c Enoc m*ei*c Can*nain*.

103.  Co*m*ad iatsi*n*, a*ch*t bec, xx muigi na Bethile i tír Íuda uli do neoch innist*er* do crechad i*n* Ier*u*salem.   Cid di*diu* a*ch*t roscailset fon cat(h)r*a*ig 7 fona muigib co romarb*ait* leo na huli m*a*cu alla[4]

---

Jerusalem on the eighth of the Calends of January, at the end of a year.   And that was the space of time he waited[5] without slaying the children at once, and he then (began) to remember the Magi telling him that the King of the Jews was born.   And this is the design he formed then, to wit, to slay all the infants who were of the same age as Christ, for he thought that (thus) Christ would be killed among them.

102.  Now Herod thereafter sends his soldiers and household to Bethlehem of Juda, and to the twenty plains that are around Bethle- hem, to the plain of Inbas, son of Jobas, son[6] of Shem, son of Noah, &c.

103.  And those are nearly all the twenty plains of Bethlehem in the land of Juda, that are said to have been plundered in Jerusalem.[7] Well, then, they spread through the city and the plains, and by

---

[1] m. IX. in MS.

[2] The flocks.

[3] This is the same as the third plain, "mag S. meic Falcheir*aid*," *supra*.

[4] I read alla(stig), inclusive of, inside.

[5] Better perhaps, "and that is what

detained him from slaying."

[6] not Shem's son: *cf.* 1 *Chron.* i. 17; *Gen.* x. 22.

[7] Obscure to me; perhaps plundered at the (time of the) sack of Jerusalem by Titus.

doib ó lamnad[1] oen oidċe co lámnad da bl*iadan*, co romarb*ait* leo .cc.
*for* da míle it*er* in cat(h)*r*aig 7 na mugi oc iarr*aid* Cr*i*st dia marbad.
At*b*erait na scr*i*benda co fil aroli mac becc dibs*in* i*n* aroli cat(h)*r*aig
beos, Colonia a ainm na cat(h)*r*ach s*in*, cen esbuid baill—a folt 7 a
trilis f*ór* fás 7 a chrú d*e*rg f*or* a ucht am*al* bid i*n*díu nomarbtha. XL
*for* c*et* mac is*ed* romarbtha i mBethil dib.

104. Bat*ar* tra an*n*sin oc maithrech*aib* gaire garba 7 gola tróga
maithnecha,[2] *gr*echa gorti, faide fan*n*a, golgaire guba, égmi mora,
dera trom*m*a, bassa d*e*rga, gruadi scr*i*ptha, fuilt scáilte, crideda
tuarcthi, ferta fenned, ócbail[3] maithnech,[2] cíche nochta, glacca i*m*
glúnib, brun*n*i bualti, ochna aidbli ċiamra toirsecha.

[141a]. Is andsi*n* ba dubaige mór don Bethil Cr*i*st do genem*ain*
in*n*te, 7 ba suba d'ai*n*glib nime. Ba lámċomairt tra 7 ba basġari do

them were slain all the children inside of those from the age[4] of
one night to the age of two years, so that two thousand two hundred were slain by them between the city and the plains (as they
were) looking for Christ to kill Him. Writings say that there is
a certain little child of them in a certain city still (Cologne is the
name of that city), without lack of limb,[5] the hair of his head[6]
grown, and his gore ruddy on his breast, as if it were to-day he was
killed. One hundred and forty children, that is what were slain of
them in Bethlehem.

104. There were then among the mothers hoarse cries, sad and
plaintive (?)[7] wailings, bitter, long, faint cries, wailings of woe, great
shouts, heavy tears, red palms, torn cheeks, dishevelled hair, bruised
hearts, deeds of soldiers (?), sad moaning (?), bared breasts, hands
around knees, stricken bosoms, great, dismal, sorrowful groans.[8]

Then a great sadness to Bethlehem was the birth of Christ in it,
and it was a joy to the angels of heaven. It was hand-clapping and
palm-clapping to the mothers of the children, and it was a pure pro-
cession towards heaven for the holy infants who were slain there. It

---

[1] O'Brien's *Dict.* has "o lamna aon uidhche go lamna da bhliadhan," from the *term* of one night.

[2] *Cf.* mifrigi 7 mainechus, § 60.

[3] Read oc(h)bad, sighings; ochal, moaning, *O'R.*

[4] *Lit.*, birth or "parturitio," *Wind.*

[5] *Dict.*; *better*, lamna, time, *O'Brien's Dict.*

[5] i.e. the body is whole.

[6] Lit., his hair and his hair.

[7] *for* mairbnecha, dirge-like (?); *see* maithnech, maithnecus, 104, 60.

[8] = ochsard *or* ochbad; possibly Conor's shield was called indochain the moan (?).

m*athréch*aib na mac he, 7 ba cemniug*ad* glan do*č*um*m* nime dona
toir*č*etul in áir sin *ut dixit in* faid n*œ*m ochéin anall, " Vox in Rama
nœmnóidenaib romarbta an*n*.    Ba fota t*r*a re*n*a thide*cht* robás oc
audita est ploratus et ululatus magnus."

105. Is an*n*si*n* atb*ert* aroli ben oc tarrai*n*g a me*í*c asa hucht don
feoldenmaid,[1] " Cid ima ṅdelige mo m*ac* g*rá*dach f*r*im ? .i.

> Forad mo brónd
> Me rothusim,
> Mo chích rosib ;
> Mo brú rosi*m*orch*uir*,
> M' in*n*e roṡúig,
> Mo chride roṡás ;
> Mo betha robé,
> Mo bas a breth uai*m*m ;
> Mo n*ert* do t(h)ráig,
> M' in*d*sce roṡocht,
> Mo ṡúile rodall."[2]

---

was long before its  coming that there  was a prophecy of  that
slaughter, as the holy prophet said long ago :—" Vox in Rama," &c.

105. It is then a certain woman said, drawing her child from her
bosom for the butcher :—" Why dost thou sever my beloved child from
me, *i.e.* :—

> The fruit of my womb.
> It was I brought him forth,
> My breast he drank it,
> My womb bore him,
> My vitals he sucked,
> My heart he satisfied,[3]
> My life he was,
> Death to me (is) his taking from me,
> My strength has ebbed,
> My speech has become still,[4]
> My eyes it has blinded."[4]

---

[1] feoldenmaig, MS.
[2] rosocht, *with* "no dall" *over* rosocht.
[3] *Or*, "my heart nourished" (him).
[4] *Or*, (it is) my voice that has been

stilled ; it is my eyes that have become
blinded, or it has blinded my eyes ;
*rodall* seems intransitive here, as *do*
*thráig* and *rosocht*.

106. Is andsin atbert aroli ben :—

> " Mo mac beri uaim,
> Ni me dogní int olcc ;
> Marb didiu me fén,
> Na marb mo mac ;
> Mo c(h)iche cen loimm,
> Mo śuile co fliuch,
> Mo lama for crith,
> Mo chorpan cen nith,
> Mo cheli cen mac,
> Me feni cen nirt ;
> Mo betha is fiu bas,
> Uch m' oenmac, a Dé!
> M'foiti cen luach,
> Mo galar cen gein,
> Cen dígail co brath ;
> Mo chiche 'na tast,
> Mo chride rochrom."

106. Then another woman said :—

> " My son thou takest away,
> It is not I that do the wrong,[1]
> Kill then myself,
> Kill not my child,
> My breasts are without milk,
> My eyes are moist (with tears),
> My hands are trembling,
> My poor body without wound,[2]
> My husband without a son,
> Myself without strength,
> My life is as death,[3]
> Alas! my only son, O God!
> My patience (is) without reward,
> My grief[4] (to be) without a child,
> Without being avenged till doom ;
> My breasts (are) silent,
> My heart is bowed down."

---

[1] Perhaps we should read Ní hé dogní in t-olc, it is not he that does the wrong.

[2] Or, fight, power of resistance; níth, mortal wounding, Cormac and O'Clery ; also battle, see Stokes' Metr. Irish Glossaries, p. 86.

[3] fiu. .i. inand, cutruma, O'Dav.

[4] Or, sickness.

107. Is annsin atbert aroli ben :—

    " Oen sirthi dia marbad,
      Sochaide marbthaí,
      Nóidin bualti,
      Na haithrecha gontaí
      Na máithrecha marbthai ;
      Iffern rolín sib
      Nem rodún sib,
      Fola fíren rodoirtsibar cen cinaid."

  Is annsin atbert aroli ben :—

    " Tair chucam, a C(h)rist !
      Ber m'anmain col-luath
      Maroen is mo mac ;
      Uch, a Muire mor,
      Máthair Meic Dé !
      Cid dogén cen mac ?
      Tret' mac-su ro marbtha

---

107. Then another woman said :—

    " One ye seek to slay Him,
      Many ye slay,
      Infants ye smite,
      The fathers ye wound mortally,
      The mothers ye kill,
      Hell ye filled,
      Heaven ye closed,
      The blood of righteous ones ye have shed, without
        guilt (on their part)."

Then another woman said :—

    " Come to me, O Christ !
      Take my soul quickly,
      Together with my son ;
      Oh, great Mary,
      Mother of the Son of God !
      What shall I do without a son ?
      On account of thy Son have been deadened

Mo chon*n* is mo chiall,
Dorigne ben boeth dim
I *n*díaid mo m*ei*c
Mo c(h)r*i*de is caep cró
A haithle in[1] áir truaig
Oṅdiu co tí brath."

108. Is ead atb*er*ait aroli scribenn*a* .i. Cr*i*st 7 M*ui*ri do beth hi tír Iúda fós i*n*tan romarb*ait* i*n* m*a*crad.[2]  Intan *tr*a bói Hir*u*ath oc arm*i*mirt[3] marbtha na m*a*craide isí si*n* aim*ser* ta*n*ic int aingel dochúm Iós*ep*h co*n*d-epert f*r*is, "Ber lat M*ui*ri co*n* a mac," ol se, "7 eirg isi*n* Égipt, 7 bíd in*n*te co*n*-abrur-sa f*r*it tide*ch*t esti; ár ata Hir*u*ath for tíí marbtha na m*a*craide d'iarr*aid* Cr*i*st dia marb*ad*, 7 soc*h*aide ele dia náimtib."

---

My reason and sense,[4]
I have become a crazed woman
After my son (who is slain),
My heart is a (mere) clot of gore,
After the miserable slaughter,[5]
From this day till comes Doom."

108. Some writings say that Christ and Mary were still in the land of Juda at the time when the children were slain.  But when Herod was with arms plying the slaughter of the children, that was the time the angel came to Joseph, and said to him :—" Take Mary with her Son," said he, " and go into Egypt, and abide therein till I tell thee to come away; for Herod is a plotting[6] the slaughter of the children, seeking Christ to kill Him, and many others of His enemies."[7]

---

[1] " in i*n*," MS.

[2] The *facs.* seems to have m*a*craid.

[3] *Sic*; read oca imirt (?); *or*, translate " a weapon-plying of the murder of the children."

[4] Perhaps these are terms of endear-ment for son; *cf.* a ćuisle mo chroiḋe, a chuisle !

[5] in i*n*air or in i*m*air, *ms.*

[6] about to slaughter.

[7] the enemies of Christ are seeking to kill Him.

# IRISH NEUTER SUBSTANTIVES:

## *ARRANGED ALPHABETICALLY.*

———◆◇◆———

IN the fourth volume of the Todd Lecture Series, the neuters are distributed under six declensions, and, in each declension, are grouped according to their terminations or formation. I complete that treatise by alphabetical indices of the final syllables and of the words, and by the addition of neuter forms since discovered by me, or pointed out by Doctors Whitley Stokes, Ascoli, and Meyer. In this index *RD.* = Rennes Dindsenchus, *HM.* = Hibernica Minora, published, respectively, by Doctors Stokes and Meyer, *L C.* = Leabar na gCeart.

## 1.—INDEX OF THE FINAL LETTERS AND SYLLABLES.

[*The final letters are*—c, ch, g; d, t, th; l, m, n, r, s; b; a, e, i, u; *never* f *or* p.]

| | | | | | |
|---|---|---|---|---|---|
| B, | .. | .. 125, 128, 170, 207. | bad, bed, | .. | 137. |
| C, | .. | .. 169, 201. | dad, | .. | .. 144. |
| lc, | .. | .. 169, 201. | fad, | .. | .. 137. |
| rc, | .. | .. 147. | ged, | .. | .. 143. |
| sc, | .. | .. 146. | lat, led, .. | | .. 142. |
| Ch, | .. | .. 128, 198, 201. | mad, | .. | .. 137, 145. |
| bach, | .. | .. 171. | nad, ned, | | .. 143. |
| cach, | .. | .. 177. | pad, | .. | .. 137. |
| dach, | .. | .. 173. | rad, red, .. | | .. 138. |
| fích, | .. | .. 198. | sad, | .. | .. 144. |
| gach, | .. | .. 177. | tud, | .. | .. 144. |
| lach, lech, | | .. 174, 177. | rd, | .. | .. 145, 205. |
| loch, | .. | .. 201. | Be, | .. | .. 181, 133. |
| mach, | .. | .. 172. | ce, | .. | .. 184. |
| nach, | .. | .. 177. | de, | .. | .. 186. |
| rach, rech, | | .. 147, 179. | ge, | .. | .. 184. |
| tach, | .. | .. 173, 181. | le, | .. | .. 193. |
| tech, | .. | .. 128. | me, | .. | .. 195. |
| D, t, th, | | .. 130, 134, 198, 202. | ne, | .. | .. 195. |

## II.—ALPHABETICAL INDEX.

airecur, 163.

aired, 138, *g.* airid; *d.* airiud, *M. Tall.*
xvi., xviii., xxviii.

aiream, 171; *g.* airṁe, *FM.* iv. 698.

airenach, 178; *d.* airenuch, *LL.* 288,
290 b.

airer, delight; *g.* airir; *nap.* airera par-
duis, *LU.* 33 b, 31 b.

airer, harbour, 162; airer n-, *AU.* 324;
*d.* airiur, *AU.* 426, *LL.* 108 b, airer,
162, territory.

airet, 138; an airet, *Todd Lect.* v. 18,
114.

airge, 186.

airgetlach, 176.

airlégend, 167.

airlim, 116; *g.* airlime, *O'Dav.* 77,
*O'Don. Sup.* 569.

airm, place; *np.* armand, *LU.* 34 b,
*HM.* p.

airmbert, 145.

airócre, 191.

Airne, 195.

airrige, 185.

airrinde, 132; foran a. *Sg. Incantatio.*

airscél, 148.

airscéle, 194; in soscele, *Wb*, 7 b.

airṡliab, 125; *g.* airṡlebi, *LL.* 243 b.

Airthech, 169; *g.* Airtig, *FM.* iv. 829;
*d.* Airtiuch, *Fél.* 53.

airther, 159; airther n-, *B. of Hy
Maine*, fo. 155, isan airther, *BB.*
272 ab.

airtherthuaiscertach, north-east, *LB.*
109 b.

airthossach, the front or prow (of a boat).

airthraig, 198.

aisleán, 165, *cf.* assil.

aiseudach, grave clothes, *Bible Focloir.*

aisléim, rebound, *O'D. Sup.* 569.

aithairec, 148.

aithbe, 182; .i. erchre, *Fél.* 127.

aithbéim, 114, *LL.* 108 a.

aithber, 161, *LB.* 111 b.

aithchumbe, 183.

aithchumme, 183.

aithe, 190.

aitherrechtaichthe, 189.

aithesc, 146; aithiusc m-bréithre, proverb, *Lismore Lives*, p. 12, 384; *ap.*
athisca, *Ml.*; = *English* proposal,
and *French*, propos; petitio, dictum,
*Todd Lect.* v.116; an aithesc, *LU.,Ir.
Texte*, i. 126.

aithgell, 154.

aithgen, 131.

aithgin, 200.

aithgne, 195, visio, cognitio, *Todd
Lect.* v.

aithirrech, aithirruch, 181; an aithirrech sin, *Ml.* 94 a.

aithléim, 116.

aithmet, 138.

aithne, 196.

aithne, 196.

aithsceinm, 123.

aitrebthach, 174.

aithrech, 180.

aithrige, dethroning, *Fen.* 68, 70.

aithriscél, 148.

aithtinol, 149.

aittreib, *ds.* to dwell, *LU.* 34 a.

álath, 142.

albéim, 114.

all, 152, dán-all, two bridles, *LU.*
105 b.

all, 130, 152; all n-ard n-, *FM.* an.
904); da n-all, *O'D. Sup.* 571; *dp.*
aillib, *LL.* 304 b.

all, 130, 152.

allas, 164.

allbach, 171.

allfid, 203.

allgaire, *LL.* 298 a.

alliath, 136.

alma, a flock, *d.* almaim, *LU.* 26 a, 57 a.

almne, 197.

alt, 146.

alt, 146.

alt, 152.

alt, (?) joint; *ap.* alta, *Rev. Celt.* xv.
485.

altar, 157, *g.* altair, *Fél.* 82.

altfad, 137.

ám, ámm, 124, 118, 170, hand, handful,
company; an am, *Ml.* 36 c.

am, 133, 170.
ambor, 160.
amnert, 145.
amrath, 202.
amre, 193.
amus, 164.
án, 165.
ana, 197.
anaccor, 162.
anacul, 153.
anad, 143, 204; *ns.* anad n-, *Laws,* i.
144; *g.* anta, *LB.,* 273.
anart, 145.
anaurthach, 173.
anblúth, 203.
anchride, 187; an ancride, "offensio,"
*Todd Lect.* v. 42.
andach, 174, 178; á n-andach, *Ml.*
80 b, 90 d; *g.* annaig, .i. feirge, *Fél.*
20.
andliged, 143.
andord, 145.
anechtar, 157.
anécne, 195.
anerdach, 173.
anfolad, 142.
anforlann, (?) *g.* anforlainn, *FM.* iv. 750.
anfós, 164.
anre, 193.
anrecht, 204.
antechte, unbecomingness; *g.* antechtai,
*LB.* 46; *v.* techte.
apach, 172.
apad, 137, 204.
ár n-, 155, 1° slaughter, *AU.* 412 *bis,*
434, 300, *FM.* ii. 596, iii. 588; 2°,
the number slain: ár már n-, *AU.* i.
418, 440, 524, *FM.* 346, 256; *nap.*
ára, *LL.* 283 b, *FM.* 346, 256.
ár, (?), ploughing, tilling; *g.* áir, *LB.*
275; *Fél.* 61.
arach, 180; *g.* araig, *Laws,* i. 144: cuibrech, *O'Dav.* 53; *pl.* airge, *O'Don.*
*Sup.* 568.
arach (?), .i. cróchar, a bier, *FM.* iii.
364; *g.* araig, *LL.* 305 b.
arag, 147.
arat, 138.

arathar, 158.
arbe, 124, *g.* arba, panis; *Todd Lect.* v.
72; *d.* arbaimm, *O'D. Sup.* 575, *nap.*
arbanna, *FM.* iii. 152, 264, 288, 346,
370, iv. 752; *d.* arbannaib, *L. Cé.* i.
636.
arbar, 161.
arcumdach, 173; *d.* arcumdaigib, *LB.*
209 b.
árd, árdd, 145, 205; Ard mBreccain,
*AU.* 57, 562.
ard, 145.
ardarasc, *O'D. Sup.* 576.
ardbéim, *LL.* 288.
árdchéim, 115.
arde, 188; airdde n-, *FM.* an. 905, 919.
árdgaire, 192.
Ardinber, Wicklow.
árdléim, high leap; *np.* ardlemend, *W.*;
*ap.* ardlémend, *LU.* 50 a.
ardrath, high luck, *Fen.* 158.
árdriched, 142.
árdscél, *FM.* ii. 572.
ardtrechém (?), .i. ar n-a trén chéim-
mugud, *Laws,* ii. 240, *cf.* céim.
argat, 143.
Argatglend, 132; *d.* Argatlinn, *LL.* 23 a,
129 a.
Arge, 186.
Argetbor, 161.
Argetros, *g.* A. rois, *AU.* i. 362, *Fen.*
22; *d.* A. rus, *Todd Lect.* iii. 156.
árim n-, *S. na R.* 7888.
arm, 171; *np.* inna arma, *Ml.* 44 a.
armag, 126, *g.* armaige, *LL.* 476, *Frags.*
*of I. An.* 44, *Mart. Tall.* 18, 27.
armgrith, 199.
armrad, 141.
aros, árus, aross, 164; árus n-ait n-
aingel, *Man. Mat.,* 123; *g.* arais, *np.*
airise, *TL.* 641, *like* dorus.
arosc, 147; arosc n-, *Lism. Lives,* 385;
árasc, *Todd. Lect.* v. 27, *Ml.* 55 a.
arpe, 183.
arra n-ail, .i. arreum aliud, an arra
n-uile, issed an arra; occurs ten times
in *Rev. Celt.* xv. p. 488; *np.* na harra,
na harrada; *dp.* arraib, *ib.* p. 491.

art, 145.
arther, *d.* arthiur, anterior pars, *Todd. Lect.* v. 115.
arthrach, 179; *d.* arthrach; *nap.* arthraige, *FM.* iii. 278, 328, 90, 230.
áss (?), growth; *cf.* forás.
ass, 164; ass n-aill; *g.* aiss, *LB.* 9 b; nu-as, nús, new milk, *Codex Lat. Monac.*, ed. by Zimmer as n, *O'Dav.* 105.
asclang, 169; *gsf.* asclainge, a piece (of wood), *FM.* iii. 80.
ascnadiu, 186.
aslach, 177; *as.* aslach, *FM.* iii. 276, iv. 732; *np.* aslaige, enticements, *LB.* 257 a; *np.* inna aslach, *Ml.* 36 a, 38 a.
asnach, 179.
asreud, 140.
assil, *ap.* particulas, *Todd Lect.* v. 116; *ap.* aisle, joints, *LL.* 300 b, *Cormac,* 17; aisleán, articulas, *Ml.* 132 d.
astar, 157; *d.* astur, *LU.* 49.
atach, attach, 173; atach n-, *Fél.* 113, 123, 126, *O'Brien's Dict.* 51.
atach, 173, refugium.
áth, 110, 202; áth n-, *Ir. Texte,* ii. 199, *LU.* 58 a, *LL.* 111 b, 111 b, 302 b, 305 a, *M'Firbis' Gen.*, Pedigree of O'Reilly, p. 483.
atharde n-, patria, *Three Mid.-Ir. Hom.*
athartír, fatherland, *LL.* 108 a, 108 a, *LB.* 256 b.
athaubae, 182.
athbach, 172; *g.* athbaig, *S. na Rann,* p. 126.
athchomarc, 147.
athchumma, slaughter, *FM.* iv. 788; *v.* aithchumbe.
atchur, 163.
athchumtach, 173; an. a, *Ml.* 135 a.
athelluch, reunion, *S. na Rann,* 109; *v.* ellach.
athérge, resurrection, *Vis. of MacConglinne,* 159.
athgairm, 123.
Athmag, 126, *Nen.* 142.
athscríbend, 167.

athtinól, collecting, *LB.* 206 a.
athtuitim, 119.
atrab, atreb, 170; atrab n-, *Ml.* 66 d, 68 b.
au, 133; *dp.* auib, *LU.* 114 a.
audsud, 204.
auiss, 164.
auraccomol, 153.
aurchomol, 153.
aurchor, 162; *gs.* urchora, *T. B. Fróich.*
auchumrech, 180.
aurdach, 173; aurtach, feast, *Cormac, v.* lugnasad.
aurdliged, *O'D. Sup.* 579.
aurdrach, 179.
aurfócre, command, *Laws,* i. 112.
aurrach, 180.
aurradus, 164.
aursliab; *d.* aursléib, mountain slope, *LL.* 198 b.
aurtech, 128; aurtach, *Cormac, v.* lugnassad.
authuile, 194.

bach, *O'D. Sup.* 579, from bongim (?)
badbscél, 148.
baethléim, 116.
baindialt, feminine declension, *BB.* 330 b.
bainferinsgne (?), epicene gender, *M'Curtin's Gram.* 70.
baistech, 128.
baithréim, 117.
balcbéim, 114; balc, .i. trén, mór, *Fél.* 45, 97, 59; .i. calma, trom, *O'Dav.* 59.
ballcéim, 115.
ballgalar, rheumatism.
ballrad, 141, *g.* ballraid, *BB.* 263 b.
banbéim, 115, *O'D. Sup.* 580.
banbíad, 135.
bánbuaid, 198.
bandscal, 154.
banecht, 205.
bángleo, 133.
bangnad, *LU.* 47.

bánmaidm, 120.

bánór, 155.

bansidach, 174.

bantellach, 175.

baoithbéim, Stokes' *Oid. Mac n- Usn.* l. 748.

barlinn, rolling sea, *O'Reilly's Dict.*

bás, 163, bás n-, *FM.* ii. 256.

bascrand, 166.

basgaire, 192.

bé, 133, bé n-, *Cormac*, 8.

bée, 133.

bec, 170.

beccán, 165.

béim, 114 ; béim n-, *LU.* 111 a ; *gp.* bemenn, *R.C.* xv. 488-9 ; *g.* béimme, *LL.* 282 a.

beidm. 122.

belach, 174; belach n-, *RD.* 98 b, *BB.* 364 b, *LL.* 194 c ; bwlch, *pl.* fylchi, *Welsh* ; *d.* beilgib, *O'D. Sup.* 582.

belat, 142 ; belat n-, *Stowe*, 992, fol. 66 aa; *g.* beluit ; *d.* belut, *AU.* ii. 322, 368 ; *ap.* belata, *Laws*, 322, *Chr. Scot.* 332.

bélbach, *g.* belṁaig, *np.* bélṁaige, *O'Begley's Dict.* 88 ; *Coney's Dict.*, bridle-bit.

belg (?) horse-bit ; *np.* beilge, bellce, *T. B. Fróich; Cog. Gaedel*, 116, *Man. and Cust.*, iii. 554.

bélre, 193.

benchopur (?), *das.* roof, *Fél.* 47.

beninsgne, feminine gender, *MacCurtin's Gram.* 70 (?).

bennmuir, 200.

beochride, 186.

bérle, 194 ; bérla mbán mbiaid, *Laws*, i. 16.

bernas, 164.

béscnae, bésgna, 196 ; vitæ ratio, *Ml.* 14 c ; mos, regula, *Todd Lect.* v. 117.

bét, 135.

bíad, 135 ; bíad n-, *O'Dav.* 92 ; *d.* bíud, *FM.* iii. 280 ; *dp.* biadaib, *LB.* 112 a.

bíadbach, 172 ; *O'Dav.* p. 57.

ble, 194.

binnscél, 148.

bir, 206 ; *g.* bero, *A U.* 242.

birín, 165.

biror, 160.

bithaitreb, 170.

bithbuaid, constant victory, *BB.* 50 a.

bithféidm, 121.

bithsamrad, 141.

biththellaig, *gs. M'Coise's Poem* on Plunder of Milscothach.

blad, 135.

bladm, *pl.* bladmanna, bragging, *O'Reilly's Dict.*

blaithlind, 208.

blaithrige, flourishing reign, *BB.* 50 a.

bléde, 186.

bled, *np.* bleda mara, *LL.* 198 a ; *nap.* bleda .i. aige alta, *Fél.* 71.

bledmall, 153.

bledmíl, 149; *ap.* bledmíl, *gl.* animalia maris, Stokes' *Laurent. Gl.* 9, 34 ; *ap.* bledmíla, *LL.* 108 a ; blaidmíl, *O'Dav.* 61.

blodbéim, 114.

blosgbéim, 114.

bloscmaidm, sudden burst, *L. Cé*, i. 168.

boár, cow-plague, *LL.* 339 a.

boccmell, row, noise (?), *LL.* 110 a.

Bodbgne (?), *d.* Bodbgnu, *AU.*, 132.

bodibad (?), cow-destruction, *AU.*, 470.

bódún, a baun (= cow-fort) *L. Cé.* i. 206, 213.

boimm, 118 boímm do bairgin, bit of bread, *Fél.* 61.

borrfad, 137, tumor, att 7 borrfad, *Todd Lect.* v. 77 ; co mbríg 7 borrfad 7 baraind, *LB.* 205 a borrfad, elation (?), *BB.* 506.

borronn, 131.

borrthorad, 139 ; *g.* borrthoraid, *LB.* 215 a.

botech, 128.

Brad-ṡliab, in Sligo, *L. Cé.* i. 409.

braenbuaid, 198.

Braenros, *Hy Fiach.* 116.

brafad, 137.

braichlinn, 208, *LU.* 107 a.

braithbéim, 114.

brangaire, 192.

brath, 202.

brathtecosc, betrayal by an informer, *HM.* 77.

breccbuaid, *Fél.* 143.

Breccmag, *g.* breccmaige, *FM.* an. 941.

Brechmag, 126, *Fél.* 90, 117.

brechtrad, 140; breecrad, *RC.* xiv. 64.

brécsith, feigned peace, *Todd Lect.* v. 7, 118.

Brecsliab, *FM.* iii. 598.

Brégmag, 126.

Brégros, *LL.* 58 aa.

breim, 118.

breince, 184.

breisim, 119, battle, onset, *FM.* iv. 858, iii. 362; bressim ngle, *O'Hartaccain's Poem.*

brenloch, 21, *np.* brenlocha, foul lake, *LU.* 33 a.

Bréntír, *Cog. G. re G.* 62.

bresmaidm, overthrow, *FM.* iv. 674.

brí, 134.

briatharécosc, 146, *LU.* 46.

bricht, 205.

briscbrúar, *as.* fragments, *LL.* 110 b, 288; *ds. LB.* 156 a.

brisim, overthrow, *L. Cé,* i. 636; *v.* breisim.

Brocros, *LL.* 297 b.

brodscuad, 136; brotscuad, *O'Dav.* 59.

bróenrad, 141.

brogne, 196.

broimm, 118.

brollach, 175; *d.* broluch, prologue, *Fél.* 5.

bronann, *ap.* 120.

broscar (?), sound, *LL.* 304 b.

brothrach, 179.

brothrach, 177, *np.* brothracha beca, *LL.* 252 b; brothrach, rug, *is fem.*

brotlach, 176.

bruar, 162.

brund, 135.

brúth, 203; bruth n-armach, *O'Dav.* 57; morbruth n-, *LU.* 106 b.

buad, 136.

buadréim, 117; *np.* buadremend, *LL.* 78 a.

buaid, 198; buaid n-, *FM.* an. 925, *LL.* 288.

buaidcéim, *Fél.* 25.

búale, 194.

buanbach, 172, *g.* buanbaig, *LL.* 289 a.

buanfach, 172.

buantadall, *BB.* 13 b.

búar, 162, *as. Todd Lect.* iv. §. 4; *g.* búair, *FM.* iii. 222; but *np.* na buair, *FM.* i. 96.

buárach, 180, cow spancelling, *LU.* 61 b, *LL.* 11 b; *d.* hi mbúaruch, *HM.* 3.

buas, 164.

bude, 186; *g.* budi, *Todd Lect.* v. 85.

budech, 174

buiderad, yellow flowers, *LL.* 120 a.

buidm, 122; *O'Dav.* 57.

buim, 118.

Buimlinn, *FM. Index.*

buinne, 197.

buirech, 180.

buiresc, 146.

bunad, 143.

bunadchenél, original stock, *Lism. Lives,* l. 3173.

búrach, 180; burach mbuaid, *B. of Lec.* 244.

butelach, fire-place, *Fél.* 180.


cabach, exaction, *Chr. Scot.* 226; *cf.* tobach.

caimchet, fair hundred; *Fen.* 356.

caemchlod, 142; c. n-, *bis, LB.* 208 b.

caemna, 197.

Caere, 193.

cáichach, 178.

cailement, 167.

caille, 193, 194.

cáinchumrech, 180.

Caindruim, 120.

caínesce, 184; *Fél.* 30.

cainforgall, 154.

caingen, 168.

cainimbed, 137; cainimmed n-, *HM.* 41.

cáinscél, 148.

cáintaidlech, 177.

cáintormach, good increase.

cairde, 189; cairde n-, g. in chairde, Ml. 91 c, 110 a.

cairechthrét, 135.

Cairlinn, 132.

caissel, 155; caisel n-, B. of Hy Maine, fo. 145.

caisleán, casᵤe⁻ np. L. Cé, i. 152; np. caisléna, FM. iii. 290.

Caladruim, g. Caladroma, AU. i. 247.

Calathros, AU. 130.

Cambas, 164 207; g. camais, O'D. Sup. 577.

camchrann, 166, pl. camchranna, gl. trabes, SG. 189 a.

Caimlinn, g. Caimlinne, Fen. 86, L. Cé, ii. 50, FM. iv. 662.

camśruth, 203.

carabuaid, 198.

carachtar, 158.

caratrad, 140; FM. iii. 158, 242, iv. 838; as. caratrad, Ml. 90 d.

a carnd, LU. 86 b.

Carnmag, 127.

cath n-, AU. i. 562.

cath, battalion; np. trí cath, Circ. of Ireland, p. 40.

cathach, 174.

cathar, 159.

cathgleo, 133.

cathgním, battle-deed, Fen. 358.

cathgréim, 117.

cathlaem, 116.

cathmaidm, 120.

caithréim, 117; gp. cathréimenn, LB. 272 c; gs. caithréime, FM. iii. 628.

cathtomaidm, 121.

caustal, 152.

cécht, 205.

cechtar, 158.

céimm, 115; gp. céimend, Fél. 101; np. cémend, LU. 32 a; ceim n-glé, LL. 107 b; rochin(g)set a céim, LL. 128 b.

ceithi n-, a pillar, AU. i. 450.

Ceithiorlach (?), Carlow, FM. iv. 784.

cél, 148.

celar, 160.

celtar, 160, clothes, LU. 79 b.

cenél, 109, 148; cenél n-, FM. iii. 132, iv. 768; np. inna cenel, Ml. 74 b.

cenéle, 194; cenela n-, Chron. of Picts and Scots, 316, 320.

cenn, 168, a c., a c. sin, cenn n-, LL. 202 a, 288 a, 288 b.

cendar, 162.

cennbart, 145.

cennchongraim, HM. 77; v. congraim.

cend-diúnach, head-washing, LB. 265 a; v. diunach n-.

cenngalar, 156.

cendlá, 189, LB. 10 a.

cendmíl, 149.

cendmullach, 175; g. c. mullaig, LB. 265 a, fo. 100 a.

cennach, 178; cendach n-, BB. 289 a; ap. cennaige, 'customs, donations, conditions,' Fen. 140, 148, 406.

Cenondas, 207.

centar, 157; g. centair, FM. ii. 1112.

céol, 149; as. an ceul, HM. 16; ns. a céul, np. inna céul, gl. carmina, Ml. 126 c, 115 b; céol, musical instrument, Ml. 26.

ceolán n-órda, O'D. Sup. 595.

ceoltech, 128.

certlár, 156, LL. 302 b.

certle, 195.

certleth, LB. 110 a.

césadcrann, 166.

cét, 135; nap. cét, BB. 9 a.

cétal, 151; ised á c. Ml. 60 a.

cétchéim, 115.

cetharde, 186; a c. Ml. 111 c.

cetharthreb, 125.

cethirríad, np. Todd Lect. iv. 220.

cethrar, 159.

cetlach, 176.

cétmír, 124.

cétna, 197.

cétnad, 143.

cétnide, 187.

cétscél, 148.

cíallrad, 140.

Cichmag, *g.* Cichmaige, *M. Tal.* xxii.

cilornn, 168.

cindruimm, 120.

cined, 143.

Claenloch, *FM.* iii. 78.

claenre (?), a pentasyllable, *Cormac,* p. 19, *cf.* bélre.

clagtige, *gs. Chr. Scot.* 336, *LU.* 33 b.

claideamtír, sword-land, *Chron. of Picts and Scots,* p. 319.

claitesc, 146.

clamar, 161.

clár, claar, 156 ; clár n-argait, *O'D. Sup.* 643.

clárimdibe, 181.

clárlestar, *LU.* p. 3.

clármag, 127.

clárríad, *LL.* 29.

clasach (?), *ds. g.* clasaig, *Chr. Scot.* 318.

clascétul, 151 ; *LB.* 109 a.

clausul, 155.

cleith n-, pillar, *AU.* i. 450.

cleithe, 189.

cleithe, 189.

cless, 206.

clessrad, 140 ; *as.* ludendi artes, *Todd Lect.* v. 119.

cliabgalar, 155.

cliabrach, *Hy Fiach.* 258 ; *g.* cliabraig ; *pl.* cliabraige, *Coney's Dict.*

cliathar (?), battle, *L. Cé,* i. 36.

clithar, 159.

clochar, clocher, 161.

clocctech, cloigtech, 128 ; *FM.* an. 948; *pl.* clocthige, *LL.* 308 a.

clochtech, 128.

Cloenath, Clane, *AU.* i. 152 ; cloénloch, 201, *R.* 123 a.

cloth, 135.

clothdelgg, 126.

clothmag, 127.

clothnem, 125.

clothonn, 131 ; *Amra C. C.* ch. 6.

clú, 134.

cluchemag, 127.

cnáimred, 141 ; cnáimreth, 2d *Battle of Moytura,* p. 115.

Cnamros, *g.* Cnaimrois, *BB.* 116, *LL.* 295.

cnocbéim, 114.

cnuasach (?), *g.* cnuasaig, *Michæas,* 7, *Parrthas an anma,* 335.

cnuastorad, *Parthas an anma,* 391.

coaccomal, 152.

cobach, tribute, *B. of Kells,* fo. 7.

cobas, 164.

coblach, 177.

coblach, 177 ; *g.* coblaig, *FM.* iii. 198 ; *d.* cobluch, *AU.* i. 434 ; *d.* cobluch, navigatio, *Todd Lect.* v. 119.

coblige, 184.

cobra, 193.

cócetal, 151.

coche, 195.

cocrann, 166 ; *d.* cocrunn, *Ml.* 37 d.

codh n-, *RD.* p. 433.

codach (?), *as.* covenant, *Fél.* 32.

coemdoirsi, *S. na R.* 8189.

coemrath, *ap.* coemratha, mild graces, *Fen.* 168.

cohuaim, *Amra C. C.* ch. 5.

cóiced, 142 ; cóiced n-, *bis,* *LU.* 41 b ; *d.* cóiciud, *LL.* 295.

cóicer, 159.

cóicthe, five things, *HM.* 95.

cóilach, 177 ; *g.* coelaig, virgarum fasciculus, *Todd Lect.* v. 120.

coilgbéim, Stokes' *Oided mac n-Uisnig,* l. 555.

cóimcne, *d.* cóimcniu, history, cognitio, synchronism, *Trip. Life,* 644.

coimfrecre, 191.

coire mBreccáin, *bis,* *Edinburg Dinnsenchus,* fo. 4 b ; coire, = caldron.

coirmthech, ale-house, *n. dual,* *Fél.* 134.

coirpdíre, 193.

coirttobe, 182.

col, 149.

collud, 142.

comaccomal, 152.

comach, dispersion, *Fen.* 246 ; *cf.* combach.

comacnabad (?), *d.* comacnabud, consuetudo, *SG.* 143 a, *Ml.* 96 a.

comacra, *O'D. Sup.* 604.

comadbar, 161.

comadnacul, 153.

comaes, 163.

comainm, 122: *LL.* 307 a; *np.* cóm-
anmand, *Fél.* 53.

comaithmét, *O'D. Sup.* 605.

comal, 152; comal n-, *FM.* an. 903,
904, *Frags. of Ir. An.* p. 48, *LL.*
144 b.

comall, comall, 152; comall n-, *LL.*
305 b, *Fél.* 33, 184, *FM.* an. 903, 904.

comallad, 142.

comalne, 197.

comarc, 147, .i. cuimniugud, *O'Dav.*;
based comarc, *RD.* p. 449.

comardach (?), *g.* comardaig, federa-
ration, *LB.* 276.

comarde, 188.

comartha, 188.

comatrab, 170.

combach, combag, 172; *d.* combuch,
*Ml.* 118 b; combach, a breaking
down, *FM.* iii. 602, where *AU.*
*has* commach; cumach, *RD.* 96 b.

combaid (?), *g.* combada, confederacy,
*FM.* iii. 452.

combar, 155, 160; *cf.* inber, and *Welsh*
cymmer.

combás, 163.

combérla, 194.

comcenél, 148.

comcét, 142.

comchetal, 151.

comchuibrech, fetter, *LL.* iii. b.

comdach (?), *g.* comdaig, *AU.* 518.

comdíre, 193.

coméirge, 185.

comérim, *g.* comérma, course, *LL.* 107 b,
111 b; *cf.* érim.

commesséirge, 185.

comét, 138.

comféidm, 122.

comfuaim, alliteration; *v.* fuaim, uaim.

comglenn, 132; *np.* inna comglinne, *Ml.*
81 c.

comgné, 196.

comgrád, 134.

comlóg, equal value, *H.* 4, 22, f. 66.

comlúd, comlúth, 203; *LB.* 208 a, to
urge, excite.

comluge, 184; *g.* comlugi, *FM.* iii. 226.

commach, *AU.* an. 602, combach.

commaidm, 120.

commaim, 124.

commant, 167.

comnacal, 153; comnacal, necessaries,
*Lism. Lives,* p. 380.

comnaidm, 121.

comnert, *d.* comneurt, great effort, *LB.*
275.

comol, 149, 152, .i. cengal, *O'Dav.*
73.

comól, carouse, *LC.* 72.

comrag, 148, 169.

comram, 207.

comrar, 160.

comríge, 185, *BB.* 13 a.

comsinm, 123.

comsuide, *Fél.* 40, consessio, *Ml.* 123.

comteclaim, 119.

comtherchomrac, 148; *masc.* Wb. 7 c.

comthinól, 149.

comthriall, 150.

comtogairm, convocation, *O'Dav.* 46.

comthuitim, falling by each other's
hand, 119; *FM.* an. 1029, *L. Cé,* 132.

comuaim, 118.

conach (?), affluence; *g.* conaich, *FM.*
iii. 406; *Hy Fiach.* 250.

conarach, 180.

conn n-, a head, *FM.* ii. 652.

condad, 144; *g.* condaid, *AU.* i. 428.

condelc, condelg, 147; condelg n-,
*O'Dav.* 62.

condem (?), 119.

congraimm, 117; a cruth, a écosc 7
a congraim, *LU.* 105 b.

conguin, 200.

conmír, 124.

connlach, 175.

coplestar, *LL.* 111, 110 ab, a cup.

cor n-, 162; cor n-, circumstance, *FM.*
ii. 612; *LB.* 260 a; cor n-, 162.

cormlind, ale, *MSS. Mat.* 616.

corplár, 156.

corrmíl, 149.

Corrsliab, 125.

corrsuide, 187, *Lism. Lives,* 388.

corrthar, 159.

corthe, 190.

cosc, 146; *g.* coisc, *LU.* 46, correptio, *Ml.* 113 d.

coschéim, 115.

coscrad n-oenaig, interruption of a fair, *AU.* i. 448.

cosrach, 180.

costad (?), maintenance, *Fen.* 360 ; drochcostud, *W.*

costal (?), gathering ; *cf.* tochustal.

cotach, *g.* cotaig, amity, compact, *LL.* 302 b.

cothad, 144.

cothinól, "collectio," *Todd Leet.* v. 121.

craeslach, 177.

craislach, 177; *d.* craisluch, a body-guard, *LL.* 263 a.

crann, 166; *d.* craunn, *S. na Rann*, viii. ; *ap.* cronna, *Todd Lect.* v. 75.

cranchur, 162.

crannlach (?), load, (*i.e.*) branches of a tree, *O'Brien's Dict.*

creachruathar, *ds., FM.* iv. 706.

crech ngur, *S. na R.* 7899.

crécht; an c., *as.*, vulnus, *Todd Lect.* v. 46.

credemgalar, 156.

creim (?), creidm, gnawing, *Chron.* 475, *Zeph.* 3.

cretem, 124.

crí, 134, *FM.* an. 911, 925, 926, *LB.* 110 b.

criathar, 158 ; *misprinted* cuathar.

criathrach (?), *g.* criathraig, *Hy Fiach.* 202.

críchdorus, *ap.* críchdoirsi, the passes into a country, *LB.* 206 b.

cride, 186; cride n-, *LL. Texte*, i. 104 ; *np.* na cride, *RD.* 95 a.

cridecán, 165.

cridín, 165.

cridescél, 148 ; *.i.* verbum bonum, *Palatine Gl.* 68, 2.

crínach, 179 .i. lignum aridum, *Todd Lect.* v. 121.

crindar, 160.

crislach, 177 ; *dp.* crislaiṡíb, *LB.* 207 a.

crith, 199.

crithdeilm, 122.

crithfeidm, 122.

crithgalar, 156, *LB.* 60 a, febris, *Todd Lect.* v. 121 ; *d. c.* galur, *BB.* 272 bb.

crochar (?), bier, *LB.* 275 ; *g.* cróchair, *Coney's Dict.*

crodh, 135.

croisbéim, 114.

crólige, 184; *d.* cróligiu ; cróligu, *LL.* 202 a, 208 a ; crolige báis, *Chr. Scot.* 318.

crólinn, 132.

crú, 134.

Cruachanmag, 127; *LL.* 107 b.

cruadbach, 172.

cruaidchéim, 115.

Cruithenchlár, *Nen.* 174.

crumdub, 170.

crumduma, 195.

cuach, 171.

cuachnaidm, 121, *Cormac*, 47.

cuachṡnaidm, *O'Dav.* 64, loop-knot, battle-axe (?), *LL.* 109 b: *pl.* cuach-snadmanna, *Battle of Ventry*, 498.

Cuailñge, 197, 186.

cuáine n-, *LU.* p. 50.

cuanlach (?), *Mart. of Tall.* xxxi.

cuairt, 200.

cuchtar, 158.

cuchtarthech, 128.

cúibrech, 180, *LB.* 111 a ; *g.* cúibrig ; *ap.* cúibrige, *LB.* 60 a, 60 b ; cúibrige, catenas, *Todd Lect.* v. 93 ; cuibrend n-éroll ; *g.* cuibrinn, *LL.* 29, 303 b ; *np.* cuibrenna, *LB.* 264 b ; *av.* cuibrendd, rations, *Fen.* 168.

cúicthe, 189.

cuile, 194.

cuimbae, cumbae, destruction, *AU.* 326 ; *cf.* aithchumbe.

cuimrech, 147, 177 ; *cf.* au-chumriuch n-, a cuibrech ; *d.* cúimrigib, *LB.* 208 a.

cuindrech, 180.

cuirm, 123 ; *.i.* cerevisia, *Todd Lect.* v. 72 ; coirm .i. ól, *LC.* 271, 4 ; *d.* cormaimm, *LB.* 12 a.

degthír, *Todd Lect.* iv. s. 4, v. 225.

degtrían, good third, *Fen.* 168.

deichthriub, 207 ; *gp.* deichtrebe, *BB.* 9 b.

deilm, 122 ; *g.* delma, *LB.* 260 a, .i. fogur, *Fél.* 208 ; *g.* delmæ móir, *LU.* 111 b ; a ndeilm, *LL.* 246 b ; *gp.* delmand, *RD.* 96 a.

deisceart mBrég, *O'Brien's Dict.* 173 ; *v.* tuaiscert.

déiscéim, measure of two paces, *O'D. Sup.* 617.

deithbir, 161.

delc, delg, 126 ; *d.* deilc, *LU.* 94.

delrad (?), brightness, *Todd Lect.* v. 122

denn (?), colour ; *d.* fordinn ; *gl* minio, *Bucolic Gl.* 122 ; *cf.* gledenn, .i. dathglan, *Fél.* 270.

dér, daer, 155 ; *np.* na dær, dér, *Ml.* 23 a, *AU.* i. 138, der n-gréine, a sun's tear (or ray), *Amergin's Third Poem.*

derbad, 137.

derbairde, 188 ; *FM.* iii. 210 ; *np.* derbairde, *LB.* 152 a.

derbarusc, proverb, *TL.* p. 646 ; *v.* arosc.

derbforgell, *O'Don. Sup.* 616.

derc mBuailcc, Bualcc's cave, *BB.* 190 ; derc m-Babuil, *bis, RD.* 92 b, *LL.* 211 a ; *d.* deirc, *RC.* xv. 489 ; *ds.* Deirc, *Cog. G. re G.* 60 ; deirc, a pit, *O'Begley*, 539.

derc, a berry; *np.* dercæ, derce, *SG.* 49 a, *Bucolic Gl. of Laur. Lib.* 101 ; an S-stem (Stokes).

dered, 138.

dérfadach (?), *g.* dérfadaig, weeping, *LB.* 208 a.

derge, 186 ; *d.* dergu .i. facbail, *FM.* an. 925, 937 ; déirge, *d.* deirgiu, *AU.* i. 436, 444, 518 ; *g.* dærgi, destitutionis, *Ml.* 118 b.

dergapad, *O'D. Sup.* 616.

dergár, red slaughter, *LL.* 299, *FM.* iii. 124.

dergór, 155.

dergruathar, 158 ; *ap.* tri dergruathar, *LL.* 78 a.

dergruba Conaill, *v.* rube.

dériad, *gl.* bigæ, *Z.* ; *cf.* cethirríad.

Dermag, Dermach, 127.

dermat, dermet, 138.

dernum, 171.

deróil, 201.

dertech, 128 ; dertech = oratorium, *FM.* an. 812, 905, *AU.* 815 ; *ap.* dertige, *Chr. Scot.* p. 172; *gs.* derthige, *LB.* 85.

descéim, 115; *np.* deiscemanda, *Laws,* iv. 276, *O'Don. Sup.* p. 648.

desíd, vengeance, *FM.* ii. 648 ; *cf.* síd.

desimrecht, desmrecht, 204.

desléim, 115, 116.

desmaig, *ds.* south plain, *Fél.* 20.

desrad, *Windisch Dict.*

dia, 133.

diabul, 150.

deithriub, *Ml.* 137 c.

diablud, 142, 204 ; diablud n-aithgina, *O'Dav.* 63.

diall, 150.

dialt, 146, 205 ; dialt n-etarléme, *BB.* 328 b, 31.

díanbás, *LB.* 112 b.

diangalar, 156.

dibad n-, *g.* díbaid, *LB.* 208 a, 260 a.

díbe, 181.

díceltar, handle of a spear ; issed an d., *LU. Mongan's Story.*

díchetal, 151, *Todd Lect.* v. 123.

dichomarcc, 147; *gs.* díchmairc, *LB.* 260 b

diglaim, 119, *BB.* 289 a ; dioglaim caor, *Michæas,* 7 ; *g.* díogloma, *Jer.* xlix.

digna, 196; *g.* dignai .i. neimgné, drochgné, *Fél.*

dílgend, 167, *d.* n-, *Ml.* 53 c.

dillat, 142.

dimbuaid, 198.

dimdibe, 181.

dímíad, 136, *LB.* 207 b.

dín, 166.

dind, 208 ; an dind, *RD.* 437 ; dinn .i. tulach, *O'Dav.* 79 ; *g.* denna, *Amra C. C.* ch. 2.

dine, 197.

dínert, 145 ; *v.* nert.

díor, 155.

díre, 193 ; *ns.* díri n-, *Man. and Cust.* iii. 572.

dírech, 181,193; direch n-dligid, *O'Dav.* 72.

diréim, 117.

dírimm, 117 ; .i. diréim .i. réim ndeda, *Cormac*, 24; dirimm, *gl.* immat, *Fél.* 208, *O'Dav.* 75 ; *ap.* dírmann, *O'Dav.* 75 ; *np.* dírmand, dírmandai ; *gp.* dírmand, *LB.* 207 a, b.

díruidigthe, 189.

disccae, 184; dísce mblechta, *Gaelic Soc.* vol. i. 32.

disceinm, 123.

dísert, 145, 206 ; a ndísert-sa, the hermitage, *LU.* 15 b.

dith n-ænmaic, *RD.* 433.

dithim, 119.

dithrab, 170.

dithrecht, 204.

diubae, 182.

díucaire, 191, 192, *Todd Lect.* v. 123.

díucræ, 191.

diuchtrad, 140.

díuderc, 147.

diumaidm, 120.

diumand, 167.

díunnach n-ind, *Cormac*, 20.

diuthach, 174.

dliged, dligeth, 143.

doacaldmach, 173.

doburbur, 161.

dochar (?), torment, *LB.* 276 ; sochar 7 dochar, *LC.* 237.

docetul, 151.

dochenél, 148.

dochraide ndaíne, *O'D. Sup.* 623.

dodamna .i. mac beg, *O'Dav.* 79, *v.* damna.

doergalar, *Fél.* 35.

dógrae, 191 ; *d.* dogru, *LU.* 49.

doimim, *ds.* (of doim?), *LL.* 147 a.

doinmech, 173.

doirtech, 128.

dolad (?), *as.*, *g.* dolaid, detriment, *Hy Fiach.* 252 ; *g.* dolaid 7 murir, a charge and burden, *C. Ros na Ríg*, pp. 16, 17, 227; dolud, moeror, is masc., *Ml.* 77 d.

domaidm, bursting, *BB.* 11 a, 11 b.

domnach, 178.

donasnach, 179.

dondnaidm, 121.

dorar, 162.

dorche, 184.

dord, 145.

dorochol, 154.

dorus, 164 ; a ndorus, limen, *Ml.* ; *ap.* torus, *Ml.* 46 a.

dos ndime, *g.* dois, *O'Dav.* 77,74, a bush.

dosbile, 194.

dosmag, 127.

drantmír, 124.

drécht, 205.

drecht, 205 ; drecht n-, *RD.* 433.

dreim, 118, from dringim, I climb, *LL.* 300 a.

drindrosc, 147; *ap.* trí drindrosc. *LU.* 111 b.

driseach (?), thorns, *das. Luke* vii. *Heb.* vi.

drocb, dá ndroch, *LU.* 105 b and *W.*, a wheel.

drochbéscne, 196 ; *g.* drochbaescni, *Ml.* 118 a.

drochdesmirecht, 204.

drochdub, 170.

drochet, 142.

drochfolad, *O'D. Sup.* 624.

drochgne, *Fél.* 45.

drochrad, 139.

drochscél, *ap.* drochscéla, *Ml.* 129 a.

drogscél, 148.

drolmach, 173 ; but *asf.* drolmuig, *Todd Lect.* v. 125.

dromchetel, 151.

drong, 169.

druimm, 109, 120, 201 ; druim n-, *LL.* 202 a, 305 b (four times, *BB.* 356 b), *RD.* 94 a ; *np.* dromman, drommann, *LL.* 29 ; *gp.* drummann, *FM.* iii. 320.

engne, 196.
énrige, 185.
erat, 138.
erbach, 172.
erbe, 183.
erchomul, 153.
erchor, 162.
erchosc, *LB*. 276.
erchre, 191.
erdam : an erdam, *LB*. 255 b.
erdibad (?), failing, extinction, *LB*.
109 b.
Ereros (?), *FM*. an. 857.
eres, 164.
eret, erat, 138 ; issed eret, *LU*. p. 43 ;
*Ml*. 107 d.
erfuacra, 191.
ergaire, 192.
érge; éirge, 185.
ergne, 196.
érimm, eraim, 117 ; erimm n-, *LB*. 111 b,
*LL*.278, col. 1 ; eraim n-, *S. na Rann*. ;
ag eirim no marcuigeacht, *Hardiman's*
*Minstr*. ii. 349 ; *g*. erma, driving (of
horses), *LL*. 110 a ; errim, a journey,
*Fen*. 280.
erriram, 117.
erlár, floor, *LU*. p. 3.
erláthar, 158.
erlim, eirlim, 116.
ermaisse, 197.
ernbás, 163.
ernn, 166.
ernach, *g*. ernaig, iron tools, *LL*. 198 a.
ernaidm, 121.
eross, 164.
erthossach, *LL*. 247 a.
erus, 164.
errach, 180.
erranda (?) particulas, *Todd Lect*. v. 69.
erred, eirred, 138, 139.
érrend, 169, 201.
érrethech, erredech, 174.
eirrige, *as*. government, *LL*. 108 a.
érscél, *cf*. airscél.
ersinm, 123.
ersliab, *g*. erslebe, *Broccan's Hymn*.
ertach, 173 ; *np*. erdaige, *LB*. 73 b.

ertech (?), protection, *as*., *Chr. Scot*.
242, 244.
erthuaiscertach, 174.
eruacra, 191.
escairde(?), *d*. escairdiu, enmity, *AU*.440.
escaire, 192.
escann, 169.
escart, 145.
ésce, æscae, 184.
escomol, *C. R. na Ríg*.
escongra, 192.
escor(ŧ), *ds*. fall, *FM*. iii. 570.
escra, 193.
escrimm, 117.
eslind, 132.
esngaire, 192 ; *np*. inna esngaire, *Ml*.
105 c.
esngarthe, 189.
éss, 163 ; eas nDuinn, *R.D*. § 80.
esrad, 144.
esséirge, 185 ; an æ. *Ml*. 38 c ; *d*. eserciu,
*HM*. xi.
essíd, 130, 144 ; síth nó eisíth, *FM*. iii.
286.
estad, *Fen*. 308, *v*. etsud.
éstosc, 146 ; *d*. estoasc, *Ml*. 97 a.
étach, 173.
etarairdbe, 182.
etarcnae, 196, an e., experientia, *Ml*.
109 a, 111 c.
etardibe, 181.
Etardruim, *M. Tall*. xxvi.
etarfuarad (?), *ap*. refrigeria, *Gildas Gl*.
etargaire, 192.
etargne, 196.
etarimdibe, 181.
etarléim, 116, *BB*. 328 b, 31 ; *see* dialt.
etarthotaim, 119.
etercne, 196.
eterdibe, 181.
eterimdibe, 181, *LB*. 205 a.
etech, 174.
étechte, 190.
etgud : issed ba étgud, *Life of Hugh*
*Roe*, 72.
ethar, 159 ; *g*. ethair, *AU*. i. 220, *as*.
ethar, navis, *Todd Lect*. v. 126 ; *ap*.
ethra, *FM*. iv. 748.

fich (?), *g.* ficha, vicus, *Fél.* 133.

fid, 203; fid nGaibli, *RD.* 95 a, *LL.*
196; *ap.* feda, *L. Cé.* i. 136; *gp.*
fede, *Hy Fiach.* 172, 270; Fid
n-dorcha, *FM.* ii. 1160.

fidach, 174.

fidach, *g.* fidaig, hunting, *Fen.* 264.

fidár, 155; *as. AU.* i. 366, 408, *FM.*
an. 1178.

fidbach, 130, 171.

fidbad, 137; *but* fidbad, forest, *npm.*
fitbuid, *LB.* 111 b; *nf.* ind fidbad,
*S. na Rann,* ix.

fidbae, 183; *g.* fidbai, *Laws,* ii. 166.

fiddruim, 120; *g.* fiddromma, woody
ridge, *LU.* 48..

fidlestar, 157.

fidnemed, 137; *g.* 3, 15, f. 3 b, *AU.* i.
502; *d.* fidnemud, *BB.* f. 245 a, b.

fidrad, 139; *as. LL.* 302 b; *g.* fiodraid,
*B. of Mag Lena,* 76.

fín : a fín, *Ml.* 45 d.

fínechar, 162.

finnchlár, *Hy Fiachr.* 270.

findchœlach, *Three M. Ir. Hom.* 76; *cf.*
coilach.

findchoire, *d.* f. choriu, *Ml.* 126 c; *v.*
coire.

finnfolad, white kine, *LL.* 295 a.

Finnglenn, *AU.* i. 179.

findlestar, 157.

Finnloch, *B. of Arm.*

Findmag, 127; *ap.* findmaige, *Hy Fiach.*
288.

findnem, 125.

Finnross, *Fen.* 86.

findscél, 148.

Finntracht, *FM.* iv. 738.

fintech, 529, 148, *LL.* 111 b; *cf.* intech; *d.* intigib, *LL.* 240 a; *d.* fin-
tiuch, *LU.* 91 a.

Finntráig, 198.

fíradnacul, 153.

fíraichne, *LB.* 151 b.

fírchride, 186.

fírdliged, 143.

fírluge, 184.

firmullag, 175.

firór, 155.

firt, mound, tomb; f. mBoinne, *BB.* f.
190, *RD.* 92 b; *gs.* firt, *BB.* 298 a.

firt, 206; an f., miraculum, *Todd Lect.*
v. 70, 94.

fír-uaim, proper concord; *v.* uaim.

fisscél, 148.

fithrach, 179.

fius, 206.

fledól, 149; *ds.* fledól, = manducare et
bibere, *Todd Lect.* v. 127; *g.* fledóil,
*LB.* 273.

fledtech, fleteg, 129; *Ml.* 86 b.

fleuchud, 137.

foaccomal, 152.

foarbbe, 183.

fobach, 172; fobach n-, .i. buain, toch-
ailt, *O'Dav.* 88, 91.

fobar, 161; *cf.* inber, combar.

fobíad, 135.

fochann, 169; *npm.* fochainn, *Ml.* 86 c,
101 a; isead fochand, *L. Lec.* 270 b.

fochéim, 115.

Fochla : isa F., into the North; *g.* ind
fochlai, *AU.* i. 398, 404.

fochmarc, 147; *g.* fochmairc, inquiry,
*B. of Lec.,* p. 11, col. 1; *d.* fochmarcc, *LB.* 136 a.

fochrod : *np.* fochrod ilarda, many small
flocks, *FM.* iii. 558.

fócre, 191; fócra n-, *O'D. Sup.* 644.

fodb, 170; *ap.* inda (inna) fodb, *gl.*
exuvias, *Laurent. Gl.* 72; *gs.* fuidb,
*LB.* 208 a; *nap.* fodba, *Ml.* 92 d.

fodbeim, 114.

fodiuba, 182.

fodmag, *g.* fert fodmaige, *B. of M.
Lena,* 156; = fotbach, 92.

fodord, 145.

fodorus, *gl.* posticium, *Vat. Regina,* 215,
f. 91 b.

fodruba, 182.

fóenlige, 185.

fóglaim, 119.

fográd, 134.

fogur, 160.

foilbéim, 114.

foiltech, 128.

foimrim, 117 ; *g.* foimrìme, *Laws,* i. 234, 168.

foimtharruṅg, 169.

foindeb, 150.

fointreb, 170.

foirchéim, 115.

foirnert, 145.

foirtbe, 182 ; foirtbe, foirddbe, devastatio, *AU.* 200, 204, 216.

foirthír, 131.

foithne, 196.

folach (?), to hide; *ds.* imfolach, *LB.* 276; folach n-, *O'Don. Sup.* 646.

folad, 142; *g.* folaid, substantiae, *Todd Lect.* v. 128; *np.* folta, *O'D. Sup.* 646.

foléim, 116.

fomet, 138.

fonaidm, 121.

fond, 167.

forad, 138, 139 ; *as.* forsa foruth n-abbaḋ (*AU.* i. 318) ; *dp.* foradaib, benches, *LU.* 52 b; stations, *AU.* i. 328 ; forad, .i. airm, *LL.* 62 b.

foraim, 123.

forainm, 122 ; *LU.* 39 a, *L. Lec.* 270 b, 242 ; = cognomen, *Stapleton's Cathechism,* p. 21 ; pronoun, *M'Curtin's Gram.,* p. 70.

foraithmet, foraidmet, 138 ; recordatio, *Todd Lect.* v. 128.

forar, 160.

forbann, 167 ; *as.* morem superstitiosum, *Todd Lect.* v. 128.

foram n-, *Stokes Metr. Glosses,* p. 17.

forás : inna f. *ap.* profectus, *Ml.* 104 d, *v.* forus.

forbach, exaction, *O'D. Sup.* 647 ; *cf.* tobuch.

forcall, forcell, 154.

forcenn, 168.

forcetul, forcital, 151 ; *np.* inna forcital, *Ml.* 107 a.

forcmachta, 187.

forcomol, 153 ; *d.* forcomul, *LB.* 207 b.

forcongre, 192 ; præceptum, *Todd Lect.* v. 128.

forcraid, 199.

fordiuclaim, 119 ; fordiuglaim, *LU.* 111 a.

fordorus, 164.

Fordruim, 120.

fóreth, 138.

forfócre, 191.

forfolach (?), *g.* forfolaích, *LB.* 260 a.

forgaire, 192.

forgell, forgall, 154.

forgemen, 118.

forgglu, 133.

forgnide, 187.

forgu, 133.

forim, 117 ; *see* fuirm.

forlés, 207.

forlóg, 126.

formaidm, 121.

format, formet, 138.

formór, 155.

fornaidm, 121.

forngaire, 192 ; *ap. Ml.* 53 c.

forod (?), *LL.* 184 b ; *v.* forad.

forodmag, 127, *LL.* 62 b ; *d.* forodmaig, *LL.* 62 b (forad, .i. airm, *ibi.*), *LL.* 109 a.

foróil, 201.

forom, 123 ; f. ngrind, *LL.* 203 a.

forscamon, 117.

fortched, 142.

fortchide, 187.

forthrum, 171.

fortormach, 172.

forthosach, 181.

fortse, 197.

fortuge, 184.

forum, 171.

forus, 165, issed inso forus, *Y. B. of Lec.* col. 217 ; *dp.* foirsib, *Laws* i. 78.

foscaige, 184.

foscél, 148 ; *np.* foscéla, *Laws* i. 46.

foscul, 154.

foṡnaidm, 121, *O'D. Sup.* 647.

fossad (?), *g.* fossaid, truce, cessation, *LL.* 302 a.

fossadlár, 156.

fótbach, 171, *O'D. Sup.* 644.

lotha, 190.

fothach, 174.

fothrand, 167.

Fraechmag, *LL.* 206 b, *BB.* 386.

fraechraḋ, heath, *H.* 2, 18, f. 73 b ; *d.* fraechrud, *Ir. Texte,* i. 106.

frecndairc, 147.

freccre, fecra, 191 ; *g.* frecrai, *FM.* an. 990.

freiteach, 174.

freslige, 185.

frestal, 152.

frithagra, 191.

frithbruth, 203.

frithḟolad, 142.

froechrad, 139.

fuacre, 191.·

fuad, fuath, 136 ; *np.* fuatha, *LL.* 207 a.

fuadach, 173 ; *g.* fuadaig, *Luke* xviii. ; *gp.* fuadaige, 1 *Cor.* v.

fuaim, 118 ; fuaim n-, *LU.* 52 ; *gp.* fuamann, *FM.* iii. 340, 364 ; *np.* fogur 7 fuamand *LU.* 28 b.

fualascach, 177 ; *np.* inna fualascach, *bis, Ml.* 48 c.

fualred, 140.

fualtige, *np. L.B.* 11 a, urine-houses.

fúan, 166 ; fuan corcra n-imbi, *LU.* 106 a.

fuargfothrom, noise, *LL.* 111 a ; *cf.* fothrom.

fuascar (?), precipitate flight; *Todd Lect.* v. 128 ; *cf.* oscor.

fuasnad, 144.

fuath nDé, hatred of God, *M'Curtin's Gram.* 120.

fuatluch (?), *ds., S. na R.* 7412.

fubæ, fuba, 182.

furfócre, 191.

fugell, 154 ; *d.* fugiull, *LU.* 38 b, 32 b, 36 a, *d.* ḟúiglib, *LB.* 211 a.

fuidell, 150.

fuilled n-ága, *LL.* 297.

fuilred, blood ; *ds.* fuillriud, *LU.* 109 a.

fuined, 144.

fuirec, 148, 180.

fuirech, 180 ; *as. LU.* 29 a.

fuirired, 148.

fuirm, *d.* fuirmim, march, *L.Cé.* 38.

fuithairbe, 183 ; *ap.* fuithairbe, *LU.* 111 a.

fulach, 169.

fulang, 169.

fulracht, 205.

fulred, 140.

furad, fureth, 138.

furḟocre, furócre ; *d.* furógru, 191.

furgrad, 139.

futharbe, 183.


gabulrind, *Cormac,* 9.

gaimbíad, 135.

gaimred, 141.

gainem, 171.

gairbthrían, *FM.* ili. 196.

gaire, 192.

gairm, 123 ; *d.* garmaim, *Fél.* 45, *Man. and Cust.* iii. 511 ; *ap.* garmann, *Keating's Hist.* p. 203.

gaisced, 142.

galar, 156 ; *np.* galara, Meyer's *Hib. Minora,* 39 ; *d.* gallraib, *LB.* 111 a, 113 a.

gallbélre, 193.

gáo, 133.

garbgreim, 117.

garbrois, *gs. AU.* i. 298.

gardrad, 140.

gass n-óir, sprig of gold, *AU.* i. 378.

géim, 118.

gein, 131, 200 ; a ngein, *LL.* 290 a, 290 b ; gein n-, *Fél.* 61 ; *a.* geinim, *Ml.* 59 a, 85 b.

geirrmíl, 149.

gelgabargraig, 198.

gelgruad, *S. na R.* 140.

gell, 154 ; *np.* inna gell, *Ml.* 123 c ; *d.* giull, *LU.* 13 a.

gelmaidm, *FM.* iv. 752.

gemel, 155.

gemred, 141.

genelach, 175 ; *np.* genelaige, *LU.* 46 ; genelaig, *Hy Fiach.* 278.

Geomag, *AU.* i. 462.

gerrétach, 173.

gibne, 197.

ginathchomarc, 147.

glaim, 118.

glaislinn, 132 ; *g.* glaislinne, *LL.* 308 a.

glamrad, 141.

glanbuaid, 198.

glanmíad, 136.

glanór, *Fél.* 114.

glasmag, 127.

glasmuir, 200, *LL.* 288, *LC.* 72.

glasrad, greens, vegetables.

gledruimm, 120.

glegraim, 117, *LB.* 111 b.

glenn, 131 ; *as.* glenn, *Ml.* 58 c.

gléo, 133 ; ferthar gliaid n-amnais, *FM.* iii. 642 ; *das.* gleó, *Fél.* 139 ; *gp.* gleo, *Fen.* 218 ; *d.* gleó *and* gliad, *FM.* iii. 362.

glés, 207.

gless, 207.

globeim, 114.

gloimm, 118 ; gloim, baying of a dog, *LL.* 110 b.

glomrach, 180 ; *dp.* glomraigib, the muzzles (of bridles), *LL.* 110 a.

glorgrad, *S. na R.* 2341.

gluair, 200.

glún, 131 ; *ap.* glúine, *Todd Lect.* v. 129.

glún, generation; *np.* glúine, *Matt.* i. 17.

gnáth, 134.

gnáthainm, 122.

gnáthbelra, 193.

gné, 133 ; gné n-aill, *LB.* 170 a, *BB.* 326 a ; gné mbróin, *Lism. Lives,* p. 116 ; *np.* gnée, *Fél.* 67 ; an gne, vultus, *Ml.* 74 a.

gním, 207 ; gním n-, *LL.* 167 b, 297, *S. na R.* 7661.

gnímrad, 141 ; *g.* gnímraid, *Hy Fiach.* 274 ; *as.* gnímrad, *Fél.* 132 ; *np.* grímrada, *LB.* 111 b.

gó, 133 ; *ds.* gói, *Todd Lect.* v. 24.

goirthbíad, 135.

góithlach, gaethlach, 176 ; *np.* gaethlaige, *LL.* 11 ; *dp.* gaethlaigib, *BB.* 272 a, b ; *LB.* 149 b.

gol : is é a ngol nglechrach ngarg.

golgaire, 192.

goscél, 148.

grád, 134 ; *nap.* gráda, orders, *LB.* 109 b, *Todd Lect.* v. 130 ; *ap.* nói ngrád, *LU.* 27 b.

grad, 134 ; a ngrad, love, *LU.* 129.

grad, 202.

graig, 198 ; *np.* na graige, graigi, *Chron. Scot.* 130, *Todd Lect.* v. 130 ; *np.* graige, droves of horses, *AU.* i. 314, 328.

grán, 165 ; *np.* inna grán ; *SG.* 184 b.

Granairet, 138 ; *g.* Granairit, *AU.* i. 202, 236.

greidm, 122.

gréim, 117 ; *d.* gremmaim, .i. vigore, *Ml.* 31 c ; greimm, sceptre, advantage, *Todd Lect.* v. 130.

grith, 199 ; *np.* gretha, .i. óenaige 7 cluiche, *Fél.* 31.

grothlach (?), gravel pit, *O'Brien's Dict.*

grúad, 130 ; dá ngrúad, *Ir. Texte* i. 80, *LU.* 106 b ; *np.* inna gruade, 'convexa,' *Ml.* 96 c ; *g. dual,* gruad, *LU.* 48 b.

gruth, 203.

guafiadnuisse, 197.

guba, 183 ; *d.* gubu, *Todd Lect.* v. 43, gubæ, *LU.* 69 a.

guforcell, guforgell, 154 ; *g.* guforgaill, *Todd Lect.* v. 130.

guide, 188.

guin, 200.

gus, 207.

guscél, 148, *O'D. Sup.* 660.

guthaigthe, 189.


iachlind, 132.

iallacrand, 166 ; *gs.* iallacraind, *BB.* 272 b, a ; acrann *is fem.*

iarbe, 183.

iarchomarc, 147, last word of a poem, *Thurn.* i. versl. 129.

iarfaigid, 199.

iarmbélre, 193.

iarmbérla, 194, any part of speech, save nouns and verbs, *M'Curtin's Gram.* 27.

iarmérge, 185, *LU.* 31 bb.

iaronn, *gp.* ; *npl.* iarnda, *Todd. Lect.* v. 120.

íartach, 173.

iarthuaiscerdach, 174.

iasgloch, 201.

íath, .i. mind, *Amra Choluim C.* (?).

íath, 136 ; iath n-, *H.* 3, 18, p. 635 c ; *B. of Hy Maine,* fo. 145, *RD.* 433 ; *ap.* iath, *O'Dav.* 109 ; a aith n-, *LU.* p. 50.

íathmag, 127.

Iabarglend, *d.* Iabarglind, *LL.* 207 a.

ích, 198.

ícht, 205.

íchtar, 157.

íchtardescardach, 174.

íchtarthuaiscerdach, 174.

id, 130 ; id, *g.* ind ide, *LU.* 62 a, da n-id, *LL.* 72 b.

idaltech, 129 ; *g.* ídaltige, .i. fani, *Todd Lect.* v. 120, *LB.* 60 b.

idna, 197.

idnacul, 153.

il, 149 ; híl, 149.

iladbar, *S. na R.* 7734.

ilanmann, *pl.* 122.

ilar, 159 ; ilar m-, *LU.* 47 ; ilur n-, *Texte,* i. 107 ; *O'Don. Sup.* 634.

ilardbe, 182.

ilbéim, 114.

ilbélre, 193.

ilceolaib, *dp. LB.* 110 a.

ilchenele, 194.

ilchéta, *ap.* several hundred, *LL.* 288 a, *FM.* ii. 102.

ilclesrada, ilclessarda, *nap. LB.* 155 a.

ildechor, 162 ; ildechraib, alternationibus, *AU.* 125 d.

ilfolad, 142.

ilgaire, *np. LB.* 151 b.

ilgne, 133.

ilimat, *g.* iliomaitt, *FM.* iv. 662, 744.

illitred, 140.

ilmílaib, *dp. LB.* 112 b.

ilmrechtrad, 140.

ilmuire, *gp., O'D. Sup.* 606.

ilséim, 118 ; *pl.* ilsemman.

ilseinm, 123.

iltech, 129 ; *gp.* iltige, *Amra C. C.* ch. 7.

imaithber, 161 ; *d.* imaithfeur, *S. na Rann,* x.

imbaire, 193.

imbe, 184 ; *g.* imbi, *Man. and Cust.* iii. 489.

imbed, immed, 137 ; an imbed, *Ml.* 56 b; imad n-, *O'Dav.* 88.

imbel, immel, 155.

imblech, 202, 177 ; imblech n-, *FM.* an. 948, *T. B. Dartada,* p. 197.

imbresan, 166.

Imchlár, 156 ; *g.* imchláir, *FM.* iii. 116.

imchosc, 146.

imdell (?), device, *FM.* iii. 244 ; *cf.* diall.

imdibe, 181.

imdorus, 164 ; *np.* inna imdoirsea, *Ml.* 92 d.

imelach, *Fél.* 37.

imfreccra, imfrecrae, imreccra, 191, 192 ; *gl.* consequentia, *Ml.* 136 c.

imléim, 116, shying.

imm, 124 ; imb., *LL.* 144 a ; *d.* immim, *Todd Lect.* v. 130, *LB.* 63 a, *O'Dav.* 90.

immadal, *Wind. Dict.*

immarbe, 184.

immarcor, 162.

immargó, 133.

immchim, 115, *LU.* 50 a, *FM.* an. 919.

immchomarc, 147, *Ml.* 46 b.

immchumdach, *LB.* 206 a.

immechtar, 157 ; dá n-imechtar, *LU.* 29 b.

immeirge, 185.

immellach, 175.

immetsad, 144.

immformat, 138.

immlind, 200.

immorchor, 162.

immram (?), *as.* ; *d.* immrum, navigium, navigare, *Todd Lect.* v. 131 ; *masc.* in t-imram, *Ml.* 126 a.

imrimm, 117 ; .i. réim in eich 7 réim in duine, *Cormac*, 24.

imnach, 178.

imned, 144 ; *g.* immnid, *LB.* 205 a.

impsuide, imsuide, impude, 187.

imrool, 149.

imroll, imrall, 150 ; *g.* imroill, *LL.* 305 a ; *as.* imroll, *Fél.* 129.

imtelgad, 143.

imthaccra, 191.

imthanad, 143.

imthinól, 149.

imthriall, *LB.* 205 a.

imthórmach, 172, *LB.* 9 b.

imtothaim, mutual killing, *AU.* 398.

imthuge, 184.

imuaim, 118, *Amra C.C.* ch. 5, *FM.* iii. 368 ; *v.* uaim.

inad, 143 ; an inad, ined, ineth, *d.* inut, *Todd Lect.* v. 79, 131 ; *pl.* inata, *LB.* 273 b.

inathar, 158 ; *as.* or *ap. FM.* an. 1186.

inber, 109, 161 ; inber n-, *RD.* 93 b, *bis*, 124 a ; *B. Lec.* 194 a, O'Dav. 62, 100 ; an inber, *Todd Lect.* v. 50 ; *np.* inbíora, *FM.* i. 96 ; inverdele = invernaele in *Charters* of years 1179, 1171, 1192, 1192.

inchosc, 146 ; *cf.* inchoisc, "indica," *Todd Lect.* v. 131 ; inchosc mbec, *Ml.* 57 b.

indarbe, indarpe, 183 ; indarba n-, *AU.* 416 ; *d.* innarbu, *AU.* i. 484 ; indorpou, *HM.* 11.

indas, 164 ; an indus sin, *Amra C. C.* ch. 7.

indbed, 137.

indber, 161, 206.

indeb, 170.

indeal, 150.

inderge, innerge, 186.

indlach, 177.

indliged, 143.

indlat (?), *d.* indlut, *Z.* 949, omitted in the Index Verborum.

indrach, 179.

indrad, indred, 141 ; indred n-Ulad, *AU.* 294.

indrosc, *gl.* proverbium.

indruth n-, 203.

indsma, 195.

infeidm, 122.

ing, 128.

ingaire, 192.

ingnáth, 134 ; ingnad, mira res, *Todd Lect.* v. 131.

ingnæ, 195.

ingraimm, ingreimm, 117.

innaide, indnide, 187.

innchomartha, 188.

innlach (?), .i. casaoid nó gearrán, *O'Clery* ; *v.* indlach.

inntech, journey ; *g.* inntig, marked neuter in *Atkinson's Glossary.*

insgne (?), gender, *M'Curtin's Gram.*, 70.

ínsuide *or* ainsuide ; dul for a ínsuide, *HM.* 71 = do filliud a glún.

intech, 129 ; *d.* intiuch, *LU.* 68 b ; *dp.* intígib, *LL.* 240 a.

intech, 130, 174.

intinscann, 167.

intinscetul, 151.

intled, 142.

intreb, 170 ; intreb n-, *Laws*, i. xli.

inturas, 165.

inunn, 168.

irfócre, 191 ; an irfocra, *LB.* 134 b.

irgaire, 192.

irgne, 196.

írnaidm, 121.

irtech, 173.

irthorad, great produce, *Fél.* 61.

isel, *d.* dundisiul, inferno, *Ml.* 107 b.

iselbéim, *LL.* 288.

isleidm, 122.

istad, istud, 144, 204 ; *np.* istoda, *LL.* 264 b ; istad, *B. of Mag Rath*, 198 ; naom-iostad ronaomtha, Holy of Holies, *Heb.* 9.

ith, 199 ; ith n-glas, *Sylva Gaed.*, p. 80.

ithlár, 156.

íthtech, ítech, 129.

itirimdibe, 181.

itsad, treasure, *Ml.* 51 d.

iúgsuide, 187.

iumat, 137.

Lachtmag, 127; *Fen.* 346.

laechlestar, 157.

laechtigib, *dp. LB.* 260 b.

laem (?), *dp.* laemannaib, *M. Rath*, 222; *cf.* ina laem tromm, *LB.* 156 a.

laemscél, 148.

laideng, 169.

Laigenmag, 127, *FM.* an. 918.

laim, *d.* drop, *Todd Lect.* v. 32; *v.* loim.

láinrige, 185.

laithe, lá, 189; al lá, *Todd Lect.* v. 8; laithi n-, *O'Dav.* 98; a laa n-, *Ml.* 108 a.

láither, 158.

Laithglend, *g.* Laithglinde, *AU.* i. 362.

Laithlinn, *g.* Laithlinne, *AU.* i. 35 4.

lamach (?), *g.* lamaig, *Fen.* 356, *Hy Fiach.* 238, 240, *L. Cé*, an. 1281.

lámchrand, 166.

lámthorad, 138; *LU.* 49, 124 b.

lán, 165; lán n-, *Gildas*, iii. viii.; *np.* tri lán, *FM.* iii. 312.

lánbruth, 203.

lánbuaid; *ap.* lánbuada, prizes, *LL.* 206 b.

lándílgend, *S. na Rann*, xi.

lándíre, 193.

lándirech, 181, 204.

lánfreccra, 192.

langnímrad, 141.

lánlóg, 126, *AU.* i. 560.

lánsíd, *LU.* 336, 34 a.

lánsuth, 203.

lántorad, 138.

lár, 156; lár, page of book, *Fén.* 358.

lath, 134.

lathach, 174, *is fem.*, *FM.* iii. 244.

lathar, 158; lathar n-, *LL.* 199, 299, 203 a; l. aill, *Ml.* 44 b; *np.* innallathar, dispensationes, *Ml.* 91 d.

Latharna, 195.

láthrach, 179; *as.* láthrach, *LL.* 306 b, *Hy Fiach.* 266; *Fél.* 19; *g.* lathraig; *d.* lathrug, *AU.* i. 416, 114; *dp.* lathraigib, *AU.* i. 408.

Leathroiss, *gs. Fél.* 77.

lebend (?), rampart, *LL.* 120 a; *g.* lebinn, platform (of a ship), *Fen.* 282; *d.* lebeunn, *Todd Lect.*, iii. 16; *d.* lebendaib, *LB.* 109 a.

Leccmag, *FM. Index.*

lecht, 146.

lechtaige, grave, *Sylva Gaed.* 372 (?).

Lee, 133, *as.* and *ngp. B. of Armagh*, and *Trip. Life*, 160.

légend, 167.

Legmag, 127, *FM. Index*; Leccmag, *Chr. Scot.* 4, *FM. Index.*

léim, 116; *d.* léimaim, lémum; *g.* lémme, *LU.* 111a; *np.* lémenna, *LL.* 207 a, *FM.* an. 1030.

leinm, 123.

léire, 190.

léna (?), *d.* lénu, meadow, *B. of Kells*, fo. 66, *B. of Armagh.*

lenomnaib, *dp.* 123.

ler, 156.

lermag, 127.

lermuir, *Fél.* 49.

lérthinól, 149, *LB.* 205 b.

lés, 207.

less, 207.

lessainm, 122.

lester, lestar, 157; lestrai, *asf. Ml.* 18 b.

leth, led, 130, side; *d.* leith, *Todd Lect.* v. 52; *g.* leithe, *LB.* 110 a; *g. dual*, lethe, *LL.* 288, *Fél.* 186; *AU.* i. 98.

leth, led, half, 135; al leth n-, *LU.* 39; al leth n-aill, *AU.* 208, *Fen.* 138; al leth n-ur, *Todd Lect.* v. 11, *FM.* iii. 214.

leth-aithgin, *O'D. Sup.* 594.

lethanmag, 127.

lethárd, 205.

leth-arra, half arreum, *RC.* xv. 488.

lethdechnad, 143.

lethdíre, 193.

lethdirech, 181, 204.

Lethduma, *LL.* 295, 299.

lethlóg, 126.

Lethglenn, 132.

lethluige, leaning, *Bible Focloir.*

lethrige, half-rule, *LU.* 39 a.

lethtagra, *OD. Sup.* 669.

leathtorad, "modicum," *Todd Lect.* v. 70.

leithtrían, 166.

lí, 134 ; *pl.* lithe, *O'D. Sup.*

liacht, 124.

liadelg, 126.

lianmag, 127.

liasrad, 146.

liathdruim, *g.* Liathdromo, Leitrim, *M. Tall.* xxiv.

lige, 184 ; lige, grave, *Frags. of Ir. An.* 66 ; in a ligu, jacens, *Todd Lect.* v. 47, 60 ; ligi n-Eothaille, *O'D. Sup.* 571.

lígdath 202 ; *v.* dath.

ligrad, 139 ; *d.* ligradaib, *BB.* 274 ab.

lín, 166 ; lassanda(la) lín, with one net, *Ml.* 137 c.

lín, 200.

línanart, 145 ; *np.* línanarta, *Todd Lect.* 93, *LB.* 60 b ; *pl.* línanart, *Sylva Gaed.* 36.

linn, 124.

linn, 132.

linn, lind, 208 ; *ggp.* lenddann, *LB.* 212 a, 211 a.

linnmuir, 200.

lith, 134 ; líth n-gaile, *RD.* 98 a.

lithlaithe, 189.

litred, 140.

lóan, 166.

loch, 109, 201 ; loch n-, *LL.* 169 b, *ter BB.* 11 b ; *nds.* louch, *Mac Conglinne,* 119, 120, Loch n-, *Ogygia,* 169 ; *g.* da locho, *AU.* i. 136, 418, *Fél.* 98.

lochán, 165.

Lochmag, 127.

lochmaidm, *pl.* lochmaidmanna, *Chr. Scot.* 6.

lochtomaidm, 121.

lóg, 126 ; ised lóg, *Ml.* 12 ad.

loim, loimm, loinb, 118, loimm n-aiss, *LB.* 9 b, 10 a ; loimm, *Fél.* 100 ; *d.* lomum, *LB.* 219 a ; *g.* lomma, lactis, *Todd Lect.* v. 132 ; *ap.* lomann, *LB.* 9 b, *BB.* 403 a ; *pl.* lomanna, *O'Don. Suppl.* ; *np.* lommann, *RC.* xv. 491.

loman, 166.

lomchrand, 166.

lomrad, 141.

longthech, 129 ; *d.* longthig, *Harl. Gl.* 1802.

lonnbruth, 203.

Lorcmag, *g.* Lorcmaige, *Syl. Gad.* 372.

lórthorad, 138.

lot(?), *g.* luit, a wound, *FM.* and *L. Cé,* an. 1283.

loth, 130.

lothar, 159.

lóthar, 159.

lothblind, 132.

lotrad, 140.

Luachmag, 127.

Luachros, *FM. Index.*

luad, 136, 204 ; luad n-, *Fél.* 125.

luad (?), *g.* luaid, tucking, *Laws* ii. 416.

luae, 195.

luag, *S. na Rann,* viii. (*v.* lóg) ; *d.* luaig, *B. of Kells,* f. 7, *bis* ; *np.* luagi, *O'Curry's Lect.* 491.

luaithred, 139, pulvis, *Todd Lect.* v. 34 ; *das.* luaithred, *AU.* i. 494.

luathcride, 186.

luathlámach, swift-shooting, *as. Todd Lect.* iv. 98.

Luathmag, 127, *LL.* 305 b.

luathtimdibe, *Tog. Troi,* l. 2230.

lubenchlár, 156.

luchtlach, 176 ; luchtlach in coiri, *Y.B. of Lect.* col. 777.

lue, 195.

luge, luige, 184 ; a luga, luga n-eithig, *d.* lugu, *Todd Lect.* 132 ; luige n-, *O'D. Sup.* 622.

lugach, 177.

Lugbad(?), *g.* Lugbaid, *Fél.* 142, 132 *FM.* an. 903.

lugléim, 116.

Lugmad, *g.* Lugmaid, *AU.* 118.

Lugmag, 127.

lugna, 196.

lugnasad, 144, *Todd Lect.* 110 ; *d.* lugnasad, *FM.* iii. 346 ; *v.* nassad.

luiberad, roots, herbage, *LB.* 113 a, 137 a ; *g.* lúibrid, *LB.* 156 b.

Luigne (?), *ds.* Luigniu, *FM.* iii. 224.

Luimnech (?), *g*. Luimnig, *FM*. an. 951.

Lusmag, 127 ; *BB*. 406 a, *RD*. 120 b.

lussrad, 140 ; *Voyage of Hui Corra* ; *gs*. lusraid, 49, *Hib. Minora*.

luisradtech, *Fél.* 143.

luth, lúd, lúud, 135, 203.

Luth (?), *g*. Lutho, *AU.* i. 118.

lutha, 190.

lúthléim, *d*. luthléimendaib, *LB*. 208 b.

macainm, 122.

macgnímrad, 141.

machad, 143.

maclestar, 157.

macrad, 139.

maell, 124.

maenmaige, *gs*. *FM*. iii. 114.

maetherge, *B. of Fermoy*, f. 52, *O'Don. Sup*.

mag, 126, 109 ; mag n-, *LC*. 92, *ter* ; am mag, *LU*. 105 b, 129, *LL*. 288 b, *RD*. 419, *voc*. a mag n-, *AU*. i. 438 ; *np*. maige, *LL*. p. 5 ; *g*. *dual*, da maige, *Fél*. 46.

Magloch, 201.

magsliab, 125.

magtráig, 196.

maided, 144.

maidm, 120 ; *d*. maidmaim, *AU*. 250, 306, 328 ; *nap*. madmand, madmanna, *Cog. G. re G.*, *FM*. iv. 752, iii. 256, 420, 116 ; *gp*. madmmann, *Keating's Hist*. 202.

maillréim, *O'Reilly's Dict*.

mailltriall, slow-going.

maim, 118.

mainbech, 172 ; a mainbech, .i. molad, *Man. and Cust*. iii. 26.

maisse, 197.

maithem n-, 207.

maithgréim, 117 ; maithgraim, *Lism. Lives*.

malach (?), load, *O'Reilly*.

mallmag, 127.

marclach, 176 ; *dp*. marclaigib, *AU*. i. 364 ; con assan ina láim 7 marclach fair, *LB*. 115 a.

márráth, 134.

martaretch, 129 ; *gs*. or *gp*. martortige, *Todd Leet*. v. 35.

mascul, 154.

maslach, 176.

matharlach, 177.

med n-, *Fen*. 348 ; *v*. mét.

meddechnad, 143.

medónlathe, 190.

medtos, 164.

melg, milk, *S*-stem (Stokes) ; melge .i. as, *O'Dav*. ; melg n-, *Eg*. 1782 ; *Cormac Translation*, p. 107 ; *g*. (bó) milge, *Bucolic Gloss*. 118 ; melg n-etha .i. cuirm, *Cormac*, 107 ; *g*. Lochmelge, *FM*. iv. 848.

mellgléo, 133.

membrumm, 171.

membur, memmur, 160.

men : an men, the stuff, *AU*. i. 110.

menmannrad, 141.

menmarc : issead bá m. leo, *FM*. iii. 284, 1706, 2016, *Fled. Bricr*. 260, 280.

mennat, 144, 204 ; U-stem; *g*. mennota, *M. Tall*. xvi.

mér, finger ; *d*. meur, *np*. mér, *ap*. méra, *Todd Lect*. v. 29, 17, 95, 96.

messred, messrad, 140, fruit, *LC*. 8.

mét, 130 ; met n-, *Cog. G.* 7 *G*. 94, *LB*. 210 b.

meth, 135, 202.

methrad, 139.

meathusrad, fatlings, *Bible Foclóir*.

miach, 171.

míad, 136, 204 ; miad n-, *LL*. 202 a ; *dp*. miadaib, *LU*. 52 a.

mialtur, 158.

mian, 165.

mianach, 178.

miaslaig, *gs*. malæ persuasionis, *Ml*. 28 b.

míchomall, 152.

míchride, 187.

mid, 203 ; *dp*. medaib, *Hy Fiach*. 216.

midbach, 172.

Midbech (?), *FM*. iii. 264.

Mide, 18*i* ; *gsf*. Mide *FM*. iii. 272.

Midemag, *FM.* ii. 644.

midglenn, 131.

midól, 149; *g.* midóil, *Hy Fiach.* 216, *BB.* 50 b, 51 a.

mígnímrad, *np.* mígnímrada, *LB.* 211 b, *BB.* 274 a.

mil, 149.

mílrad, 141; *g.* mílraid, *Fen.* 178, 184; *d.* mílruth, *LL.* 272 a.

mílte, 190.

mímaslach, 177.

mímír, 124.

mínbach (?), *ds. O'D. Sup.* 587.

minchombach, *LB.* 151 b.

mind, 169; minn n-aine, *AU.* i. 392; *np.* minna, treasures, *AU.* i. 552.

mindlestar, 157.

mindloch, *Fen.* 154.

mínluaithred, powder; *v.* luaithred.

minmír, 124.

mír, 124; *nap.* mírenna, *LL.* 303 b, 304 b, *Fél.* 36; mír n-immi, *Y.B.* of *Lec.* col. 245; *ap.* mírend, *LL.* 280 a.

mírath, 202; mírad, *B. of Kells*, fo. 6.

mírind, evil point, *Bodl. Cormac*, 16.

míscél, 148, *LB.* 273.

mithórmach, 172.

míthurus, 165; *pl.* míthurussa, *LB.* 260 a.

mochæirge, mochérge, early rising (for war or prayer), *LL.* 107 b.

mochbás, early death, *LL.* 147 a.

mochlige, 185.

mod, 135; mod n-, *S. na Rann*, p. 34; *LL.* 111 a; mod 7 monar, *LB.* 112 b.

Moenmag, 127.

moethal (?), fruit produce; *ap.* maethle, *LL.* 187 c.

Moidlind, *Oss. Soc.* v. 286.

móirécht (?), great lamentable deed, *FM.* iii. 588.

moirtchenn, 169.

monar, 157; monar n-, *LB.* 111 b, *LC.* 8.

móraenach, *LU.* 52 a.

mórán, 165.

mórár, great destruction, *S. na Rann*, p. 34.

mórbroscar, *Lism. Lives' Index.*

mórbruth n-, *LU.* 106 b.

mórbuaid, 198.

mórchol, *ap.* forsnam-morchol, scelera, *Ml.* 91 a.

mordeilm, 122.

morenglaim, great woof, *LL.* 47 a.

mórgalar, *FM.* iii. 236, *Chr. Scot.* 316.

mórimned, *d.* mórimniud, *Todd Lect.* v. 57.

morlestar, 157.

mórlinn, 132.

Mórloch, 201, .i. Loch Ree, *FM.* p. 1780.

mormuir, 200.

mórnert, 145.

morsaethar, *FM.* iii. 150.

mórscel, 148.

morseser, morfeser, 159.

mórsliab, 125; *np.* morslebe, *Fél.* 20.

mórsoethar, *Todd Lect.* v. 58, *FM.* iii. 150.

mórtuile, *np.* great floods, *LL.* 168 b.

mothar, 159; fid 7 m., *LL.* 165 b.

mrath, 134.

mrechtrad, 140; *g.* mrechtraid, *Ml.* 90 c.

mucár, *AU.* i. 324.

muineach : d'eirgeadar an m., *Mark.* 4; *g.* muinig, *Matt.* 13.

muinbech, 172.

muinde, 188.

muinmech, 172.

muinnech, 178.

Muintech (?), *LU.* 47 b.

muir, 200; muir n-,*Reeves' Culdees*,124; *np.* muire, *AU.* i. 314.

muiragu, *ds.*, 184.

muirfecht, naval expedition, *AU.* i. 356.

muirlinn, 132.

muirloch, 201.

muirmíl, 149.

muirn, 201.

mullach, 175; *Todd Lect.* v. 133; *gp.* mullach, *FM.* iii. 340; *np.* mullaigi, *LB.* 156 b.

Mumaintír, 131.

múnloch, 201.

mur, 156; mur n-ollaman, *Skene's Chron. of Picts and Scots*, 320.

murbach, 171; *d.* Muɩbauch, *FM.* iii. 416, 578, *L. Cé,* i. 470; *g.* Murbaig, *Hy Fiach.* 296, 298, 288.

murbruth, 203.

murchoblach, *FM.* an. 639.

murchrann, 166.

murear, 160.

murmag, 127, *LC.* 92.

murmíl, *gp., O'Dav.* 105.

muirthorad, 139.

murtola n-, *Chron. Scot.* 6 ; *v.* tolae n-.

murtraig, 198.


naidm, 121, *AU.* i. 430.

nás, new milk, *O'D. Sup.*

nasa, 197.

nasad, 144, ba ed n. Loga, *LL.* 194.

nascar, 162.

neaṁagra, *O'D. Sup.*

neb, 125.

nebimdibe, 181.

nebthóbe, 182.

nech, 130, 177; neich, *np.* nechi, *LU.* 58 a, 32 a; *gs.* neich, *Fél.* 144 ; *gp.* nech, *LB.* 133.b.

néimer, 162.

nél, 149.

nem, heaven, 125 ; an n., *Ml.* 42 b ; *agp.* nime, *FM.* an. 908, *LB.* 110 b.

nem, poison, 125 ; an neim, *Todd Lect.* v. 134; *ngp.* nime, *LB.* 110 b, 257 a.

nem, precious stone; *dp.* némannaib, *LB.* 209 b.

nembéscna, *O'D. Sup.* 582.

nemchomal, *Frags of Ir. Ann.* 32.

nemdialt, *BB.* 330 b.

nemed, 137 ; *ap.* nemed, *Fen.* 302.

nemforbann, 167.

nemfreccra, 192.

nemgné, *Fél.* 45.

nemiath, 136 ; nimíath, *Amra C. C.*

nemrath, 202.

nemthech, 129.

nemthess, 207.

nemthor, 157.

nenaidm, 121.

nepadæ, *see* adae.

nepetarscne, 196.

nephaccomol, 152.

nephdéirge, 186.

nephdíall, 150.

nephescide, 187.

nephní, 195.

nephtóbe, 182.

nert, 145, 206.

neutor, 157.

ní, 195.

niamlestar, *RD.* 451.

níth, 199.

nóchoblach, *g.* nóchoblaig, *AU.* i. 426.

nóebtogairm, 123.

nóemneb, 160.

noenbar, 160.

nóilathe, 190 ; *np.* noilathe ; *gl.* ɩʋndinum, *SG.* 116.

Nóindruimm, 120 ; *g.* Naendroma, *Fél·* 107.

nos, 163.

nuabés, *gs.* nuabésa, *Fél.* 53.

núall, 159.

núas, *g.* nuis: bainne, núis, bee-stings, *O'Reilly's Dict.*

núathorad, 139, *Hy Fiach.* 266.

núefiadnisse, núiednisse, 197.

núescae, 184.

nús, new milk, *Cod. Lat. Monac.* ed. by Zimmer.


ó, 6a, 133; *gs.* óe, *LL.* 318; da n-ó n-, *Fél.* 113.

ob, 125 ; *ap.* oibe, *Stapleton's Catechism,* 122.

ocbad, 137.

ochbad, ochfad, 137.

ocht: da n-ocht déc, *Chron. of Picts and Scots,* 319.

ochtar, 158, 160.

ochtrach, 179.

óded, 136.

oenar, 159.

óenlá, 190.

offrend, 167.

og, 126 ; og, .i. ob, *Cormac.*

óg, 169.

ógdílgend, 167.

ógdíre, *O'D. Sup.* 684.

Ogmag, *g.* Ogmaige, *FM. Index.*

ognarathar, 158.

ogthindnacal, *Wb.* 1 a.

Ogum, is marked neuter in *Wind. Dict.* Why ? *gs.* oguim, *LL.* 258 b.

oigrecht, 204.

oigred, 139.

óigsíd, *FM.* iv. 930, *LL.* 277 b.

oigthech, 129.

oilbéim, 114, disgrace, *Hy Fiach.* 206.

oilethir, *LB.* 256 b.

ói-melg .i. imelg, *Cormac's Gl.* p. 133, sheep's milk ; *v.* melg.

óinach, 178 ; aenach n-, *LB.* 264 b ; *d.* oenuch, *LL.* 20 a ; *np.* oenaige, *Fél.* 31, *Hy Fiach.* 226, 268 ; the old name Nenagh shows the *n* of the article *an.*

óinbíad, *Ml.* 97 d.

óimbéim, 114 ; *d.* óenbémim, *LL.* 60 a, *LL.* 300 b.

oirbelach, *g.* oirbelaig, *FM.* iii. 566.

oirer, 160, abundance, pleasure; *v.* airer.

oirleach (?), *ns.* slaughter, *FM.* iv. 788 ; *ds. Oided Chloin. Tuireann,* p. 164.

ól, 149 ; *d.* oul, *Ml.* 118 c.

olachrand, 166.

olc, 147.

olfoirbthe, 189.

olgrád, 134.

ollach, 175.

ollchóiced, *v.* cóiced ; *pl.* ollchóiceda, *Todd Lect.* iv. 242.

olor, 157.

óltech, 129.

onn, 131, .i. cloch, *Amra C. C.* ch. 6.

ór, 155.

órarget, *Bucolic Gl.*

orbe, orpe, arpe, 183 ; orba., heritage, *Todd Lect.* v. 134 ; an orbae, *Ml.* 100 c.

orclaigib, *LB.* 156 a.

ord, 145.

ordd, 144.

orddan : a n-orddan, the grandeur, *LL.* 290 b.

orddain (?), dá n-ordain, two junks, *LL.* 110 b, *Stokes' Death of Goll and Garb,* p. 397.

ordlach, 177 ; *np.* ordlaige, *AU.* an. 1498 ; *Laws,* iv. 276 ; *Ir. Texte,* i. 112, *O'D. Sup.* 648, *LB.* 149 b.

orlár, 156.

oss, 163.

osailcim (?), 119.

osnad, 144.

ossad, 144 ; osad, peace, *AU.* i. 430.

ossar (?), burden, *Stokes' Met. Glosses.*

óthad, 136.

othar, 159.

othar, 159.

otharlige, otharlige, otharlaige, grave (?) *LL.* 121 b, 165 b, 288.

óthatnat, 144.

othrach, otrach, 179.

plágbéim, 114.

pólaire, 193.

praintech, prointech, 129.

prímbelra, *LB.* 150 b.

prímmbíad, 135.

prímdorus, *dp.* dóirsib, *LB.* 109 a, b.

prímdun, 131 ; *g.* prímduine, *LB.* 264 a.

prímesci, *gs.* first day of the moon.

prímgrád, 134.

prímistad, *C. M. Rath,* 198 ; *v.* istad.

prímloch, *g.* prímlocha, *AU.* an. 1234, *Chr. Scot.* 316.

prímmaigib, *LU.*

prímrath, 202.

prímscél, 148.

prímsruth, *Nen.* 30.

prímsuide, 187.

prímsuidiu, *ds., Todd Lect.* v. 56.

prímtheglach, 176.

prímthellach, 175, *H.* 3. 17, p. 732.

psalmthech, 129, *FM.* an. 987.

pudar, 206.

rabad (?), warning ; *np.* raibthe, *FM.* iii. 276, iv. 698.

rad, 134.

rád, ráth, 134 ; rad n-, *LL.* 109 a, *Tigern.* an. 520.

Raithlinn, 132 ; *gs.* Raithlinne, *FM.* an. 903.

rangabalda, 187.

rath, 202.

rath, 202.

rath, 202 ; *g.* ratha, grace, *LB.* 61 a, *Fen.* 294 ; *np.* rath, ratha, successes, *Hy Maine*, 13 ; *nap.* ratba, *Fél.* 2.

rathlind, *Fair of Carmam, rann*, 67.

rathtech, 129.

ré, 133.

réc, 133.

rebrad, 139.

recht, 204 ; recht n-, *LB.* 211 a, 256 a, *Thurn.* i. versl. p. 21.

rechtrath, *BB.* 50 a.

rechol, 149.

récomarc, 147, *BB.* 307 b, .i. desellabach, *Fél.* 2.

réim, 116, 117 ; réim n-, *FM.* an. 904 ; *d.* réimim, *LB.* 209 b, *Nen.* 134, *Hugh Roe's Life*, pp. 16, 28, *FM.* iii. 366 ; *gp.* remmend, *Fen.* 68, *FM.* an. 904, *BB.* 51 a.

rémainm, 122.

rembélre, 193.       [*Gram.* 76.

rembérla, 194, a preposition, *M'Curtin's*

rémeperthe, 189.

rémfius, 206.

rémmíad, 136.

rémscél, 148.

remthaircetul, 151.

remthóchim, a preceding, *LU.* p. 84 a.

rét, 203 ; *np.* raeta, *BB.* 274 a.

reud, 136, 203.

riathar, 159.

ribar, 161.

riched, 142 ; *d.* richiud, the kingdom of heaven, *Fél.* 53.

rícht : frissa r, *Sg.* 197 b.

ríge, 184; rige n-, *LB.* 264 a, 265 b, 274, *LL.* 147 a, *BB.* 148 ; rigi, *gs. BB.* 5a, 8 a, *L. Cé*, 642 ; *d.* rigu, *LL.* 291.

rige (?), 186.

rígdál, 150.

rígdaltech, 129.

rígdomna, 197 ; rígdomna n-, *AU.* i. 416, 456.

rígdorus; *np.* rígdoirse, *LB.* 109 a, b.

rígdún, 131.

rígiáth, 136, *Fél.* 82, 166.

rígráth, 202.

rígsossud, *ds. LB.* 109 b.

rígscél, 148.

rígsruth, 203.

rígsuide, 188, *Todd Lect.* v. 21, 91 ; *i masc. in LU.* 27 b.

rígthech, 129, *Todd Lect.* v. 4 ; *gs.* rígthige, *LB.* 109 ; *gp.* rígthige, *LU.* 111 b.

rígthorad, 139.

rígthreb, 125.

rím, 116.

rind, 169.

rinde, 188.

rinn, 109, 132, 169.

Rinn mBeara, *Ogygia*, 176.

rinn, 201 ; *np.* inna rinn, *Ml.* 145 d.

rindnem, 125 ; *d.* rindnim, *Fél.* 82.

ríochtainm, *pronoun, OR.*

ró, 134.

roas ndeda, *Dallan Forgaill's Poem, H.* 3. 18, p. 2.

robar, 161.

rochetal, 151.

rodiall, 150.

roeimbed, 137.

roemag, 127.

roenmag, 127

roga, 133 ; r. ndealba, *L. na gCeart*, 290.

rogu, 133.

rogním ; *np.* na rogníma, *L. Cé*, ii. 138.

roithréim, rushing, *Bible Foclóir.*

romaidm, 120 ; *g.* romadmai, *LB.* 206 a.

romuir, 200.

róráth, exceeding luck, *BB.* 50 b.

rorba (?), .i. toirmesc, *O'Dav.*

ros, ross, 183 ; ros n-, *LL.* 305 b, *bis, BB.* p. 233 a ; *B. of Lismore*, f. 187 a ; Ross Commain ustum est, of *AU.* i. 318, seems to show the neuter of *ros.*

rosaiglige, 185.

roscbéim, 114; rosg n-, *Sylva Gad.* 249.

rossar, 163.

rosscél, 148.

róstae (?), *gl.* rosarium.

rotach, rotaigib, *dp., LU.* 28 b, *LB.* 254 b.

rout, 135, a roud-si, *LU.* Story of Mongán.

ruag (?), *Hy Fiach.* 228; *d.* ruaig, ruaicc, *FM.* ii. 1164.

ruathar, 158; ruathar n-, *Fen.* 218, 354; *ap.* ruathar, *Fen.* 398, *LL.* 78 a, *gs.* ruathair, *LL.* 240 a.

rube, 182; *d.* rubu, *LL.* 109 a; *AU.* an. 932; rubu .i. marbad, *O'Dav.*

rube (?), point of land, *O'Donovan's Supp.*; *d.* Rubu, *AU.* i. 452, 454.

rucce (?), *d.* ruccu, *gl.* confusio, verecundia.

rudrad, 139.

ruidléim, 116.

ruithen, 131.

ruithned (?), flame; *g.* ruithned, *Gernon,* 475.

rún, 131; rún nDé, rún siorraidde nDé, *B. of Common Prayer,* p. 589, *np.* rúine, *LU.* 27 a; *is fem., Ml.* 38 c, 45 a.


saebforchetal, 151.

saebléim, 118.

sægulrad Crist, *LB.* 132 a.

saerchenel, 148.

saerchetal, 151.

sai (?), sai n-dána, sai n-enig, 7 n-engnama, *L. Cé,* i. 634, 636.

sáibairde, 188.

sáibchore, *gp., gl.* syrtium, *Cr.* 34 b; *v.* coire.

sáibfirt, 206.

sáibscél, 148.

sáigul, sáegul, 154.

saile, 194.

saimbíad, 135.

saimgné, 133.

sainbás, 61.

sainchenelae, 194.

sainchomarde.

saine, 197.

sainecosc, 146.

sainfolad.

saingné, 133.

saingrad, *Lism. Lives' Index.*

sainlaa, 190.

sainlinn, *O'D. Sup.* 584.

sainól, 149.

sainred, 141; sainred n-, *Ml.* 37 b.

sáithar, saethar, 158.

sál, 131.

salchar, 162.

salmcedal, 151; sailmchetul, *Fél.* 84.

salmuir, 200.

samlá, 190.

samsíth, *Amra C. C.* ch. 7 a, summer place.

samrad, 141.

sárchuimrech, 180.

sarlóg, 126.

sásad, 144; sássad n-, *Fél.* 65.

sathe, 190; saithe, swarm is *masc.*; *np.* int sathi, *Ml.* 90 b; *ap.* saithiu.

scath, 134.

scéim, 115.

sceinm, 123.

scél, 148; scél n-, *LU.* 39, *O'Dav.* 98; a scél cetna, *LL.* 289 b; sgél, bad tidings, *FM.* iii. 586.

scíathrach, 179.

scibar, 161.

scichlim, disappearance (?), vanishing, *Lism. Lives' Index.*

scíthfeidm, 122, *LC.* 36, 274.

scíthlim, 116; *LB.* 256 b, *Lism. Lives' Index.*

scoitbeurla, Irish language, *Keating,* p. 80.

screchgaire, 192.

scretgaire, *Trip. Life,* 657.

scríbend, 167; *d.* scríbunn, *AU.* an. 438; *nap.* ínna scribenda, *Rawl. B.* 512, fo. 45 a.

scriblinn, 132.

sechim, 116, 119.

slúag, 147, 169 ; *ns.* slog n-aile, *L. of
Hugh Roe*, p. 164 ; *but* in slóg, *LU.*
29 b, *ap.* ilslogu, *Tur.* 2 c.

sluagad n-aill, *ns.*, another hosting ;
*AU.* i. 504, *FM.* iv. 740, 748 ; slogad
n-, *AU.* i. 288, 290.

sluagthech, 129.

smachtgell, 154.

smir, 206.

snaidm, 121.

snechta, 190.

sneddechnad, 143.

sóaltar, 157.

sóas, 164 ; soas n-, *Cormac*, p. 8, *O'Dav.*
8.

sobérla, 194.

sochar, 163 ; *g.* sochair, *Lism. Index* ;
sochar 7 dochar, *LC.* 237.

sochenél, 148.

sochosc (?) ; *g.* sochoisc, *gl.* docibilem,
*Wb.* 30 b ; seems gen. of a noun used
adjectively.

socomul, 153.

sodath, 202.

sofoirchetal, 151 ; soforcetal, *Lism.
Index.*

sogairm, *LL.* 517.

sogne, good form, *Fél.* 141.

soilestar, 157.

soimrim, *g.* soimrime, of easy riding,
*R.I.A.* 43 b, f. 20 a.

soindsce, oratory, *Lism. Lives Index* (?).

soinmech, 172.

solad (?), solace, *Todd Lect.* iv. 227.

somíad, 136 ; *LU.* 336.

sonn (?), troop (of horse), *FM.* iv. 750.

sonnach, sondach, 178 ; *dp.* sondaigib,
*LB.* 207 a.

soól, 149.

sóscél, 148.

soscéle, 194, *masc.*, *Wb.* 7 b.

sossad, 144 ; *g.* sosaid ; *ap.* sosta, *LB.*
109 a, 109 b.

sotech, 129.

spirdide, 187.

spruigleach (?), morsels, *Bible Foclóir.*

spuirech, 180.

sraigell, srogell, 154.

sruaim, 119 ; a sruaim, *Wb.* 11 a.

sruithléim, 116.

sruithred, 139.

sruth, 203 ; sruth n-imbath n-ard,
*O'Dav.* 56 ; sruth n-Iordanen, *LB.*
73 b.

sruthair, 200 ; *g.* sruthra, *LL.* 298.

sruthlind, 132, *LL.* 263 b.

sruthmaidm, *FM.* iii. 130, where it is
used figuratively; "sruthmaidm dia
muintir."

stuadléim, 116.

stuagdorus, 164.

stuaim (?), device, 2 *Chron.* 2.

suaicned, 143.

suan-bás, *Amra C. C.*, ch. i.

subae, 183 ; *d.* subu, *LU.* 29 a ; a subæ,
*Ml.* 146 d.

suide, 187 ; sude, *Todd Lect.* v. 29.

súilbéim, 115 ; bewitching with the eye,
*Coney's Dict.*

suithred, 139.

suithe, 190.

sundred, 141.

suth, 203.

suthinsíd, *g.* suthinsíde, *Ml.* 89 b.


tabach, *ds.* rescue, *FM.* iii. 646.

tabéim, 115.

tachim, *LL.* 247 a, 265 b.

tachor, tachur, return, 163, *BB.* 9 b, 10 a.

tachor, combat, 163 ; *g.* tachair, *FM.* iv.
756.

tacre, 191.

tadall, 150 ; *d.* tadall, *Texte*, i. 9 b,
"adire," *Todd Lect.* v. 16 ; *LL.*
fo. 72.

tadbéim, 115.

taebán, 165.

tagraim, 123.

táibréim, 117.

taidbech, 172.

taidlech, 177.

taidmech, 172.

taidm, 121.

Tailtenmag, 128.

taipe, 182.

tairchetal, 151.

tairgaire, 192.

tairgell, 154, *Man. and Cust.* iii. 489.

tairgille, 194.

tairlimm, 116.

tairm, 124.

tairmchetal, 151.

tairmchless, *Wind. Dict.*

tairmoircniu, *ds.*, *SG.* 63 b.

tairngere, 192; *Ml.* 122 d.

tairred, 138.

taistell, 150; *g.* tastil; *d.* tastiul; *LL.* 55 a, 133 b.

taithesc, 146; *Wb.* 27 c; *cf.* aithesc.

taithlech, 177.

taithmech, *as. LL.* 87 a, 303 a.

taithmet, 138.

talland, 168.

Tamanrind, *Ossian Soc.*, vol. v. 288.

Tamnach, 179.

taoibréim, 117, digression; genit. case, *M'Curtin's Gram.*, 41.

taoicreidm, dizziness, *O'Brien's Dict.*

tarall, crossing, *BB.* 404 a.

tarcadach, 174.

targlaim, 119; tarclaim, *RD.* 449.

tarmmorcenn, 168.

tarsno, 197.

tartbéim, 115.

tarthar, 158.

tascair (?), *gs.*, things cast ashore, *Laws* ii. 166.

tasgur, 160.

tatalc, 147.

tech, 128; tech n-, *LL.* 279, *Fen.* 268, *L. Cé*, i. 130; a tech, *AU.* i. 124, *Ir. Texte*, i. 126, *LU.* 45, 102 a, *Todd Lect.* v. 11.

téchte, 190.

téchtmuir, 200.

teclimm, 119.

tecmang, 169.

tecosc, 146.

teglach, 176; a teglach n-, *LU.* 107 a.

tegnach, 178.

teidm, 122, tedmmaim, *Todd Lect.* v. 99, *LB.* 61 a.

teinm, 123; *cf.* teinmndech, *LL.* 304.

teiscléim, *O'D. Sup.* 711.

telach n-epscop, *Letter of Pope Urban*, an. 1186.

telchube, 184.

tellach, 175, .i. lucht tige, *FM.* iii. 241; *np.* tellaige, *Fen.* 158, *BB.* 200 a, *RD.* 96 b.

tellach, 169, 175; a tellach, fornacem, *Todd Lect.* v. 49; *np.* tellaige, *LL.* 72.

tellach (?), tellach na scor, *LB.* 206 a.

tellfuaim, 118.

temel, 153, 155.

Temenmag, *Frags. of I. An.* 216, 218.

ten, 131.

tenlach, 175.

Tenmag, 128.

tepe, 182, *LL.* 61 a.

terca n-etha, *F. Mast.* an. 969.

tércital, 151.

terloch, *Tigern.* an. 4166.

terúacra, 191.

tess, 207; imman rothess, *LL.* 135.

tescertleth, 135.

tét: tri tét, *LL.* 288 a.

tidnocul, tindnacul, tinnacul, 153, traditio, *Ml.* 96 d.

timarcc (?), *g.* timaircc, *F. Mast.* ii., p. 1162.

timchetol, 151.

timcre, 191.

timmcride, 186.

timdibe, 181; *Fél.* 143.

timgaire, 192; timgaire n-, *Gildas*, iii. (viii.).

timne, timpne, tinne, 197.

timthach, 173; *d.* timthuch; *pl.* timthaigi, *Tog. Troi*, 1671, 596, 889.

tinchetal, 151.

tinchor, 163.

tinchosc, 146, *Wb.* 5 c, 16 a.

tindlech, 177.

tindrem, 117; *but* in béstindrim, *Ml.* 48 c.

tinfed, 137.

tinól, 149; *g.* tinóil 7 toichestail, *FM.* iii. 178, *Laws* ii. 346, 356.

treduma, 195 ; tredumi, *RD.* 91 a.

trell, 152.

trénaithbe, 182.

trénféidm, 122, *B. Lismore*, 219 a.

trenlamaig, *gs.* strong shooting, "might of arm," 198.

trénmid, *g.* trénmeda, strong mead, *LL.* 111 a.

trénothath, *SG.* 56 b.

trénrige, *Fél.* 68, 70.

tréntogairm, 123.

trét, 135 ; *ap.* tréta, *LB.* 213 a.

trethantracht, *LU.* 39 ; *v.* tracht.

tríall, 150, *pl.* trialla, devices, *Isaias*, 66.

trían, 165 ; trian n-, *O'Dav.* 62, 100 ; *g.* triuin, *AU.* i. 422.

trian, 159.

trichem, 116, trichim, *O'D. Sup.*

trichtaige, 184.

trocur, 163.

tromaife, tromaithbe, *BB.* 476.

tromchnuasach, *Parrthas an A. last* p.

trommchride, 186.

tromgalar, 156 ; *g.* tromgalair, *BB.* 506; *np.* tromgallra, *AU.* i. 302.

tremlach (?), weight *or* bulk, *LL.* 292 b, tromthinól, *FM.* iii. 230.

tromtuile, 194.

tromualach, burden.

trost, 145.

trostán, 145.

trostbéim, 115.

trotchor, 163.

trúalned, 144.

tuagmíl, 149 ; *d.* tuagmílaib, *O'Curry's Lect.* 507.

tuaim, 119 ; t. n-, *LC.* 277, 278 ; *g.* tuama, *Mart. Tall.* xxii., *Todd Lect.* v. 35.

tuaiscert, 145 ; t. n-, *LL.* 304 b ; tuais-rinn, 201.

tuar, 162.

tuaréim : fa n-a thuaréim soin, "quam ob rem," *Stapleton's Catech.* Pref. § 33.

tuaristal, 152 ; *d.* tuarastul, "stipendia," *Todd Lect.* v. 88.

tuathmag, 128; *d.* tuathmaig, *O'Curry's Lect.* 492.

tuathtír, *S. na R.* 5147.

tudrach, 179 ; *as.* tudrach, *Fél.* Epil. 329.

tuba, 182.

tuba, 182, attack, *Laws*, i. 269.

tuibreim, 117.

tuile, 194 ; tuile n-, *LL.* 168 b ; tuile m(B)aile, *RD.* 437 ; *d.* tuliu, *Fél.* 25 ; *g.* indintuli (*read* in tuli, *gl.* redundantiæ, *Ml.* 129 d.

tuilreim, dative case, *M'Curtin's Gram.* p. 41.

tuindtuiliu, wave-flood, *Fél.* 21.

tuirléim, 116.

tuirthim, 119 ; *g.* tuirthime, *O'Dav.* 168.

tul, 152.

tulgairm, loud call, *M'Curtin's Gram.* 32.

tulmag, 128.

tulrech, 180.

turba, 182.

turim, 117.

turlach (?), value, *Chr. Scot.* 286.

turlach, *g.* turlaig, *LB.* 275 ; *as.* turlach ; *g.* turlocha, *FM.* iii. 288.

turlaim, 116 ; turléim, *LC.* 2, 271.

turloch, 201 ; *v.* turlach.

turnaidm n-, *O'Don. Sup.* ; *v.* adall.

turrscar (?) ; t. in mara, *Fél.* 38.

tuslestar, 157.

tuthle, 195.

uabar, 160 ; *g.* uabair, *LL.* 304 a.

uachtar, 158.

uachtmag, *LC.* 92.

uadath, 136.

uaimm, 118 ; uaim n- (*Colum Cille's Rule*), sewing ; *g.* uamma, uama, of knitting, uniting, *L. Cé*, an. 1281, *FM.* iii. 368 ; uaimm n-étaig, *LB.* 11 b.

uaim, 118 ; *gp.* uamann, *LB.* 154 b, 155 a.

uaimmbrechtrad (*Lism. Lives Index*).

uaircride, *d.* uaircridiu, *FM.* i. 292.

uairthech, 129.

uaithne, 146.

úalach, burden; *ap.* ualuige, *Numbers,* iv. 26 ; dá úalach, *Gen.* 49.

uall (?), *ap.* ualla, " clamores," *Todd Lect.* v. 91.

uanbach (?), *LL.* 297 b ; *masc.* int úanbach, *LL.* 96 a.

uasaldliged, *O'D. Sup.* 723.

uath, 136.

uath, 136.

úathad, uathed, 136.

huathfecht, 205.

uathonn, 131.

ub, 125.

úbull, 154 ; *nap.* úbla, *Todd Lect.* v. 75, 83, 11 ; *np.* úbla, *Hy Fiach.* 284, *LU.* 105 b.

uccu, 133.

ucht, 204.

ugra, 191 ; cen ugra cen agra, *FM.* ii. 1164.

uide, 188 ; *d.* uidiu, *Laws,* ii. 390-2.

uiscilestar, 157.

Uisnech, 178.

upad, 204.

úradach, *LB.* 205 a ; *cf.* ertach.

urbach, 172.

urchomul, 153.

urchor, 162.

urchra, *v.* erchre.

urdligéd, 143.

urdún, *pl.* urdúne, *Windisch Dict.*

uréirge, 185, *Lism. Lives Index.*

urfuigell, arbitration, *O'Don. Sup.* ; *g.* urfuigill (*G. Corca Laide,* 324), " eloquence."

urgaire, 192.

úrimb, *g.* úrimbe, *HM.* 49.

urlár, 156, plain, *Fen.* 246 ; floor, *Numb.* 5.

urmaisse (?), *LB.* 276.

urmór, 155.

urnaidm, 121 ; *FM.* iv. 834.

urrathas, 164.

úrsnaidm, 121.

urthabach, 172.

urthach, 173 ; an u., *Laws* i. 180.

urthobach, *LB.* 258.

urthorad, *Lism. Lives Index,* *opposed to* lethorad.

urthriall, *LB.* 210 b ; *FM.* an. 228.

urtlach, 176 ; *np.* urtlaige, *Fél.* 32.

utlach, 176 ; *g.* utlaig, *Todd Lect.* v. 46.

# INDEX OF WORDS.

*[The appended numbers refer to the numbered paragraphs in text.]*

nirgabad, 58.
gabalaib, 4.
Gaill, 20.
gairdechais, 53, *gs.*
gairfes, 91.
gári, 10.
gelchorccra, 88.
rogellsam, 94.
rogened, 96.
genelaig, 13.
genfithir, 83.
rogiallsat, 72.
glangríbdai, 40.
glóir, 62.
glormaraigther, 71.
glúinech, 58.
gnáithche, 39.
gnáthugud, 27.
goborchind, 12.
Goedil, Goedelach, 12, 13.
góesach, 101.
gola, 104.
gortach, 54.
gorti, 56, *ds.*
gráine, 40, *nas.* and *gp.*
grecha, 104.
grianta, 89.
guilbend, 91.


iach, 53, *nsf.*
ídnaide, 79.
imnedaig, 91.
imráti, 84, *np.*
inarbach, 54.
imbuid, 60.
inchosc, 33.
indail, 66.
ingantaig, 77.
inísiul, 43.
inne, 105.
inse, 3, *np.*
irfuacarthid, 63.
isa, 34, 46, whose.
isat, 87, thou art.
Iúdaide, *in full, LB.* 133 b.
iumentib, 69.

laigid, 44.
laim: fril, 35; d'oenláim, 98.
lámchomairt, 104.
lámnad, 103.
lánbrudechas, 28.
lánchomaiditiu, 28.
lat: Dia latt, 87, = " ave."
legaib, 43, *dp.*
legdais, 89.
lénti, 80.
lethi, 77, *compar.*
lethimel, 61.
lige, *g.* ligi, 69.
roligsium, 78.
línanart, 88.
lógmairite, 31.
logtha, 44, *gs.*
loind, 36.
loscandaib, 38.
lott, 97; in cathraig do l.
luperac(h)an, luchrupain, 10, 12.
luiberad, 78.


máelanu, 21.
mairned (?), 71.
maithiges, 41.
maithiusa, 52, *gsf.*
maithneeh, 104; maithnecha, 104;
    maithnechus, 60.
margrent, 88.
menmnaigi, 30.
merachta, 55.
meraigthi, 55.
methmerchurdacht, 80.
michairdig, 55.
mifrigi, 60.
milse, 77, *compar.*
mirbuldacht, 93.
miruin, 55.
misniges, 56.
mlais, 34.
mongtheindtech, 92; mongthenntacha,
    89.
mordataig, 75.
morecin, 36.
muich, 56, *ds.*
muichnig, 52, *ds.*

muincend, 8.
muinigin, 98.
Muire, in full, 58, *ter*.


nech, 59, *gp*.
némdibaide, 88.
nemlogatha, 44.
nemscithach, 82.
nertadbul, 66.
nith, 106.
nochtaid, 44.
nóemas, 41.


ócbail, 104.
ochna, 104.
óclach, 81.
oelscugud, 41.
oendán, 98.
oibne, 94, *compar*.
oigride, 55.
oilithír, 54.
ro-oircset, 98.
oirmitin, 60.
oirriga, 62.
oisínech, 81.
olcugud, 41.
ongaine, 45, *gs*.
ordan, 86.


págáin, 26.
péin, 64, *for* féin.
point, 33.
prímchenela, 3, 4.


ra n-a, 13.
rebrad, 74.
recus, 54, 55.
rena duthracht, 32.
rethi, 33.
rétla, rétlu, 69, 71, 93; rétlaind, 82,
  *asf*.; rétland, 88, *gp*.; rétlanda, 93,
  *ap*.
risna, 46, 58; risnad, 37, 43, 56, 58.
Ródii, 3.

roich, 77.
Sabrinne, 24, *gsf*.
do sáss, 94.
Saxain, 2.
sceith, 43.
scélaigecht, 74.
roscenntis, 89.
scithlim, 57, *as. synon. of* erchra.
scríptha, 104.
roselbsat, roselbsatar, 3, 8.
seolbrat, 16.
sét na samail, 75, 85.
sethar, 58, *gsf*.; *pl*. sethracha, 13.
sessib, 61.
sib: (rodán, rolín) sib, 107.
sída, 57, *gs*.
sílne, 39, 40; *cf*. Sílnán.
sírluad, 57.
sírrechtach, 75.
siublach, 93.
slánchutruma, 46.
slechtain, 88.
smuaintigthi, 84, *np*.
snimche, 52, *gs*.
sobésa, 56.
soccumla, 49, *gs*.
rosocht, 105.
soeri, 77, *compar*.
rosoither, 60; śous, 39.
solusnél, 68.
son, 45; ina son-sa, 83, *ds*.
srátib, 73.
staraidecht, 75.
stól, stol, 62, 64.
subaigi, 70.
rosúig, 105.
suiscelach, 58.
sulbair, 70.
suthaine, 55, *gsf*.


tacmong, 91.
tæniud, 46.
taifnitir, 20.
taircsin, 69.
tairmisceb, 87.
thaisbenait, taisbentair, 43.
tan, 67.

tarraid, 30.
roteich, 17 ; roteichsetar, 26.
tegdaise, 63, *gsf.*
tendius, 69 ; *cf.* tenn, .i. ledrad, *O'Dav.* ;
    tinneas cloinne, "labour," *O'Begley.*
tennte, 55, *ʒp.*
ticcid, 78, 2 *pl.* for 2 *sg.*
timmarcte, 16.
tocu, 49.
tóduchtach, 29.
toga, 94, *gs.*
togail, 96, 97.
toidlenach, toidlenacha, 93, 89.
torothor, 10.
Traconitidi, 10.
rothráig, 105.
tráthaigtech, 37.
treblíadnach, 34.
trebraid : fige t., 88.

trelma, 63, 64.
tremdíriges, 29.
trill, 100, *gs.*
tromdacht, 40.
truallnide, 36.
tuarcthi, 104.
rothubtís, 31.
thuicebair, 92.
ni-thuill, 77.
turcharthi, 90.
tusmiud, 61.


uair : arn-u, 29 ; ar uairib, "some-
    times," *Donlevy,* 422.
ugain, 69, *for* u(n)gain ; *cf.* ongaine.
ullán, 74 (?).
usaiti, 61.

END OF VOL. VI.

# IRISH MANUSCRIPTS—FAC-SIMILES.

*[Editions limited to 200 copies.]*

THE accurate study and critical investigation of the ancient literary and historic monuments of Ireland have hitherto been impeded by the absence of fac-similes of the oldest and most important Irish Manuscripts.

With a view of supplying this acknowledged want, and of placing beyond risk of destruction the contents of Manuscripts, the Academy has undertaken the publication of carefully collated lithographic or photo-lithographic copies of the oldest Irish texts still extant.

---

### In folio, on toned paper.—Price £3 3s.

LEABHAR NA H-UIDHRI : a collection of pieces in prose and verse, in the Irish language, transcribed about A. D. 1100 ; the oldest volume now known entirely in the Irish language, and one of the chief surviving native literary monuments—not ecclesiastical—of ancient Ireland ; now for the first time published, from the original in the Library of the Royal Irish Academy, with account of the manuscript, description of its contents, index, and fac-similes in colours.

---

### In Imperial folio, on toned paper.—Price £4 4s. ; or £2 2s. per Part. Parts I. and II. ; or in One Vol., half calf.

LEABHAR BREAC—the " Speckled Book "—otherwise styled " The Great Book of Dun Doighre " : a collection of pieces in Irish and Latin, transcribed towards the close of the fourteenth century ; " the oldest and best Irish MS. relating to Church History now preserved."—(*G. Petrie.*) Now first published, from the original MS. in the Academy's Library.

---

### In Imperial folio, on toned paper, with a Photograph of a page of the Original.—Price £6 6s.

THE BOOK OF LEINSTER, sometime called The Book of "GLENDALOUGH": a collection of pieces in the Irish Language, compiled in part about the middle of the twelfth century. From the original MS. in Trinity College, Dublin, with introduction, analysis of contents, and index, by ROBERT ATKINSON, M.A., LL.D., Professor of Sanskrit and Comparative Grammar in the University of Dublin, Secretary of Council, Royal Irish Academy.

The Book of Leinster is one of the most important of the fragments of Irish literature that have come down to us. In addition to copies of the native prose historic accounts of the Táin Bó Cualnge, the Bórama, &c., it contains a large fragment of an early prose translation of the Historia de Excidio Troiae of Dares Phrygius ; a great number of the poems and prose introductions of the *Dindsenchas* or legendary account of the origin of the names of places in Ireland ; very many historic poems, in which the legendary and traditional accounts of the early history of the country are preserved ; Irish genealogies and hagiologies ; and a great number of interesting stories, illustrative of the manners and customs, the modes of thought, and the state of culture, &c., of the people of Ireland just about the period of the Anglo-Norman Invasion.

*In Imperial folio, reproduced by Photo-lithography.—Price £5 5s.*

THE BOOK OF BALLYMOTE: a collection of pieces in the Irish Language dating from the end of the fourteenth century; now published in **Photo lithography** from the original Manuscript in the Library of the Royal Iris Academy. With Introduction, Analysis of Contents, and Index, by ROBERT ATKINSON, M.A., LL.D., Professor of Sanskrit and Comparative Philology in the University of Dublin; Secretary of Council, Royal Irish Academy.

The Book of Ballymote contains numerous articles of interest to the Scholar and to the Antiquary. The original portion consists of—Genealogical Lists; Histories and Legends; a fragment of the Brehon Laws; a copy of the *Dindsenchas;* Treatises on Grammatical Topics, &c. The other portion contains translations from Latin originals: the Destruction of Troy, the Wandering of Ulysses, the Story of the Æneid, and the Life of Alexander the Great.

## THE IRISH MANUSCRIPT SERIES.

Volume I., octavo.—Part 1.—Containing: (1) Contents of The Book of Fermoy; (2) The Irish MS. in Rennes; (3) Mac Firbis on some Bishops of Ireland; (4) Tain Bo Fraich; (5) Tochmarc Bec-Fola, &c. Price 5s.

Volume I., quarto.—Part 1.—WHITLEY STOKES, LL.D.: On the Felire of Œngus. Price 14s.

Volume II., octavo.—Part 1.—ROBERT ATKINSON, M.A., LL.D.: Τρί διορ-ξαοιτε αn Όάιρ ["The Three Shafts of Death"] of Rev. Geoffrey Keating. The Irish Text, edited with Glossary and Appendix. Price 3s. 6d.

## THE TODD LECTURE SERIES.

Volume I., octavo.—Part 1.—W. M. HENNESSY: Mesca Ulad. Price 4s.

Volume II., octavo.—ROBERT ATKINSON, M.A., LL.D.: The Passions and Homilies from Leabhar Breac. With an Introductory Lecture on Irish Lexicography. (Pages 1 to 958.) Price £1 10s.

Volume III., octavo.—B. MAC CARTHY, D.D.: The Codex Palatino-Vaticanus, No. 830. Texts, Translations and Indices. (Pages 1 to 450.) Price 7s. 6d.

Volume IV., octavo.—REV. EDMUND HOGAN, S.J.: Cath Ruis Na Rig for Bóinn. Text, Translation, Preface, and Indices, &c. (Pages xxxii. + 282.) Price 3s. 6d.

Volume V., octavo.—Rev. EDMUND HOGAN, S.J., F.R.U.I., M.R.I.A.: The Latin Lives of the Saints as Aids towards the Translation of Irish Texts and the Production of an Irish Dictionary. (Pages xii. + 140.) Price 2s. 6d.

Volume VI., octavo.—Rev. EDMUND HOGAN, S.J., F.R.U.I., M.R.I.A.: The Irish Nennius from L. Na Huidre and Homilies and Legends from L. Brecc. Alphabetical Index of Irish Neuter Substantives. (Pages viii. + 130.) Price 2s. 6d.